ADVANCED PRAISE FOR *INSIDE THE TEXAS CHICKEN RANCH*

Jayme Blaschke has done a superb job in telling the story of the famous (or infamous, if you prefer) Chicken Ranch of La Grange, Texas. He delves into the perhaps mythical history of its ancestor, Mrs. Swine's establishment. He deals affectionately with civic benefactor Miss Edna and her boarders, as well as their protector and civic leader, Fayette County sheriff Jim Flournoy. This is the best account of the "Best Little Whorehouse in Texas" ever written.

—*former five-term Texas Lieutenant Governor William P. "Bill" Hobby Jr.*

Broadway and motion pictures popularized—and trivialized—the story of the famed Chicken Ranch brothel in La Grange, Texas. The real story is far more interesting, presenting a mirror to mores and conventions not just in that one locale, but for much of America. From its heyday to its ignominious demise, the Chicken Ranch was the story of enterprise, politics, power and even patriotism, writ in the garish hues of cheap makeup. Jayme Blaschke's Inside the Texas Chicken Ranch *is a compelling and brilliantly researched exploration of a unique icon of Texas history and society and what its rise and fall says about America. One comes away with the feeling that when outside pressure finally closed down the Chicken House, it was an act of cultural vandalism.*

—*William C. Davis, author of* Three Roads to the Alamo *and* Lone Star Rising

INSIDE THE
TEXAS
Chicken Ranch

The Definitive Account of

the Best Little Whorehouse

REVISED, EXPANDED AND UPDATED

JAYME LYNN
BLASCHKE

THE
History
PRESS

Published by The History Press
Charleston, SC
www.historypress.net

First published 2016
50th Anniversary Edition 2023

Manufactured in the United States

ISBN 9781467153935

Library of Congress Control Number: 2016934536

Notice: The information in this book is true and complete to the best of our knowledge. It is offered without guarantee on the part of the author or The History Press. The author and The History Press disclaim all liability in connection with the use of this book.

For Aunt Jessie, Miss Edna and every other woman who ever found herself at the Chicken Ranch through fate or circumstance.

CONTENTS

ACKNOWLEDGEMENTS

No book is ever written in isolation, but this project in particular has brought me into contact with an amazing array of people who have been exceptionally generous with their time and assistance. Without their assistance and cooperation, this book would not exist. I am forever grateful to the following:

Lisa Elliott Blaschke, Edna Milton Chadwell, Robert Kleffman, Mike McGee, Dan Beck, Jay Briones, Robert Hardesty, Bill Hobby, Kaitlin Hopkins, Cait Coker, Leerie Giese, William "Trigger" Rogers, Thad Sitton, Scott Cupp, Ronald W. Jeffrey, Bill Henry, Mark Finn, Willie Pankoniem, Red O'Neil, Ron Smith, Robbie Davis-Floyd, Ken Walters, Virginia Pritchett, Kathy Carter, Sherie Knape, Allison MacKenzie, La Grange Chamber of Commerce, La Grange Visitor's Bureau, Fayette County Heritage Museum and Archive, Paula Sanders-Hollas, Yvonne Stryk, Harvey Dipple, Robert Anderson, Erin Maxey-Whilhite, Jim Walton, Randy Sillavan, Lee Martindale, Ray Prewitt, Sue Owen, Debbie Rivenburgh, Diana Wilson, Jimmy Margulies, Herb Hancock, Oliver Kitzman, Stan Kitzman, Ray Grasshoff, Pete Masterson, Larry Conners, Patrice Sarath, Elizabeth Moon, Marc Speir, Bill Crider, Sara Cooper, T. Cay Rowe, Mark Hendricks, Steven Davis, Michele Miller, Bill Cunningham, William Davis, Tim Buchholz, Christine Buchholz, Joy Jones, Mark Carlson, Charlie Duke, Bill Anders, Jess Nevins, Chris N. Brown, Derek Johnson, the Scarlet Hens, La Grange Episcopal Women, Cait Coker, Gary McKee, Wittliff Collections, Seraphina Song, Bob Mauldin, Gary Cartwright, Terre Heydari, Ramiro Martinez,

Jennifer Reibenspies, Delores Chambers, Halley Grogan, Michael Gross, Irwin Thompson, David Guzman, Gregory T. Bailey, Roy Bragg, Linda Barrett, Cathy Spitzenberger, Jose Chapa, Nancy Naron, Katharine A. Salzmann, Linda Hass, Carolyn Heinsohn, Joe Southern, Steven Kantner, Elizabeth Haluska-Rausch, Mike Cox, Al Reinert, Travis Bible, Peggy Dillard, George Frondorf, Rox Ann Johnson, Terry Baer, Gene Freudenberg, Sherri Knight, Tina Swonke, Terre Heydari, Nick Rogers, Joan Gosnell, Ralph Rosenberg, Laurie Rosenberg, Thomas Van Hare, Timothy Ronk, Tom Copeland, Hilary Parrish, Christen Thompson, Penny, Donna Morris, Ruth, Victoria Bates, Myrna Thiessen, Stacey Norris, Ben Gill, John Kamenec, Vince Lee and Emily Deal.

INTRODUCTION TO THE 50TH ANNIVERSARY EDITION

Fifty years have passed since the infamous Chicken Ranch, purportedly founded in 1844, closed its doors for the last time.

When I reluctantly started research for this book a year or so following Marvin Zindler's 2007 death, I expected the endeavor to take no more than six months, tops. Everyone already knew the story of the Chicken Ranch, after all. How much more story was left to tell?

Turns out, there was a whole lot more story to tell. It took me six years. That movie with Dolly Parton and Burt Reynolds? Not a documentary. Hard to believe, I know.

I learned so much along the way. Astonishing things. Facts and stories and truths ready to be discovered at any time, if only someone bothered to look. But nobody looked, because everyone already knew the story. Or thought they did.

Still, when the first edition of this book went to press, many gaps in the history remained, scores of questions left unanswered. I could have researched for the next sixty years and still not have all the answers. What I did have, though, was the most complete history of that pissant country place possible at the time.

And readers responded. At book signings and lectures, many folks thanked me for finally setting the record straight. More importantly, the book piqued the interest of amateur historians. They'd approach me at signings, through email and honest-to-gosh stamped letters to share little bits of Chicken Ranch lore they'd uncovered. All of this, bit by bit, helped fill in some of those remaining gaps in the history. To them, I will always be grateful.

Then one day, I received the most extraordinary telephone call from a woman named Ruth.[1]

"I don't know if this is of any interest to you or not," Ruth said, "but Edna Milton worked for me managing a massage parlor in Oklahoma City."

Yes, I would be interested. The years 1982 to 1984 were a big gap in Miss Edna's history. I was very interested indeed.

Miss Edna's fortunes had waned quickly since *The Best Little Whorehouse in Texas* hit cinemas in 1982. In urgent need of a job, she fell back to what she knew best and approached the Capri Massage Salon, smack dab in the middle of Oklahoma City.

"When I opened the door, I thought she was an angry wife of one of our clients," Ruth explained. "She said she wanted a job, and I didn't believe her. Women at that age just didn't show up there. It was really strange."

Warily, Ruth let her in and started a decidedly awkward job interview.

"I just said, where have you worked before? She named off some places; I can't remember all of them. And then she said La Grange. I said, 'La Grange? You mean the Chicken Ranch?'"

"Yeah," Miss Edna answered.

"Did you work there?"

"I ran it."

Ruth looked at her closely, realization dawning. "I said, 'You're Miss Mona?' It came down like that. Oh, she just grinned real big!"

As proof, Miss Edna showed her the back album cover for the original Broadway cast recording of *Best Little Whorehouse in Texas*. There she was, wearing a tiara and waving to the audience with the rest of the cast.

Miss Edna had arrived at a fortuitous time. Ruth was stretched thin. In addition to the Oklahoma City massage parlor, she'd had to start running a second in Duncan, Oklahoma, after her husband died. Having Miss Edna in Oklahoma City allowed her to concentrate on running, and eventually selling, that second property.

"I needed somebody desperately to run that place, and it's like she just fell out of the sky, you know?" Ruth said. "I needed her so desperately at that time. When she first came to work there, she worked on the floor with the girls for a few weeks before I put her in charge.

"I remember her as very fair and honest. And it's very difficult to find somebody to run one of those places for you that is honest. They're usually not. I'm most certain that she was honest," she said. "There was a Pakistani peddler that came around occasionally, selling the girls jewelry, scarves and such. He was also going to college. A real nice guy. I saw him after Edna had left town, and he told me that Edna gave him five $100 bills and that he refused to take them, but she kept insisting. He was just amazed that she would do that. She told him to spend that on his schooling.

"Of course, she knew he would come in contact with other girls from other parlors and recommend her place to work in," she said. "I only wish she had kept more money over the years for herself."

Miss Edna proved herself to be a model employee—most of the time. After years of giving the orders, it wasn't always easy for her to take them.

"I had a little conflict with her once, just barely. And I absolutely saw the devil in her eyes," Ruth said, laughing. "Edna carried a snub-nosed .38 in her purse all the time. She was complaining about the girls one time, and I said, 'You've got to get along with them.'

"I mean, she was ready to fight [when I said that]. She just didn't like any authority over her. She pounded her fist on the desk and shouted, 'I'm getting along with these girls!'" Ruth said, well aware of the pistol Miss Edna kept handy. "Like I said, I kinda saw the devil in her eyes. I backed off a little bit and said, 'Oh, okay. I hope so.'"

Ruth saw that devil reappear one other time. Miss Edna arrived in town driving a baby blue Cadillac with Texas license plates she'd bought back in the 1970s. Unfortunately, a notorious pimp from Texas drove a similar car, and Oklahoma City police didn't want him in their town.

"I was at the parlor giving one of the bedrooms a new coat of paint when I heard a commotion in the office area where Edna and another girl were. I thought we were maybe being robbed, but soon, cops were all over the place," Ruth said. "They had been looking for [the pimp] for some time. Said he was working underage girls. Said it looked like his car.

"When they kicked the door in, they knocked Edna to the floor. Once again, I saw the devil in her eyes. She sure did have a temper!" she said. "We helped her up, and we were all surprised when one of the cops came right back in and sincerely apologized. That sure softened the blow a bit.

"About that temper, she said she had a girl at the ranch who kept bringing in drugs and lying about it," Ruth said. "So [Edna] sailed a .38 bullet over her head as a warning! I thought that was funny, but probably scary."

The end of Miss Edna's time in Oklahoma City came swiftly, with none of the fanfare that accompanied the Chicken Ranch's closure.

"We were sitting there listening to the album that had her picture on it. We had a glass door in the parlor—you could see out but couldn't see in," Ruth said. "All of the sudden, I saw four or five cops coming across the street. They were headed right for my front door, so I knew it was a problem.

"I got to the door as quickly as I could because always, those cops want to kick your door. I opened the door as quickly as I could and let them in," she said. "They said, 'We're closing all the parlors in town. You be closed by tomorrow. We'll be back, and there will be consequences.'

"Edna just packed up and left, and that's the last time I saw her. However, we were sitting there listening to that album, the stage play, and there was a picture of her playing the original madam, and I thought it's sure coincidental listening to that when they came here to close us.

"And a tear ran down her face. Edna said, 'Every place I've been has closed,'" Ruth said. "See, these places were like home to her. I think that's mostly all she ever knew."

I can hardly wait to see what new stories I'll have to share for the bicentennial edition of this book in 2044.

—Jayme Lynn Blaschke
New Braunfels, Texas
October 2022

Chapter 1

A History that Grows in the Telling

The Chicken Ranch was a brothel, pure and simple. Not so pure, and nowhere near as simple, were the motives of those who closed it down. Therein hangs this tale.

Not that this story hasn't been told before, after a fashion. Five decades removed from its spectacular, primetime closure by a crusading Houston television station, the "Best Little Whorehouse in Texas" remains one of the most infamous brothels ever to operate in the United States, if not the world.

Yet the trappings of the tawdry, media-driven sex scandal—titillation, notoriety, celebrity—are ill suited to what never amounted to anything more than an unassuming little country whorehouse tucked back amidst the post oaks and cedar trees just beyond the city limits of La Grange, Texas, less than a mile off State Highway 71 on an unpaved county road.

The Chicken Ranch, unlike the personalities that came to dominate its final days, was never larger than life. The owners kept their heads down and noses clean, paid their taxes and stayed on the good side of the law and politicians. The brothel's relations with the community at large were helped immensely by its madams being generous civic benefactors.

The fact that prostitution flourished in La Grange for well over a century did not make the town unique. In that aspect, at least, La Grange claimed no different pedigree from the scores of other cities and small towns across Texas that found a booming trade in illicit sex.

The Chicken Ranch, circa 1973. *William P. Hobby Sr. Family Papers, 1914–1997, 2011, Dolph Briscoe Center for American History, University of Texas at Austin.*

What set the Chicken Ranch apart was its venerable history. By 1973, it was the last man standing, so to speak, the lone holdout against changing times that shuttered pretty much all of its one-time contemporaries. The story of the Chicken Ranch is very much the story of Texas, in a literal as well as metaphorical sense.

FROM THE EARLIEST DAYS of the Republic of Texas, long before vast oilfields covered the landscape and "black gold" made the state rich, the Texas economy depended on three industries: cattle, cotton and timber. A casual observer of the time could not be blamed, though, for thinking of prostitution as a fourth major cash crop.

As Texas' frontier society developed, sex followed settlements. One of the earliest records of prostitution dates to 1817 in what eventually became San Antonio, when nine women were run out of the Spanish colonial outpost for whoring. Unsurprisingly, that did not end vice in San Antonio, or anywhere else in Texas for that matter.[2]

Prostitutes soon appeared in every Texas settlement of note. El Paso, the westernmost city in Texas and a crossroads of the Spanish empire in the New World, had to contend with prostitution on an ongoing basis, but the newer, Anglo-American settlements found out firsthand that commercial sex was not a genie easily kept in the bottle. Houston, established following Texas' 1836 independence from Mexico, grew so rapidly that by 1840, the Harris County Commissioners' Court licensed scores of bordellos in a futile attempt to keep the city's rampant vice under control. Galveston, which developed into an important seaport after its founding in 1830, attracted prostitutes right from the start to satisfy lusty sailors. Despite this statewide precedent, prostitution did not find its way to La Grange quite so quickly or directly.[3]

For thousands of years prior to the arrival of European settlers, a variety of Native American tribes continuously inhabited the land that would compose Fayette County. At the time of Stephen F. Austin's colonization efforts in the 1820s, Lipan Apaches and Tonkawas predominated, but

Modern La Grange retains a conflicted relationship with the Chicken Ranch. To the chagrin of some, a La Grange Area Chamber of Commerce billboard welcomes visitors to "The Best Little Town in Texas," a direct nod to Broadway musical and motion picture *The Best Little Whorehouse in Texas. Author photo.*

Waco and Comanche raiding parties were also common. It didn't take any great imagination to see why the region so appealed to the various tribes. The fertile Colorado River Valley bisected the land west to east, rich with pecan, black walnut and oak trees. To the north stood an arm of the Lost Pines Forest, with the rest of the area dominated by rolling blackland prairie and post oak savannah. Wild game abounded, with buffalo, white-tailed deer, black bear, beaver and countless other species thriving in the forests and fields.[4]

La Bahia Road, an important route through Texas since at least 1690 under Spanish colonial rule, cut through the heart of the region, crossing the Colorado below a prominent, two-hundred-foot limestone bluff. Enterprising Anglo pioneers from the United States set up trading posts near the crossing, taking advantage of the regular traffic, but not until 1822 did settlers of European descent—members of Austin's "Old Three Hundred"—arrive in significant numbers.[5]

Almost from the start the whites and the natives clashed. The first recorded battle occurred in 1823 on Skull Creek, when a hastily assembled troop of twenty-two settlers destroyed a Karankawa camp harassing whites along the river. The Karankawas, more commonly associated with the Texas Coastal Bend, were generally reviled by settlers and rival tribes alike for their reputed cannibalism. At the end of the fight, twenty-three Karankawas lay dead, without the loss of a single settler.[6]

The settlers and the Lipans remained on relatively good terms for the next decade, with Lipan warriors often serving as scouts for the whites and both groups uniting against the ever-present threat of Comanche raiders. Relations with the Tonkawas were cooler. Indian attacks constantly threatened the isolated farms and homesteads. Many settlers died in raids, but far more natives died through the settlers' retaliations. During the years of the Republic of Texas, the influx of newcomers from the United States and Europe displaced the tribes, forcing them westward. The last recorded Indian raid casualty in Fayette County came in 1840, when a party of Wacos ambushed and shot Henry Earthman.[7]

For nearly twenty years prior, however, the isolated settlers viewed Indian attacks as a most serious threat. To guard against the danger, in 1826 Tennessean and Old Three Hundred settler John Henry Moore built a fortified blockhouse half a mile from where La Bahia Road crossed the Colorado River. Over the course of the following decade, newcomers took advantage of the protection offered by "Moore's Fort," as it was called, and by the time of the Texas Revolution, the town of La Grange had coalesced.[8]

In the heady aftermath of the Battle of San Jacinto, with Texans reveling in their independence from Mexico, La Grange experienced perhaps its closest brush with fame prior to the closure of the Chicken Ranch more than a century hence. Formally created during the Second Congress of the Republic of Texas in December 1837, Fayette County was carved from the existing counties of Bastrop and Colorado. Formally platted at that time, La Grange was designated the county seat. The following year, the Texas congress voted on a permanent location for the young nation's capital. La Grange won on the second ballot, beating out eight other communities, including Bastrop, Nacogdoches and Richmond.

Celebrations in La Grange were short-lived, however, as President Sam Houston unexpectedly vetoed the legislation, and congress failed to muster sufficient votes to override. Instead of a capitol building, La Grange settled for a mere courthouse.[9]

Still, things changed rapidly for La Grange, capital or no. The nascent Texas republic, thinly populated and vulnerable to Mexican invasion from the south and hostile tribal raids from the west, threw open its doors to European immigrants. Thousands of Germans answered the call, lured as much by the promise of free land as by overcrowding and lack of opportunity in the mother country. The fractious German states organized the *Adelsverein*—an administrative body charged with establishing a "New Germany" in Texas— and the influx of immigrants quickly led to the founding of New Braunfels and Fredericksburg, with five other smaller settlements established along the Llano River. In 1843, the *Adelsverein* purchased more than 4,400 acres in Fayette County, naming the land Nassau Farm. The land never became the hub of German activity in Texas as intended—the *Adelsverein* ultimately designated New Braunfels for that role—but immigrants making their way to the frontier settlements along the Llano River used Nassau Farm as a welcome way station. Many of these early settlers liked what they saw and chose to homestead in Fayette County instead of the frontier.[10]

A decade later, a wave of Czech immigrants followed the Germans. Rather than a formal, government-sponsored movement, the Czech influx came as more of an individual, populist response to the letters of Reverend Josef Arnošt Bergmann, an early settler of Cat Spring, Texas. Bergmann's glowing reports published in *Moravské Noviny* (*Moravian News*) about available land and opportunity inspired many poor Moravians to strike out for Texas, with Bohemians soon following. The influx of new immigrants had an immediate and lasting impact on the population of Fayette County. The newcomers founded the communities of Dubina, Praha and Nechanitz, while many more moved into the existing towns of Fayetteville and La Grange. By the end of the decade, Fayette County had grown to become the epicenter of Czech culture in Texas.[11]

"Most of the population was German or Czech," said Oliver Kitzman, a former district attorney who served Fayette County. "If you look around the country, you'll see when the Czechs came over they settled in the blackland prairies and the Germans settled in the hills, the more rolling places. I don't know why that is, but it's true. They were a frugal, hardworking people."[12]

A frugal, hardworking people who knew how to have a good time. A mix of Catholic, Lutheran and Moravian brethren, their ideas on proper observation of the Sabbath—with feasts, celebrations and lots of music and dancing—clashed with the more austere, Puritanical views of the Anglo settlers from the United States. Significantly, they also brought with them a general European tolerance of prostitution. The Americans viewed the newcomers as aloof, an understandable conclusion considering the language barrier and the fact that the Germans and Czechs shared more in common with each other than with the Americans. On the other hand, the Anglos were nothing short of patronizing toward the Europeans. Before long, it didn't matter: increasing numbers of Germans and Czechs steadily displaced the early Anglo settlers, forever altering the culture of Fayette County and La Grange.[13]

No contemporary records documenting the opening of the first brothel in La Grange exist. Why should there be? The arrival of prostitutes was not something breathlessly reported in the pages of the *La Grange Intelligencer*, and even if it were, a fire in 1850 destroyed most of that newspaper's archive as well as its successor, the *Far West*.[14]

Lack of evidence didn't prevent Jan Hutson from providing plenty of detail in her 1980 book, *The Chicken Ranch: The True Story of the Best Little Whorehouse in Texas*. As Hutson tells it, the very first madam to run a brothel in La Grange arrived in 1844 on La Bahia Road from New Orleans, that infamous Sodom-on-the-Mississippi, with a covey of three "soiled doves" in tow. A full two years would pass before the violent, tumultuous existence of the Republic of Texas came to an end with its annexation as the twenty-eighth state of the Union. From then on, prostitution operated continuously in La Grange for the next 129 years.[15]

Of these women's lives in New Orleans, or whether they made any detours along the way, nothing is recorded. It strains credibility to suggest that they set out from New Orleans with the actual intent to settle in La Grange, a tiny frontier town barely known to anyone east of Nacogdoches, if even that. It is far more likely that their intended destination was San Antonio or possibly the new capital of Austin. In any event, circumstances forced them to stop in La Grange, and in La Grange they stayed.

The newly arrived madam came to town sporting the most unfortunate name of "Mrs. Swine." It's doubtful this was her real name, or even an alias willingly chosen, for obvious reasons. Short, obese and unkempt, with an unattractive upturned nose and "piggy" features, she claimed to be a widow fallen on hard times. Wearing only black garments of mourning that had seen better days, Mrs. Swine's sole connection to a life of wealth and luxury—past or present—was a diamond ring encircling one pudgy finger.[16]

Whether or not Mrs. Swine actually existed is debatable, to put it kindly. While the origin of the Chicken Ranch—or, at the very least, a brothel that eventually became the country whorehouse known as the Chicken Ranch—is consistently dated to the 1840s by oral histories and local lore, the same cannot be said of Mrs. Swine. In fact, the earliest reference to her appears *no earlier* than Hutson's 1980 book, a full 130-plus years after the assumed founding of the brothel and 7 years after the Chicken Ranch closed its doors for good.

In short: Mrs. Swine is a complete fiction.

The fact that Mrs. Swine is often cited in post-1980 articles and literature as the original madam in La Grange does nothing to change the fact that no evidence exists supporting the idea that she ever lived. By the same token, no conclusive evidence exists disproving her, either. If the widowed Mrs. Swine is a likely fiction, then she is a convenient one. Prostitution certainly flourished in nineteenth-century La Grange, as it did throughout Texas and the Old West. *Somebody* had to be first, it stands to reason, and if nothing else, the homely, crude widow dressed in black makes for a good story.

An alternative version of the Chicken Ranch's origins told by Edna Milton Chadwell, the last madam of the brothel, makes no mention of Mrs. Swine, although it pegs the date close to 1844. According to Miss Edna, two women were traveling across Texas in a covered wagon with a hired hand along to handle the driving and also serve as protection. The travelers got as far as La Grange, approaching the ferry landing, when the wagon broke down, beyond the hired man's ability to repair. Stranded, without money or shelter, the two women resorted to selling themselves to get by.[17]

"Those girls did it right there in that wagon," Miss Edna said. "I don't know what the man was doing right about then. Maybe he was just trying to find a job, too. Or maybe he was letting the men in town know there was some women out there. I don't know what the deal was. This is all hear-tell stories because there's no way to verify any of it."[18]

After a while, the trio abandoned any plans they had to repair the wagon and continue their journey. Instead, they took up residence in a saloon on Lafayette Street near the river. Efforts a century later by Miss Edna to locate the original site ended in failure; the building and any signs of where it once stood were long gone.[19]

A third—and possibly the most interesting—version dates the origin of the brothel to 1842. Or, not the brothel exactly, but rather, a track along the Colorado River flood plain at the end of Colorado Street, adjacent to Lafayette and the ferry landing. Head-to-head match races between horses were held there, along with the requisite gambling. A brothel soon followed as a matter of course. The racetrack (and, by extension, the brothel) was established by a La Grange businessman in partnership with a senator of the Republic of Texas representing Fayette County. James Seaton Lester of Winchester—who just happened to be one of the first trustees of Baylor University—served in the Texas senate during the first, second, fourth and fifth congresses and in the house during the third congress. James Webb of Austin served in the senate for the sixth and seventh congresses. Both had strong ties to La Grange, and either could be the brothel-owning senator of lore.[20]

At the time, Lafayette Street served as the main thoroughfare through town, one leg of the historic La Bahia Road, running northeast to southwest. It extended all the way to the Colorado River, where a ferry operated until 1883. The steady flow of travelers proved irresistible, and before long, at least one wood-frame saloon went up between Water Street and the river, just a stone's throw beyond the city proper. The saloon's prime location took advantage of the abundance of thirsty, road-weary travelers and, as a matter of course, offered several rooms to rent. It is here the mythical Mrs. Swine— or Miss Edna's stranded whores—took up residence. The saloon operated continuously as a brothel for at least the next fifty years.[21]

That nobody took particular notice of a brothel setting up shop in a backwater saloon is hardly surprising. The decade-long existence of the Republic of Texas was an eventful time for La Grange and Fayette County, and the years of statehood prior to the Civil War no less so. The republic's near-constant state of war with Mexico led to the spilling of much Fayette County blood. Many men from La Grange participated in the ill-fated Dawson and Somervell Expeditions, dying in the subsequent massacres.[22]

A ferry operated until 1883 at the end of La Fayette Street, where the Kalamazoo vice district flourished. As early as the 1840s, horse races were held at the end of Colorado Street, between La Fayette and Travis. *Augustus Koch,* Bird's Eye View of La Grange, Fayette County, Texas, 1880. *Courtesy Fayette Heritage Museum and Archives.*

The remains of the Somervell dead—those decimated in the notorious "Black Bean Affair"—were brought to La Grange in June 1848, and by September, the remains of the Dawson company were acquired as well. The two sets of remains were then interred with full military honors in a vault built on the bluff overlooking the Colorado River. Over the years, the site became known as Monument Hill, one of the most important shrines of Texas history.[23]

Despite the nearly continuous conflict, La Grange showed steady growth and prosperity. One of the most prominent signs of this was the opening in 1840 of Rutersville College, seven miles northeast of La Grange. The first chartered college in Texas, this coeducational institution enrolled a modest sixty-three students at first, but by 1850, its alumni numbered more than eight hundred. Mismanagement led to a decline in enrollment and the school's fortunes after 1850, and by 1856, Rutersville College had merged with the Texas Military Institute, the former enticing the latter to relocate from Galveston. Funding originally intended for a permanent monument at Monument Hill was used to subsidize the merger, and the ensuing controversy further destabilized the college. Following Texas secession in 1861, the entire graduating class enlisted, and most undergraduates followed. Without students, Rutersville College closed its doors for good.[24]

Secession offered yet another opportunity for Fayette County to differentiate itself from the rest of the state. Although a black flag on the courthouse flagpole greeted the election of Abraham Lincoln, pro-Union sentiment ran strong in the community. Indeed, when it came time to vote to secede, the measure was rejected by Fayette County voters 580 to 626—the only county in Texas to do so. By this time, the area was one of the most prosperous in the state, with a growing population of more than 11,600. One thousand farms filled the county—most of them homesteaded by German and Czech immigrants—but a number of successful plantations had taken root as well, with nearly 3,800 slaves.[25]

The growing importance of slavery to the local economy couldn't tilt the scales in favor of secession at the ballot box. The Germans and Czechs were largely responsible for that outcome, with both sets of immigrants by and large opposed to slavery. The Germans, in particular, already had their fill of war, with many of them fleeing to Texas to escape the widespread revolutions of 1848, which wracked the various German states. One German family went so far as to hide their son in a muddy wallow among their hogs in order to evade conscription. La Grange did not greet the specter of war with enthusiasm.[26]

Nevertheless, once fighting broke out, three volunteer companies quickly formed, and roughly eight hundred men from the Fayette County area fought for the Confederacy. This late-blooming Southern patriotism may explain the story of Mrs. Swine's abrupt end as reigning madam in La Grange. With the war intensifying and hardships on the homefront mounting, whispers and suspicions grew that she was a Yankee sympathizer and a traitor. More than seventeen years had passed since she supposedly arrived in La Grange. The town had tripled in size during that time, and her girls had serviced many of the newcomers, transients and old-timers as well. Whatever goodwill she'd built up through the years didn't last long once her loyalties came into question. By 1865, the fictitious Mrs. Swine had fled La Grange, never to return.[27]

The brothel left behind endured, however. All across Texas, prostitution thrived in the aftermath of the Civil War as the population increased. Freed black women joined the ranks of poor Mexican and European prostitutes, but self-imposed segregation formed in a caste-like system. In San Antonio, with a growing military presence, prostitution was considered both inevitable and necessary for the entertainment of the soldiers stationed there. Austin took a similar stance, only instead of the US Army, it was the Texas state legislature that demanded easy access to carnal pleasure. Unlike the rowdy clientele in San Antonio, the state representatives and senators demanded more discretion. Madams like Miss Sallie Daggett learned to navigate the nuanced system effectively, rarely running afoul of the law. As Austin police focused most of their attention on streetwalkers and black prostitutes, Daggett had no hesitation about calling in the law when confronted with theft or disruptive behavior in her house. Such a cordial relationship between police and brothel eventually developed in La Grange as well.[28]

To deal with the seemingly inexhaustible male demand for prostitution and women willing to accommodate, Texas cities followed the lead of others across the nation and established sprawling vice districts in the hopes of containing the sex industry, if not legitimizing it. The names of some districts were whimsical, such as Austin's "Guy Town," Houston's "Happy Hollow" and Dallas' "Boggy Bayou" and "Frogtown," while others, such as Fort Worth's "Hell's Half Acre," were simply bleak. Others eschewed memorable names in favor of geographic description, as was the case with Galveston's infamous Post Office Street and El Paso's Union Street.[29]

Waco, known today as the home of conservative Baylor University, the largest Southern Baptist–affiliated college in the United States, led the vanguard of this movement. Along the south banks of the Brazos River near Waco's famed nineteenth-century suspension bridge, a red-light district alternately known as "The Reservation" or "Two Street" thrived for more than forty years. Waco blazed a trail, becoming the first city in Texas to legalize prostitution. Brothels had business permits and paid taxes while prostitutes were licensed and—like the women of the Chicken Ranch decades later—submitted to regular, mandatory medical examinations. Although the political establishment ostensibly supported Two Street as a means of keeping vice segregated from more respectable parts of the city, the vast amounts of revenue generated by taxes and licensing fees levied upon commercial sex held far more sway over public policy than moral concerns.[30]

Prostitution proved no less prevalent in rural Texas. Thousands of women, ranging in age from teens through early thirties, struck out for the western frontier in hopes of finding opportunity, freedom or at least a good husband. Often lacking skills, literacy and money, these women found themselves facing a stark choice: whore or starve. Ranch brothels were common throughout the West, where white owners offered minimal room and board to white women in exchange for a percentage of their earnings. "Hog ranches" were another

The Old Fayette County Jail was constructed in 1883 of native limestone and operated until 1985. *Courtesy Fayette Heritage Museum and Archives.*

kind of brothel altogether. Wherever the US Army established a garrison, a hog ranch sprang up within easy walking distance for the enlisted men. The buildings were hastily built, put up by local saloon owners who showed little concern about the races of the women staffing it. High-volume affairs, women working hog ranches serviced as many men a day as necessary to maximize the owner's profits. Hog ranches, viewed by commanding officers as breeding grounds of disease and corruption, were strictly off-limits to troops. Troops widely ignored such orders.[31]

The sad truth is that, by and large, women on the frontier existed as disposable commodities, generating significant profit for their bosses with little for themselves beyond subsistence survival. Nineteenth-century whores faced a staggering degree of hardship. Rigid Victorian-era prejudice against premarital sex led to the rationale that all prostitutes, regardless of their circumstances, were "ruined women" and therefore something less than human, shorn of even their most basic human rights. Abused and assaulted women learned quickly to make peace with whatever justice they could find on their own rather than look to the law. The rape of a prostitute was, by definition, impossible as far as the public was concerned.[32]

The job itself was filled with occupational hazards easily capable of taking the prostitute's life. The constant specter of pregnancy loomed over every tryst. It's hard to imagine a working woman not sighing in relief at the first appearance of menstrual blood each month. Misguided modesty led to widespread ignorance and misinformation about reproduction and birth control. Condoms were available but rarely used. Instead, an assortment of medicines ranging from outright quackery to drugs and herbal mixes purported to induce miscarriage or "eliminate obstructions," as the prevailing euphemism went. Any woman desperate enough to take one of these "medicines" gambled with her life. Surgical abortion hardly offered a safer alternative, with poorly trained clinicians conducting the procedure in deplorable conditions. Infection and hemorrhaging were common, with a correspondingly high death rate. Despite this—not to mention the illegality of it—abortion remained the most common form of birth control among prostitutes, a situation exacerbated by the Comstock Act of 1873, which effectively outlawed all contraceptives and even information on birth control.[33]

Disease constituted the other lurking horror for prostitutes. Syphilis, gonorrhea and like afflictions constituted an inescapable fact of life for whores, and women working in the sex trade long enough were certain to contract something. Again, a skewed version of modesty contributed to the spread of venereal disease throughout the West. Until the latter years of the nineteenth century, neither party undressed for intercourse. The client opened his fly, the whore hitched up her skirt and a few minutes later they'd part ways. Eventually, the threat of disease grew so severe that houses implemented policies requiring men's genitals be washed with soap and water prior to sex, giving the women a chance to look for any outward sign of disease. Such measures were necessary—in New Orleans alone, syphilis claimed the lives of close to 3,900 in a single year at the turn of the twentieth century, a very steep price to pay for a two-dollar screw.[34]

It is difficult for someone from modern society to fathom the very real scourge of venereal disease in the nineteenth century. Prior to the discovery of antibiotics, contracting syphilis was every bit a death sentence. Syphilis afflicted its victims with grotesquely disfiguring lesions followed by excruciating pain and very often insanity. Gonorrhea seldom resulted in death, but symptoms in severe cases included fever, vomiting, inflammation and often permanent sterility. Medical treatment often proved as dangerous as the diseases themselves. Bloodletting to "balance the humors," cauterization of chancres, steam baths and a host of other remedies offered brief but false hope of cure as the diseases passed into natural remissions. When other treatments invariably failed, quicksilver mercury treatments often served as the first, second and last line of defense for suffering patients. Doctors injected mercury into the penises of afflicted men, applied it directly onto lesions or even made patients breathe mercury vapors. By the 1910s, medicine had progressed to the point where arsenic, in the form of Arsphenamine (or Salvarsan), was the treatment of choice to combat syphilis. One of the biggest breakthroughs prior to antibiotics came in 1927, with the discovery that the intense fever brought on by malaria infection was hot enough to kill the syphilis bacterium—if it didn't kill the patient first. The extreme health hazards inherent in these treatments—which were willingly endured—stand as testament to the real horror syphilis represented.[35]

AWAY FROM THE CITIES, in smaller, rural agricultural communities like La Grange, prostitutes tended to enjoy a better life than their urban sisters. Pimps, those men who lured women into prostitution and then exploited and often abused them in parasitic relationships, were far less common in the country. The brothels were smaller, unpretentious but clean. The farmers, cowboys and other common men who patronized the country whorehouses were rarely wealthy but were more open to marrying a soiled dove—no small consideration.[36]

In 1849, German stonemason Heinrich "Henry" Kreische purchased a 172-acre tract, including the bluff overlooking La Grange to the Colorado River below—a purchase that brought with it the tomb of the Somervell and Dawson dead. By 1860, Kreische had built an elaborate, three-story stonework brewery in a ravine halfway down the bluff, taking advantage of a free-flowing natural spring to provide water for the brewing, which also naturally cooled the beer stored in the lower cellars. The brewery filled what could only be considered a glaring need for the German and Czech immigrants, and by 1879, it had grown to become the third largest brewery in the state, shipping Bluff Beer as far as San Antonio.[37]

For the brothel operating at the far end of Lafayette Street—as well as the other saloons in town—the Kreische Brewery was like manna from heaven. Alcohol and sex had a long-standing affinity for each other, and now local sources existed for both. Beer was a marvelously effective lubricant when it came to separating a customer from his hard-earned dollars. Whenever a saloon ran low on drink, it simply put in an order and a wagon loaded with barrels of cellar-cooled beer would arrive shortly, helped along its short journey by a ferry Kreische's sons operated across the river.

Tragically, the happy arrangement did not last. Kreische died in a wagon accident in 1882. His sons continued the operation of the brewery, but that same year, a tap line of the Galveston, Houston and San Antonio Railway Company connected La Grange for the first time to the rest of the state. While this came as a boon to the cotton farmers of Fayette County, who now had an easy way to ship their produce, it also opened up La Grange to cheap beer, shipped in from St. Louis on refrigerated cars. By 1884, the brewery had closed its doors, and Bluff Beer was no more.[38]

While the isolated location at the end of Lafayette Street provided the brothel with a steady flow of customers, as well as enough separation from the town proper to maintain decorum, it came not without peril. A massive flood of the Colorado in 1869 utterly swamped the saloon housing the brothel. Most of La Grange suffered terribly, with countless acres of crops destroyed in the surrounding countryside, venomous water moccasins driven into homes seeking dry ground and water standing five feet deep on the courthouse square. The brothel, literally a stone's throw from the ferry landing on the river, was all but destroyed. The following year, another flood almost as large did a comparable amount of damage.[39]

Despite the back-to-back floods, the brothel rebuilt once the waters receded. Times were changing, though, and despite picking up the euphemistic nickname "Kalamazoo" from the local populace, the riverside location that had served well for close to forty years grew steadily less viable. In 1883, La Grange built a long-discussed iron bridge across the Colorado River, and Kalamazoo suffered immediately. The bridge, several blocks south of Lafayette Street, spelled the end of the old ferry. The brothel remained an easy walk from the new bridge, but the literal as well as symbolic bypassing hinted at bigger changes to come.[40]

Local lore holds that the elevated bridge undermined the business of Kalamazoo in a second, more devastating way. Because of the bridge's height, it supposedly offered a direct and revealing view of the brothel and saloon patrons as they came and went. As brothel-watching became a popular pastime, business suffered a corresponding decline. Faced with such direct economic pressures, the owners adapted by relocating to the east corner of the Jackson and Travis Street intersection. This location was safely within the boundaries of the segregated "black part of town," where such business would be tolerated while also avoiding unwanted spectators.[41]

Except…the relocation of Kalamazoo did not happen so neatly. While the modern bridge across the Colorado River is only a couple blocks downstream from the old ferry landing at the end of Lafayette Street, the *original* bridge built in 1883 crossed the river farther downstream, close to the

Prior to the construction of flood control dams, the Colorado River flooded La Grange with devastating regularity. Deluges in 1896, 1870 and 1900 destroyed countless homes, businesses and crops. This photo of the 1913 flood shows the river swamping city streets. *Courtesy Fayette Heritage Museum and Archives.*

current boat ramp. The intervening distance—not to mention any trees and brush—would have made brothel-watching a poor sport.[42]

By 1897, a second brothel *had* opened in the northeast part of town, near the intersection of Jackson and Travis Streets. Kalamazoo, too, continued to operate at the far end of Lafayette Street. Despite La Grange's historical tolerance of prostitution, the townsfolk did not greet this twofold increase in the sex trade with joy. The second brothel caused such scandal that the subject—normally taboo in polite company—spilled over into the pages of two of the town's three newspapers:

> *We understand that several of the "soiled doves" of the city have grown weary of the secluded locality known as "Kalamazoo," where they can hold their nocturnal orgies and make night hideous without disturbing the peaceful slumbers of the virtuous, and have moved up in the north east part of town among the residences where they are carrying on their nefarious traffic with a high hand. But there is a place recognized as their abode and the officers should see to it that they have to stay there. But this official can break up the "joint" recently established on the hill.*

Now why should they be allowed to stay in the west part of town, where it is only about three or four blocks from the courthouse? They have no more right there than in the eastern or any other portion of the town, and as for the officers running them out of the eastern part of the town, of course they could [sic] them all out of the city limits. Again, the News says: "The so-called 'K' does not disturb the neighbors," yet it can be proved that the so-called "doves" have been heard as far as the new Casino.

They say break up the "joint" on the hill; why not break them up in the western part also. Hoping when the officers put in their work, they will do it right; put them in a place where they will not disturb anybody out of the city limits.

WEST PART OF TOWN [43]

Prostitution may have established itself in La Grange in the days of the republic, but the dust of time shrouded memories of the frontier and the "anything goes" attitudes that accompanied it. Grown into a modern town of more than two thousand residents, La Grange boasted electric and water utilities, an opera house, four schools, three banks and five churches. With the progressive era of a new century dawning, there seemed little chance that the status quo—enjoyed by the brothels for so long—could continue.

Chapter 2

AUNT JESSIE

The turn of the century brought with it another devastating flood, with the Colorado River surging out of its banks on December 4, 1900. The rising waters inundated La Grange, forcing families to use flatboats to navigate the submerged streets. Nearly 160 homes were lost or damaged by the deluge, which was every bit as destructive as the floods of the previous century. The floodwaters were another blow to the vice district still hanging on at the end of Lafayette Street, exposed as it was on the river's flood plain. The rising waters even disrupted business at the newer brothel at Jackson and Travis Streets.[44]

As opening salvos went, the great flood of 1900 was a doozy. But bigger challenges than nature could muster awaited La Grange's brothels in the early twentieth century.

During the late nineteenth century, the predominant view of prostitution considered it a necessary evil, an inevitability of human nature that must be regulated for the public good. This was buttressed by the idea that female and male sexual natures were vastly different—that women were, at best, delicate and sexually indifferent creatures, whereas men were driven by uncontrolled, bestial lust. Prostitutes provided a needed outlet for such rampant libido, protecting virginal maidens from rape and wives from relentless sexual servitude. Men could not help it that they were consumed by such enormous sexual appetites; this was their nature, and only through profound feats of self-control could they resist ravaging any woman to cross their paths.[45]

The idea that legalized prostitution prevented rape and the spread of venereal disease was perhaps the most persistent argument used by those in favor of a regulated sex trade and, not coincidentally, commonly invoked to defend the Chicken Ranch. These so-called regulationists consisted mostly of police and medical practitioners, those who interacted and dealt with prostitution on an ongoing basis. From their perspective, the world's oldest profession had thrived despite centuries of eradication efforts by countless cultures. The prohibition approach, in their view, persistently failed. If prostitution could not be eliminated, then might containment and segregation protect polite society from corruption? A regulatory environment had the advantage of licensed brothels and prostitutes who underwent regular medical

August Loessin was born in Prussia in 1952 and immigrated to Texas with his parents as an infant. He won election as Fayette County sheriff in 1894 and served until 1920. *Photo by Louis Meleher. Courtesy Fayette Heritage Museum and Archives.*

exams, thereby cutting down on the incidence of sexually transmitted diseases. By the first decade of the twentieth century, practically every major American city had at least one official vice district, as did many smaller cities and towns.[46]

The inevitable backlash rode the same powerful wave of righteous indignation that fueled the temperance and women's suffrage movements. A much more persistent anti-vice campaign than any of the nineteenth century resulted. During the previous high-water mark of anti-prostitution fervor, the reformers' efforts were remarkably naïve, rooted in the notion that women who sold themselves were simply ignorant of their immorality or corrupted by outside influences. Mid-nineteenth-century efforts to counter these perceived causes of vice often centered on prayer meetings and the distribution of Bibles. Unsurprisingly, the reformists' efforts met with little success.[47]

Social purity advocates found the ground much more fertile for their cause by 1910. Hysteria over "white slavery"—not entirely unfounded— swept the nation, with the idea of unwilling women forced into sexual bondage horrifying many Americans. For their part, the sanctioned brothels and red-light districts did little to allay such fears, fostering all manner of petty crime and corruption, not to mention drunkenness and gambling. The prostitutes themselves, forced to pay off corrupt police and split their take with madams, pimps and landlords, often found the only way to survive was to become very adept at relieving customers of excess wealth, either through subterfuge or outright theft. Because of the existing system of bribes and protection payments, the authorities more often than not came down on the side of the women. In one instance, a visiting Canadian accused an Austin prostitute known as Duckie Belcher of stealing sixty-five dollars. Madam Sallie Daggett backed up Belcher's testimony in court that the man drank a lot and simply forgot he'd spent the money. The court sided with Belcher. Such cases were not uncommon among Austin's well-oiled brothel operations.[48]

Although the legalized brothel system offered a degree of protection, a woman's value only amounted to her ability to bring in money. One Austin police officer took note of a well-known prostitute, Georgetown Ella, who had fallen deathly ill. With their mother unable to work, Ella's four children faced the likelihood of starvation. Nobody expected the brothel's owner, Charley Cooney, to show compassion to any of them. Society in general didn't show much compassion, either.[49]

The twentieth century's social purity movement now understood the ineffectiveness of moral arguments to turn prostitutes away from their lives of sin—money put more food on the table than piety. Even so, their efforts at rehabilitation still fell short. Despite the harsh conditions and precarious social standing of a prostitute, brothel work still promised better prospects for a financially stable life than the few types of low-paying, menial jobs available to most women. Kitchen and domestic help, for instance, worked grueling hours and earned only a pittance for their labor.[50]

Nevertheless, the tide had turned against segregated vice. Even the famed Everleigh Club, an opulent Chicago landmark that played host to American millionaires, politicians and European royalty, found its doors permanently padlocked in October 1911. The rest of Chicago's tawdry Levee District suffered a similar fate the following year. Across the country, the social purity movement had gained popular support—and with it, the upper hand. Clearly, business as usual would no longer be tolerated.[51]

La Grange reflected the national mood when Jessie Williams arrived in town. Yet another newcomer generated little attention in the growing town, but in short order, "Aunt Jessie" gained control over all local prostitution, becoming one of La Grange's most influential citizens. Her impact on the community proved deep and lasting.

Of course, with the Chicken Ranch, nothing was as straightforward as it appeared at first glance. Aunt Jessie didn't enter the world as Jessie Williams.

Born Fay Zulema Stewart in February 1885 or 1886, she was the youngest of two children, after sister Alfa May.[52]

According to the most widely repeated story of her life—popularized by Jan Hutson's book—Stewart grew up on a marginally productive farm outside Hubbard, Texas. Around the age of eleven, she contracted diphtheria, with lasting negative effects on her health. At the age of fourteen, she moved with her family to Waco. Petite, with a round face and curly hair, a pale complexion and large eyes, Stewart worked a number of menial jobs until she found herself one of the more successful prostitutes in Waco's Two Street district by the time she turned eighteen. Within five years, she owned her own house with several prostitutes working under her. In 1905, at the age of twenty-five, she abruptly departed Waco and relocated to La Grange, where she either ran a brothel in a downtown hotel or purchased a house near the river for that purpose.[53]

An alternative version of Aunt Jessie's history agrees that her early years were spent in Hubbard but dates her arrival in La Grange to 1904. Rather than inexplicably abandoning her Waco operation, Aunt Jessie came invited, recruited by a local businessman to operate the Travis Street brothel. With public mood turning against the operation, the owners gambled that putting a woman ostensibly in charge of the brothel might counter the rising hostility, thus ensuring the brothel's continued profitability.[54]

In truth, Fay's parents came from Georgia or possibly Nashville, Tenn., not Hubbard, moving to Waco well before she was born. Her father, Andrew James Stewart, ran a grocery store in town until mounting debt forced its closure in 1882. Thereafter he worked as a clerk and a printer in town. A faulty 1900 census erroneously indicates he died in 1886, but Andrew James lived until 1924, when he passed away in Oklahoma City. It was Fay's mother, Amanda Stewart (née Tippens), who died young in 1896. Fay and Alpha lived with their widowed father for the next few years, but when he remarried in 1903 to Emma Gilcrease, herself a widow, life changed dramatically for Fay.[55]

Fay, all of 18 years old, moved out with Alpha. While it is entirely possible that Fay learned the ropes of prostitution on Two Street, no evidence backs that up. Instead, it's Austin where Fay first runs afoul of the law. In July of 1903 Fay—now going by the name Jessie Williams—was fined $5 for prostitution, euphemistically referred to as "vagrancy." Working under an assumed name comes as no surprise, as it was customary for women in the sex trade to do so in order to protect their families' reputations.[56]

In 1908, Alpha abruptly died at the age of twenty-five, leaving the younger Jessie truly alone for the first time in her life. Partnering with

The Loessin family poses in front of the Fayette Country Jail. *Back row, left to right*: Katie Stiehl Loessin, Will Loessin, unknown woman; *middle row*: Ruth Loessin, August Loessin, Louise Loessin, unknown boy; *front*: Wilburn Loessin. *Courtesy Fayette Heritage Museum and Archives.*

a woman named Francie Walker, Aunt Jessie took up residence in an Austin boardinghouse—the preferred front for most brothels—listed as a housekeeper. Her listing was a subtle but meaningful distinction from the regular prostitutes, identified as boarders. Aunt Jessie didn't stay a housekeeper for long. The 1912–13 Austin city directory showed that Aunt Jessie and her partner had opened their own house at 200 West Second Street, in the heart of the infamous Guy Town vice district. The brothel, modest by Guy Town standards, employed only four women as prostitutes: Lillian Fry, Leona Wright, Irell Logan and Etta Hartman.[57]

Unfortunately for Aunt Jessie, her rapid climb to the elite levels of the Austin vice scene came crashing down abruptly. Bolstered by a fear of syphilis as well as concerns that the red-light district corrupted students from the nearby University of Texas, social purity activists led by Mayor Alexander P. Woolridge succeeded in forcing a city council vote in 1913 to shut down Guy Town once and for all. Thus, Austin became the first city in Texas to disband its previously legal vice district. Guy Town's many brothels were ordered closed on October 1. By October 3, prostitutes were leaving the city in droves.[58]

While other women headed to the still-thriving vice districts of San Antonio, Waco, Houston or Galveston, Aunt Jessie instead relocated to La

Grange. Locals may well have recruited her to front the Travis Street brothel, but having run her own successful house in Austin, Aunt Jessie certainly had grander ambitions than serving as someone's proxy.

What she found waiting for her would give anyone pause. Guy Town had more than its share of squalid cribs intermixed with middle- and high-end houses, but La Grange had *nothing* nice to offer. Instead of an idealized Old West–style bordello, Aunt Jessie found herself in charge of a wretched hotel in a shanty town straddling the segregated black neighborhood, extending south and east from the intersection of Travis and Jackson Streets. Rather than working in the relative safety of a boardinghouse, the prostitutes here serviced their clients in hovel-like cribs—the lowest strata of city prostitution but the *only* strata in La Grange. Even the name of the place conveyed a sense of bleak hopelessness: the Shacks.[59]

Almost immediately, Aunt Jessie came under pressure from the community. Unlike Kalamazoo, which kept prostitution, gambling and liquor safely hidden away down by the river, the Shacks sat square in the middle of town,

By the late 1890s, with Kalamazoo rapidly fading, a new brothel (or brothels) had established itself near the intersection of Jackson and Travis Streets. As La Grange grew and expanded, this area of vice and blight acquired a new name: the Shacks. *Augustus Koch, Bird's Eye View of La Grange, Fayette County, Texas, 1880. Courtesy Fayette Heritage Museum and Archives.*

a blight that fostered crime and corruption, some of the same charges that helped put an end to Guy Town. The city wanted the Shacks gone. The residents wanted the Shacks gone. Having learned from her experience in Austin, Aunt Jessie didn't give the reformers a chance to build up a head of steam against her.

On July 31, 1915, Aunt Jessie and a new business partner, Grace Koplan, purchased a modest farmhouse on eleven acres from O.K. Zapp for $700. The land, dotted with post oak and cedar trees, proved ideally suited for a brothel. Part of the Eblin League, one of the first surveyed tracts in Fayette County dating to Spanish colonial times, the property lay northeast of town, less than half a mile off the main road between Houston and Austin. A right-of-way across neighboring property led straight to the front door, and a dusty dirt road out back offered a more circuitous route for customers concerned about privacy.[60]

As summer waned, Aunt Jessie realized the leaky, ramshackle farmhouse as it stood could not get her or her girls through the winter. She pitched some tents as a stop-gap measure until her carefully cultivated network of personal contacts saved the day.

After Aunt Jessie moved the brothel out of town, La Grange built a new high school on the property in 1923 to ensure vice would never return to the area bordered by Jackson and Travis Streets. *Courtesy Fayette Heritage Museum and Archives.*

"Well Mr. Temple down in the lumberyard said, 'Jessie, I tell you what. You pay all the men, the carpenters and everything and I'll finance the materials needed to build this house,'" said Edna Milton, who worked for Aunt Jessie and later bought the brothel from her. "So that's what happened there. He didn't charge her any interest or anything. From what I hear about him, he was a good man. He wasn't an ass about things the way some people could be. I never heard one thing about him trying to take advantage of any of the women."[61]

A small, one-room building on the opposite end of the property became the first of many additions, moved and attached to the main house during the renovations to provide a much-needed additional bedroom. The new house—a no-frills affair to be sure but ready to withstand the winter, far cleaner than the Shacks and infinitely more secluded—proved a resounding success. Aunt Jessie named it "Jessie Williams' Fashionable Boarding House," and booming business enabled her to buy out the recently married Koplan for the princely sum of $1,200 in 1917.[62]

La Grange, for its part, tolerated the new arrangement. The city soon tore down the Shacks that blighted Travis Street and, in 1923, built a new school on the block to ensure the area wouldn't fall back into vice.[63]

Although tensions with La Grange eased considerably, the brothel remained vulnerable. Her house operated beyond the reach of the city, true, but the county could still shut her down at any time. With that in mind, Aunt Jessie set about protecting her investment by convincing the Fayette County sheriff, August Loessin, that her brothel would cause no trouble and could even be an asset to the county.

Sheriffs in Texas at the turn of the century were generally known as "high sheriffs." Although a throwback to an earlier time, the term reflected the sheriff's vast political power at the county level. If Aunt Jessie wanted to operate long term, she had no choice but to win over the sheriff.[64]

Born in Prussia on February 19, 1852, Sheriff Loessin immigrated to Texas with his parents just three weeks later. He grew up near Fayetteville and Black Jack Springs, winning election for Fayette County sheriff in 1894. Loessin, a balding man with a thick mustache, served as sheriff for twenty-six years—notably keeping the Ku Klux Klan out of Fayette County—until retiring in 1920.[65]

When Aunt Jessie approached the sheriff's office, she did her best to win over both Sheriff Loessin and his brother, William, as allies. Mr. Will, as

Top: As sheriff, August Loessin established a departmental policy of tolerance toward the Chicken Ranch, one that would be continued by future Fayette County sheriffs, including his brother, Will Loessin, and J.T. Flournoy. *Courtesy Sandy Otto*.

Bottom: Will Loessin served as chief deputy for his brother, August, from 1894 until 1900, when he became La Grange city marshal. In 1924, he won election as Fayette County sheriff in his own right. *Courtesy Sandy Otto*.

William was known, was born on August 20, 1872—young enough to be August's son. After Mr. Will completed studies in 1894 at Blinn College in nearby Brenham, Texas, August hired him as chief deputy. In 1900, Mr. Will won election as La Grange city marshal, and over the years, August relied on him more and more as the sheriff's health declined.[66]

Cooperation, mostly, seemed key in forming a lasting alliance between the brothel and the sheriff's office. Law enforcement everywhere maintained useful networks of informants who would pass along information overheard from the underworld. In La Grange, this boiled down to the fact that petty criminals tended to brag about their exploits to impress whatever pretty boarder they happened to be bedding. Aunt Jessie made sure to relay any such confessions. The arrangement proved so effective that Mr. Will made nightly visits to Aunt Jessie's, ostensibly to check up on the latest gossip. The sheriff spent so much time there that deputies began referring to the Chicken Ranch, tongue-in-cheek, as his "office."[67]

To get elected sheriff in his own right, Mr. Will needed to develop his own political savvy. After August's retirement, Charlie Grint served a four-year term as sheriff. At the time, a resurgence of the American Party—an anti-Catholic, anti-immigration movement prone to conspiracy theories and commonly referred to as the Know-Nothings—gained control of Fayette County government. Mr. Will, along with his friend Pete Nichol, approached the politically powerful Joe Wagner about recruiting a slate of strong progressive candidates to oppose the incumbents. Wagner agreed, and in 1924, the progressives swept the Know-Nothings from power in Fayette County, with Mr. Will winning election as sheriff.[68]

Mr. Will came into the sheriff's office already owning a reputation as a clever detective from his years as deputy and city marshal. He distinguished himself as a deputy in 1902 by recovering a businessman's stolen $1,700 and arresting the thief, despite a lack of witnesses or obvious clues. In 1905, he and two constables tracked down and arrested a black man accused of raping a white woman in the far reaches of the county. Word spread of the arrest, and a mob soon formed, intent on lynching the suspect. Mr. Will stood up to the mob, forcing them to momentarily back down. Seeing an opportunity, he recruited half a dozen of the men to serve as guards to ensure the suspect reached La Grange safely. The suspect was later tried, convicted and hanged.[69]

"Loessin was no damn fool. He was a super sleuth. He solved more damn mysteries," said Leerie Giese, a longtime La Grange resident and banker. "Loessin could sit down and talk to anybody and talk out of them a confession, no damn coercion whatsoever. A real con man."[70]

Will Loessin, or Mr. Will, as he was called, managed the Fayette County Sheriff's Department from his office in the Fayette County Courthouse. *Courtesy Fayette Heritage Museum and Archives.*

As sheriff, Mr. Will crossed paths once with the infamous Raymond Hamilton, a one-time ally and partner of the murderous Bonnie Parker and Clyde Barrow. Following Hamilton's capture in Sherman, Texas, in 1934, the courts ordered him transferred to La Grange to stand trial for his 1933 robbery of the Carmine Bank.[71]

"When they put Raymond Hamilton in this jail, [Mr. Will] put an old boy they had in there [with Hamilton] who'd been indicted for murder," Giese said. Hamilton's cellmate, M.K. Simmons from the Rio Grande Valley, had accidentally killed a man while shooting at a hawk. "I don't think they wanted to try [Simmons], because damn, they knew he was innocent. Old man Will put him in the jail with Raymond Hamilton, same cell, to keep track of Hamilton."[72]

Since Simmons was facing potential murder charges, Hamilton treated him as a confidant. Simmons, for his part, kept Mr. Will updated on his conversations with Hamilton and eventually won acquittal. Hamilton probably owed Mr. Will a debt of gratitude—he sat safely in the Fayette County Jail as a posse made up of Texas and Louisiana lawmen ambushed and killed Bonnie and Clyde on May 23, 1934.

With that kind of background, Mr. Will wasn't about to let Aunt Jessie's house operate as an unchecked den of iniquity. If La Grange *must* have a whorehouse, then it would operate as a fine, decent, *upstanding* whorehouse. Mr. Will laid down a series of conditions: Firstly, although Aunt Jessie served beer, there would be no drunkenness tolerated. Second, that other staple of brothel revenue, gambling, was strictly prohibited. Third, taking a page from the red-light districts that still operated in the state, Mr. Will required medical examinations of the working girls on a weekly basis—subsequently pushing the creation of the office of county medical examiner to ensure the exams took place. Finally, Mr. Will would report to the Fayette County Grand Jury twice a year on the goings-on at the brothel, including any complaints, arrests and estimates of revenue, as well as instances of intelligence passed along to law enforcement, all to ensure the unique relationship with the sheriff's office stayed on the up-and-up. Aunt Jessie agreed to each and every condition.[73]

Only once did Aunt Jessie run afoul of the law after that. In the early years of Prohibition—as widely unpopular in La Grange as in the rest of the nation—the brothel continued selling beer, just as always. A pragmatic man,

Sheriff Will Loessin and his horse, Noebuck. *Courtesy Fayette Heritage Museum and Archives.*

Mr. Will tended to look the other way with folks home-brewing for their own consumption but took an axe to a still the moment he caught wind of moonshine sales. Eventually, common knowledge of Aunt Jessie's beer sales grew too widespread to ignore, and Mr. Will made the drive out to the house.

"Aunt Jessie, I don't like it any more than you do," Mr. Will warned, "but the drinkin' has got to go."[74]

After the repeal of Prohibition, with booze flowing freely across the country once again, Aunt Jessie kept a tight lid on her house. Even so, she still managed to turn a tidy profit.

"You could not come in there drunk, and you could only buy one beer," Giese recalled. "Beer was, at that time, fifteen cents to a quarter, and they were getting fifty cents to a dollar for it. And the nickelodeon—originally those were nickels, that's where the name came from—that one was always twenty-five cents."[75]

With the local law now firmly in her corner—significantly, *without* the onerous bribes and protection money that ensured police disinterest during the two-year run of her Guy Town brothel—Aunt Jessie set about shoring up relations with the La Grange population itself. One of the first opportunities to ingratiate herself with the community came with America's entry into World War I. As plenty of young Fayette County men headed overseas, joining the legendary doughboys of the American Expeditionary Force, Aunt Jessie had her handful of girls write encouraging letters to the guys, sometimes even sending along care packages filled with home-baked cookies. That show of compassion went over well in La Grange.[76]

Unfortunately, the War Department wasn't nearly as impressed.

Concerned with the debilitating impact venereal disease could have on the troops, the US government launched a full-on war against prostitution. Following the advice of Teddy Roosevelt, Secretary of War Newton Baker spoke softly and carried a very big stick: any Texas city that wanted an army post (or wanted to keep one it already had) must shutter any and all vice districts, period. During the summer of 1917, Baker succeeded where two decades of anti-prostitution crusaders had failed, as El Paso, Fort Worth, San Antonio and even "segregated vice" trailblazer Waco shut down their brothels, arresting prostitutes they had cheerfully licensed months before.[77]

Despite the fact that La Grange didn't have a military post, Aunt Jessie voluntarily enforced the army's prohibition on patronizing brothels…sort of.

"During the war, no soldier could come in that place," said Giese, "*unless* you were local, so that she would recognize the name."[78]

Aunt Jessie revived that policy when World War II flared up, although at the time it stemmed more from the need of crowd management rather than fear of running afoul of the War Department. With the establishment of Camp Swift in nearby Bastrop and Bergstrom Army Air Base outside Austin, the number of GIs in the immediate area had grown far beyond the capacity of a small country whorehouse to service.

"Shit, she couldn't have controlled it," Giese said. "Everyone from Camp Swift came down here [to La Grange]. This damn square was just loaded with soldiers every weekend, and a lot of times during the week."[79]

Once World War II ended and peacetime stability returned—Korea notwithstanding—Aunt Jessie relaxed the restrictions on GIs. Knowing they made dependable repeat customers, during the 1950s she lowered the prices for soldiers from the middle of the month until payday came around. Aunt Jessie had a distinct knack for spurring business while simultaneously engendering goodwill.[80]

Sometime prior to 1920—1913 or 1917 or even 1905, depending on which version of the local lore is accepted—two sisters took up long-term residence as boarders at Aunt Jessie's. Or they opened their own bawdyhouse on the hills south of the river in direct competition with Jessie's place. Experienced prostitutes, the "freckle-faced young pixies" hailed from Beaumont, where they did well for themselves servicing the roughnecks who worked in the booming Spindletop oil fields. Over the decades, versions of the story included Aunt Jessie as one of the women, arriving with her sister to open the brothel in 1917. This is improbable, as Aunt Jessie is documented as a La Grange resident from 1913 on, and Alpha had died years before. These sisters, though, showed they had a good head for business right from the get-go. Before long, Aunt Jessie grew confident enough in their abilities to promote them to "middle management." One sister married a wealthy San Antonio businessman and departed the brothel some years later. The other stayed on, managing the operation for Aunt Jessie until her death at the age of eighty.[81]

Little evidence backs up this story. Any woman living to eighty at the Chicken Farm would have had to be at least fifteen years older than Aunt Jessie— hardly the definition of a freckle-faced young pixie. If two sisters ever lived at the brothel, they weren't around when Uncle Sam came counting heads. The 1920 federal census identifies two women (Trixie Roth, thirty-three, and Evelyn Harris, twenty-four) as lodgers at the boardinghouse, with two black women (Augusta Dotson, twenty-eight, and Ada Poole, twenty-one) listed as cook and chambermaid, respectively. The 1930 census shows Aunt Jessie expanding operations to include six lodgers: Kitty Curtis, twenty-seven; Mildred E. Storey, twenty-one; Daisy Brooks, thirty-two; Cleo Williams, twenty-eight; Katherine Guthrie, thirty-four; and Estella Barrows, twenty-two.[82]

Barrows, at least, stuck around for more than a decade, eventually earning the nickname "Deaf Eddie." A relative of Aunt Jessie's remembers visiting the Chicken Farm with her family when she was no more than nine years old. Although Aunt Jessie closed the gates and business shut down during family visits, many of the boarders remained at the Chicken Farm. Barrows was one, and she always showed Aunt Jessie's young relative special kindness.

"I remember going out there a couple of times. The ladies there were always very nice," the relative recalled. "I do remember one of her workers, Eddie Barrows. There was one time [she] took me to where the jukebox was. It was rather dark in there. I think that she did buy me a Coke. People would've danced in there."[83]

The family lived in neighboring Bastrop County, close enough for the young relative's older brother to run errands for "Cousin Fay," like picking up supplies or driving the women someplace if needed. Just like everyone else in Texas, the family called Cousin Fay's boardinghouse the Chicken Farm—although it would be years before the young relative figured out why there weren't any chickens around. She just knew that everyone liked Cousin Fay.

"[Cousin Fay] was a very private person. She was a good person. Unfortunately, the profession she was in was not so good," the relative said. "It served a purpose. In fact, my grandmother…always said it should be legalized. It would prevent a lot of crime if it were legalized. That was the way the family looked at it.

"We accepted her, and there was no problem as far as we were concerned. We were very quiet about all of it. I knew that. I didn't really understand why, but we were," she said. "Even when my mother passed away, many years ago now, she didn't want people to know about it. I'm kind of the same way. I don't want to share with people around here because some people didn't like it, some people thought there was no problem, and I don't know the difference.

"I've just always grown up that way. We don't publicize it," she said. "There's a time, though, that you've got to start, if you want to make sure it's remembered correctly, you have to [speak up]."[84]

During this time, Aunt Jessie continued to work her diplomatic magic, implementing policies designed to win favor with the people of La Grange. She made a point of purchasing everything the boardinghouse needed

The Chicken Ranch's phone number was listed publicly in the Southwestern Bell telephone directory under "Williams, Jessie." In the era before area codes, simply dialing 283 in Fayette County would directly connect the caller with the state's most famous brothel. *Courtesy Gary McKee.*

locally, spreading business around so that all merchants in town benefited. She required the same of her girls, albeit with rules in place to ensure deference to the locals. When her women visited the local beauty salon, for example, they always took chairs in the back, leaving the front seats open for the townswomen. It didn't take long before local businesses decided the brothel outside town wasn't such a bad place after all.[85]

"The merchants appreciated them. They came and paid cash, very courteous, never intrusive," Giese said. "Miss Jessie was a *strict* disciplinarian.

"Those gals, they paid for everything. Back in the early '30s, the deputy sheriff brought the girls to town every Saturday afternoon. He let them out and he'd take them back," he said. "When [the deputy's son] graduated from high school, those girls gave him a twenty-one-jeweled Bulova wristwatch. Shit, that was unheard of!"[86]

Generosity, it turned out, made for great public relations. This fact did not escape Aunt Jessie's notice. If the granting of indulgences worked for the Vatican for centuries, then why couldn't La Grange use the same model? "*Indulgentia a culpa et a poena*," indeed.

"Miss Jessie was extremely good to this community. The banks were instructed to charge her account equal to top giver on anything," Giese said. "When they built the swimming pool in 1952, it was going to cost $7,500. She gave them $5,000."[87]

The showstopper, though, involved Fayette Memorial Hospital and cemented Aunt Jessie's image as a pillar of the community. The hospital opened in 1921, housed in a white two-story home on East Guadalupe Street originally built in the 1870s. It started with twenty-five beds and in 1927 added a nursery and obstetrics unit. By 1948, running short on space, the hospital trustees launched an ambitious renovation campaign to expand capacity to fifty beds.[88]

"When they got ready to rebuild it and were starting to raise money, she called my dad [hospital administrator Roy Giese] and said, 'I'm sending $10,000, right now,'" Giese said. "Now you can see why the people liked her. Very generous. Any charitable drive or fundraiser, Aunt Jessie was the top giver."[89]

Even Roy Giese, a socially conservative man with little tolerance for vice of any sort, gradually softened his opinion on Aunt Jessie.

"One day he told me, 'You know how I feel about Miss Jessie's place— [but] I wish I had a hospital full of them. Those gals, they are the nicest patients we could have,'" Giese said. "Miss Jessie takes the best room, pays a week in advance, leaves $250 and says, 'If you need any more, give me ten minutes and I'll have it.'

"Then [Roy] said, 'The only thing is, they mess up my nurses,'" he continued, chuckling at the memory. "'The way they tip, the nurses are always hanging around that room!'"[90]

Almost anyone who came into contact with Aunt Jessie's girls told a similar story. A high school sweetheart of Giese's went to work after graduation for a doctor who handled the weekly examinations of the prostitutes and developed a deep respect for the women.

"She said the same thing—'I wish we had nothing but those gals. They are absolute ladies in every respect. It's a pleasure just to have them in there,'" Giese said.[91]

If Aunt Jessie won over the people of La Grange with her largesse, it wasn't purely altruistic on her part. She'd navigated the ins and outs of the sex trade for decades and found La Grange's soft spot—which she shrewdly exploited to the best of her ability.

"She was a manipulator. Didn't make much difference who it was," remembered Edna Milton. "Somebody would say, 'Oh, she was a sweet, gracious old lady.' Uh-uh.

"I got on with her all right. You had to get along with her," she said. "It was her house."[92]

Aunt Jessie, the kindly philanthropist, was not the same Aunt Jessie the Chicken Farm boarders knew. Tenderhearted people did not run brothels— at least, not well or for very long—and Aunt Jessie could be as hard as she needed to be.

"The most I ever saw of that, some tense nervous tearful one, who in the privacy of her own room with only me and one other girl, would tell me weepingly that 'She's mean to us, demands, gives orders we have to do,'" recalled Gene Schulze, a Schulenburg doctor who occasionally treated the

Chicken Farm women. "One said, 'She's a devil; her name isn't Jessie, it's Jessie-bell.'"[93]

In the early 1950s, Aunt Jessie suffered a stroke of bad luck. While staying in a hotel in Kyle, Texas, she fell and broke her hip. The break was severe enough that she was taken to Scott & White Hospital in Temple, Texas, nearly one hundred miles distant, for treatment. Although she eventually healed, her hip troubled her greatly, and Aunt Jessie remained confined to a wheelchair from then on. Her family visited at the hospital and at the Chicken Ranch once she was discharged, and her relative remembered Cousin Fay as bedridden.

"Her bedroom—if I remember correctly—was very large and, well, *great*," her relative recalled. "Everything was elegant. I will say that. It was elegant. Expensive things were there. I just remember her being there in bed the last time I saw her, because of her hip."[94]

The broken hip proved Aunt Jessie's biggest challenge in more than two decades. One had to go all the way back to the Great Depression to find the madam as hard-pressed. She'd spent the previous fifteen years cultivating goodwill among the community, but all the goodwill in the world couldn't spare Aunt Jessie's girls from the ravages of the Great Depression. Texas depended heavily on agriculture in the 1930s and suffered terribly during the Dust Bowl, compounding the impact of the Depression. The humble farmers and cowboys who made up the bulk of Aunt Jessie's customers simply could not afford even the modest fees of the simple country whorehouse. Business dried up, and even though Aunt Jessie owned the title to her boardinghouse free and clear, that didn't put food on the table.

Desperate times called for desperate measures, and, as legend had it, Aunt Jessie hit upon a solution almost as old as the oldest profession itself: barter. Area farmers didn't have money, but they *did* have livestock. The brothel began accepting stock in trade. Before long, the going exchange rate became jokingly known as the "poultry standard"—that is, one chicken, one screw. Needless to say, Aunt Jessie's girls were up to their eyeballs in chickens in no time. Between the eggs and the butchered birds, they never went hungry, even at the height of the Great Depression. The enormous flock of poultry gave the men of Fayette County a convenient euphemism for the brothel as well, and they happily discussed visiting the "Chicken Farm" or "Chicken Ranch." The name stuck.[95]

It is a well-known story in Texas, as hallowed as the famed line in the sand drawn by Colonel William B. Travis at the Alamo. And just like Travis' line in the sand, it is the stuff of myth.

By the middle of the century, the Chicken Ranch—or Chicken Farm—had become so well known throughout the state that Southwestern Bell made a sly acknowledgement of it on the cover of the April 1958 telephone directory. *Courtesy Gary McKee.*

Fay Stewart, otherwise known as Jessie Williams, died on March 27, 1962, in San Antonio, just four months after selling the Chicken Ranch to Edna Milton. Stewart was interred in San Antonio's Sunset Memorial Park. Her simple grave marker makes no mention of her infamous past. *Author photo.*

"'Chicken Ranch' was just a nickname, made up for bullshit reasons," said Miss Edna. "It wasn't a ranch, it wasn't a farm, but it was out in the country. It was a boardinghouse. You don't feed people and let them sleep there if you're not boarding.

"I'm going to tell you the truth about those chickens. I heard it so damn many times, people asked about it," she said. "Every now and then, there's an investigation that goes on with a grand jury. Well, some of the men around there was telling Jessie, 'Jessie, you know there's going to be a grand jury investigation into everything that's been going on. You know somebody's always got to bring up your place out here. We've been thinking about how you might get around it. If you got you some chickens out there, a chicken ranch, they might just let it slide…'"[96]

So Aunt Jessie went out and bought one hundred chicks, raising them and giving them the run of her eleven acres. "Going to the Chicken Farm" became a popular euphemism in La Grange, but the customers didn't get by with offering pullets in trade.[97]

"There was no sales of chickens. You could go down to the hatchery and buy fifty or whatever you wanted and put out there, so that when the foreman on the grand jury wanted to [investigate], all they got out there's a bunch of chickens. Got a little chicken ranch. That's all. That's how that name got started," Miss Edna said. "The old lady hadn't had chickens there for years and years. That was just one year that went on, and that was just for the grand jury's benefit and nobody else's. There's more hockypoo about that place than anything else."[98]

Aunt Jessie, savvy as ever in publicity matters, recognized a good story when she heard it. She encouraged the misconception, even repeating it herself when necessary. But that didn't make it real. The name of Texas' most famous brothel, the Chicken Ranch, was based on nothing more than a silly, misguided fantasy perpetuated by generations of Texas schoolboys and men who wanted it to be real.

Chapter 3

MISS EDNA

The first time anyone called Edna Milton "Miss Edna," she got angry. Very angry. Working in a Fort Worth brothel at the tender age of nineteen, the house's black maid, Lou, made the mistake of addressing her as "Miss" and lived to regret it.

"See, the only ones I'd heard called 'Miss' when I was a kid growing up was a schoolteacher. When she was a child, they were making homemade soap, lye soap, and she fell in this great big kettle," Miss Edna explained. "It was a miracle she didn't die, but she was scarred for life. It made her very ugly. Well, you know somebody like that will probably never get married, and she didn't. So, they called her Miss…

"Well, when that Negro woman called me Miss Edna, I hated her from that day forward. Because, to me, I thought she was making fun of me. Like I was an old woman," she said. "I said, 'I'm nineteen years old and I've already been married, and you call me Miss?' Oooh, it really got to me."[99]

From that point on, Miss Edna treated Lou with a coolness bordering on contempt. Their interactions noticeably lacked civility. It got so bad the madam of the house finally intervened.

"Edna, why do you dislike Lou?" she asked.

"Because she's an insulting bitch," Miss Edna answered.

"What do you mean, 'insulting'?"

Miss Edna wouldn't say, not for a long while. Frustrated, the madam warned her that she needed to make an effort to get along.

Edna Milton. *Courtesy Edna Milton Chadwell.*

"Well, I wasn't trying to start no problem, I just didn't want her around me! Just because you don't want to associate with somebody doesn't mean you're mistreating them," Miss Edna said. "I just wanted her to stay away from me. Is that too much to ask, if you don't want somebody around?"[100]

Eventually, the fed-up madam demanded answers, and Miss Edna had no choice but to provide them.

"You have to answer the boss' question soon or you won't have a job. So I finally told her, and she kind of laughed."

The madam said, "Edna, you weren't brought up in the South, were you?"

"Oklahoma's not really very far north," Miss Edna answered.

"Well, in the South, all women are called Miss. Even little girls. Little boys are called Mister."[101]

That revelation gave Miss Edna something to think about.

"Huh. I didn't know about this southern crap. I didn't know about that—I thought she was just being very insulting to me," she said. "It didn't mean too much; I just didn't like it. I finally told her, 'I'm not Miss anything. My name is Edna, and I'd appreciate it if you called me by my name instead of making fun of me.' She didn't understand that.

"If I'd known what I know today, I'd have shown her respect and went on," Miss Edna said, with a touch of regret. "I wouldn't have gotten upset about it. It's not worth it. Nothing's worth getting upset about, really. Life's too short."[102]

Prostitution in Fort Worth had changed considerably since the days of "Hell's Half Acre." The traditional boardinghouse-style brothel no longer existed, driven to extinction by more aggressive enforcement of vice laws. Instead, flophouses, liquor stores, pawnshops and massage parlors took over Hell's Half-Acre. The flophouses became the new brothels, with women renting tiny rooms on a week-to-week basis. The conditions were better than cribs, but not by much. Some flophouses had madams, others just landlords, with bellhops, porters and cabdrivers making extra money from referrals. As usual, the prostitute turned over about half of her daily income to the house. If there happened to be a café within walking distance, the residents took their meals there. If not, then one of the tiny rooms served as a makeshift, communal kitchen.[103]

Despite the low-rent working conditions, the clientele represented a cross-section of Fort Worth society. Uptown customers found their way to the flophouse brothels just as easily as downtown clients, which is where Miss Edna met James Cash Penney, founder of JCPenney department stores.

"He'd hand you $100 to start with. He'd sit there and talk to you a while, then he might hand you another $50 or another $100," she said. "He'd always want to know where you'd worked, besides that [brothel], you know.

"What he was really trying to do…he must've not had it wonderfully easy growing up himself, and he was just trying to help the girls make a buck if they treated him nice," Miss Edna said. "He was an old man, white hair. You ended up getting more money from him than ten or fifteen others."[104]

Clients as generous—and compassionate—as Penney were few and far between, however. Working in a flophouse brothel offered only marginally better conditions than streetwalking, and some women didn't see the benefit.

"A little girl that'd been working the streets came into this house. [She] said, 'You can make more money on the streets,'" Miss Edna remembered. "I said, 'Yeah, but it's not safe.' She didn't think it was so unsafe.

"She hadn't been gone a week and she was dead," she said, still troubled by the memory a half century later. "She'd gotten on a corner and some other gal didn't like her—they must've been dope fiends. I can't figure it otherwise.

"These streetwalkers, there's nobody to help guide them in any way, shape or form—you know, as far as a woman that's been there, done that," she said. "To me, streets are dangerous. I would never consider that. I know I almost died there in Fort Worth."[105]

For Miss Edna, that woman's death signaled that it was time to move on and put Fort Worth behind her. Streetwalking, needless to say, was out of the question— she needed a house, one offering a measure of security and stability. Those types of old-style brothels hardly existed in 1952, yet as impossible as it sounded,

James Cash Penney, founder of JCPenney department stores, in 1953. *Courtesy J.C. Penney Papers, DeGolyer Library, Southern Methodist University.*

rumor held that a country whorehouse in La Grange called the Chicken Farm was all that and more.

"A boy that went to school at the University of Texas came home to Fort Worth, told me about it. He exaggerated a little bit too," Miss Edna said, shaking her head. "It didn't sound natural what he was saying. If it's not natural…If it doesn't sound right, it's not right. That's the way you can go with most things."[106]

Suspicious of the Chicken Farm, Miss Edna instead moved to Houston briefly before heading to Austin, where legendary Texas madam Hattie Valdes operated several houses catering to horny University of Texas students and Texas legislators in equal measure.

"She didn't have any openings at that moment, but she asked me if I knew about La Grange," Miss Edna said. "The lady in Austin was telling me about it, then she called down there and they said somebody's going to be gone a week. I said, 'Well, at least I'll go down there and see what it's about. I may not even want to stay.' But you can tolerate almost anything for a week."[107]

Miss Edna didn't own a car, so a bellboy from a nearby hotel borrowed his brother's car and drove her to La Grange, dropping her off at the bus station. From there she caught a ride out to the Chicken Farm.

"It was pleasant driving up to that old thing, seeing the trees and everything, you know?" she said. "After having looked at the city for a few years, that white house in the distance, among those green trees, it looked real pleasant. I didn't know how it'd be like inside, you know, but I went from there.

"I showed up and this little old lady with gray hair opened the door," Miss Edna recalled. "It was about coffee time, in the afternoon, and the girls were just sitting around."[108]

That little old lady, of course, turned out to be none other than the legendary Aunt Jessie. While Miss Edna got on tolerably well with Aunt Jessie, she ran afoul of another woman at the Chicken Farm almost immediately. The woman happened to date the brother of the bellboy who'd driven her to La Grange, and the car Miss Edna had come to town in didn't go unnoticed. The woman accused Miss Edna of messing around with her boyfriend. That infuriated Miss Edna, who dated a medical student from Galveston off and on at the time.[109]

Despite the rocky start, Miss Edna had faced far worse in her previous twenty-four years of life. She stuck it out, and before long, her jealous rival packed her bags and moved on to greener pastures. Miss Edna didn't know it, but that tentative start at the Chicken Farm would grow to twenty-two years, by far the most stability she'd experienced in her life up to that point.

Miss Edna's Milton ancestors arrived in the United States at the time of the Civil War, settling in Springfield, Illinois. Her grandfather set out for Texas but only made it as far as Indian Territory. There he established a hardscrabble family homestead, where Miss Edna's father was born. She herself was born in Caddo County, Oklahoma, on January 3, 1928, the eighth of eleven children, with seven sisters and three brothers. The Great Depression and Dust Bowl hit the family hard, as it did pretty much everyone in the Midwest, and the family bounced among Oklahoma, Texas and Arizona throughout her childhood.[110]

With that many children, it's not surprising squabbles broke out, and Miss Edna clashed repeatedly with an older sister.

"That sister…The crap that she pulled when she was a kid!" Miss Edna said, shaking her head. "If I had a hair ribbon and she wanted it, she'd just take it. Just a bully. That's what you'd call her. One time, I must have been about eleven years old, I don't remember what it was about—nothing real important, just enough to agitate me to death. I was angry. I slapped her as hard as I could slap her.

"If I'd had sense I'd have done this to her," she said, folding her fingers into a fist. "You ever see on television when women fight, well, hell, it looks like they're trying to swim or keep from drowning or something. If you're going to hit somebody, the best surface is your [fist] or if you have a rock or at least a roll of nickels, hit them as hard as you can right in the head. Knock them out!"[111]

If the clashes with her sister annoyed Miss Edna, an incident with her eldest brother during their time in Arizona gave rise to lasting bitterness and resulted in her never learning to swim.

"My oldest brother was an ass. He tried to teach me how to swim. Picked me up and threw me into the pond," she said. "You know what happens when that water gets up your nose, you almost feel like you're choking to death. That water getting in your nose like that makes it kinda burn. He did me that way twice."[112]

After the family returned to Texas, when Miss Edna was eight or nine years old, the local public swimming pool offered swimming lessons. Her parents signed her up, but when it came time to submerge her head and open her eyes under water, her experience with her brother came back to haunt her.

"Well, I wasn't sure I wanted to do that. About that time, those assholes walked by where I was. My head wasn't under the water, so he took his foot and put it atop my head and pushed it under," she said. "Well, that scared me to death. Consequently, I never really learned how to swim.

"It's not that I didn't want to, but I knew if I had to go through this crap twice with my brother and once with a lifeguard, who in the hell's going to protect me?" Miss Edna said. "If Daddy could've been around, he'd be the best one to've had. He was a good swimmer and everything, but hell, he had to work all the time."[113]

Miss Edna stopped attending school around the fourth grade, and by the time she turned sixteen, she'd left home and had a full-time job making sandwiches at a pharmacy's soda fountain in Pampa, Texas. Aptly named the Crystal Palace, all the surfaces were glass or chrome. For a simple country girl, it was a lovely place to work, all shiny and sparkly, but her weekly salary of fifteen dollars wasn't so shiny, even for 1943. She grew tired of that job quickly. When an older brother returned to Texas after a tour guarding the Panama Canal with the US Army, it didn't take Miss Edna long to make up her mind when he invited her to travel with him back to Oklahoma, where their parents were then residing.[114]

Her visit to Oklahoma lasted just a few days. An older sister, who by this time was married with three children, invited Miss Edna to come out to California, where her husband worked in the shipyards. Enticed by the perceived wealth of opportunity awaiting her on the West Coast, Miss Edna readily agreed and set out on her grand adventure.[115]

California's golden promise proved a false one.

Miss Edna's brother-in-law had a friend on a nearby naval base named Elva Arthur Hutson, who everyone simply called "Larry." Miss Edna quickly figured out her sister and husband intended to marry her off to Hutson, never mind her age. The prospect horrified her.[116]

"My sister practically forced me into it. I told her, '*I don't want to get married!* He's a sorry son of a bitch, and I don't want him,'" Miss Edna said emphatically. "He's no damn good. Why would I want to get married? I said, 'I'm too young to get married—sixteen is much too young to get married. There's no way.'"[117]

Miss Edna took some measure of security in the fact that under California law, she was underage and unable to marry without parental consent. This barely gave her sister pause, though. She wrote to their parents in Miss Edna's name, professing love for Hutson and requesting parental consent. With their daughter living on her own and supporting herself for more than a year by this time, her parents saw no reason to object. Their return letter included formal permission for Miss Edna to marry Hutson.[118]

"I said, 'I don't give a damn.' I said, 'I don't want him,'" Miss Edna said. "You're already married, or I'd tell *you* to get married to him!"[119]

Edna Milton, age sixteen.
*Courtesy Edna Milton
Chadwell.*

Under pressure from her sister and brother-in-law, with no help coming from her parents, Miss Edna felt trapped. Seeing no escape, she gave in and married Hutson.

"I had to. He was a sorry son of a bitch. He was. I'll tell you what made me know it for sure. If you're in the military, you follow orders. You *never* strike an officer," she said. "Well, he did. They put him in the brig for thirty days. He should've stayed forever—it didn't teach him anything."[120]

The marriage, forged under false pretenses and lacking anything resembling love or even civility, quickly broke down into open hostility. Miss Edna took a job as a cashier and waitress, trying to earn enough money to maintain an apartment and feed herself. Her husband, living on base, didn't concern himself with her welfare. Instead, he went through her purse for money whenever he wanted to hit the town for a night of drinking and hell-raising.

"He was going to take my money out to spend on booze or whatever he wants? I told him, 'Look, *you* can go back to the base. *I* can't go back to the base. I have to have this money to pay the damn rent. You don't need that stuff to drink.' It never made anyone prettier or more handsome or beautiful or wealthier. I can't see where the booze did one thing for anybody," she said, her anger coming to a boil. "Uh-uh. Not my way of thinking. I didn't mind working for whatever wages people could afford to pay. It's all right. But if I can't make it on that, get two jobs then. I've done that too. I've worked sixteen hours many times."[121]

Miss Edna worked constantly but had less money. With Hutson taking most of her income, she struggled to pay the rent. Hustling all day waiting tables, she came home foot-sore and exhausted, too poor to even afford a comfortable pair of shoes. Hutson, for his part, seemed to go out of his way to make her life miserable.

"It wasn't even two weeks and he came home with the biggest dose of gonorrhea you'd ever seen in your life. I don't think I'd ever seen one that was that ugly," she said. "You know you might see some you suspect having it, but this looked worse than a real bad cold. It was almost orange it was so yellow and green looking. It was a horrible-looking mess. And I should actually love *that*? I'm wrong for leaving *that*? I'd have been crazy if I'd have *stayed*!

"My sister fucked herself. She didn't have control over me no more."[122]

The sham collapsed after barely three months. Miss Edna walked out with few prospects but certain that anything would be better than a hellish married life with Hutson.

Underage, divorced and without any education, family or friends for support, California looked less and less like the land of opportunity from her dreams. Surprisingly, amid the turmoil and uncertainty, she actually found happiness for a time.

"I've only been in love one time in my life, really. I was very young, I was seventeen," Miss Edna said, her voice taking on a dreamy, wistful tone. "Well, we were both too young, truthfully. He was twenty, but he was a B-29 pilot. I never knew whether he came back or not."[123]

Miss Edna met Benjamin D. Groves, a young bomber pilot out of West Virginia, in late 1944. He was training to fly the new B-29 Superfortress bombers that hadn't even seen combat yet. The two hit it off and began dating. Miss Edna fell hard for the dashing young airman, dreaming of an idyllic future together.[124]

"It wasn't much of a relationship. It was more romantic than it was a sexual deal," she said. "I'm not going to say he was a virgin, but I'm not going to say he wasn't, either. I thought he was a great guy. I would've been happy with him."[125]

World War II, which brought the two together, doomed the fleeting romance. In early 1944, Groves shipped out to the Pacific Theater. They made promises to stay in touch—unrealistic, perhaps, under the circumstances. Miss Edna never heard from him again, never even found out if he survived the war. He never left her heart, though, and even in her eighties, stooped and suffering osteoporosis, Miss Edna grew animated as she spun romantic plans of traveling to West Virginia and seeking out the long-lost love of her life.

"If he's alive and single, I'm going to try and take him home," she said, eyes sparkling with a youthful fire. "I don't give a damn if he's lost both arms, or both legs, or both eyes. I don't give a damn. If he made it back, whatever condition he's in, if he's not married, I'm going to try and take him home."[126]

"She pined over him for years, and I think especially so these past ten years, possibly wondering 'What if…?'" said her nephew Robert Kleffman. "Every time she talks about him, she lights up like a schoolgirl. There is no doubt that, in her mind at least, she loved this guy very deeply. She must have, to carry a crush for sixty-plus years!"[127]

Sometime after Groves' deployment, Miss Edna learned she was pregnant. Alone and more of an outcast than ever, she suffered through nineteen excruciating hours of labor before giving birth to a son, whom she named Freddy Joe. The hardships of the previous nine months—and nineteen hours of labor—melted away at the sight of her child. Miss Edna had someone she could love unconditionally and who would love her back. That makes her ensuing heartbreak all the more wrenching.[128]

"My little boy died when he was two months old. Jaundice. *Jaundice.* Today it doesn't matter. At that time…" she said softly. "I did not want any more children; there's too much pain involved.

"I thought, before I had that one baby, I wanted at least four children: two boys, two girls. I thought you could order them. I thought I could order me two girls. Mm-hmm," Miss Edna said. "Yeah, you give me enough money and a house big enough, a husband worth being with, there'd been ten or more of them. But no, I'm glad I did not have any. Ten or twelve would be too much for anybody. When a man and a woman care for each other, want children together, you've only got two hands and he's only got two hands, so there can't be more than four kids. When you go to cross the street you need to hold those [little] hands."[129]

Her life continued to spiral steadily downward. While holding down a string of menial jobs, she tried to learn a legitimate trade. She found herself unsuited for interior decorating after taking a few classes and later failed as a real estate agent when the housing market declined.

"I wanted to be able to work, I wanted to go to school. I wanted a good education, but I knew I would have to work like hell to get that, too. It wouldn't be just a gift to me, you know," Miss Edna said. "I knew I wanted it. I wanted to be a straight-A student. You know, if I had been, if I'd finished high school, I might've gotten a small scholarship or something. That's what I really wanted to do."[130]

That kind of life was out of reach for a divorcée who'd already buried a child at seventeen. Penniless and desperate, scorned by polite society, one day Miss Edna simply gave in, accepting payment in exchange for meaningless sex. The money was good, though, and morality and self-esteem always seemed more important to those with full stomachs than to those without.

"I had a habit," Miss Edna related years later. "Yeah, a habit of eatin' three times a day.

"If you're a teenage girl with not much education and no trade, it don't take long to learn you can make more money on your back than you can on your feet. How many waitresses you know that drive Cadillacs?"[131]

Shame haunted her. Although whoring allowed her to survive, she took care to hide her secret life from her family.

"I thought it was degrading," Miss Edna said. "But you need the money and men are going to mess around, so you might as well get the money."[132]

That easy money didn't come without consequences. Two years after burying Freddy Joe, Miss Edna unexpectedly got pregnant again. A full-time prostitute at nineteen, she'd long since given up on romantic dreams of white picket fences. The pregnancy threatened the only income she had. It was impossible to know who the father was—not that the knowledge would do her any good. And the memory of nineteen hours of labor, plus the anguish of burying her son, terrified her. The people around her at the time suggested she get an abortion—still illegal in 1947. The idea didn't sit well with Miss Edna. Her familiarity with abortion was tenuous; growing up, she'd known one older, pretty neighbor girl who had one, and the memory troubled her.

"She went to college in New Orleans—I believe it was New Orleans—and got pregnant. Somebody told her about abortion," Miss Edna said solemnly. "Well, abortion's not good anytime, but in those days, that was pretty much of a death sentence. That's what she got out of it. She was young, like eighteen, twenty at the most. That's what was so sad about it. She was a nice girl and their family was a good family."[133]

In the end, despite such misgivings, Miss Edna opted for the abortion. The experience was a disaster on every level. The doctor who performed it did a poor job, leaving her bleeding and in pain. Complications set in. Infection. Eventually, she recovered, but her reproductive organs were irreparably damaged and troubled her for years. In 1954, still suffering from the effects of complications, she underwent a hysterectomy. Her previous medical treatment infuriated Dr. John Guenther, Miss Edna's physician in La Grange.

"He said, 'You didn't have a surgeon, you had a butcher' that got ahold of me when I was nineteen," she said. "I said, 'I don't know what's going to be wrong inside, and when it happens, you're the only one that's going to know. So, it's up to you.'"[134]

Since prostitution didn't come with a health plan, necessity forced Miss Edna back to work at the Chicken Farm long before she'd fully healed. She had no business being back on the floor, but for a whore, not working is perilously close to not eating, and medical bills wiped out what little savings she had. Physically incapable of intercourse, she made do with the reduced income she could earn by offering hand and blow jobs. Such limited activity only lessened her discomfort slightly, and a drunk veteran who'd lost both legs in Korea sorely tested her tolerance one night—for both pain and insensitivity.

"A lot of men come back from overseas and end up a pain in the ass. I know right after I had major surgery and went back to work, in comes a guy with [artificial] legs. He was drunk, falling around. The guy grabbed ahold of me, damn near pulled me to the floor!" Miss Edna said. "Hell, I was still weak myself. So I said, 'Hey, Mister, I didn't cut your legs off, and you didn't cut my belly, but I just had major surgery myself, and you pulling me almost to the floor like that does not make me feel any better about you because of injury.'

"When you're not well yourself and somebody's pulling on you, those stitches aren't all that strong. Yet you mean to say you're going to cause me to have injury again? No thanks," she said. "There's a few people that are like that. They think, well, I got hurt so I might as well go out and hurt everybody else."[135]

Her body did eventually heal following the hysterectomy, and Miss Edna's health returned to normal—after five years of suffering. The *emotional* scars from her ordeal reached far deeper, though.

"She has told me, I don't know how many times, of all the things that she has done in her life the only thing she regrets, and the only thing she's afraid of that God might not forgive her for, is that one abortion," said Kleffman.

"That haunts her, bad. And that messed her up so she can't have any kids. So that's the one thing that she just wishes she hadn't done, out of everything."[136]

Despite her medical problems, Miss Edna settled in at the Chicken Farm, working under Miss Jessie. For the first time in her life, she bought a car—a used '51 Ford sedan. Previously, she'd had no need of a car, living in cities, as she could take the bus or a taxi to get around. At the Chicken Farm, with no local bus or taxi service, a car was essential to get around the rural communities of Fayette County.[137]

Miss Edna changed in another way following her surgery. After medical expenses all but wiped her out, she began to save more money. Her newfound thrift—insurance against the unforeseen—turned out to be a savvy move on her part just a few years later.

Aunt Jessie, well into her seventies, found her health failing. Wheelchair-bound because of the broken hip she suffered in the early 1950s, she also suffered arthritis and in her later years developed diabetes. She craved sugary food and candies, though, and her undisciplined diet made controlling her disease impossible.

"She didn't want anything except something sweet to eat, and the doctors kept telling her, no, no, no," Miss Edna remembered. "They'd give her a decent diet to eat. She didn't want to do that."[138]

At the same time, Aunt Jessie's extended family saw less and less of "Cousin Fay." As she slowly lost her grip on operations at the Chicken Farm, Miss Edna stepped in to fill the power vacuum.

"After Edna came, it seems like we were blocked from seeing Cousin Fay," a relative recalls. "I didn't know Edna, but I have no love lost for Edna. I know that [Cousin Fay] did have to eventually leave the Ranch."[139]

Diabetic complications set in, and in the late '40s, Aunt Jessie underwent surgery with Dr. Guenther to amputate her leg. She struggled to find the energy to manage day-to-day operations as her body betrayed her, and her mental sharpness declined as well. Her once-iron grip on the Chicken Farm slipped, and it didn't take her street-smart boarders two seconds to notice. By the middle of 1961, the sedate country whorehouse had turned downright wild and rowdy as Aunt Jessie completely lost control and the inmates took over the asylum.[140]

That was more than enough for the current Fayette County sheriff, T.J. "Big Jim" Flournoy. La Grange had only tolerated the Chicken Farm for so long because Aunt Jessie made sure her girls didn't cause any problems in the community. With the Chicken Farm now causing one problem after another, Big Jim dealt with it in the most direct way possible: he drove over in his

Edna Milton in the famed Chicken Ranch parlor. Note the ubiquitous cigarette in her hand. *Courtesy Edna Milton Chadwell.*

patrol car and ordered Jessie to close up shop and send her girls packing. He didn't have to add "or else."[141]

Sensing opportunity, Miss Edna made an offer to buy the Chicken Farm. Aunt Jessie, forbidden by the sheriff to operate a brothel and faced with the prospect of living there alone, agreed to sell. After some haggling, Miss Edna bought the Chicken Farm for $28,500 on November 27, 1961.[142]

"She came back two months later, wanted to buy it from me. She said, 'I'll give you $2,000 more than you paid for it,'" Miss Edna said. "I said, 'No, ma'am. You're too old to run it, so I wouldn't even consider selling it to you. But if you really want to be here, you can have the same bedroom you had before and live here the rest of your life, if that's what you want. But never will I sell it to you.'

"Mentally, she was entirely too old. Eh, if she'd had all her marbles she'd have been all right," she said. "But she didn't have all her marbles to start with."[143]

Aunt Jessie didn't take her up on the offer to live at the Chicken Farm. Instead, she went to San Antonio, where she moved in with a longtime friend. By that time, Miss Edna's payments for the Chicken Farm constituted the bulk of Aunt Jessie's remaining wealth, the rest eaten up by uncontrolled generosity, poor financial management and constant medical expenses. Her rumored vast real estate holdings amounted to a single duplex in San Antonio that she collected rent on.

Jessie Williams, otherwise known as Fay Stewart, died in San Antonio on March 27, 1962. Her sister-in-law, Eddie Ledda Moody, traveled from McLennan County to oversee Aunt Jessie's burial in Sunset Memorial Park.[144]

FOLLOWING THE FUNERAL, MISS EDNA had big decisions to make. She owned the Chicken Farm, sure enough, but the brothel stood empty. None of the women stuck around once Big Jim ordered its closure. An even bigger potential problem was Big Jim himself. The sheriff only closed the Chicken Farm in the first place because Aunt Jessie lost control of the women, but he hadn't given any signal to Miss Edna that she could reopen. And she'd owned the property for several months by that point.

"It was closed. It wasn't worth nothing. It was no value unless you could open it, and I couldn't open it for a while. Jim never told me I could open it back," Miss Edna said. "I didn't have it wide open. I didn't have eight or ten girls there. I had me and one other for a while.

"Some men told me, 'Edna, why don't you go ahead and open up?'" she said. "I said, 'I was told to close, not to be open.'

"[They said,] 'You can get in just as much trouble for two girls as you can twenty. They can do just as much to you, so since you're here, you might as well open. You're here to make money.'

"I took their advice."[145]

Chapter 4

TRIXIE, THE THROW-AWAY DOG (AND OTHER SOCIETAL REJECTS)

Trixie arrived at the Chicken Ranch in much the same way as the women did—a castoff, looking for shelter and safety. Given its location just a mile or so outside town in a mix of woods and farmland, people habitually abandoned unwanted pets along the back road near the brothel.

"A lot of strays were dropped off there. You know *people*," Miss Edna said, contempt dripping from her words. "That little white dog was one of them. I got Trixie, she was a little throw-away dog. Another little dog was with her, white and had some brown spots on her."[146]

Trixie showed up shortly after Miss Edna bought the place and soon became the Chicken Ranch's unofficial mascot. She lived to about thirteen years, and Miss Edna took the little white dog along with her whenever she went on trips. Trixie, for her part, never failed to entertain.

"You know how a dog will get on their back, scoot around rubbing their back? I got to where she'd be on her back and I'd get ahold of her back feet, and say, 'Show 'em how the good girls make money,'" Miss Edna explained with a devilish gleam in her eye, pantomiming how she'd pump Trixie's hind legs back and forth. "Well, it got to where I could finally just say it to her and she'd do it. She'd just go flop down and go *'ooooh'* [excitedly kicking her hind legs]."[147]

"Right! Exactly! [Trixie] was totally precious and friendly," said Robbie Davis-Floyd, PhD, a senior research fellow in the Department of Anthropology at the University of Texas. "Edna would make this circular motion with her finger and say, 'Come on, Trixie, show us how the good girls make their money!'

Edna Milton with Trixie,
a stray dog adopted by the
Chicken Ranch women.
Courtesy Edna Milton Chadwell.

"Trixie would circle, go *'ruff'* and roll over and then she would wave her feet up in the air," she said, laughing hard at the memory. "'Show us how the good girls make their money!'"[148]

Trixie stayed by Miss Edna's side almost the entire time she owned the Chicken Ranch. Trixie loved everyone, basking in the attention showered on her by the women and customers alike. And Trixie had no shame in demonstrating how the good girls made their money.

"Any man that's been to Texas A&M that ever went down there, the University of Texas, Rice University or half the businessmen across Texas, you know, when they see that dog, they're going to recognize her," Miss Edna said. "Little old Trixie, I miss her."[149]

The ribald humor behind Trixie's entertaining tricks permeated the Chicken Ranch. In some ways, the women working there turned the brothel into their own version of a sorority. For the most part, the women avoided joking about the customers—something Miss Edna frowned upon—and they tended to keep things strictly business when working. Behind the scenes, however, when they let their hair down and weren't playing to the customers, their tongues loosened considerably and the dirty jokes flowed relentlessly.

"Do y'all know the difference between an old prostitute and a young one?" asked one prostitute known as Carol. "A young prostitute uses Vaseline and an old one uses Poly-Grip."[150]

Another whore, Gloria, tended toward jokes featuring the ever-popular sex-and-religion combination.

"There were three nuns, and they were goin' to confession, and the first nun went in and she says, 'Father, I have to confess—I, uh, jacked a man off.' And he says, 'I'm ashamed of you, sister—go put your hand in the holy water.' So she went in and put her hand in the holy water," Gloria said. "And the next nun went in, and she says, 'Father, I have to confess, I had intercourse with a man,' and he says, 'I am *really* ashamed of you.' He says, 'Go sit in the holy water.' And the third nun says, 'Be sure you don't 'go' in it, because I'm gonna hafta gargle!'"[151]

Miss Edna herself kept an arsenal of bawdy jokes at the ready, using them for various purposes depending on what the situation called for. Crowd management topped her agenda. One well-timed joke might break up testosterone-fueled tension and defuse a potential fight, whereas another might reassure a customer suffering performance anxiety. Some were simply amusing, told to focus attention on Miss Edna and remind everyone that she remained in charge. To maintain control over the physically stronger—and potentially drunk—men who were their clients, prostitutes learned to deftly use language to manipulate and control the situation. Miss Edna mastered this art thoroughly, and her women greatly admired her for her skill.

"Miss Edna could walk out on this floor right now, take any man to the bedroom and talk him out of even the deed to his house," gushed one of Edna's boarders. "She really knows how to handle men."[152]

Tellingly, while women played the butt as often as men in the prostitutes' jokes, in all of Miss Edna's jokes the woman came out on top, so to speak. This deliberate strategy fit in alongside Miss Edna's other policies—such as her intolerance of pimps on the premises—which helped further define her role as a defender as well as employer of her women at the Chicken Ranch: "This guy has his head down between this girl's legs, and he says, 'Honey, you've got the roughest pussy!'" Miss Edna said. "She says, 'Well, why don't you move up a few inches; you've been licking the carpet!'"[153]

One dirty rhyme was a particular favorite, and she repeated it almost as a defiant affirmation of the brothel and their status as prostitutes:

> *Two old whores, walkin' down the street*
> *No hat on their heads, no shoes on their feet*
> *Too old to fuck, and too proud to suck*
> *Just two old whores, shit outta luck.*[154]

Trixie was abandoned by her owners near the Chicken Ranch. The women took the pup in and made her an unofficial mascot. *Courtesy Edna Milton Chadwell.*

Not all the jokes traded were short and pithy. Some had elaborate set-ups, such as a sailor joke told by Bonnie to April and Gloria. Sometimes the reactions to the jokes were funnier than the actual punchlines:

"Well, this service boy had been out on the ocean for two years and he hadn't even seen a woman," Bonnie began. "And they were all real horny, and there were about five of 'em around talking and he said, 'Well I tell you what, when we dock, I'm having the first girl I see, regardless of age, looks or color…I don't care. I'm horny. I'm taking her.'

"Well, this one guy, he says, 'Well I bet you $100 it'll be something you don't want. She'll be colored, or she'll be too old or somethin'. And you won't take it.' And he said, 'No man, that's a bet—the first one I see when

I step off—that's it!' He was that horny," she explained, drawing laughter from her audience. "Well they docked and these other guys were gonna follow him to make sure that was what he did and everything.

"He was walkin' down the street and here comes the first old lady. She was 90, 98 years old—man she was about ready to die. All wrinkled up. She had a cane and was all hunch-backed and everything," Bonnie elaborated to more laughs. "And he was thinkin' 'Oh my God,' and everything. But $100 is a lot of money to a service boy. So he goes up to her and puts this story on her, the old lady, and he's shocked as hell—the old woman's rarin' to go—'Yeah Sonny.'

"So he takes her to this motel room, and they're followin' him to make sure…it's funny to them 'cause she's so old and everything. So they get in the room and they get undressed and get in bed, and he's gettin' it on, and gettin' it on, and after a while—Here's the punchline, are you ready?—he smells this awful odor and he says, 'My God, what is that smell?'

"She says, 'Well I'm too old to come, so I shit to show my appreciation!'" Bonnie concluded amidst howls of laughter. *"I wonder if it really gets that way when you're 98."*

"Well I hope not!" said April.

"I hope not!" Bonnie agreed.

"I hope not, too!" Gloria.

Then Bonnie, after considering for a moment, added, "I can see fartin' maybe…"[155]

Through facial gestures, skillful use of jokes and dominating the conversation, Miss Edna maintained control of her house, her whores and her customers. She respected her customers but fiercely protected her women. She refused to let herself or any of the whores feel shamed or demeaned by their profession. They'd all suffered in life, but at the Chicken Ranch, Miss Edna called the shots, and under her leadership the brothel would remain a proud haven for prostitutes.[156]

Lest anyone doubt where things stood, Miss Edna had no problem reminding them with a raucous, well-worn toast:

Here's to the girls of the golden west
they've got tits like a hornet's nest
the skin on their belly is tight as a drum
and they got a puss that'll make a dead man come![157]

The Chicken Farm wasn't always so bawdy (even if the women only cut loose behind the scenes, away from customers). In most cases, "straight-laced whorehouse" is a mighty profound contradiction in terms, yet under the early rule of Aunt Jessie, no other phrase could do the Chicken Farm justice. The madam lived her life as a God-fearing woman who kept her Bible close at hand. Her soul sported a conservative streak a mile wide, and her reputation as a strict disciplinarian extended into the bedrooms of her working women.[158]

The implications can be pondered to irony and back.

Aunt Jessie's strict sense of decorum made an impression, however, and stuck with the women even when they weren't working at the brothel. In the mid-1940s, two men in their early twenties—Leerie Giese and a friend named Bo—were driving back to La Grange from Austin when they came across a car pulled over to the side of the road with steam rising from the radiator. Because of the late hour—approaching 1:00 a.m.—and the fact that the driver, a young woman, was alone, the two boys offered her a ride into La Grange.

"She said, 'First let me tell you, I work out at Miss Jessie's. And if it's going to reflect on you in any way just let me sit right here,'" Giese recalled. "Well, we said, 'No, no, no. Come on.' We brought her in to this gas station and she was going to call a cab."

The woman had planned for a weekend getaway in Austin and had a packed suitcase with her. The breakdown of her car scratched those plans, so she'd decided to return to the Chicken Farm.

"Both of us said, 'We'll take you out there.' We drove out and got there about two o'clock in the morning. She invited us to come in, but I didn't want to go in because my dad was in politics and he was intolerant of prostitution," Giese said. "Well, Bo went in and came out damn quick. I said, 'What the heck did you do?'"

"Oh, I got a tree burst," Bo answered sheepishly.

Giese explained, "In the service, if an artillery shell hit a tree, it would explode," showering the area with shrapnel and splinters. "And that's what he called it—a tree burst."[159]

Fortunately for the brothel's cash flow, most prospective customers didn't experience such premature tree bursts very often. In truth, there wasn't much of anything exotic enough to trigger such an embarrassment. To Aunt Jessie's thinking, prostitution as God intended consisted of a straight lay with the man on top, period. Actual nudity amounted to little more than an unfortunate side effect best avoided if at all possible. She viewed slight deviations from the basics with suspicion, and any requests even approaching fetish or kink territory met swift condemnation if Aunt Jessie caught wind of it, no matter what the customer offered to pay.

One La Grange regular found out the hard way when he tried to talk a prostitute known as "Deaf Eddie" into serving up an entree not on the main menu.

"See, we called her Deaf Eddie 'cause she really was hard of hearin', so I was havin' to talk pretty loud," the regular said. "Well, what happened is that Miss Jessie heard me and come a-crashin' into there, hitting me with a big iron rod and hollerin' 'bout turnin' her girls into French whores! She throwed me out and wouldna' let me in for a month."[160]

Once, during Deaf Eddie's monthly vacation, Jerome "Sonny" Mazoch paid a visit to the Chicken Farm, and the woman he selected took them into Eddie's vacant room. As they were undressing, Sonny noticed a picture of a football player hanging on the wall and asked if it was a patron from the Texas A&M football team.

The woman laughed. The player was neither an Aggie nor a patron but rather Deaf Eddie's nephew, an All-American at Rice University playing for legendary coach Jess Neely. The player in question eventually graduated and became a successful executive with Humble Oil and later Exxon.[161]

The careers of prostitutes are measured in years, not decades, as age takes

Edna Milton sits at a vanity in one of the brothel's nine bedrooms. *Courtesy Edna Milton Chadwell.*

its toll. As Deaf Eddie got older, she transitioned out of the bedrooms. She took over answering the door, taking care of the girls and handling matters when Aunt Jessie wasn't around.[162]

"Miss Jessie had an old matron out there, Deaf Eddie. She was outside of that damn Chicken Ranch, and these two drunk sonsabitches wanted to get in," said Leerie Giese, recalling the scene he witnessed during a ride out to the Chicken Farm with some friends. "She just said, 'I'm sorry, you're not going to come in.' They said, 'You can call the damn tin badge and he can shove it up his ass.'

"And the drunk bastards were throwing rocks on that damn tin roof.

Now, that's about as low as a son of a bitch can get—throwing rocks on a damn whorehouse and defying Deaf Eddie," he said.[163]

Another time, one would-be patron walked up to the house packing a bottle of whiskey. Although Aunt Jessie sold beer at the brothel, she had a hard-and-fast one-bottle limit and tolerated no drunkenness.

"That woman says, 'You can't bring that bottle in here, but if you're not drunk you can come in. If you've been drinking, you can't come in,'" Giese said. "She had to watch who was coming. She wouldn't let [drunks] in, along with any rough-looking bastards, they couldn't come in, either. And no blacks. It was a first-class whorehouse is what it was."[164]

Such a colorful character as Deaf Eddie could easily be fictitious, like so much common folklore surrounding the Chicken Farm. They didn't come any more real than Deaf Eddie, though. Born Estelle Faith Fisher, a Polish Jew from tiny Olin, Texas, she moved with her family to Houston at a young age. Her father, a doctor, died a few years after that, and Estelle's mother eventually remarried to the owner of a dry cleaning business in the Houston area.[165]

"I do remember her, quite well. Estelle married a man who had a Mercury dealership [in Houston]. I don't know how long she was married to him," said Miss Edna, providing a glimpse of Deaf Eddie's life before the Chicken Farm. "Anyway, later there was a divorce. He apparently still liked her because every now and then when he'd be out in that general area he'd come by [the Chicken Farm] and say hello to her. She apparently still liked him too, but I guess the love affair was gone, you know."[166]

Even after Estelle became Aunt Jessie's top lieutenant, her years as a working boarder gave her a certain insight and compassion that won over many of the women at the Chicken Farm. To put it bluntly, she didn't snitch.

"She was a pretty nice old gal," Edna remembered. "[Some of the women] were drinking around there at night after work and everything, and one time someone asked me to get some whiskey for them, a pint of this and a pint of that, you know.

"I fixed it up for them and brought it in, even though I knew that was supposedly against the rules. Estelle came in about that time I had it in my hand, and it slipped. Down on the floor it went," she said. "She didn't say a damn thing, and I didn't either. Hell, I knew she wasn't blind."[167]

The circumstances that led Estelle to the Chicken Farm weren't clear, but life in the brothel suited her surprisingly well. Like Miss Edna after her, Estelle saved up her money and, when the time came, went out on her own terms.

"She left before I bought the place. She'd left before that, and she bought a place down on the other side of Houston, a little beach cottage," Miss Edna said. "She'd go out crabbing and water skiing. Somebody taught her how to water ski. She had a hell of a good time.

"Somebody was running a speed boat and they hit her while she was water skiing and hurt her. Hell, she was in her seventies at that time. She didn't want to go back water skiing after that," she said. "It wasn't that she didn't want to—she was afraid to. That damn speedboat run into her and hurt her, what would it do next time? Might kill her. She wasn't ready to die."[168]

After Miss Edna bought the Chicken Farm and made the decision to reopen, finding boarders became her primary concern. Miss Jessie's rules had fallen by the wayside as the old madam lost control of the brothel, and Miss Edna viewed that as intolerable.

"My first year, about 500 of them was in and out of that house in less than one year," Miss Edna said, quoting a number so astronomically high that roughly 1.4 prostitutes had to arrive *every day* for an entire year to meet it. For reference, the 1960 census pegged the entire population of La Grange at 3,623, and a confidential Department of Public Safety report for Texas governor Preston Smith in 1971 identified 764 prostitutes working the entire state, along with 62 madams and 392 pimps.

The definitive "unreliable narrator," Miss Edna's grandiose claims nevertheless gave insight to her mindset and the workings of the Chicken Farm at the time. "Well, that's the way that went. The second year, about two hundred. Three years? I don't think I ran off two to three. Fifth year, I'm not sure I ran any of them off.

"It took a while for the information to spread. Different ones wanted to come in. I said, 'Well, you want to stay and follow orders, or do you think you should pack your things and been gone yesterday?'" she said. "Well, they wanted to stay. I said, 'Just remember who owns this place and who gives the orders and who's going to follow them or they're not going to stay here. Take your choice.' That's the way I felt about it, too."[169]

Like Aunt Jessie before her, Miss Edna provided her women with room, board and maid service—for a fee. They also paid for their own medical services during their weekly checkups, despite rumors to the contrary. Some of Aunt Jessie's policies had always rubbed Miss Edna the wrong way, so as soon as she could, she put her own rules in place. When Miss Edna first arrived in 1952, she paid rent of five dollars a day or thirty-five dollars a week whether she was there or not. Miss Jessie reasoned that normal boardinghouses charged regardless of a boarder's circumstances, and maids and utilities still had to be paid. Miss Edna thought the policy unfair, since Miss Jessie's boarders normally had one week a month, during their menstrual cycle, where they couldn't work, or at least didn't want to. Aunt Jessie, for all her conservative nature and biblical leanings, expected her prostitutes to entertain customers during their period. Miss Edna changed that, giving each of her women one week off a month.[170]

Despite the changes Miss Edna made to improve the working conditions of women at the Chicken Farm, she doubled-down on enforcing other rules to maintain discipline. Illegal drugs, in particular, counted as a hot-button issue for her, and Miss Edna's fervor bordered on religious.

"Hell, no! I wouldn't put up with narcotics, then or now. Somebody walk in this house with narcotics, I'd tell them, 'Get that shit off my property and don't come back, because I'm through messing with you. I will call the law on you in a damn minute,'" she said. "I told them that at the Chicken Ranch. I said, 'If any of you think, just get the idea, that you're going to bring something in here, I say you're not. If you bring 'em, I tell you what, you're going to have a visitor from the law, either county or city or state. No narcotics will be allowed on these premises!'

"You see, they can take your property and everything else for narcotics. They can take your car, they can take your home, your jewelry and if they really wanted to they could probably take the clothes you're standing in," she said. "No, I won't put up with that at all."[171]

Newcomers to the Chicken Farm often tested Miss Edna, but they quickly learned that she wasn't joking about "my way or the highway." Miss Edna had no choice, really. She had a firm policy that newcomers to the Chicken Farm be veteran prostitutes before she'd hire them on—she had no desire to recruit inexperienced women into the unforgiving life of prostitution.

"The minimum [age] was eighteen, but you really didn't want them eighteen. You rather had them about middle twenties, because they're still young enough the young boys don't care," Miss Edna explained. "They still look good, and yet they've developed a few brains. That way, you don't have to babysit them all the time. Less work for me."[172]

"Most of the women there were married and had families. Every bit of the money they made went into their farms or their house payments, stuff like that," recalled one former prostitute who worked at the Chicken Farm under the name "Penny" from 1966 to 1969. "It wasn't anything like most people think a prostitute's going to be. You know what I'm saying? 'They're all on drugs, or they're all alcoholics.' That was not the case at the Ranch. None of that was allowed."[173]

Because of that, the women coming to Miss Edna weren't lost little girls who'd wandered off the family farm. They were hardened prostitutes from society's lowest rung who knew firsthand that the world was a harsh and unforgiving place. Although Miss Edna had a famously low opinion of pimps, she wasn't above using them to her advantage. For most of the time she operated the brothel, she wouldn't take on a new woman unless that woman had a husband or a pimp to answer to. When a woman showed up looking for work escorted by a man, Miss Edna separated the two and spoke to the woman privately to find out if she was a willing participant or not before making any hiring decisions. Those showing reluctance were turned away. As for those who found work at the Chicken Farm, Miss Edna kept them in line by using those men in their lives as leverage.

"I was the only 'outlaw' there because I didn't have a husband or a pimp," Penny said. "That was one of her requirements, to have someone who was in charge of the girls there, so if they stepped out of line, she had somebody to go to, to straighten out the situation.

"That was just a threat. That's all that was. I've never known her to do it while I was there," she said. "That's the reason she took to me so much, because I didn't have one. I just needed one to get in there. But once she felt that I wouldn't cause her any trouble, that's when I was allowed to stay.

"And the other girls could not believe it. They could not believe it. Needless to say, I gave a couple of them some ideas, I think," she said. "I know one girl in particular tried to go home and disassociate herself with her partner there, and she came back with a lot of bruises and knots on her head. It's hard to break away from these men. They're so controlling, and they're used to that money coming in."[174]

Unfortunately, Penny knew that type all too well. Originally from a rough area of Houston known as the Heights, a local pimp kidnapped Penny in 1960 and put her to work in a Galveston whorehouse on Market Street. To make sure she stayed in line, the pimp held her infant son hostage.

"They just kind of threw me in there. There was a big ol' black woman in there, and she was *wonderful*. She knew I was green as grass, and so she tried to explain a lot of the details about what would happen and what I was supposed to do and what I wasn't supposed to do and stuff like that," Penny said. "He would come by once a week, and if I hadn't made enough money, he would beat the crap out of me. Usually with a coat hanger, because they don't leave wide marks. That was the experience. It took me years to get away from him. Just years."[175]

Penny fled to Dallas for a few years and then returned to Houston when her pimp ended up in jail. She'd given birth to two more children and moved to Austin by the time her mother fell ill and moved in with her around late 1965. Her sister soon followed with her two kids, and then her mother's invalid husband joined them. Suddenly, Penny found herself expected to support a household of eight, something she couldn't come close to doing as a waitress in Austin.

"Everything sort of mushroomed. I said, 'Well, I've done it before, maybe I can just do it again. But I don't want to have to give all my money away,'" Penny explained. "That's when I plotted to get to work at the Chicken Ranch, because I'd already heard of it. I was young. I was stupid. I didn't have an education, so I did what I could do."[176]

To get on at the Chicken Ranch initially, Penny had to find herself a pimp. Penny made a deal with one man she knew, agreeing to earn enough to buy him a convertible if he'd pose as her pimp. Once she'd paid him off, Penny went to Miss Edna and explained her situation, at which point Miss Edna agreed to let her continue working sans pimp. By that time, Penny had already developed a friendly relationship with the madam. Miss Edna herself gave Penny her working name the day she interviewed.

"When I went in there, my face was shiny from perspiration. It was real hot," Penny recalled. "And [Miss Edna] said, 'You are just shiny as a new penny—come on in here!'"[177]

While some prostitutes may have viewed the Chicken Ranch with as much suspicion as Miss Edna had when first she heard of it, most knew it by reputation as a safe place to ply their trade. Others likely saw it opportunistically—a hayseed whorehouse ripe for manipulating to their own advantage. These women tested boundaries to see what they could get away with by gossip and double-talk.

"Everyone liked to tell different stories: 'Well, so-and-so told me this,' or 'I was told this or that,'" Miss Edna said. "I said, 'Weren't you in here when I had everybody in here?'

"'Yes.'

"'Now what makes you think I would go behind your back and tell somebody different than what I told you?'" Miss Edna said, getting on a roll. "'Don't fuck with me. All you is, is a mind fucker, and you're trying to fuck with my mind. And I'll tell you what, you're about to make me mad. If you can't listen to what I tell you and let it go at that—If you don't like living here, you don't have to stay here. *Nobody* has to stay here. Just pack your shit and get the hell out of here! If you want to drive me crazy, I'm not going for it.'"[178]

Most women quickly learned the pecking order and chose to follow the rules, although a few—not too many—persisted in trying to finagle the situation until Miss Edna got fed up and showed them the door. For any whore foolish enough to openly challenge the madam, retribution came swiftly and served as an example for every other woman in the house.

"There was one night when some little girl was telling Edna back in the kitchen we need to do this that and the other," said Robert Kleffman. "I was sitting back in Edna's office watching TV, and I heard the darndest commotion you ever heard. I went in there and said, 'What's the matter?'

"That girl was *going* down the hall. And I heard Edna—she'd thrown a *table* at the girl—she said, 'This is *my* G.D. whorehouse! I'll run it the way I want! If you want one, you go start your own somewhere!'"[179]

Miss Edna's no-nonsense, take-no-prisoners management style may have come off as cold and harsh, but she had to maintain an iron grip lest she lose control of the brothel as Aunt Jessie had before. Ruling with an iron fist did have the advantage of keeping conflicts between the women to a minimum.

"The girls didn't ever fight. She didn't allow it," Penny said. "If one even raised her voice, she would call them into her office and give them a talking to and [ask], did that girl there want to call her male person and have him come pick her up? Because that [behavior] would *not* be tolerated. And that's just for raising their voices, much less anything else."[180]

That they tested the rules and probed for weakness to exploit was only to be expected—that's how they'd managed to survive elsewhere. Troublemakers departed sooner rather than later. Those who ultimately bowed to Miss Edna's way of doing things surprisingly found not only quiet sympathy but also a fierce defender in their new madam. Miss Edna never fit the "hooker with a heart of gold" cliché—that would be a disservice to Miss Edna's complex character as well as the truth. She was a businesswoman out to make money and knew far too many people were eager to take advantage of her at the first opportunity. Her prostitutes could spin golden sob stories out of straw if they saw any advantage in it. But Miss Edna *did* have compassion for her women, even if she didn't always show it. She'd worked her way up from nothing and knew firsthand how close to the edge many of them lived.

"I wouldn't have tolerated anyone mistreating my women. I'd say, 'Look, you may mistreat your mother or your sisters or your wife, but you're not coming out here mistreating these women. They're here for one purpose and one purpose only, and if you treat them for any other reason, it's your own ashes,'" Miss Edna said. "They've been mistreated enough in their lives. I knew they had. You know, different uncles take advantage of a young girl—her uncle or her dad or this and that. After a while you just get sick listening to that crud!"[181]

Many of the women arrived at the Chicken Ranch as damaged souls, abused, hurting and lost, in search of some sort of security, of safety. Often they needed a confidant, someone to confess their darkest secrets to, share their shameful burden. Sooner or later, they sought out Miss Edna.

"Not right away. They were embarrassed. But it bothers them, mentally," Miss Edna said solemnly. "There for a while I was finding they'd tell me just about everything that ever happened to them. But you don't betray the confidences, because if you do, then you never hear from them again. They may leave and go someplace else and then they'd keep their mouth shut for sure. They'd never tell another person.

"They need to get that out, for their own selves. There are different things that happened to persons but you wouldn't go tell your momma or sister or next-door neighbor," she said. "Yet you want to be able to confide in somebody, the things that's bothering you. It's hard to be able to confide in somebody about all the things."[182]

If Miss Edna couldn't do much to heal their damaged souls, at least she could help strengthen their bodies. Prostitutes at the Chicken Ranch ate well.

"They always had really nice meals there. The food was fantastic!" Penny recalled. "And it was healthful and nourishing. You know what I'm saying? There was always some form of dessert."[183]

Miss Edna insisted on two good meals every day, with dinner featuring two vegetables, a salad and dessert, plus a main meat entree. On slower days, the kitchen turned out a fish or poultry dish, but for busy weekends the women got steak, roast or some other beef. Greasy, fried foods turned Miss Edna's stomach and were rarely served. Bowls full of fresh fruit—oranges, peaches, pears, apples, grapes—awaited the women if they needed a snack anytime during the day or evening. Under Miss Edna's watchful eye, the women working at the Chicken Ranch probably ate healthier diets than many of their customers.[184]

"When the girls first come in there, they've been places where they didn't give a shit what the girls ate or didn't eat," Miss Edna said. "They could be starving to death. And they'd eat and they'd eat. Those girls would eat their self to death.

"I said, 'See what they're doing now? Come back and talk to me in about a month, tell me what they're doing,'" she said. "They'll be over their hunger. They're not going to be hungry anymore. They'll have some food in them that's good for them. They'll be healthy women."[185]

Miss Edna may have loosened up some of Miss Jessie's restrictive rules once she reopened, but that's not to say she didn't have her own firm convictions about right and proper behavior. When her boarders got a little too comfortable in the house, showing up to meals in sheer, see-through gowns or even topless, Miss Edna put her foot down in the name of decorum. She saw no reason for the women to prance around half-naked. Nudity, she reasoned, should be reserved strictly for either work or pleasure.

"I told them, 'Don't you have a thicker gown? No? You got a robe? Buy one next time you're in town.' I don't like for anyone to come to the table without any clothes on," Miss Edna said. "I don't appreciate it and I don't know of anybody else that does. There are all women here, and I'm not interested in sleeping with any of them. I always liked boys myself. Maybe that made me a freak to some people. Me, I always thought that men were God's gift to the world's women.

"Always come to the table with at least a robe on if you're not going to get dressed. Nobody wants to look at that," she said. "If there's men here, they might not mind it. But I don't know of any men that live here, and I don't know of any woman that wants to look at it unless they're queer. And to my knowledge there's not anybody around here that's queer.

"I hadn't planned to find out whether a woman might be fun or not—I was having too much fun with the boys," Miss Edna said. "To me, the thought of two men together or two women together, to me that was just always real repulsive."[186]

For some of the boarders, Miss Edna evolved into an almost mother-like figure—although she was careful never to let any of the women get so close as to blur the line between employer and employee. Life had left others so embittered and jaded, however, that they never could bring themselves to trust Miss Edna—or anyone else. Some carried such deep hurt and anger that Miss Edna wondered if they even had mothers or merely sprang to life fully formed, scars and all.[187]

Still, for Texas prostitutes during the 1960s and early '70s, no place else offered working conditions as favorable as the Chicken Ranch. Miss Edna's rules stated that there were no assigned bedrooms, but in practice, each woman had her own private bedroom where she lived as well as worked and decorated it as she saw fit. Each of the nine bedrooms had a double bed with a floral bedspread and a dresser on which the women displayed photos and other personal items. During their monthly menstrual periods, boarders got one week off to go wherever and do whatever they pleased. For many, the Chicken Ranch was the closest thing to home they'd ever had.

"To have women on the streets is so dangerous. If there is going to be prostitution, Edna's style of it was the safest for the girls. Absolutely," said Davis-Floyd. "They had a family, they were protected. They had a big den [that] none of the customers ever went in. It was a huge family room. They would do Christmas and Thanksgiving dinners in there.

"It was a combined kitchen/family room with paneling, with big sofas and a television. That was their hangout room," she said. "Then at Christmas, they would draw straws for who was going to give who a present. It was like a family."[188]

Like family, maybe, but that didn't change the bottom line. By the 1970s, Miss Edna charged boarders fifteen dollars a day for room, meals and laundering sheets and towels. For their personal laundry, the women had the option of doing it themselves or paying one of the maids to do it—one way Edna saw to it that the black maids picked up a little extra money on the side.[189]

"The maids there, you could hire them to wash your clothes for you and stuff like that. I tipped the maids. Once you keep the maids tipped, they'd do extra things for you," Penny explained. "They'll keep your place cleaned for you and they're nicer to your customers, you see what I'm saying? You've got to keep the palm greased. You take care of them, they take care of you. Edna knew it was going on, but she didn't like it. She didn't like favoritism. But I did what I felt was good, because I worked as a waitress before and if you have an area, you split your tips with the busboy so he keeps your area clean then you get more people in there. Well, it's the same thing with that business, too.

"When you had a customer come in, if they gave you any indication they was going to be rowdy, there was a signal you could give to one of the maids there at the door. One of them would stand outside your door until he left," she said. "Because you had a vent in the bottom part of your door where they could listen to what went on in the room. So if you said anything to lead them to think this guy was going to give you problems, they would just knock on the door and tell them, 'Time's up!'

"It was necessary sometimes. They're very, very protective of you and wouldn't allow any shenanigans going on," Penny said. "I have seen them turn away carloads of boys because they thought they'd be too boisterous."[190]

Miss Edna pauses in the den area of the Chicken Ranch, the only room Miss Edna added during her ownership of the brothel. Customers were not generally allowed in the den, which served as a private refuge and gathering place for the women. *Courtesy Edna Milton Chadwell.*

One of the most-recognizable faces at the Chicken Ranch was Trudy, Miss Edna's most veteran employee. The large black woman acted as gatekeeper and was the first person any customer saw when they arrived at the brothel. The screen door did not have an outside handle—if Trudy did not like the look of a fellow, she did not let him in. In the segregated '60s, men far and wide learned quickly to treat Trudy with politeness and respect regardless of the color of her skin.

"She came to work for me just before I reopened the place. Because when I bought the thing, I was letting a few customers in," Miss Edna said. "You know, she'd been around there with her grandmother and her mother and her aunts and everyone. Everyone worked there, the whole family.

"She answered the door. I kept it locked because I didn't want some drunk just walking in. Then later I'd had to draw her some money so she could make some change if she needed to make change," she said. "If it was just simple change, the girls could do it. If it had to be more than that, if they had to unlock [the money box], she had the key. It's safer that way.

"You have to trust somebody for God's sakes."[191]

Years later, Miss Edna explained just how important Trudy had become to the brothel's daily operation.

"This girl could run my place good as me," Miss Edna said. "If she hadn't been the wrong color I might have been workin' for her."[192]

Trudy lived with her family just a mile or so away from the Chicken Ranch on the so-called back road. Her children stayed home alone many times as she went off to work, with her eldest daughter watching over them. Trudy's mother and grandmother had both worked for Aunt Jessie, and by the 1970s, Trudy began bringing her teenage daughter along to help out. Being black, even in post–civil rights era Texas, meant they always entered by the back door where no potential white customers could see them, ironic since none of those white men could enter through the front without Trudy's say-so.

The teen made extra money doing sewing and laundry work for the prostitutes at the Chicken Ranch. She planned to buy a car with her savings. Her mother promised to match half the down payment, and by the summer of 1973, she had saved enough for her share. In an effort to cut down on the size of monthly payments, though, she decided to continue saving up her money for a few more months. In the interim, crusading television reporter Marvin Zindler came to town, the Chicken Ranch closed and Trudy lost her good-paying job. Instead of a car, the teenager's savings went toward keeping the family afloat.[193]

Despite Miss Edna's professional respect for Trudy, she held on to the deeply ingrained attitudes regarding racial segregation she'd grown up with. Occasionally, men from Trudy's family came around to do yard work or other manual labor, but Miss Edna didn't make a habit of hiring them and made sure customers never saw the men.

"I really didn't want Negro men hanging around there under the circumstances," she said. "I didn't want the story to get out they were coming in and having sex with the girls. I wasn't going to tolerate that at all. I'd close that house up faster than they'd ever thought if that kind of story had ever got out, you know."[194]

WHEN MISS EDNA TOOK over the brothel, she simplified the calculation of the house's take from each act of prostitution.

Under Aunt Jessie, every time a woman entertained a customer, she paid two dollars, keeping three dollars for herself. If the visit lasted longer than normal, she paid four dollars, keeping six dollars. Miss Edna thought counting minutes a ridiculous waste of time and instituted a straightforward 40/60 split, with the women keeping 60 percent for themselves.[195]

"Just do it that way, and we're not going to argue over minutes then," Miss Edna said. "If you go in there, you're with a guy two minutes, that's all it took for him, you still got as much if you'd been ten or fifteen minutes. I finally made them up a damn rule book. My way or the highway, you know."[196]

To drive the point home, Miss Edna wrote all of her rules down so she would have them handy if anyone proved foolish enough to call her on them. In the end, she had a bona fide booklet on her hands. To save time and trouble, she started giving every new boarder a mimeographed copy and prominently displayed a condensed version of the rules on painted sheets of plywood hanging in the kitchen. Never in the history of prostitution had a brothel so thoroughly dotted its Is and crossed its Ts.[197]

Miss Edna crafted her rules to ensure she'd maintain tight control over the brothel but also as a means of protecting the women who worked for her. She allowed her women to accept out-call dates only if Miss Edna personally knew and approved of the customer. Consequently, these happened rarely. She also instituted fairly limited business hours of 1:00 p.m. to 3:00 a.m.

"I have been so tired as a prostitute I've gone to sleep on a customer," Miss Edna explained. "I don't let the girls put in that many hours here."[198]

"You slept in the morning, and then you got up in the early afternoon. You would take turns working days. They had to have somebody on call in case people came in during the day," Penny said. "Every now and then, you'd get a farmer that'd come in during the day—supposed to be out buying feed or something, I don't know. He'd come by there and you had to be able to get up and make yourself presentable enough to where he would want to have a date with you. So we all took turns doing that.

"When you was there long enough where you had your regulars, sometimes they would come by during the middle of the week when there wasn't as many people there. That way you could make as much money during the week as you would on weekends, once you had people coming back and asking for you," she said. "That was your goal, to get—as the girls used to call them—come-backs. A lot of the people, I know for me, would sit and wait for me if I had a customer. Sometimes I'd have a couple of them waiting. That's how I made my good money—with my tips."[199]

Limiting the hours her women worked didn't significantly cut into profits—Miss Edna cultivated other revenue streams to make up the difference. She put in a Coca-Cola machine, charging fifty cents a bottle at a time when the going rate was a nickel. She also added a jukebox and cigarette machine, likewise with inflated prices. As per Miss Edna's instructions, the prostitutes all encouraged their customers to buy them a drink or smoke or play some music on the jukebox.

"They had a jukebox going all the time, and you had to solicit quarters from the guys to keep it going. They had all kinds of different music on the jukebox," said Penny. "A couple of the girls were musical, and they would sing along with it, which would get some of the guys sometimes singing some of the old songs. That led to a better communication between them, I think."[200]

Despite claims to the contrary, Miss Edna didn't count the number of bottle caps at the end of the night to keep track of the number of customers her women entertained.

"That had nothing to do with customers. There's no reason to check bottle caps if you have the bottles there and you had the cases to set 'em in," she explained, pointing out that in the 1960s and 1970s, Coke machines still dispensed bottles for the most part, which had a deposit at the time. "You didn't sell a Coke to everybody, anyway. It's like the quarter jukebox: might as well say, 'Count all your quarters and see how many played the damn thing.'

"I know I made a pretty good amount of money on those Cokes, because nearly everybody that came in bought at least one," she said. "Most of them bought two—one for him and one for the girl."[201]

As far as contraception went, birth control pills were a latecomer to the scene and played a relatively minor role in the brothel's later years. Prior to that, most prostitutes at the Chicken Ranch used diaphragms and spermicidal jelly, although condoms were available if the customers wanted them. Lots of myths surrounded birth control for prostitutes—some even made the ludicrous claim that the semen from many men would cancel each other out, although any woman relying on that strategy soon found herself as pregnant as she would from just one man. Other claims were equally strange.

"I heard a lot of women say this—but I think they're lying because they'd have sold a lot more Vaseline: 'A greased egg won't hatch,'" Miss Edna said. "Well, maybe a greased egg won't hatch, but we're not talking about chickens or anything. We're talking about children.

"They say, 'Well, use Vaseline and you won't get pregnant.' I'm not going to buy that," she said. "There's a lot of people in the world, and Vaseline's been around a long time."[202]

Edna Milton at age forty-two in this photo dated March 2, 1970. *Courtesy Edna Milton Chadwell.*

Because of their weekly medical check-ups, any sexually transmitted diseases the prostitutes picked up from clients were treated quickly and rarely spread. Despite popular belief, by 1970 streetwalkers contributed only about 5 percent of annual STD transmission cases, said Dr. Don Miller of the Center for Disease Control, while call girls and brothel prostitutes like those at the Chicken Ranch had an insignificant role in the spread of disease.

"Really none," said Joe Pair of the Texas Health Department. "They take care of themselves better than the streetwalker."[203]

When Miss Edna's women did get a diagnosis of gonorrhea or syphilis, a quick shot of penicillin cleared it right up. Prior to the widespread adoption of penicillin to combat bacterial infections in the late 1940s, most treatments relied heavily on sulfa drugs.[204]

Married men made up a large percentage of the Chicken Ranch's clientele, and Miss Edna had no problem with infidelity. In fact, she had a quick defense of the men's behavior at the ready.

"Just because a man goes out there doesn't mean he loves his family any less," Miss Edna argued. "If you stop and think about it, if his wife is not well, if she can't have intercourse with him, I think it'd be logical if that is what he's going to do, rather than to go out and get somebody in a honkytonk. That wouldn't be good, because if he went out with some of these other tramps, got a disease and brought it home for his family to get… it may be he's showing his family more respect and love than he would be otherwise."[205]

While few housewives likely would buy into that logic, Miss Edna nevertheless respected and defended the wives of her customers—albeit in her own way. She considered sex and love two very different things and had no problem with married men paying her women for the former. If a romantic relationship developed, however, that crossed a serious line.

"I wouldn't tolerate it. The wife will know about it," Miss Edna said. "Even if she is a sorry wife, a sorry woman, everyone will say she is a wonderful person. I still think marriage is sacred.

"[Maybe] the poor woman's pregnant. She's got children…she's tired. She's been keeping house…working over that damn hot stove," she said. "Okay, this other girl, she's been sitting on her can all day and she's got time to go to the beauty shop and make up her face, slept all day long, so hell, she's fresh, huh? Here she comes powdered and perfumed, and what a contrast."[206]

Despite Miss Edna's strong feelings on the matter, her rule seldom, if ever, got put to the test. The men coming to the Chicken Ranch weren't looking for romance. At least, not the long-lasting kind. Stories abounded of one prostitute or another hooking up with a particularly enamored client and eventually getting married. Those stories took on an almost urban legend quality, though—they always seemed to happen to a friend of a friend.

"I heard about them, but I've never seen it. I'm not going to say it didn't happen, but who knows?" Miss Edna said. "They usually don't send you a wedding invitation if they did. They'd already checked out and gone. You don't know what they do after, and you don't have time to keep up with them.

"The only thing I can do is wish them the best."[207]

For the vast majority of women who worked at the Chicken Ranch—or any other brothel in Texas, for that matter—no knight in shining armor rode in to carry them away. Happily ever after never entered into it.

Chapter 5

HULLABALOO!

Throughout the twentieth century, in good times and bad, the Chicken Ranch had no client base more loyal than those students attending the Agricultural and Mechanical College of Texas seventy miles to the north, just outside Bryan.

Even today, no institute of higher learning is as closely associated with the Chicken Ranch as Texas A&M University. Indeed, in the whole of American history there's hardly another institute of higher learning as tightly linked with *any* brothel, anywhere—much to the chagrin of the university's modern administration.

Texas A&M enrolled its first class of 106 students in 1876 as an all-male institution with mandatory membership in the Corps of Cadets ROTC program. The school grew slowly, attracting poor farmers' sons from rural areas of the state, many of whom were the first in their families to ever pursue higher education. Their shared country backgrounds, isolated campus, Spartan living conditions and military discipline forged a unique and enduring bond among the male students.[208]

It also created *intense* competition for dates with the few eligible women available in nearby Bryan—the school wouldn't go fully coeducational until 1971. To deal with this scarcity, a sister-school agreement developed with Texas Woman's University in Denton, fully two hundred miles away. On certain weekends, coeds were bused in for dates.

"That's how we got dates—you wrote letters and they brought a bus down. That's how you luckily got a date every now and then," said Willie

Pankoniem, a 1974 A&M graduate. "They had the same situation. I mean, they didn't see guys all week, and we didn't see women all week. It's a different mentality all the way around."[209]

For those unlucky Aggies unable to secure a date for the weekend, the Chicken Ranch beckoned. Of course, the students first had to scrounge up a ride and gas money, not to mention what it would cost to party with one of the Chicken Ranch ladies. Ironically, those Aggies lucky enough to get a date faced pretty much the same problem—how to pay for the date.

"We always needed money. It's hard to imagine how poor we were. It was a poor boy's school," said Dick Ghiselin, a 1960 A&M graduate. "We had to get a corsage. We had to pay for this motel [for the dates to stay in], and if you wanted to have any drinks, you had to go get some and the nearest place was Burleson County, because it was the nearest wet county."[210]

Dates were bused in for every home football game in the fall and for two big dances in the spring—the Combat Ball and Ring Dance. To fund these dates, enterprising Aggies hit upon a raffle system that proved popular and enduring. Cadets took the cardboard stiffener placed in their shirts by the campus laundry and then cut the cardboard up into one hundred squares. Each square was marked with a number, one through one hundred, and then placed in a hat and taken around the dorms.[211]

"It was young guys playing, mostly, because they couldn't get liquor. And there was always some who wanted to go down and visit the Chicken Ranch, so either way it worked," Ghiselin said. "They'd draw a number out of the hat, and whatever number they drew, they'd pay in pennies. If you take the numbers one through one hundred and you add up the sum of all the digits, it comes to five thousand pennies, or fifty dollars. It was easy to sell one hundred squares at A&M. I mean, there were five thousand cadets, and they always had pennies in their pocket and wanted a bottle of whiskey or a trip to the Chicken Ranch—whatever the prize was.

"We would hold the drawing, and whoever's number was drawn, they would get whatever the prize was. Sometimes the prize was just a fifth of whiskey. The twenty-one-year-olds would go down to Whiskey Bridge in Burleson County and buy a fifth of Old Crow or something, and that usually cost about five dollars," he said. "You'd come back and give the guy the fifth of whiskey, and then you'd keep the forty-five dollars. It was a tremendous return on your investment.

"Whenever a trip to the Chicken Ranch was the prize, that cost a little bit more money. For twenty-five dollars you could afford a round-trip bus ticket down to La Grange and you could afford the favors of a young lady at the

Cadets in formation on Military Walk, May 13, 1928. For much of Texas A&M's history, the student body was exclusively male, and participation in the Corps of Cadets was mandatory. *Courtesy Cushing Memorial Library & Archives, Texas A&M University.*

Chicken Ranch. That's what it was, that's what you got. You'd give the boy twenty-five dollars and send him on his way," he said. "But those who ran the raffle got to keep the other twenty-five dollars, and in those days you could have a pretty good date for twenty-five dollars."[212]

The raffles remained popular among the cash-strapped cadets because A) the prizes were in high demand, B) the 1:100 odds were fairly good and C) the most anyone could lose was one dollar and there was always the chance of winning with just a single penny.

"I just thought that was ingenious, that you could make that money with so little effort. It was the ultimate win-win situation, and the next week you could do it again," Ghiselin said. "All through football season that was done, usually for the whiskey. Really, nobody got burned too bad because the biggest loser was the guy who paid one hundred pennies and didn't win. Even a poor boy could afford that, because there was always a chance you could pick out number one, which means you'd only have to pay a penny."[213]

Others made their spending money by more direct methods. Pankoniem, for one, inadvertently started up a taxi service to the Chicken Ranch while he was still in high school. He worked the graveyard shift at a filling station outside Taylor, Texas, and at that time very few stores of any sort stayed open so late. High school and college students would stop in, drinking beer and raring to go to the Chicken Ranch, a ninety-minute drive away.

"Instead of them driving drunk and everything, I basically took off, because business wasn't very heavy after midnight," he said. "Usually there was a larger colored lady at the front door; she was just as sweet as she could be. She took care of everybody. I'd sit there and drink coffee and shoot the breeze with her while everybody else had a good time and I'd, you know, transport them back."[214]

A few years later, Pankoniem graduated from Taylor High School and enrolled at Texas A&M himself. By that time, the rules had relaxed so that freshmen were allowed to have their own vehicles on campus, and Pankoniem found out quickly that having a '70 Chevelle made him very popular. A group of Aggies would get together for a trip to the Chicken Ranch, pool their money to pay Pankoniem for his gas and time and they were off.

"I had the '70 Chevelle and a friend of mine had that 442 Cutlass, and we'd either take one or the other, unless it was more [students than could fit in a car], then we'd take a truck with the Chevelle and would always carry a keg of beer in the back," he said. "I guess in those days, you weren't as conscious about driving drunk, but the parents said, 'You're going to do what you're going to do, but somebody drive sober.' That's how I made my living, I guess. I was a poor boy who had to work to go to college.

"You know, five dollars would get you there and back. In those days, it wasn't anything. But usually I'd get ten dollars or fifteen dollars—I was working for one dollar an hour. That was pretty good money for just taking off a few hours and driving down and coming back," he said. "If I wanted something to eat, Miss Edna, she'd take me back there and they'd have something on the stove. She made sure I got something to drink and had something to eat. Once she made sure everybody got in the car and everybody was fine, she'd send us back. It was kind of like your momma sitting there, you know? A motherly thing, to always send us on our way."[215]

That little country whorehouse greeted all comers equally over the years, whether they paid three dollars in the early 1950s or ten dollars in the early 1960s. A wood-paneled pony wall divided the main parlor into two waiting areas, with a jukebox, Coke machine and cigarette machine in the larger of the two. Here the customers waited for their turn with a prostitute. Garish pink-and-green flowered carpet covered the floor, matched by flowered curtains along the walls sparkling with pink and green sequins. Black vinyl bucket seat bar stools ringed the room in pairs with an upright black industrial ash tray between each set. Cigarette smoke hung in the air, Hank Williams played on the jukebox. They'd ring a bell whenever a new customer arrived, and any women not already in the parlor or otherwise engaged with a customer would come out to present themselves.[216]

Once a customer selected a girl, they'd both retreat to one of the nine bedrooms. Once inside, they'd undress, and the women would examine the customer's penis for any obvious signs of sexually transmitted disease—a syphilis chancre or gonorrhea drip—as she washed him with soap and water from the bedroom sink.[217]

Miss Edna looked back on her student clients with a fondness that grew into nostalgia over the decades. Many came from Texas A&M, but plenty of others came from the University of Texas, University of Houston, Rice University—pretty much every college in the state that admitted men represented at the Chicken Ranch at one time or another. Then, after they'd graduated and transitioned into the business world, they'd return to relive some of their college memories.

"Remember this—they were all young one time. They were all students at one time. Students come here. One day they graduate. They live, they get jobs. Most of those jobs they get are fairly well-paying jobs," Miss Edna said. "I found that out to be true for most of them, those that have any ambition at all, you know. They become men, they're passing through, they stop by for old times' sake.

"A lot of them are still single, and some of them are not. Those that are not, they still stop for old times' sake, but you don't think they're going to be stupid enough to go home and tell their wife, do you? Hell no!" she said. "But you know, she's not stupid either. She knows what the hell's going on, if it is happening. That's what that whole deal is."[218]

For those college boys grown into men, Miss Edna made a lasting impression. She showed a hard edge whenever somebody tried to start trouble but offered sympathy and reassurance for any fellow intimidated, shy or experiencing technical difficulties. What's more, Miss Edna came across to the young men as genuine, someone who enjoyed their company.

"She'd always ask, 'What are you boys up to today?' She tried to keep up with the youth of the time, I think," Pankoniem said. "We were just country boys. There were a lot of rich kids that went in there too, but with the country boys, you worked all week and spent it all that weekend.

"I remember a couple of times, the younger guys come in there, just embarrassed to stand and couldn't do any good. The girls just got them a little excited, I guess," he said. "She came out and said, 'It's OK, young man.' She'd sit there and talk to them and have another girl come back in there. You could tell it meant something to her, too. I just got a kick out of that, I guess.

"You had rough people come in there, too, but it's amazing to me how she could just straighten it out in a heartbeat," he said. "I mean, she had a way about her that just—She deserved respect, and she didn't tolerate things. As long as you were decent, she was decent to you."[219]

Mixing that much testosterone together in one place, with cadets from Texas A&M and fraternity brothers from the University of Texas, plus however many other customers—most of whom had at least a little beer in them—practically guaranteed fights on occasion. Mostly, those involved posturing for a bit before one party backed down, but sometimes scuffles broke out. If things got out of hand, a quick phone call brought out a deputy from the sheriff's office, but the majority of fights sorted themselves out long before the law arrived.

"Most of the people who were involved in fights, they had buddies with them. Most of the time their buddies broke them up," Miss Edna said. "Okay, say he went to A&M. And say for instance he had been there with three or four of his buddies. Some of his buddies get into a fight, well, he sees it's not going right, so he and his buddy get in there and break it up.

"Well, that's what most of them do. You know what kids fight about," she said. "They're still kids, honey! I have to love 'em."[220]

If the Aggies didn't like the fact that their Longhorn counterparts also frequented the Chicken Ranch, they felt just the opposite about University of Texas coeds. For decades, common knowledge held that sexy girls intent on getting a degree—but short on cash—earned their tuition money the old-fashioned way at the Chicken Ranch. An Aggie took particular delight in bedding a Longhorn coed, viewing it as a sort of status symbol to have sex with a girl from the arch-rival school. That same girl wouldn't normally give him the time of day outside the brothel. It elevated the concept of "screwing their rivals" to an entirely different level.[221]

"I remember that one there, she was a blonde-headed girl and she went to the University of Texas," said Red O'Neil, a wide-eyed seventeen-year-old when he first visited the Chicken Ranch in 1959. "She said she's a college student. Of course, I believe her. Wow! A college girl!"[222]

In truth, few, if any, of the prostitutes working at the Chicken Ranch ever so much as set foot on the University of Texas campus—any coed prostitutes were far more likely to work for Hattie Valdes in Austin. A significant part of the brothel prostitute's job lay in creating a fantasy for the customer, affirming his manliness and sexual prowess, not to mention his desirability. Sex with an upwardly mobile, educated woman strongly appealed to many of the rural customers with little formal education. Traveling businessmen and elected officials could privately justify their visits to the whorehouse with the notion that they were doing the girls a favor, helping pay for college and a better future.[223]

The popular idea of a poor coed earnestly working her way through school horizontally amounted to nothing more than an appealing myth. If a whore could talk herself into a bigger tip by leveraging sympathy for a poor schoolgirl, why wouldn't she? Miss Edna demanded strict adherence to working hours, and her boarders stayed at the Chicken Ranch for months at a time, allowing only a narrow window over summer vacation when any coeds could conceivably work. Even that limited arrangement was

Texas A&M's original mascot, Reveille, was smuggled into the dorm rooms one night in 1931. She earned her name the next morning when the bugler woke her up and she began barking furiously. *Courtesy Cushing Memorial Library & Archives, Texas A&M University.*

preposterous, Miss Edna said, because college boys would quickly expose any genuine coed working as a whore. The social stigma at the time was far too great for a girl to take such a risk.[224]

"How long do you think any [administrator] would put up with that shit? Having those whores going to the university? Uh-uh. That would *never* happen. Couldn't have happened. That's just an impossibility there," Miss Edna said emphatically. "The only one I ever knew did anything at all while she was there—She was getting up into her thirties. She knew it wasn't going to be long she had to be leaving, so she knew she wanted to do something to make a living. Everybody likes to eat and pay the rent, huh?

"She decided she wanted to go to work in a grooming parlor, you know, a poodle parlor or whatever. The place she wanted to go to school, they let her go to school two weeks out of the month and be off a couple of weeks. I don't know what kind of arrangements they had, but that's the way it turned out: she came to work for me two weeks and she'd be off for two weeks and could go there.

"Well, I could tolerate that. That's just an arrangement to be made," she said. "I just didn't want them to work over three weeks [consecutively], because it's too hard on them."[225]

As far as Miss Edna remembered, only one Chicken Ranch boarder ever earned a degree, outside of the woman who completed her dog grooming certificate. After the brothel closed in 1973, one of the girls moved back in with her parents in San Antonio and went to nursing school. That made for a grand total of *two* throughout the twenty-one years Miss Edna spent in La Grange.[226]

Most customers of the Chicken Ranch probably wouldn't fret much about it one way or the other, Aggies included. They tended to be forgiving that way. In fact, the Chicken Ranch generated more warm feelings and loyalty among its clientele than a brothel had any right to expect. Decades later, Aggies, Longhorns, businessmen and state legislators alike would look back on the Chicken Ranch with a striking degree of nostalgia.

"You know, it was an Aggie's part of the rite of passage that everybody go to La Grange. It depends on your views of prostitution, I guess," Pankoniem said. "It was just a good, old-timey cathouse.

"If you go back through history, some of the cathouses weren't very fancy, but this was what a young man would like a cathouse to be, let's put it that way. It was just a good place to sow your oats."[227]

A big part of that perception arose from the view that the women working there were part of the community—albeit a marginalized part—

and concerned themselves with their customers' well-being. They weren't just whores or businesswomen but actual human beings capable of showing and receiving compassion. A prime example occurred late one evening when Pankoniem taxied a buddy out to the Chicken Ranch to celebrate his birthday. The friend was due to ship out to Vietnam within a few days, and the women's response to this forever shaped Pankoniem's view of the Chicken Ranch.

"We probably got there about two o'clock in the morning, but basically, the gals said, 'Hey, let's shut the place down,'" he said, marveling at the concern shown by the women to a young man who might never return from the bloody, unpopular war. "Just the kindness out of them…they basically all took a little break. We had a keg on the back of the truck. We had barbecue and everything else. Early in the morning we all sat there and drank beer and told stories.

"That was one of the few times I know that they actually just took a break and said, 'This is not about business, this is about being good to the troops,'" he said. "That really made an impression on me, that they were just nice ladies in there."[228]

NOT EVERYONE HAD SUCH positive experiences at the Chicken Ranch—or, rather, had any experience, period. Through failure of nerve, failure of planning or failure of competence, some would-be customers never quite managed to seal the deal.

For Jim Walton, having grown up in College Station, the Chicken Ranch took on almost mythic status. Every classmate in high school knew about the brothel, and as high school boys are prone to do, they often spoke of it with bravado. Despite all the talk, nobody he knew had ever actually gone there. That changed for Walton in the summer of 1963, when he and several buddies, all aged twenty or twenty-one at the time, spent the better part of a week on the Texas coast near Corpus Christi. It wasn't until they were well on their way home that someone realized their route took them through La Grange.

"So we decided we were going to try and find the infamous Chicken Ranch," Walton said, admitting it took about one hundred miles for the guys to talk themselves into it. "We didn't know where it was, exactly, but somehow we tracked down where we thought it was."[229]

They finally found the Chicken Ranch along a dusty county road, tucked back in the woods. Sitting in the gravel parking lot, Walton couldn't help but feel somewhat let down. The palace of sin he'd heard about all his life amounted to little more than an inauspicious, green-trimmed farmhouse with white wood slat siding on a jumble of rooms added on in haphazard fashion.

"We sat in the parking lot, and the four of us decided who's going to go in first. We sat there for about ten minutes—we couldn't quite decide who was going to go in," Walton said. "We talked about it, joked about it, so we decided we was going to look for money, first.

"We started digging around in our wallets for money. As it turned out, everybody said, 'Well, I don't have any money.' 'I don't have any money, either.' Finally, somebody said, 'You reckon they'll take a check?'" he said, laughing. "The bottom line of the whole story is, we sat there in that parking lot for about thirty minutes and never went in the place. We sat there and looked at it and said, 'OK, we've been here,' and then we left. But that's a story that I've carried with me all my life, because I can always say I went to the Chicken Ranch. I just didn't go in!"[230]

The majority of men who made it all the way out to the Chicken Ranch *did* go in, however. After a few beers, Aggies didn't need much of an excuse to head out to La Grange. As Ken Walters remembers it, one group of inexperienced cadets viewed the November 1, 1970 inauguration of Jack Williams as president of the university reason enough to celebrate at the brothel.

"We had two carloads of Corps buddies, and off we went," recalled Walters. "We went down there and really didn't know what we were going to experience."

Trudy, as usual, answered the door. One of the freshmen, masking his nervousness with bravado, started talking to her.

"Which one of those girls is good?" the freshman asked.

"How the hell do I know?" Trudy answered loudly for all to hear. "I don't sleep with them!"[231]

By 1970, the price for a straight lay had climbed to a whopping twenty dollars. Anyone asking for the legendary eight-dollar "Aggie Special" came away disappointed. That bargain-basement bedroom deal secured the customer the services of a Chicken Ranch prostitute lasting the duration of a Four-Get: Get up, get on, get off, get out. Hardly emotionally satisfying, the deal remained popular with the perpetually cash-strapped students from College Station, hence the name.[232]

"Aggie Special? They were *all* special, honey," said Miss Edna, a sly twinkle in her eye. "They was all a bunch of good kids.

"Shit, they could come in any time they wanted to for eight dollars. Well, maybe not the last couple of years it was open. I'll put it this way: for nearly a hundred years, they could've come in any time they wanted for eight dollars. Now, toward the very tail end, they had to come up with a couple more bucks," she said. "Honey, that was a little country place out there. People's tried to make it into something it wasn't. It was just a little country whorehouse is what it amounted to."[233]

Although Miss Edna downplayed the Chicken Ranch's overall significance, everyone else tended to play it up, whether warranted or not. One story told on the A&M campus held that in the 1950s, so many Aggies visited La Grange that the student health center started offering free penicillin shots. While the health center may have offered penicillin, it was unlikely in response to the Chicken Ranch, specifically, given the long-standing county efforts made to keep the women there disease-free.[234]

Another tale holds that a group of cadets driving a Model T Ford in 1931 took one of the most celebrated road trips in Texas A&M history. On their way back to campus, the car hit a dog on the road, a little black-and-white

All versions of Reveille's origins begin with cadets returning to campus in a Model T, accidentally hitting the dog and then sneaking her into their dorm to nurse her back to health. One variant of the story claims the students were returning from a trip to the Chicken Ranch. *Courtesy Cushing Memorial Library & Archives, Texas A&M University.*

mutt. The students, feeling guilty, snuck the dog back into their dorm to nurse it back to health.

"When morning came, in the person of the bugler, the pup's sleep was interrupted by the notes of Reveille," wrote Dwight H. McAnally in 1945. "She set up such a fuss about this intrusion on her sleep that the problem of a suitable name was solved. Her foster parents simply dubbed her 'Reveille' and the name stuck."[235]

This story, related to all incoming freshmen at tradition-obsessed Texas A&M, has a curious epilogue. After the story was told at orientation or one of the other spirit-building events that precede the start of the academic year, upperclassmen would seek out freshmen and promise, in conspiratorial tones, to tell the "real" story behind Reveille.

Those Model T–driving students? They were actually on their way home from a night at the *Chicken Ranch*.[236]

The fact that the details of the university's "official" story changed regularly lent credence to the Chicken Ranch tale. In that evolving official narrative, the students were variously returning from a basketball or football game; a party in nearby Navasota, Texas; or visiting relatives in Houston. Since the unofficial account referencing the Chicken Ranch remained consistent, students generally accepted it and had little trouble believing university administrators invented sanitized alternatives to suppress the awkward truth.

The truth, though, is more mundane. The reason the university could not settle on a single coherent story was because, over the years, multiple graduates had claimed they were a part of that road trip, and each gave a slightly different tale. No official records were kept at the time, so there was no way to determine which was the one true account.[237]

Of these earliest conflicting stories, though, one thing is clear: not a single one mentions the Chicken Ranch. In fact, graduates of Texas A&M who attended prior to 1980 generally expressed surprise at any connection between the Chicken Ranch and Reveille's origin. Since the motion picture version of *The Best Little Whorehouse in Texas* opened in 1982 and featured Texas A&M prominently, it isn't too big a stretch to speculate that Aggies on campus got a little caught up in the hype, embellishing an already-uncertain piece of school history to further enhance the ties between the school and brothel.[238]

Of course, while neither the stage play nor theatrical version of *The Best Little Whorehouse in Texas* made mention of Reveille, they did prominently feature another big tradition involving the Chicken Ranch: every year, arch-rivals Texas A&M and the University of Texas played each other in football

Legendary coach Paul "Bear" Bryant restored Texas A&M's football fortunes. He coached the Aggies to their first-ever victory in the University of Texas' Memorial Stadium in 1956. Student lore holds that the football team celebrated at the Chicken Ranch afterward. *Courtesy Cushing Memorial Library & Archives, Texas A&M University.*

on Thanksgiving. The winning team got more than just bragging rights: well-heeled alumni rewarded players with an all-expense paid trip to the Chicken Ranch afterward. Around College Station, the game was informally known as the Pussy Bowl.[239]

Throughout the 1950s and 1960s, the Aggies didn't win the Pussy Bowl very often. The teams fielded by Texas A&M were generally awful in those years, but in 1956, legendary coach Paul "Bear" Bryant led his famed Junction Boys to a historic victory over the Longhorns in Austin.

"My freshman year, we beat [Texas] 34–21 in Memorial Stadium, and that was fantastic because we never had beaten them in Memorial Stadium before," said Ghiselin. "Bear Bryant was the coach, and the big star was Jack Pardee. John David Crow was a junior at that time, and the next year he won the Heisman Trophy.

"That famous trip to the Chicken Ranch was probably exaggerated. It sounded like all of them went, and I don't really believe that all of them did go," he said. "Well, them that wanted to. I don't know how many wanted to go. That's the other thing you don't see so much anymore—a lot of these kids were pretty fundamental about things. My roommate, who was my roommate for all four years—I loved him like a brother—he was a fundamental Baptist and he didn't drink, smoke, chew, go with girls that do, he didn't go in for mixed swimming…what else didn't he do? Dancing, he didn't do dancing, either. See? He was very inhibited. Probably a lot of football players fell into that same mold, and they probably wouldn't have gone.

"Of course, the other thing is, a lot of them were married. You know, Crow was married, and some of those other guys were married, and that would've gone over like a lead balloon," he said. "So, there would be some that didn't go for that reason, too. But on the other hand, we had some pretty rough characters, and I'm sure they went."[240]

Aggie football players were much more likely to get a free trip to the Chicken Ranch as a recruit in those days. Assistant coaches would take promising blue chippers down to La Grange in hope that a lusty evening with the women might sway them to sign letters of intent. The college didn't officially condone such practice but, at the same time, did nothing to stop it. The only problem with the Aggies' recruiting strategy was that Texas, Rice, Houston and other competing colleges did the exact same thing.[241]

By the time Miss Edna purchased the Chicken Ranch, the post–Thanksgiving Day game celebrations by the winning team had largely ended—if such celebrations had ever amounted to anything more than a bunch of exuberant Aggies celebrating a rare victory over their rivals in '56. Football players still patronized the Chicken Ranch, but their visits were hardly akin to high school field trips.

"One thing they put in the show about the Aggies—you know, about getting on the bus and riding out to La Grange and all that bull? That was baloney!" said Miss Edna, shaking her head in exasperation. "They didn't get no bus. They got in their own cars and came.

"That's why it's all a bunch of bull!" she said. "Yeah, that's really what you call theatrical license, huh?"[242]

Chapter 6

BIG JIM

S heriff T.J. Flournoy came by his nickname of "Big Jim" the old-fashioned way: he grew into it. Standing six feet four inches tall, with a craggy face and a large, bulbous nose, he cut an imposing figure, but in his custom-made cowboy boots and Stetson hat, he looked closer to seven feet, towering over practically anyone. Townsfolk and criminals alike addressed him respectfully as "Mr. Jim."

"He was very large, a very tall man, six-foot-four or thereabouts," said former Texas Lieutenant Governor Bill Hobby. "He looked so much like Lyndon Johnson that there was just an incredible…of course, he was the same size and general build. They were both big, tall men. But in addition to the size, he looked in the face like L.B.J."

"I mentioned to my daughter the other day that I had an appointment to talk about Jim Flournoy," he said. "Her comment was, 'I remember Jim Flournoy. I remember him as larger than life.' I said, yes, that's a very good description."[243]

Big Jim's intimidating reputation as a tough-as-nails sheriff no doubt had a great deal to do with La Grange's reputation as a law-and-order community—the Chicken Ranch notwithstanding. Nobody aspired to get on the sheriff's bad side, but if they did, they took great pains thereafter to stay out of his way.

"I was prosecuting a case where a habitual felony criminal had escaped from the Fayette County Jail," said Oliver Kitzman, a former district attorney who served La Grange. "I was getting ready to present it, to get it brought

During his seventh year as sheriff, T.J. "Big Jim" Flournoy reclines in his Fayette County Courthouse office—the same office occupied by his predecessor, Sheriff Will Loessin. *Courtesy La Grange Chamber of Commerce.*

to trial. The defendant's attorney filed a motion for a change of venue, and I thought that was frivolous.

"In the presence of the defendant, I asked the lawyer why he wanted a change of venue. His client spoke up and said, 'Mr. Jim don't like me!'" Kitzman explained, breaking down in a fit of laughter. "So, even though the sheriff, of course, would have no participation in the trial, I just did not contest the motion, and we moved it over to Columbus and tried it there. The respect over there for [Big Jim] was just a wonderful thing to see."[244]

Big Jim put in a lot of long miles to earn such deference. He started life—as did most everyone in Texas at that time—from humble beginnings. He was born to Tom and Etta Flournoy on September 22, 1902, on a ranch near Rock Island, Texas. The Flournoy family was a large one, with six brothers and a sister, and Tom worked as a rancher and deputy sheriff in Colorado County to make ends meet. The hardworking father was practically the embodiment of the Old West carried over into the

"I just wanted to be a cowboy," Big Jim once said. His work as a ranch hand in South Texas, a Texas Ranger in the Big Bend region and sheriff of Fayette County gave him plenty of opportunity to live that dream. *Courtesy La Grange Visitors Bureau.*

twentieth century, and he made a tremendous impression on his sons—especially young Jim.[245]

"At first I just wanted to be a cowboy," Big Jim said years later. "My father and brothers were already in law enforcement, and I guess I always knew I'd end up there too."[246]

He attended school in Rock Island through eighth grade. His family then moved to Three Rivers, Texas, for several years before settling in Yoakum, Texas, where Big Jim earned his high school diploma. Upon graduation, he immediately began pursuing his dreams of becoming a cowboy and a lawman.[247]

Big Jim worked as a ranch hand in Colorado County briefly before heading south to Kenedy County on the Texas Coastal Bend. In short order, he landed work on the Santa Rosa Ranch, owned by Claude and Frank McGill, two brothers originally from Flatonia, a small town in Fayette County. When not working cattle, Big Jim took up an unusual hobby well suited to his cowboy inclinations: he trained his ranch horses to be cutting horses, skilled at separating specific cows from the herd.

On a working cattle ranch, cutting horses were obviously valuable property. That soon led to conflict. Once he got the horse fully trained, the McGill brothers promptly sold it for a tidy profit—the animal belonged to them, after all, and Big Jim was just a hired hand. Annoyed, Big Jim set about training a new horse. And the McGills sold that one as well. Incensed, Big Jim delivered an ultimatum: "If you sell another horse out from under me, I quit."

The McGills sold the next horse he trained up, and true to his word, Big Jim promptly quit, catching on with the famed King Ranch right up the road.[248]

In 1925, at the age of twenty-three, Big Jim talked his way into the job of deputy sheriff, thus beginning a career as a lawman destined to last nearly seventy-five years. For the next three years, when Big Jim wasn't working cattle, he kept busy earning every penny of his meager deputy's salary by chasing down cattle rustlers, thieves and other assorted lawbreakers. The few roads cutting through the county were by and large unpaved and primitive. The best—and sometimes only—way to get the job done was to saddle up and enforce the law from horseback.[249]

Big Jim stayed on in Kenedy County until 1927. After turning in his deputy's badge, he worked a brief stint in Sugar Land, Texas, as a prison guard before catching on with the Lavaca County Livestock Sanitary Commission. The following year, the job transferred him to Fayette County, where he worked to rid local herds of deadly fever ticks that plagued Texas cattle.[250]

"We'd run a thousand head of cattle through the dipping vats each day," he said. "We cleaned up most of the central part of the state."[251]

Even though eradicating ticks for the sanitary commission was honest work that served the public good, there were two significant drawbacks to it: 1) it was damned hard labor and 2) if any single job sat at the polar opposite of both "fun" and "glamorous," de-ticking cattle fit the bill. Big Jim started looking to get back into law enforcement, and by the middle of 1928, Sheriff Will Loessin had added the imposing young Flournoy to his roster of deputies.[252]

Big Jim didn't know it, but big changes in his life loomed right around the corner. One day, not long after Mr. Will had deputized him, Big Jim pulled up to the country store in tiny West Point, Texas, just a few miles west of La Grange, and spotted a young woman by the name of Gladys Daniels sweeping off the front porch.

"I just sat there and stared at her," he said. "I guess it was love at first sight."[253]

Big Jim set about pursuing Gladys with all the gusto he'd formerly reserved for chasing down mavericks from the herd. At the time, box-lunch auctions were popular social events, with single men bidding for the lunches—and de facto dates with the eligible young women who'd prepared them. When the box lunch fixed by Gladys went up for auction—prettily decorated with ribbons and bows—the new deputy in town bid so aggressively that lots of tongues set to wagging.[254]

Big Jim didn't waste the opportunity that box lunch gave him. On January 12, 1929, he married Gladys at the First Baptist Church of West Point. For Gladys, a deeply conservative woman who'd lived a sheltered life, marriage to a lawman was a jarring experience.[255]

"At first I was scared whenever he'd go out on the job," Gladys admitted years later. "That's just natural for any policeman's wife the first few years you're married. But after a while you get used to it.[256]

"I can't say it isn't hard at times, but I know that the Lord is watching over him, and it's all in His hands," she said.[257]

Despite that early period of adjustment, it didn't take long for the Flournoys to find their place among the other married couples in rural Fayette County, building a circle of friends in the community and participating actively in their church.

"His wife, Gladys and he, were so vividly devoted to each other that it was remarkable," Kitzman said. "He respected that lady, thoroughly, and she, you could tell, adored him. She was a—I wouldn't say exactly *polished* person—but very kind and personable lady and was respected greatly.

"My understanding is that she taught Sunday school class in the Baptist Church for many, many years," he said. "He and his wife had no children. They lived in a nice but modest home right there in La Grange. His family were the people of Fayette County."[258]

The Flournoys were not childless by choice. Early in their marriage, they faced their first real crisis together when Gladys miscarried. Complications set in, and she underwent surgery. Once all was said and done, she could no longer bear children. They coped, as so many families do, and remained married another five decades.[259]

Like all young men, Big Jim had a bit of growing up to do before he became the well-regarded lawman of his latter years. Even during his years as sheriff, Big Jim showed an ostentatious streak, with his pearl-handled revolvers and custom-made boots of his own design. Early on, as deputy under Mr. Will, he learned a great deal about law enforcement, but just as important, he learned how to control his impulse to show off. One particular case—in which a local teacher raped a girl—illustrated this dramatically.[260]

"That son of a bitch kept running and getting away from them. They'd locate him and get ready to get him, and Flournoy would just open his mouth and the guy would disappear," said Leerie Giese, a longtime La Grange resident. "Flournoy was a flamboyant guy. Oh, hell yes.

"So, one Monday morning, old man Will did not show up, and nobody knew where the hell he was, other than his immediate family, and they said he went to get somebody," he said. "At ten o'clock Monday morning, [Loessin] called and said, 'I've got [the suspect] and I'm bringing him back.' He'd slipped off on his own. He brought him back here, and they tried him and sent him to the pen."[261]

The fact that Mr. Will apprehended the fugitive only after keeping his plans secret from Big Jim was an uncomfortable lesson for the young deputy to learn but a valuable one. He began choosing his words more carefully after that, a habit that served him well for many years thereafter.

If that rape case chastened the young deputy, one incident that followed laid the foundation for Big Jim's redemption as a lawman, with everything that came after in his career merely building upon it. The mythology distorting it over the years underscored its importance in the "Legacy of Big Jim." In short, Big Jim shot a man dead.

It happened like this: Nelson Saunders, a black man with a reputation for trouble, got himself into some. When a Fayette County deputy arrived at Saunders' home to make the arrest, Saunders pulled out a shotgun and sent the terrified deputy screaming back to town in a cloud of dust. When the deputy reported the events to Sheriff Flournoy, Big Jim first fired the weak-kneed deputy and then promptly drove out to Saunders' place to handle the matter himself.[262]

That's how one popular version of the story goes. The truth, as usual, is somewhat different. Big Jim *did* drive out to confront Saunders, but as a mere deputy, nearly two decades away from being sheriff. And he didn't fire some hapless predecessor, either; those embellishments came much later. Still, the basic facts of the story serve well enough on their own to illustrate Big Jim's instincts as a lawman. As he arrived and got out of his vehicle, Saunders confronted him and raised his shotgun as if to shoot. Big Jim had only an instant to react. Grabbing his pistol, Big Jim fired without ever removing it from the holster. Saunders dropped to the ground, dead. Remarkably, in a violent and often bloody period of Texas history, Saunders' was the only life taken by Big Jim over the entire span of his career as a peace officer.

"That was once too many for me," Big Jim said, "but I knew it was him or me."[263]

After that, Big Jim proved himself repeatedly, earning his position as Mr. Will's top deputy. The bank in tiny Carmine, Texas, proved a magnet for bank robbers. Raymond Hamilton and Gene O'Dare, violent criminal associates of the Barrow gang—led by the notorious Clyde Barrow and Bonnie Parker—robbed it in November 1932. When the call came in about a bank robbery in progress, Big Jim answered the call.

"Mr. Will and myself went over there, but we missed 'em," Big Jim said. "They abandoned a stolen car in Smithville. We got the car, took fingerprints and checked against pictures in Austin. [We] took the pictures to Carmine and identified the robbers."[264]

The notion that Bonnie and Clyde—or at least their gang members—could rob and plunder Fayette County at will didn't sit well with anyone. The county commissioners ponied up to purchase a 1932 Thompson machine gun to counter the heavily armed gang. With the Tommy gun ready, Big Jim twice kicked in the doors to empty motel rooms over the next year, finding his tips on the whereabouts of Bonnie and Clyde nothing more than dead ends.[265]

Even though the Barrow gang moved their banditry to parts farther north, other criminals showed a great willingness to pick up the slack. Less than a year after the Hamilton-O'Dare robbery, Big Jim got a tip from an informant that another gang of bandits planned to hit the Carmine bank again. Although there's no direct evidence to support the fact, this advanced warning may have come from the ladies at the Chicken Farm.[266]

"He discovered that whenever some crook knocked over a bank, the first thing the crook was likely to do was rush over to Miss Jessie's and spend his money on one of the girls," said Lester "Buddy" Zapalac, publisher of the *La Grange Journal*. "And while he was at it he'd brag about how he'd done the robbery, how much money he got and who was with him when he did the robbing."[267]

It's not much of a stretch to imagine some would-be bandits bragging about a bank job *before* they pulled it off. In any event, Big Jim wasted no time. Along with another deputy, he raced the thirty miles to Carmine and actually beat the robbers to the bank.[268]

"We laid on the floor of the bank 'til 10 minutes before closing time but they didn't show," Big Jim said. "A farmer came in and said a strange car was out on a back road. We went to see about it. When we got back, the robbery was in progress. One guy was outside in a car with the motor running."[269]

They'd caught the robbery at a dangerous time, with potential hostages to worry about. While one bandit plundered the bank, the second waited outside as a lookout—although not a very good one, apparently.

"I sneaked up behind the guy who was keeping watch. He was sitting there looking the other way with a .45 automatic on his lap," Big Jim said. "I pulled out my gun and got him covered good, and then I reached around real quiet and just lifted that pistol right off his lap."[270]

After handcuffing the lookout, Big Jim had the second deputy cover the exits, and then he himself kicked in a side door of the bank, startling the bandit inside. When the robber spun to aim his gun at Big Jim, the bank teller had the opening he needed to pull his own pistol from where he'd concealed it beneath the counter and shot the robber in the head.[271]

"When we lifted his body off the floor he was still holding on to a bag full of $1,200 and his gun," Big Jim said.[272]

While the failed bank robbery proved more violent and bloody, the earlier robbery of the Carmine bank by Hamilton and O'Dare grew into the highest-profile case ever to run through Fayette County. With the outlaw gang of Bonnie and Clyde blazing a trail of terror from Texas to Minnesota, the capture of Hamilton in Sherman, Texas, on April 25, 1934, following a bank robbery and high-speed chase, made headlines across the nation. Hamilton had busted out of the Eastham state prison farm that prior January, where he'd been serving an aggregate sentence of 263 years. Barrow planned that dramatic escape, which left one guard dead.

Hamilton's recapture did little to settle anyone's nerves. Even though authorities locked Hamilton up in a high-security death row cell surrounded twenty-four hours a day by dozens of officers in the imposing Dallas County Jail, expectations ran high that the Barrow gang would attempt another jailbreak. Security concerns were exacerbated when a mob of more than 1,500 stormed the jail to gawk at the infamous criminal.[273]

"If I had a machine gun this afternoon, I would have shot it out with them," Hamilton threatened after his capture. Once he realized the seriousness of his situation, however, the killer soon changed his story.

"People have me all wrong," Hamilton insisted. "I'm not a killer. I'd always give up at the showdown instead of fighting it out."[274]

After much discussion, the various prosecutors and law enforcement agencies with jurisdiction in the matter decided the best course of action was to transport Hamilton to Fayette County, and try him in La Grange for the

Carmine robbery. That set into motion one of the highest-security prisoner transfers in Texas history. They loaded a shackled Hamilton onto a train in Dallas with a heavily armed contingent of guards and set out for La Grange.

With memories of the Eastham state prison farm breakout still fresh in everyone's minds, however, paranoia ran high. Word soon spread that Clyde Barrow and his heavily armed gang planned to intercept the train outside Temple, Texas, and stage another bloody breakout. Barrow posed such a huge threat at the time that Texas police took the rumors seriously—so seriously, in fact, that an emergency change in plans kicked into motion. Big Jim was the first deputy Mr. Will turned to, taking him to meet the train in Waco, where they quickly spirited Hamilton off and into a rented car. At that point, Big Jim became Hamilton's custodian, presumably because Flournoy was the biggest, most intimidating guard they could find. They then took off, hell-bent for leather along the rural Texas backroads, with Mr. Will driving and Big Jim literally riding shotgun, constantly scanning the roads for any sign of the Barrow gang. Finally, after several nerve-wracking hours, they met up with the train again in Granger, Texas, on the other side of Temple and beyond the threat of the rumored Barrow gang ambush. Big Jim delivered his charge to the waiting guards, and Hamilton continued the rest of the trip by rail without incident.[275]

Once the train arrived in La Grange, a spectacle every bit as chaotic as that left behind in Dallas greeted them. Thousands of spectators from around the county and beyond filled the courthouse square, hoping to catch a glimpse of Hamilton. To make matters worse, the railroad tracks ran a block north of the courthouse square, while the county jail stood a block to the south.[276]

"All of us snotty-nosed farts had to come down and see, because they were bringing Raymond Hamilton in on the four o'clock train," Giese remembered. "And God dang, they had [armed] men on top of all the buildings on the square, and they walked him from the old depot.

"They walked him down here with a deputy chained to each leg and each arm, and they walked him right down the middle of the street," he said. "Shit. He had a hell of a bunch of [deputies around him]. He had four *chained* to him."[277]

The resulting media circus put La Grange in the spotlight for several weeks, ending with Hamilton's conviction and ninety-nine-year sentence. For his other crimes, Hamilton eventually received convictions and a death sentence, meeting his execution in the electric chair on May 10, 1935. Big Jim didn't shed any tears for any of the Barrow gang members' deaths.[278]

Big Jim could view the Old Fayette County Jail from the front porch of his house down the street, but his department operated out of offices in the courthouse one block away. *Courtesy Fayette Heritage Museum and Archives.*

"[Big Jim] had some very strong words about Clyde Barrow," Kitzman said. "He was a ruthless killer. Killed officers for no reason, in his view."[279]

Through all of these high-profile cases and many smaller, routine matters, Big Jim won over the citizens of Fayette County and earned their respect as an able second to Mr. Will. But not only did they respect him, the people of La Grange grew to like the deputy.

"You know how teen-agers can hate people? Well, when I was a kid all the teen-agers liked Jim," said Zapalac. "Some lawmen are stuck up and look at you like they're getting ready to throw you in jail. But whenever a group of us were sitting around the courthouse lawn back in the 1930s, Jim, who was a deputy then, would stop and chat with us real friendly."[280]

As Flournoy matured as a lawman, he caught the eye of Captain Ernest Best of the Texas Rangers, "because I had made a good record as a law officer," Big Jim said. Before the Texas Department of Public Safety underwent a series of reforms in the 1970s, one thing, and one thing only, qualified an officer to join the legendary Rangers: if a Ranger captain wanted someone, he was in. No tests, no prerequisites, no seniority. In 1941, on the eve of World War II, an appointment offer from the Rangers came through. Big Jim accepted, submitting his resignation to the Fayette County Commissioners Court on September 5, 1941.[281]

Newly minted Ranger Flournoy joined Captain Best and the rest of Company E in San Angelo, Texas, which served as their base of operations. He found a small house, and Gladys soon joined him. Then the work began. As a deputy, Big Jim responded to calls from the length and breadth of Fayette County. As a Texas Ranger, though, his responsibility covered forty-four counties in the Big Bend region of West Texas, an enormous expanse of rugged desert stretching from El Paso to Del Rio.[282]

Even in the twenty-first century, roads crisscrossing the region are few and far between, and many of the unpaved routes become impassable after flash floods that regularly occur throughout the year. For Texas Rangers charged with guarding the border region throughout World War II against smugglers, cattle rustlers, foreign nationals and other potential threats, the only realistic way to patrol such a vast area was on horseback. In this, at least, Big Jim's earlier experience as deputy in sprawling, undeveloped Kenedy County served him well.[283]

"I'd hook up a trailer to the car to carry my horse and we'd drive out into the Big Bend country," Big Jim said. "When we'd gotten as far as we could go by car, we'd get the horses out and ride the rest of the way.

"We watched for smugglers. There were these big mercury mines where they dug mercury out of the ground to use in the war effort, and Mexicans would come across and steal it. They put the mercury in saddlebags and smuggle[d] it into Mexico on mules," he said. "Then they'd bring it across the border again and try to sell it back to the U.S. government.

"To catch them, a Ranger would ride along the Rio Grande looking for hidden trails and wait until the smugglers came along so you rush in and arrest them," he said. "It got pretty tedious."[284]

Not to mention dangerous. Big Jim and his fellow Rangers had more than one shootout with smugglers along the border, and during a particularly nasty fight, he suffered a deep knife wound on his left leg while subduing a prisoner.[285]

In 1944, Big Jim abruptly resigned from the Texas Rangers, a surprisingly short stint at the pinnacle of Texas law enforcement. The reasons remain unclear, although a vague notion persists that Big Jim developed a personality conflict with someone higher up the command chain. This is certainly plausible, given his low tolerance for taking any kind of guff from anybody. Regardless of the cause, Big Jim didn't have any trouble finding work as an ex-Ranger. In short order, he started working as a deputy for legendary Sheriff T.W. "Buckshot" Lane in Wharton County, where his brother, Mike Flournoy, would later succeed Lane as sheriff in 1952.[286]

Big Jim never intended the Wharton County deputy job to be anything more than temporary—just something to put food on the table until a more suitable position opened. The opportunity he wanted presented itself in late 1945, when his old mentor, Mr. Will, retired. Big Jim immediately packed up and moved with Gladys back to La Grange that November to run for Fayette County sheriff, a job seemingly tailor-made for him. There was just one problem: two other men wanted to succeed Mr. Will as well.[287]

To complicate matters further, one of those men was Charlie A. Prilop, an old friend of Big Jim's and fellow Fayette County deputy who'd become Mr. Will's right-hand man once Flournoy left to join the Texas Rangers. A tall, imposing man in his own right, Prilop always wore a big Stetson hat like Big Jim but, unlike his friend, had a more relaxed, laid-back personality. Prilop made a pact with Big Jim once they finished as the top-two vote getters in the election and headed toward a runoff: whichever man won would guarantee the other a job as chief deputy. The runoff became a surreal spectacle, with neither candidate offering anything but praise for his opponent. In the end, though, Big Jim's Texas Rangers résumé helped him edge the well-liked Prilop at the ballot box—or it may be that Big Jim's craggy face and hard,

Big Jim (right) with Travis County Sheriff Truitt O. Lang at the Texas Sheriff's Association, November 15, 1956. *M-420, Texas Department of Public Safety photographs, 1937–1965, undated. Archives and Information Services Division, Texas State Library and Archives Commission.*

towering presence simply fit voters' expectations of what a sheriff should look like more than Prilop's more polished looks. True to his word, Big Jim made Prilop chief deputy as one of his first acts as Fayette County sheriff, a position he'd hold for the better part of four decades.[288]

"I've pondered a lot of times how to describe Sheriff Flournoy's presence," mused Kitzman. "Let's see, how did I put that? 'His presence and his bearing made John Wayne look like a sissy!'"

Kitzman laughed hard for a moment, then continued.

"And that's not knocking John Wayne! Some people in the world, the air pressure changes when they walk in the room. He was one of those," he said. "That's one thing I think is sad, so many people have never met somebody like that. They can't imagine there really are people that have that kind of power and character, so they believe that it's fake. There *are* strong people in the world, there *are* people who have a personal power, and Sheriff Flournoy was one of them."[289]

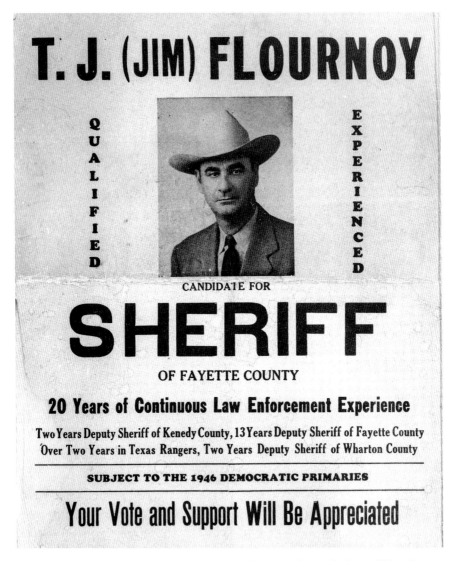

A cardstock handbill from Big Jim's first campaign in 1946. *Courtesy La Grange Visitors Bureau.*

As for the brothel outside town, the new sheriff didn't waste much time fretting about it. Aunt Jessie's Chicken Farm operated quietly without causing any trouble, as it had for Mr. Will and August Loessin before. Big Jim knew Aunt Jessie from his earlier stint as deputy, and moving to close down the brothel amounted to imposing a solution on a problem that didn't exist. Besides, the new sheriff had a far more pressing challenge to deal with: the county commissioners.

In 1946, the Fayette County sheriff still counted among those considered "high sheriffs," a historical holdover from earlier centuries that concentrated much political power in the county's top officer of the law. As sheriff, Jim Flournoy occupied the single most powerful office in Fayette County, yet even he found himself at the mercy of notoriously miserly county commissioners.

Big Jim drew a respectable salary, but to ensure a living wage for Chief Deputy Prilop took some serious horse-trading. With the commissioners loath to approve anything that cost actual money, Big Jim kept the peace and maintained an adequate force of deputies largely through sleight of hand. In addition to Prilop, he had one town deputy stationed with him in La Grange, the county seat. In other Fayette County towns—Schulenburg, Round Top, Hammondsville and Flatonia—he maintained part-time deputies who could respond more quickly to local issues, although their salaries amounted to little more than token payment. Big Jim also recruited a handful of "special deputies," essentially unpaid volunteers who worked Friday night high school football games and Saturday dances in Swiss Alp or at the Round Up Hall in exchange for the prestige of carrying a badge and a gun. Occasionally, these special deputies worked traffic and directed parking at the Chicken Farm on particularly busy evenings.[290]

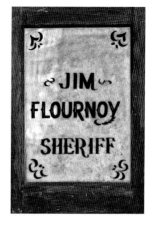

The door to Big Jim's Fayette County Courthouse office. *Courtesy La Grange Visitors Bureau.*

First and foremost, primitive communications hampered the sheriff department's law enforcement efforts. Lacking two-way radios, patrolling the county's roads was a luxury they couldn't afford because it would leave them out of touch for extended periods of time. Instead, the sheriff and whatever other deputies might be on duty at the time waited for the phone to ring in the sheriff's office so they could then respond to the call. Determined to modernize, Big Jim went to the Commissioner's Court in 1949, asking for a short-wave radio. He came away smarting from the sting of their rejection.[291]

Defeated but not deterred, Big Jim took his case straight to the people of Fayette County. Their response overwhelmed him. Donations piled up to the tune of $5,100, and when all was said and done, Big Jim had enough to buy not only a transmitter for the central office but also six mobile units for his and his deputies' cars. That alone testified to the growing popularity of the new sheriff.[292]

"One night we were [at the sheriff's office], and he had a gun he'd confiscated. He gave me that little nickel-plated .22 pistol. He said, 'Every boy needs to have a gun. Here you go,'" recalled Robert Kleffman. "He was a nice fellow. Very matter-of-fact.

"When you first met him, he was kind of gruff acting, you know what I mean. But once he knew who you were, he was just as good as he could be. But he was the sheriff. First and foremost, he was the sheriff. I just, yeah… Mr. Jim was okay."[293]

IN THE LATTER HALF of the 1940s, the expansion of telephone coverage across the United States resumed after the disruption of World War II. Like thousands of other rural homesteads across Texas, Aunt Jessie's Chicken Farm got a visit from Ma Bell, whose workers strung up the phone lines and connected the brothel to the outside world. Local lore holds this came at the behest of Big Jim so that he might discontinue his regular visits to the Chicken Farm to gather tips on crimes both planned and committed. The oft-repeated claim that the Chicken Farm's telephone included a direct line connecting it to the sheriff's department, in the mold of the famed Washington-to-Moscow "hotline," is exaggeration. In an era when most residential customers made do with a party line if they wanted telephone access at all, the technical and logistical challenges of erecting a direct line between two small, rural customers would be too much to overcome. It simply cost too much. It is entirely plausible, however, given the nature of the business conducted at the Chicken Farm and the ease of eavesdropping on a party line, that the brothel enjoyed fast-track status in getting a dedicated line that didn't have to be shared with curious neighbors.[294]

Maintaining open lines of communication with the Chicken Farm—whether through personal visits, party lines or two tin cans with a string running between them—certainly paid off for the sheriff over the years. All new arrivals at the Chicken Farm paid a visit to the sheriff's department first thing, where they were fingerprinted to check for outstanding warrants or criminal history. That way, Big Jim weeded out any outside criminal infiltration on the brothel and kept the locals satisfied the place remained under control. For their part, the women kept their ears open and shared whatever information they might hear about crime in the community. While it's impossible to know how many criminals ended up behind bars because of the intelligence gathered by the women working the brothel, ultimately the sheriff's department solved more cases with their help than it would have without it.[295]

"One time Sheriff Flournoy brought a case to me. He wasn't real big on writing reports—[he gave me] just a little bit of information and he wanted me to take the case to the grand jury," Kitzman said. "It was a burglary of a gun repair shop. He told me he had recovered the guns and whatever. But nothing in his report really told me what the evidence was.

"So, I asked him, 'Do we have any witnesses to this?' And he said, 'Yes, there are some ladies here in town that told me about it.'

"The idea [the witnesses might be from the Chicken Ranch] never crossed my mind, so I said, 'Well, we need to get them in here to testify before the grand jury,'" Kitzman said, holding back laughter. "Jim said, 'That'd be a little *embarrassing*.' I got the message!"[296]

Big Jim endeared himself to the people of La Grange by handling all manner of problems, big or small. In one odd case, an honest-to-goodness *banana thief* plagued a grocer in the downtown area. The thief would hit the business in the early morning hours, during the confusion as delivery trucks unloaded produce for the day. Instead of dismissing the grocer's complaints as beneath a sheriff's notice, Big Jim treated it as if it were a big game challenge. With all the deliberate care of an avid deer hunter (which the sheriff certainly was), Big Jim settled himself in a vantage point with a clear view of all the approaches to the market. Concealed by predawn shadows, he held ready a shotgun loaded with buckshot.[297]

"I could see him coming down the railroad tracks," Big Jim said. "He passed by the trucks, grabbed a handful of bananas and didn't even stop. I yelled at him to drop it, but he started running full speed. So I shot him square in the butt with that buckshot.

"He dropped those bananas real fast, and I never had any more trouble out of him," he said. "Matter of fact, the whole town started calling him 'Bananas' as a nickname."[298]

Big Jim continued building his reputation with popular actions like that throughout his career. Unfortunately, popular actions aren't always on the right side of history. Although Fayette County, under August and Mr. Will's leadership, avoided the worst of the racial violence and lynchings that plagued Texas in the early part of the twentieth century, the people of La Grange were neither more nor less racist than their neighbors in Bastrop, Colorado or Lee Counties. Segregation existed as both law and custom in schools as well as the community, so it caused no small amount of upheaval when two black parents tried to enroll their children in the whites-only school. Big Jim, the law and order sheriff, put his big boots down firmly against integration.

"I can't say all of what happened, but we had a little sit-in with 'em at the school," Big Jim recounted years later.[299]

Rebuffed by the community and local law, the parents took their case to Austin. Their pleas and complaints fell on deaf ears, and one decade gave way to the next before Texas—and La Grange—grudgingly integrated.[300]

If ugly incidents like that proved Big Jim had feet of clay, plenty of others showed his sincere commitment to the community. In June 1954, a frantic father arrived at Fayette County Memorial Hospital with a choking boy who'd gotten an object lodged in his throat. The doctors at the country hospital had no way to remove the obstruction, but Hermann Hospital— one hundred miles away in Houston—did.[301]

Big Jim took the stricken boy and his father in his patrol car and personally rushed them to Houston at speeds topping one hundred miles an hour on the marginal, two-lane state highways that existed before the interstate era. Knowing the challenges of driving the narrow highways, Sheriff Flournoy called ahead and got the Colorado County sheriff out of Columbus to run interference, racing ahead to clear the road of traffic all the way to Houston.[302]

As the years rolled by, the people of Fayette County elevated their sheriff to almost mythical status. The legend grew beyond the man, and while Big Jim normally spoke of himself in modest terms, when he spoke of himself at all, he did little to discourage his celebrity. Over the door of his office in the courthouse he had a trophy case of sorts, displaying myriad guns, knives, clubs and ammunition confiscated from criminals over the years, not unlike a comic book superhero. He loved the attention, true, but worked hard to live up to those high standards.

"He's exactly what he says he is—law and order. I've never doubted that gun on his hip is cocked," said Vera Ellis, a clerk at the La Grange 7-Eleven. "But he's ready with that handshake, too. He's the county itself. He knows us by our names and our modes of thinking. In the respect of the community, he'd almost be a god. I know to an outsider that seems strange, but here, he's number one."[303]

"He's an advisor, counselor, law enforcer, just everything. He knows our problems, knows when a family's in need, knows when a drunk ought to be taken to jail, or home to his family," said Zapalac. "Jim's a big part of what this community is all about, and the motto here is 'Don't upset the apple cart.'"[304]

In short, Big Jim enjoyed all the goodwill in the world from the people of Fayette County, his people. He would need every ounce of that goodwill— and more—in just a few short years when a certain reporter decided spilling that applecart across a national stage would make for gripping television.

Chapter 7

EVERYBODY WHO'S ANYBODY

As the 1950s gave way to the 1960s, the obscure Chicken Farm gradually became the most famous—and widely tolerated—illegal brothel in Texas. As other brothels around the state shuttered for one reason or another, the whitewashed farmhouse with green trim outside La Grange went from being just another commonplace, country whorehouse to an attention-getting rarity, a curious holdover from an earlier era. The Chicken Farm's profile grew through no effort of its own but by virtue of belonging to a vanishing peer group.

During this period, the Chicken Farm nickname fell into disuse, replaced by the more familiar Chicken Ranch. It is unclear how or why this happened. Perhaps the word "ranch" implied more drama and romance than the comparatively pedestrian "farm."

Regardless of the name, the inarguable fact remained that the Chicken Ranch was most definitely *not* the worst-kept secret in Texas. "Worst-kept secret" assumes a secret existed in the first place. Nobody ever tried to keep the Chicken Ranch a secret. The whorehouse operated openly for so long that common knowledge flourished at every level of society. Law enforcement agencies from the FBI and Texas Rangers on down knew of the brothel, politicians joked about it, college students wrote research papers on it and newspapers published articles about it. Yes, the brothel operated illegally, but it conducted its business well within the unspoken parameters society had placed upon it. Because of this, hardly anyone saw any reason to shut it down.

An aerial photo of the Chicken Ranch, circa 1971–72, taken by a surveillance flight crew out of Bergstrom Air Force Base while on a training mission. *Courtesy Edna Milton Chadwell.*

"I've never heard or never was aware of any citizen's movement to close it down," said La Grange school superintendent C.A. Lemons, who formerly served with the FBI. "Maybe some newcomers, but to us old folks, the Chicken Ranch was just a way of life."[305]

Once he became district attorney, it didn't take long for Oliver Kitzman to figure out area lawmen just didn't view whorehouses as a pressing issue. His district included both Fayette and Austin Counties, so in addition to the Chicken Ranch in La Grange, the lesser-known Wagon Wheel outside Sealy, Texas, also fell under his jurisdiction.

"When I was appointed DA in '67, I went about locating people I could depend on to bring me up to date," Kitzman said. "Now, Hollis Sillavan had retired from the Rangers, but he wanted to keep a badge, so he worked for me for fifty dollars a month. Now, him and Jim Ward of the FBI both told me that they regularly used the Chicken Ranch as a source of information."[306]

Shortly thereafter, Kitzman got a stronger signal that the State of Texas—or, at the very least, the Texas Department of Public Safety—had no interest in cracking down on the area brothels.

"When I first became a district attorney, I had two officers from DPS intelligence come to my office in Hempstead. They visited for a while, and one of them asked me what I was going to do about the houses of prostitution in my district," Kitzman recalled. "I just told them, 'As long as I don't have any complaints, I don't plan to do anything about them.'

"And they left," he said. "I think they just wanted to know that they didn't have to worry about me surprising them with some embarrassing thing."[307]

If any doubt persisted that the Chicken Ranch was an established and accepted part of Texas culture, it got erased once and for all during Sheriff "Big Jim" Flournoy's 1956–57 term as president of the Texas Sheriffs Association. La Grange hosted the annual state convention, and many of the lawmen took the opportunity to visit the county's most famous tourist attraction.

"I remember the time sheriffs from all over the state were gathered here," recalled L.A. Giese, a retired La Grange farmer. "It was for a state sheriff's convention. Someone went to the Chicken Ranch and said they never saw so many guns in one place in their whole life."[308]

With the law content to turn a blind eye toward the illicit goings-on, in some ways the Chicken Ranch became the most downright egalitarian business in the state. Rich or poor, young or old, businessman or dirt farmer, the Chicken Ranch welcomed them all with open arms—as long as those potential clients were white. Egalitarianism only went so far in Jim Crow Texas.

"How old do the customers have to be?" an investigative reporter asked Edna Milton in 1971.

"Eighteen, I don't want any children in here," Miss Edna answered. "The parents would chop your head off right down to your rear."

"How old is the oldest customer?"

"Eighty-seven."

"What if a girl doesn't want to have intercourse with a man that old?"

"Then she's not in the right business," she said. "There shouldn't even be any consideration of age. Take restaurants. Do they ask that type of thing—your age—when you order coffee?"[309]

Miss Edna viewed herself first and foremost as a businesswoman, and a successful one at that. Her approach to running her brothel reflected a desire to appeal to as broad a customer base as possible while maintaining a reputation inoffensive to her clientele—generally white, male and conservative.

"What kind of men come here?" the reporter continued.

"All kinds, except the degenerate, sadistic or masochistic," Miss Edna answered. "I want reasonably normal men. If they're not, they need a psychiatrist."

"Can you read men's characters pretty well on first impression?"

"I don't make mistakes. You can tell by the facial expression. Does the smile go to the eyes or stay at the mouth?" she said. "Some of them are pretty good with poker faces. For example, you have had a poker face with me half the time, but that's okay."

"Can blacks come here?" the reporter pressed.

"No, this is not an international house. This is a straight house."

"Mexican-Americans?"

"If they behave themselves."

"Hippies?"

Incredulous, Miss Edna shot back, "Whoever heard of hippies spending money?"[310]

If hippies represented one end of the social spectrum in 1960s Texas, Boy Scouts most certainly represented the other. Miss Edna's age requirements ensured that most lusty, teenage Scouts didn't have a prayer of getting in through the front door of the Chicken Ranch. The same couldn't be said about the Scout masters and fathers accompanying the boys on camping trips to the La Grange area.

"We went on weekend campouts at a ranch owned by our Scout master's father-in-law near Muldoon—about ten miles from La Grange. One Saturday night, the Scout master and a couple of the chaperoning dads discovered the need for some emergency items that we failed to bring and had to go in to town," recalled Robert Anderson, who, as a twelve-year-old Boy Scout in troop 746 from the Sharpstown area of Houston, went on many camping trips to Fayette County during the late 1960s. "One of the older boys told us the dads had gone to the Chicken Ranch, and I remember one Scout questioning innocently, 'But Mr. Loomis doesn't raise chickens here, just cattle. Why would he be going to a chicken ranch?'"[311]

The fact that the troop almost always camped out in Fayette County when there were other options much closer to Houston struck Anderson as curious, as did the fact that inevitably some important supplies were forgotten, prompting all the adults to drive off to town together, leaving the boys alone for several hours at a time. At the very least, they failed spectacularly at living up to the Boy Scout motto of "Be prepared."

"Our troop, we must have camped there six times a year. We never could figure out why we had so many dads that wanted to go on the weekend camping trips in La Grange," Anderson said. "It was always kind of funny. 'Oh, we've got to go into town for something.' We always kind of wondered.

"To me, it was always kind of in the back of my mind, that I would imagine somebody's dad—possibly *my* dad—made a trip [to the Chicken Ranch] because they certainly had plenty of opportunities," he said. "They probably weren't at the Dairy Mart getting shakes!"[312]

DESPITE THE BROTHEL'S WIDESPREAD fame, pockets of people here and there remained in the dark about the Chicken Ranch. Ironically, some of the most unknowing were among Miss Edna's relatives, from whom she kept the exact nature of her business concealed. For much of his life, Robert Kleffman knew Miss Edna only as "Aunt Edna," his mother's older sister. Shortly after he turned thirteen, his mother and a younger brother and sister were killed in a tragic auto wreck. Miss Edna started sending occasional checks to help support the family after that, but Kleffman never met her until a family reunion in Guymon, Oklahoma, around 1967.

"All my life growing up, I had heard about my Aunt Edna. To my knowledge, nobody knew where she lived. She just lived down around Austin, and she had a club," Kleffman said. "But I'd never heard what kind of club or anything about it."[313]

About two weeks after graduating high school, Kleffman lost a hand in a meat grinder accident. He planned to enroll in college but also needed a car. His savings couldn't cover everything, so he decided to ask his aunt for a car loan. She agreed to discuss it with him, and Kleffman flew down to Austin, where his aunt met him at the airport and then drove him to La Grange.

"Before I take you to the club, I want you to get a haircut," Miss Edna said, reaching over to slip some folded bills into his shirt pocket. "Go over there and get you a haircut, and I'll pick you up in a little bit."

"I got some money," Kleffman protested.

"No, here, you just go get your hair cut."

"So, I went in there and doggone—she gave me $200 to get a haircut with!" Kleffman said. "For an eighteen-year-old kid, that was a lot of cash in 1969!"[314]

By then, Miss Edna had already made up her mind to help her nephew buy a car and make tuition, although he didn't know that. She picked him up after his haircut and announced that she was taking him out to "the club."

"We went out there and pulled up to this little white building, and there was this small box trailer backed up to the front door. And there were girls running around *everywhere*," Kleffman said, chuckling at his youthful bewilderment. "They were in their night coats and house coats and underwear and stuff, running in and out of that trailer, back and forth into the house, and I thought to myself, 'Well, this is a modeling agency or these are showgirls or something,' because I still thought it was a club. I thought they were getting costumes to change clothes and stuff. Turns out there was some guy with discount clothing there, and he was selling all the girls clothes.

"I *still* hadn't figured out that this was a brothel, know what I mean? I'm dumber than grass," he said. "We go in there, and my aunt sits down there at the dinner table and she says, 'Y'all have met my nephew. Robert, this is the girls. Girls, this is my nephew Robert.'

"So, we sat back down and I said, 'Hi,' to everybody and all that, and we're sitting at the table eating, and she got this devilish look in her eye, you know? When Edna gets this twinkle in her eye, you know she's up to some mischief," he said. "She took her knife and stood up and tapped on her glass. She said, 'I've got one other comment to make.'

"Now, I don't want to burn your ears, but my Aunt Edna could talk like a sailor. She said, 'This is my nephew, and if he fucks with you, that's his business. If you fuck with him, it's mine,'" Kleffman said. "[That] made me feel about an inch and a half tall. I shrunk down in that chair a way. That's when I figured out there's something more what's going on here—and I *still* hadn't heard the term 'Chicken Ranch.'"[315]

Not until he moved to Austin in the spring of 1973 and got a job at Capitol Chevrolet did he hear references to the Chicken Ranch and put two and two together. Even then, he didn't think it lived up to the hype, as he found it a somewhat dingy, run-of-the-mill farmhouse—albeit a sprawling one with a maze of added-on rooms. Occasionally he'd spend the night there in an empty bedroom if one of the girls happened to be away, and in the morning Miss Edna would roust him for a vitamin B12 shot, just like she administered to all the women staying there.

"It was kinda surreal for a nineteen- or twenty-year-old kid, you know?" he said. "Especially growing up out in West Texas. I never heard no such thing as this. I mean, it was *different*."[316]

Kleffman's blood relation to Miss Edna didn't give him free rein at the Chicken Ranch, though. His aunt ran the place as a business and wasn't keen on offering up free samples, except for one time…

"I got laid *one* time at the Ranch. I guess it was one of the first nights I spent there—there was this girl, I think her real name was Reba, but she went by Joanne. Edna gave me a room, and I went in the room to go to bed," Kleffman said. "They'd shut the place down, and I went in there and crawled in bed, and the next thing I know, here's this girl crawling in bed. And she was *pretty*. She was! And she took care of me!

"The next morning, she was up and she was gone. She'd spent the night, but early in the morning she was up and out," he said. "I'd thought my Aunt Edna had sent her in or something, know what I mean? I thought Edna sent her in.

"Well, twenty years later I'm telling Edna the same story, and she gets so mad she can't speak straight!" he said. "'I didn't send them in there! I told them not to mess with you!' She said, 'If I'd have known this twenty years ago, I'd have fired her ass!' Well, I've been laboring under misconstrusion. I thought I'd gotten a present or something from my Aunt Edna."[317]

Kleffman may have not gotten a Chicken Ranch gift from his aunt, but Red O'Neill clearly remembered the present he got from his uncle on his seventeenth birthday in August 1958. Growing up in Gonzales, Texas, O'Neill had often heard of the Chicken Ranch but hadn't ever made the drive over to La Grange. His uncle thought that a crying shame and opened up his wallet to send his nephew on a road trip of debauchery.

"My cousin took me. He was a year older than I was. We'd heard stories about it, but we never went—we didn't have the money," O'Neill said, laughing. "Well, we started off, we went to the one in Cuero. You know, they had [a brothel] in Cuero.

"It was a long weekend; I don't remember all that. We started off there because Gonzales is about thirty-two miles from Cuero. We went there first, me and my cousin," he said. "My uncle paid for it all. He just gave us the money—he didn't go, he told us where to go. He'd been there. It was all right. [The Cuero brothel] was outside city limits. Then we left there and went out to La Grange to the Chicken Ranch."[318]

The boys cooled themselves in the hot Texas summer night by consuming vast amounts of beer as they covered the seventy miles between Cuero and La Grange. O'Neill's cousin knew the way because he'd gotten the same present from their uncle the year before. When they finally reached the Chicken Ranch, O'Neill didn't find the house itself much different from the farmhouse brothel in Cuero, but it was a lot busier, with more women to choose from. He ended up spending about twenty-five dollars over the course of a couple of hours.

"It was just a house, like you walk into anybody's house. I mean, it wasn't like walking into a bar or a saloon or anything like that. All the people were respectful. There wasn't no cussing going on, no fighting, no arguing, strictly business," O'Neill said. "Other guys were in there too, you know. It was the weekend. How many, I have no recollection. The woman that was the madam of it—I don't know what her name was—she just said what the cost was and introduced the girls, and we picked out the ones we wanted."

Unsurprisingly, the women themselves were what stood out most from the beer-fueled road trip. The country boy from Gonzales soon found himself bewildered by the various delights offered at the Chicken Ranch—a level of sophistication he hadn't contended with in Cuero.

"I can remember the girls working there. They were all pretty. They was all nice-looking. I remember this one, let's see, she said she was going to school in Austin, college. You know that story, 'Working my way through college,'" O'Neill said. "Of course when you get into the room, it was a multiple choice. It was like a menu when you got into the room: 'What do you want to do and how much do you want to spend?' I didn't know what they were talking about! You want an 'around the world' trip or whatever? Well, what's that? I don't know! I came from a ranch, I didn't know that much about it."[319]

BY THE 1950s, THE Chicken Ranch's reputation as a clean, respectable brothel had spread far and wide. In addition to the traditional clientele of college students and farmers, the Chicken Ranch started seeing more high-profile customers who trusted the brothel's discretion. During this period, famed entertainer Bob Hope toured the country regularly, performing live shows in all the major cities. Hope held a special place in his heart for Houston and famously declared that the view from the old Warwick Hotel was the most beautiful city view he'd ever seen.[320]

Early in the decade, following one particularly successful concert in Houston, Hope decided to do something special for his veteran, overwhelmingly male road crew. He loaded the stage hands into the tour bus and took them all to La Grange, where Hope treated the appreciative guys to an evening with the ladies of the Chicken Ranch. If stage hands didn't serenade Hope with "Thanks for the Memory" on the ride back to the hotel, they should have.[321]

In most cases, however, the future movers and shakers were years away from making their mark on the world when they set foot inside the Chicken Ranch. Legendary Texas attorney Dick DeGuerin, while an undergrad at the University of Texas, preferred to spend much of his time drinking beer, reading Shakespeare and visiting the Chicken Ranch rather than attending classes. Future millionaire and Republican gubernatorial candidate Clayton W. Williams Jr. made regular visits to the Chicken Ranch during his years as a student at Texas A&M in the early 1950s.[322]

Probably the two patrons who contributed the most to the Chicken Ranch's eventual national fame were Billy Gibbons and Dusty Hill. The pair, along with drummer Frank Beard, rose to prominence in the 1970s as the Houston-based rock trio ZZ Top. One of their earliest recordings to earn major radio airplay was a growling, blues-heavy rocker simply titled "La Grange."

"It's the endearing anthem to this house of ill repute that was so popular in Texas," said Gibbons.

"Did you ever see the movie *The Best Little Whorehouse in Texas*? That's what it's about," said Hill. "I went there when I was 13. A lot of boys in Texas, when it's time to be a guy, went there and had it done. Fathers took their sons there.

"You couldn't cuss in there. You couldn't drink. It had an air of respectability," he said. "Miss Edna wouldn't stand for no bullshit. That's the woman that ran the place, and you know she didn't look like Dolly Parton, either. I'll tell you, she was a mean-looking woman. But oil field workers and senators would both be there.

"It was a whorehouse, but anything that lasts a hundred years, there's got to be a reason."[323]

Acclaimed Texas journalist and author Gary Cartwright also patronized the Chicken Ranch during his misspent youth. Growing up in Arlington, he'd heard of the Chicken Ranch, but it remained a sort of mythical brothel Promised Land off in the wilds of Central Texas. When he transferred to the University of Texas his sophomore year, however, the Chicken Ranch suddenly became *the* topic of conversation.

"I lived in a boardinghouse with a bunch of horny guys, and *everybody* had been to the Chicken Ranch, or had a story about it, or claimed to have gone," Cartwright recalled. "This guy in my boardinghouse was a Sigma Chi, his last name was Weiser, so he became 'Bud' Weiser. He was pressing me to pledge Sigma Chi, but I *hated* fraternities. I grew up thinking fraternities were a bunch of chickenshit bastards. I didn't want to have anything to do with them. I told that to Bud, and he said, 'You ought to go to pledge week anyway, because the parties are great!'"[324]

Cartwright found it impossible to argue with that logic, so he jumped into pledge week feet-first. The first party he attended didn't stand out as anything special, but the second left a lasting impression.

"A bunch of guys said, 'Let's go to the Chicken Ranch.' I thought, 'Wow! This is getting pretty good!'" he said. "We piled into a couple of cars, probably about ten to twelve guys, and went out to the Chicken Ranch."[325]

After an hour's drive down Highway 71 and turning onto an unpaved backwoods road, Cartwright finally got his first look at the Chicken Ranch. The one-story, whitewashed wooden farmhouse left him unimpressed. They parked alongside a handful of other cars and pickups, and the fraternity pledges piled out.

"We went in, and it was an old, modest farmhouse with a living room or sitting room that'd been enlarged to accommodate the people sitting around," Cartwright said. "A lot of people went out there to sit and visit just for the experience. They wouldn't have sex; they'd just enjoy the company of the girls.

"There weren't many girls, four or five at the most. Everybody just kind of sat around the living room. Sometimes a girl would come over and sit next to you and say, 'Would you like to go to a room?' Sometimes a guy would make a move," he said. "It was very informal, no protocol that I was aware of, you just sort of let it happen."[326]

Growing up between Dallas and Fort Worth, Cartwright was no stranger to brothels. The lower end of Fort Worth had more brothels than anyone could shake a stick at, with a handful of prostitutes working each of the old flophouse hotels that dominated that part of the city. The big thing to do for boys in high school in Arlington was to drive over to Fort Worth and pay the going rate of three dollars to spend a few quick minutes with one of the flophouse whores.

"It seems like nothing now, but at the time three dollars was fairly dear. At La Grange the price was five dollars, and I remember thinking, 'Oh, my God, this must really be a classy joint!'" Cartwright said. "This one girl came over and started talking to me. Her name was Patsy, and she was from Highland Park in Dallas. Highland Park was kind of the ritzy, silk stocking area of Dallas, so I was impressed. Here was this hooker from Highland Park! That added a little cachet to the situation.

"She was skinny, blond, not particularly attractive but not unattractive. The other girls in the room were about the same—no real knockouts but no dogs, either. Eventually, we went to one of the rooms, and the whole thing lasted three minutes, four minutes, then it was over," he said. "I went back and sat in the waiting room. The socializing in the living room section was probably more memorable than the actual sex, which, as I said, lasted almost no time."[327]

On the busiest weekends, students, farmhands and roughnecks had to contend with airmen from Bergstrom Air Force Base outside Austin. Having no shortage of pilots needing to log flight hours, a helicopter ferry system occasionally came into service when the need arose, with up to sixteen airmen delivered or collected each trip.[328]

US Air Force personnel have never been known as quiet, retiring types, so the potential for out-of-control mayhem loomed large. Fortunately, Miss Edna figured out a way to keep them in line far more effectively than calling in the sheriff.

"Somebody told me about…Captain Lucas out there at Bergstrom. I don't think he was the base commander, but he had some authority there. If some of the boys from that base show their ass, I threaten them with Captain Lucas," Miss Edna explained. "I told them, 'Have you heard of Captain Lucas? You'd better behave yourself or I'll tell him to take you out behind the barracks if you don't behave yourself.'

"I didn't have to say too much. I didn't want to overstep my ass, either. Hell, suppose I'd been talking to someone and they'd be Captain Lucas' son or something? Ah, that'd been nice, wouldn't it?" she said. "So, I had to be kinda careful what I said and how I said it, because you never really know who you're talking to."[329]

Miss Edna perhaps downplayed her working relationship with Bergstrom just a bit. Even decades later, she still exercised restraint and discretion to protect those she worked with, but behind the scenes, she expressed great pride in the friendly ties that existed between the Chicken Ranch and the base.

"Airmen would show up and knock on the door and give her a tube of papers. She'd take them and spread them out, and it was aerial photographs of her place," Kleffman said. "She knew the commander at Bergstrom Air Force Base, and she'd want information, so the guys doing their routines and practice flights—they had to take pictures anyway—so they did flyovers of the Ranch and they'd take photographic pictures and bring them to her.

"She had the military doing surveillance on her place for her!" he said. "I mean, she had that state wired down."[330]

Folks stationed at Bergstrom weren't the only people arriving at the Chicken Ranch via helicopter. In at least one instance, La Grange was a detour on

Right: William "Bill" Anders served as lunar module pilot on the historic Apollo 8 mission to orbit the moon. He attended La Grange High School as a freshman. Years later, as an astronaut, he piloted a helicopter over the Chicken Ranch. *Courtesy National Aeronautics and Space Administration.*

Below: Calbraith Rodgers climbs out of his airplane, *Vin Fiz*, at the finish of his epochal transcontinental flight in 1911. His flight allegedly included a close encounter with the Chicken Ranch. *Courtesy George Grantham Bain Collection, Library of Congress.*

the way to the moon. Bill Anders, who served as the lunar module pilot during the Apollo 8 mission in 1968, had attended La Grange High School as a freshman years before. In 1965 or '66, the school invited Anders—now a member of NASA's famed astronaut corps—back to campus.

"I was on my way to speak at a commencement, and I always wondered what the Chicken Ranch looked like," Anders said. "So I flew the helicopter over it to take a look. As I was hovering there, a woman came out and started gesturing for me to land.

"I got to thinking, you know, this would *not* be a good place for me to crash, because I wanted to go to the moon!" he said, laughing. "So I went on to La Grange High School, where I gave the commencement address at graduation.

"I saw it, but I never went in there," Anders said. "That's my story, and I'm sticking to it!"[331]

Stories of pilots and aircrews visiting the Chicken Ranch dated back to the earliest days of aviation—although most are almost certainly apocryphal. For example, during the historic 1911 transcontinental flight of the *Vin Fiz*, a modified Wright Brothers biplane piloted by Calbraith Rodgers, engine trouble forced an emergency landing near Kyle, Texas, on October 20. Rodgers holed up in a passenger car of the train carrying the support crew

Vin Fiz takes off from Sheepshead Bay, New York, on September 17, 1911. *Vin Fiz* attracted large crowds at every stop along its transcontinental flight. An emergency landing in Kyle, Texas, due to engine trouble, proved no different. *Courtesy George Grantham Bain Collection, Library of Congress.*

for his expedition, first waiting for installation of the *Vin Fiz*'s spare engine and then for the weather to clear after a blue norther roared into Texas, bringing with it frigid wind and torrential rains. The following day, a group of local young men, hoping to raise Rodgers' flagging spirits, offered to take him to the Chicken Ranch in La Grange.[332]

Rodgers declined, but for three members of his ground crew, the temptation proved too strong to resist. They snuck out at 9:30 p.m. and "borrowed" the expedition's car to drive the sixty miles to La Grange. They returned seven hours later, profoundly drunk, with two prostitutes in tow. After wrecking the car, one of the trio, obviously feeling quite generous, rousted Rodgers at five o'clock in the morning to proudly present him the women for his personal entertainment. Rodgers—sharing a stateroom with his wife, Mabel, and exhausted from his grueling flight schedule—was less than amused.

"Get those two chippies out of here!" Rodgers snapped at his drunken ground crew. "What would mother think—or Mabel?…Now, I want everybody—and I mean everybody!—to cease this tomfoolery."[333]

Any and all tomfoolery came to a screeching halt whenever customers of substance visited the brothel. And at the Chicken Ranch, that meant one thing and one thing only: politicos. Whenever the students, roughnecks, farmers and truckers experienced a sudden corralling that kept them quiet and bottled up, they knew a police raid wasn't in the offing, but rather, some powerful mover-and-shaker had arrived to demand the brothel's undivided attention.

"Old John Connally, he used to be one to drive through there, too," said Willie Pankoniem. "The thing is, they would always come up in the limos, and, seemed like to us peons, they tried to keep the young kids away from the older establishment. But you just heard that's who was there. As to personally seeing them? I couldn't verify it.

"When you had nothing but limos lined up from one end to the other, well…when people came in, heads of state and everything else that came to Texas, that was a part of seeing Texas. They'd bring them right out from the capitol, and the chauffeurs were sitting out there and there was no telling who would be in them," he said. "It was funny how it was respectful. Usually they were kind of reserved. It was very seldom that you'd have a mixture of us young guys and everything else. They'd kind of pre-plan their get-togethers, but there would be some times that you might just have one pull up. No telling who got out.

"That's why I say the little black book of the names, that would be a treat to have," he said. "I'm sure it's probably not around anymore. She wasn't that kind of lady."[334]

Miss Edna considered herself a businesswoman, but she was a born politician, cultivating and working her political allies as effectively as any party whip. Colonel Wilson "Pat" Speir, the head of the Texas Department of Public Safety as well as the famed Texas Rangers, received a brand-new silver-belly Stetson hat from Miss Edna every Christmas. W.T. "Bill" Moore, the long-serving state senator from Bryan, Texas, worked as a tireless advocate for Texas A&M during legislative sessions. His forceful legislative style earned him the nickname the "Bull of the Brazos," and with so many Aggies making regular pilgrimages to the Chicken Ranch, he considered it part of his job description to keep the brothel free of legislative interference. US representative Charles Wilson, widely known as "Good Time Charlie" for his relentless partying and womanizing, denied ever visiting the Chicken Ranch, although he allowed that he may have "driven past it a time or two."[335]

The parade of state lawmakers passing through the doors of the Chicken Ranch grew so numerous that a Dallas-area representative who served in the legislature during the 1950s felt compelled to immortalize the phenomenon in poetry:

"Nostalgia"
Twenty years have come and gone
Yet I remember still
A fateful night in the Granite House
That stands on Capitol Hill.
Important business had come up,
Where could the members be?
A hundred votes were required
Instead of eighty-three.
One solon held the microphone,
His countenance all red,
(It was indeed a crucial vote),
And this is what he said:
"Mr. Speaker, drastic is the action here
For us to have decorum,
If you'll kindly poll the Chicken Farm
I think we'll have a quorum."[336]

Never one to let an opportunity pass, Miss Edna worked to cultivate friendly relations with all the high-powered political figures who frequented the Chicken Ranch. Even before she'd bought the place, back when she worked the floor as just another whore, she'd met future Texas governor John Connally and his brother Wayne, a future state senator, and struck up a cordial relationship with the pair.

"They were nice people, and they treated me nice," Miss Edna said. "If I asked something of them that wasn't unreal or wasn't unreasonable, maybe they'd consider. I don't know. They did what they damn pleased. If they wanted to help you, they would; if they didn't, they wouldn't."[337]

Miss Edna never claimed friendship with the Connallys, instead describing them as nice acquaintances. In any event, those connections came in very handy a few years later once she'd bought the Chicken Ranch from Aunt Jessie. A small-time racetrack

John Connally, governor of Texas from 1963 to 1969, was one of the many powerful political figures in the state who patronized the Chicken Ranch. *Courtesy of Texas State Library and Archives Commission.*

opened up outside La Grange, not too far from the brothel. That in and of itself wasn't a problem, but the manager quickly made one of himself.

"The son of a bitch that was running it—I don't know what part he owned in it, but he'd been running it—he kept telling people, 'Come out to the Chicken Ranch, do this, do that,' as if he owned the damn place," Miss Edna said, fuming at the memory of people arriving expecting free sex. "I said, 'Who in the hell are you talking to? I don't know him. How in the hell can he tell you anything about this place?'

"Well, anyway, I got tired of that shit. I'll never know to this day which one it was. The Connallys—I'm not sure which, they looked so much alike, I couldn't tell them apart," she said, her voice dropping low in an embarrassed whisper. "He kinda liked me, and I was telling him about that shit, about this racetrack. I was telling him every damn thing I heard about that place, you know, and how his track was too short for the horses and this, that and the other, but I said, 'They need to get off my ass, first thing.'

"Well, do you know what? I don't know, but that racetrack wasn't there. A couple weeks later it was closed," she said. "I always kind of suspect one of the Connallys did something. But I'll never know which one it was."[338]

Occasionally, the mutually beneficial relationship between the Connallys and Miss Edna played out in odd ways. Normally, the Chicken Ranch was strictly a cash-only operation. Miss Edna didn't accept credit cards, and the risk of getting burned with a hot check was too great. She did make at least one exception, however. State Senator Wayne Connally brought in a party of bigwigs to entertain one evening but did not have enough cash to cover the bill. He asked Miss Edna if she would take a check.

"That was one of the few checks she'd ever taken at the Ranch. She said because of the signature, she just pulled the money out and paid the girls herself," Kleffman said. "She said, 'I could swallow that little bit of loss just to have that souvenir here.'

"She had that check signed by them that she hung over her desk at the Ranch for a long, long time."[339]

The Connally brothers were regular patrons of the Chicken Ranch, at least as much as any other Texas politicos. But the politically powerful brothers certainly received deferential treatment and made an impression on the prostitutes with their hard-partying ways.

"Ah, yes. The Connallys were something else," said Penny, who worked at the Chicken Ranch from 1966 to 1969. "They were real loud and boisterous, they liked to have a good time. They had special girls they saw all the time that Edna would make allowances for, time-wise, when the boys came out. We were told ahead of time if any bigwigs were coming to the house.

"She would even let me go out with some of them and stay out all night and come back the next day. She knew she wouldn't have any trouble with me doing that. In fact, one of the local politicians' son used to come pick me up and we'd go dancing at the Broken Spoke [in Austin].

"He was in college, and I looked a lot younger than I was. I put on my boots and jeans, and we'd just go dancing," Penny said. "So, one time some of his buddies had dates, and afterward we got something to eat. The girls they were saying, 'What college do you go to?' This guy cracked up and said, 'The college of hard knocks!'"[340]

State Senator Wayne Connally, brother of Governor John Connally, was one of a select few customers the Chicken Ranch allowed to pay by check. *Photo by Bill Malone. Courtesy of Texas State Library and Archives Commission.*

The Chicken Ranch also had a very real and lasting impact on Texas politics—eighteen years to be precise. William P. "Bill" Hobby Jr. won election as Texas lieutenant governor in 1972 and went on to serve for a record five terms, unmatched in state history. Nobody realized at the time, however, that a certain brothel directly helped put him in office.

"When I started running for office in 1971, there were maybe a dozen counties in Texas that were one-stop shopping," Hobby explained. "If *The Man* was for you, you got 70 percent of the vote. If *The Man* was against you, you got 30 percent. Either way, your business in that county was done. *The Man* might by a mayor (Pepe Martin, Laredo), a judge or a sheriff (Jim Flournoy in Fayette County).

"My Fayette County campaign manager was Clyde Luck of West Point [Texas]. She introduced me to Jim," he said. "Jim and I got along fine, and he supported me. Jim publicly anointed his candidates by having them join him in his convertible in the July Fourth parade. I rode with Jim for several years."[341]

Texas Lieutenant Governor William P. "Bill" Hobby Jr., who held that office for an unprecedented five terms, is possibly the only politician in history to have won election with the Chicken Ranch actively campaigning in his favor. *Photo by Bill Malone. Courtesy of Texas State Library and Archives Commission.*

Afterward, Big Jim asked Hobby if there was anything else he could do to assist the campaign. Hobby replied that he had campaign literature—postcards and the like—he needed mailed out to all Fayette County voters. Big Jim immediately volunteered to take care of the mailings himself, so shortly thereafter, Luck delivered the campaign literature to the sheriff. The mailings went out as promised, and Hobby went on to win the Democratic primary and subsequent general election.[342]

"After the campaign, my wife, Diane, was in charge of sending thank-you notes to all who helped us. She telephoned the sheriff to ask who addressed my campaign literature," Hobby said. "He stuttered and stalled and wouldn't say. Diane persisted. Finally she told me of the situation, and I called Sheriff Flournoy.

"'Well, Governor, I tell you,' the sheriff said. 'I give them pamphlets to Miss Edna. Her and her girls addressed 'em for you. But I think we ought to keep that between ourselves.' I agreed with him."[343]

The Hobby campaign achieved an astounding 100 percent coverage rate in Fayette County, and the longtime lieutenant governor had no hesitation in expressing his gratitude to the prostitutes who spent slow afternoons at the brothel hand-addressing his campaign postcards.

"I was glad for whatever help I could get!" Hobby said. He added—with a deep belly laugh—that although he never knew for certain if any of the women of the Chicken Ranch voted for him, "I certainly hope so!"[344]

Governors, state senators and congressmen were small potatoes, though, in comparison to the president of the United States. Lyndon Baines Johnson, a lifelong Texan and alumni of Southwest Texas State Teacher's College (now known as Texas State University), returned to his home state often during his presidency and consequently spent much time in Austin. L.B.J. certainly wasn't the first president to engage in extramarital affairs while in the White House, but L.B.J., being an over-the-top Texan, lived up to his over-the-top reputation. As early as his college days, he proudly nicknamed his penis "Jumbo" and would brag to his roommates that "Jumbo had a real workout tonight!" following dates. He'd then recount said date in graphic detail, devoting particular attention to describing his date sans clothing.[345]

Other young men leave such sexual braggadocio behind when they leave college and gain maturity. L.B.J. was not other young men. If anything, pride in his sexual prowess increased as he gained more political influence. He took to showing off his penis at every opportunity. After urinating, he'd turn to a companion with it still in his hand and proudly ask, "Have you ever seen anything as big as this?" His secretarial pool consisted exclusively of young, attractive women, which Secret Service agents referred to as his "harem." Intensely jealous of President John F. Kennedy's "ladies' man" reputation, L.B.J. would bluster, "I had more women by accident than Kennedy had on purpose." Once, after his wife, Lady Bird, caught him *in flagrante delicto* in the Oval Office with a secretary, L.B.J. had an alarm buzzer installed so the Secret Service agents could warn him in the future. Under those circumstances, it's hard to believe L.B.J. wouldn't visit the Chicken Ranch, given the opportunity.[346]

One of the managers at KTBC channel 7, an Austin television station owned by Lady Bird, regularly visited the Chicken Ranch in the early '60s. When L.B.J. assumed the presidency following the assassination of John Kennedy, the station manager moved to Washington, D.C., to work as a presidential aid.[347]

"I can't think of his name. It doesn't matter," Miss Edna said. "He was down one night, and he called me.

"Edna, have you got any enclosed cars out there? Good, enclosed cars?" he asked.

Lyndon Baines Johnson, thirty-sixth president of the United States. *Photo by Arnold Newman. Courtesy L.B.J. Library and Museum.*

"I said, 'Mine's not here. One of the girls has a convertible.'"

"No, it has to be a closed car."

"Why?" Miss Edna asked, her curiosity piqued.

"Well, someone's wanting to come out there, but they don't want to go in their car," he said. "They want to go in a closed-in car, but a safe one."

"I said, nope, not at this time. In a day or two my car will be back," said Miss Edna, who expected the repair shop to complete its work soon. Used to the discreet ways of politicians, her suspicions grew as the cryptic conversation continued.

"I got the opinion, the conversation went in such a way, I feel like it was Johnson who was there and wanted to come out," Miss Edna said. "But he wanted to come out there in a safe way. There were security people knowing everything, too. They'd have still had to known it if he came. They'd have followed him even if they didn't come in the same car, you know.

President Johnson cultivated a reputation of sexual prowess for himself, going so far as to nickname his penis "Jumbo." *Photo by Yoichi Okamoto. Courtesy L.B.J. Library and Museum.*

"I always kind of felt like [it was L.B.J.], but there was a lot of 'em. Just state senators and state legislators, that kind of shit," she said. "Diplomats, a lot of them came out. Different counties, different towns, makes no difference."[348]

The upshot to the failed automotive shell game was that the president didn't actually make it to the brothel. But if L.B.J. would not come to the Chicken Ranch, then the Chicken Ranch would come to L.B.J.

Penny remembered that fateful day when Big Jim dropped by the brothel with the news that President Johnson was visiting a ranch nearby.

"Would you like to meet him?" the sheriff asked her. "He likes brunettes."

"He sent a car for me. I went out the back door and got in a car, and the car took me to wherever he was," Penny explained. "And that was just the first of many times I did meet up with him."[349]

Turns out, L.B.J. really *did* like brunettes.

Penny never heard if any of the other women at the Chicken Ranch ever spent time with the president, but if they had, it's doubtful they were as well prepared as she was. The previous year, Penny had dated a wealthy, prominent professor from the University of Texas, and because of his research contracts with the federal government, he warned her that the FBI would conduct a background check on her.

When Big Jim broached the same subject, Penny couldn't help but laugh.

"I said, 'Well, I've already got a FBI file, so they won't have far to check!'" she said, leaving the sheriff dumbfounded. "When they wanted to check me out to go see L.B.J., they didn't have a problem because they already had a file set up. They [already] knew I was a mother with kids and a big family who just happened to have an unusual job."[350]

Over the next couple of years, Penny met with L.B.J. as many as eight times, always on private ranches between Austin and La Grange. Because she had a clean-cut, girl-next-door look about her, Penny was always introduced as a "friend of the family" before the president would slip away with her to the privacy of a guest room in a convenient ranch house.

"I remember being surprised at how lanky Johnson was," Penny recalled. "Oh, he was huge, and I wasn't even five-two. When he had his hat and boots on, he was very impressive. *Very* impressive, that's for sure. I'd always seen him on TV, but when he stood up next to me, I just didn't realize how big he was. But he was a gentleman. He had manners like a southern gentleman.

"[It was] an extremely stressful time [for his presidency]. He was more anxious than I'd thought he'd be. Of course, I know the guy had so much on his mind and on his plate," she said. "He just needed to break away from everything and everybody that he had to see all the time, you know what I'm saying? He just needed a clean break to where he didn't even have to think about anything like that or discuss it or anything like that at all.

"We talked about ranching and a lot of stuff to do about Texas. He liked Texas history—that was one of his things. He told me about his life, how he'd worked in a service station. You know, little background stuff," she said. "He was a little rough around the edges, but he had a sharp wit—a very sharp wit."[351]

While Penny always met L.B.J. off premises, and Miss Edna insisted the president never actually visited the brothel, that's not exactly the last word on the matter. Miss Edna had one more story she occasionally shared to impress a very select audience.

President Johnson met with Penny, a prostitute from the Chicken Ranch, as many as eight times during the closing years of his presidency. *Photo by Frank Wolfe. Courtesy L.B.J. Library and Museum.*

"I just remember the picture. She showed me a picture one time," said Kleffman. "There were no cars there. There was her brown Lincoln and the presidential limousine parked in front of the Chicken Ranch.

"What she told me at the time, as I remember it, she got a phone call and was asked how many cars, how many people was there, and she told them," he said. "They said, 'Get rid of all of them but yours.' So she went and told the girls, 'Everybody out. Get rid of the customers, all the customers go home, get away, get gone, and everybody move your car to the back.'

"The next thing you know, here comes the president," he said. "I don't know if he was a customer or if he wanted to visit and talk politics. I don't know what happened there. That's the end of the story, and that's all I know."[352]

Even forty years after L.B.J.'s death, Miss Edna, ever the businesswoman, remained judicious and discreet with her words, taking the thirty-sixth president's secrets with her to the grave.

Chapter 8

WHAT DOESN'T KILL ME...

Not too long after Edna Milton bought the Chicken Ranch and reopened for business, a group of La Grange ministers gathered together to voice their ire. Sheriff "Big Jim" Flournoy's closure of the brothel when Jessie Williams grew too old and infirm to manage it properly had heartened them. That moral victory proved short-lived, though. Miss Edna began peddling lust again before any of the old customers even had a chance to forget the way to the Chicken Ranch. It didn't matter that the sheriff hadn't given the brothel permission to resume business—the fact that he didn't just toss Miss Edna in jail provided evidence enough of his tacit approval.

So the ministers did what ministers do, confronting the sheriff en masse to demand he take action.

The Chicken Ranch, they argued, had made La Grange a laughingstock. The statewide notoriety of the brothel brought shame on the townsfolk. It corrupted every person in Fayette County, and the children—there was simply no telling how badly it warped their sense of decency, what with such perversions going on right outside town. The brothel, a moral cancer in the community, simply had to go.

Big Jim patiently listened to their arguments and then, much to the ministers' delight, announced that he agreed with them. In fact, the sheriff proposed a new anti-vice campaign on the spot. Not only would he run off the prostitutes, but he also planned a major crackdown on illegal gambling, including every single bingo game and raffle in the county.

The ministers, suddenly in a forgiving mood, asked that Big Jim show a little sympathy toward the ladies out at the Chicken Ranch. After all, La Grange boasted a long history of tolerance, not to mention the fact that the Chicken Ranch's history stretched back a hundred years and never caused any real trouble…[353]

In 1966, Ben Gill was hired as pastor of the First Baptist Church in La Grange. Fresh out of seminary, the Baylor graduate was cautioned by the search committee that preaching against the Chicken Ranch would only lead to regret. Gill initially turned a blind eye to the brothel, but by September 1968, he couldn't stomach it anymore. He first spoke against it during a Rotary Club meeting and then, the following Sunday, from the pulpit. Both times, he was met with stony silence.

Shortly thereafter, Big Jim—a personal friend and silent member of the congregation—paid Gill a visit.

"Preacher, I can't protect you if you say anything else," Big Jim warned. "I can't. They'll get ya before the week's out if you keep talkin'. Hell, I may have to kill you myself. Please, I beg of ya, don't do this."

By the fall of 1969, Gill had accepted a job with the Southern Baptist Convention and departed La Grange for good.[354]

The Chicken Ranch survived those abbreviated campaigns to shut it down, but plenty more threats to the brothel waited in the wings. Despite the Chicken Ranch's tolerated status and, to some extent, open support from the community, the fact that it operated illegally left it vulnerable to attacks from reformers and criminals alike. During the latter years of Miss Jessie's rule, when arthritis and the loss of a leg to diabetes confined the old madam to a wheelchair, the brothel became an especially tempting target for robbers.

In January 1958, two habitual criminals from Houston saw it as easy pickings and staged a late-night holdup near the end of working hours, ensuring full coffers and few witnesses. After emptying the till and stripping the boarders and a few straggling customers of valuables, the robbers demanded to know where Aunt Jessie kept the rest of her money. She directed them to her cluttered closet, where she'd squirreled away stashes of cash over the years. The robbers promptly forgot about the invalid madam, judging her no threat. As the thieves rummaged through her things, Miss Jessie quietly phoned the sheriff to report a robbery in progress. Big Jim and Deputy Charlie Prilop arrived a few minutes later to find one robber holding the women at gunpoint as the other stuffed the money from the closet into a pillowcase. The lawmen arrested the surprised robbers without a fight.[355]

Colonel Homer Garrison Jr., director of the Texas Department of Public Safety (right), pins the distinctive Cinco Peso on new Texas Ranger Hollis M. Sillavan, former chief deputy in Washington County, on April 4, 1956. *R-430, Texas Department of Public Safety photographs, 1937–1965, undated. Archives and Information Services Division, Texas State Library and Archives Commission.*

Most robberies didn't even make it that far. In the early 1960s, Randy Sillavan, a young officer with the Houston Police Department, got an odd request: a newly jailed prisoner was asking to see him. When Sillavan approached, the forty-something inmate began to laugh.

"I believe that one of your relatives come pretty close to killing me a few nights ago," the inmate said. "I don't believe I have been any closer to death."[356]

That relative turned out to be Sillavan's father, Texas Ranger Hollis Sillavan. The prisoner explained he and a buddy had made a lucrative trade in knocking over Houston-area whorehouses the past few months. Their success attracted the attention of Houston-area law, however. To avoid the heat, they decided to redirect their criminal enterprise to rural areas outside Houston. Right before Christmas, they hit the Rice Street brothel in Sealy, Texas, right off US Highway 90. That robbery went off without a hitch, so they decided to knock over the Chicken Ranch a few days later.

Shortly after driving through Columbus, the duo passed a car parked alongside Highway 71. The car pulled onto the highway, paced them a bit and then suddenly flashed police lights, pulling them over. The criminals pulled their pistols, ready to shoot it out. Then one recognized the approaching officer as Hollis Sillavan. He'd first run into Hollis, a no-nonsense, tough-as-nails cop, during an encounter in Houston years before. He immediately threw his gun on the floorboard and his hands out the window, surrendering.

After Hollis got the two cuffed, the crook managed to get a closer look at the *Cinco Peso* badge on the lawman's chest. Realizing that Officer Hollis

Sillavan had graduated to the famed Texas Rangers, the crook promptly peed his pants.[357]

"I later talked to my dad about the encounter, and he kind of laughed," Sillavan said. "Dad said he had worked on the Sealy hijacking and had been in touch with the Brenham Police Department and Harris County officers. They had believed these two guys were hitting a bunch of places. He had gotten a call at home from one of the Houston officers, who had told him they had information that the La Grange whorehouse was going to be hit.

"Dad said he had driven out on Highway 71 and pulled off to check out the traffic for a while," he said. "He had been sitting there for only a short time when a car passed, fitting the description of the car he had been given. The same prisoner I had talked to had said, 'Mr. Sillavan, don't shoot me!' and dropped to the ground."[358]

Neither the Texas Rangers nor the Fayette County sheriff could be counted on to defend the Chicken Ranch all the time, though. The isolated country whorehouse, first under Aunt Jessie and then under Miss Edna, had to take care of itself in most situations. Anyone setting foot in the Chicken Ranch looking to start trouble quickly found more than he bargained for.

Based out of Columbus, Texas Ranger Hollis Sillavan used the Chicken Ranch as a source of intelligence. He was also involved in breaking up illegal casinos in Galveston and Sealy early in his career as a Ranger. *R-432, Texas Department of Public Safety photographs, 1937–1965, undated. Archives and Information Services Division, Texas State Library and Archives Commission.*

"I was in the dining room, and I heard gunfire. I went out to the parking lot," Robert Kleffman said, recalling one particular event from early 1972. "Edna was standing out there, and there was a car *fishtailing*, I mean getting *out* of the driveway.

"A couple old boys had come in there and told Edna that they was going to take over, that they was going to run her ranch," he said.

"No, you're *not* going to run my place," Miss Edna roared at them. "If you want to run a place, get you a bucket of grease and bend over, because you ain't running mine!"

"She pulled a .38 out of her handbag, out of her purse! She fired at that car a couple of rounds," Kleffman said. "Yeah, my Aunt Edna was very direct and to the point."[359]

Most threats to the brothel weren't so dramatic or quite so life-threatening. Big Jim's reputation as a hard-nosed sheriff kept most of the riffraff away from Fayette County, and the high-profile nature of the Chicken Ranch—not to mention stories of failed robbery attempts—acted as a deterrent in its own right. The only real, persistent challenges facing the brothel came from moral crusaders. These seldom lasted long or gained much traction, but there never seemed to be a lack of some new face willing to pick up a lance and tilt at La Grange's biggest windmill.

D.C. Wiley, a devout Baptist who made no secret of his disdain for the Chicken Ranch, opened a Montgomery Ward catalog store on the downtown square in La Grange in 1968. Within six months, the Chicken Ranch had a $10,000 line of credit. Wiley quit the business the following year.

"I have become as dependent as everyone else in town," Wiley said. "I don't want to raise my boys with whorehouse money."[360]

An oft-repeated story tells of a new merchant setting up shop in town, whose wife sported a particularly puritanical outlook. The wife, upon learning of the Chicken Ranch's presence, very nearly boiled over with offense and outrage. When Sheriff Flournoy declined to act on her many vocal complaints against the brothel, she took it upon herself to organize the decent folk of the town to action against the place.

The next morning, she and her husband awoke to find their lawn heaped high with all his wares returned from his various accounts in town. The message came through loud and clear: if you insist on stirring up trouble, your business is no longer welcome.[361]

Over the years, the story has evolved like a game of telephone. In some versions, the husband is a vendor of Tom's Snacks or Frito-Lay, with other tales holding that he took over as editor of a local newspaper, with all the week's editions piled up on their lawn. Still another take casts the husband as the new Baptist minister in town, with garbage fouling the lawn. In each of the versions, the gist of the story echoed a common theme in La Grange: outsiders weren't welcome to decide what was best for locals. Locals were fully capable of taking care of themselves.

"That's oral history for you. It totally varies by who's telling it," said Robbie Davis-Floyd, PhD, a senior research fellow in the Department of Anthropology at the University of Texas. "It's interesting how the townspeople allowed it to exist. The townspeople were split between the newcomers and the old-timey, European-oriented people, like the Czechs and Poles. They were used to institutionalized prostitution from Europe, so they had no problem with it. They were glad their sons could go there instead of getting some girl pregnant. Their daughters didn't have to have sex with the guys because the guys could go to the Chicken Ranch.

"It was the newcomers—that meant anybody who'd been there less than ten years—that hated the place and thought it was a disgrace and a scandal and wanted to get rid of it," she said.[362]

Once, a newly elected district attorney who'd spent many a night indulging in the Chicken Ranch's various entertainments found himself pressured by local church women to close down the brothel. He knocked reluctantly on the front door, prodded on by the mob of righteous women at his back. The madam shattered his wavering resolve by shouting from inside, "Not now, George! The law has got me surrounded."[363]

Those events were true and accurate enough—had the Chicken Ranch actually resided in the Central Texas town of Belton, one hundred miles to the northwest. The Chicken Ranch legend had grown to the point where it began absorbing the stories of other, lesser-known brothels. Again, oral history at work.[364]

ON OCCASION, HOSTILITY TOWARD the Chicken Ranch stemmed not from moral or legal arguments but more personal reasons. When relationships developed problems, sometimes blaming a scapegoat was too tempting to pass up. Miss Edna recalled one woman in La Grange who worked at a local clothing store. The wife of a highway patrolman, she grew increasingly suspicious of his long hours away from home and believed he spent much of that time at the Chicken Ranch. Finally, she confronted Miss Edna outright.

"She was upset. I knew as soon as she started opening her mouth, she was trying to quiz me. She was wanting information," Miss Edna said. "I knew what she was trying to find out. She suspected her husband of going out there.

"Her husband worked highway patrol. She was always calling to find out where he was, this and that. I said, 'I don't know, I only met the man once in my life, and that was when he first came to La Grange. Everyone was showing him around different places. They brought him [to show him the Chicken Ranch]. I only saw him once, so I wouldn't know him,'" she said. "I said, 'I don't know where he is. I have no idea.' Because she was saying he was out there.

"He was on call over in Schulenburg. He'd been called out to a big wreck over there," Miss Edna said. "She found that out, and of course that made her feel like a chickenshit."[365]

Following that incident, the woman grew friendlier toward Miss Edna, as if to make up for her earlier accusations. Before long, she'd started inviting

Miss Edna to dinner, which made the cynical madam roll her eyes. The brothel maintained its acceptance in La Grange by adhering to unspoken social rules, and the highway patrolman's wife—surprisingly naïve despite her earlier suspicion—wanted to blunder through several of them by publicly socializing with the madam.

"I said, 'I'll tell you what: not here. The work your husband does, you have children…no. If you're going to be out of town, and I'm going to be out of town, like Austin or Houston or somewhere, we might have dinner together. But not in La Grange,'" Miss Edna recalled. "I said, 'The closest we'll ever have dinner together is Austin or Houston, because you have a family and he has a political position, he's highway patrol.'

With ambitions for higher office, Texas Attorney General Will Reid Wilson launched a major anti-vice campaign in 1957 that closed most of the state's illegal casinos and brothels. *Courtesy of the Tarlton Law Library, Jamail Center for Legal Research, University of Texas School of Law.*

"I said, 'No. I will not embarrass you, or him, or those children,'" she said. "I won't ever embarrass a child."[366]

Politicians presented their own set of distinctive problems. Most who patronized the Chicken Ranch conducted themselves in a cordial manner, but occasionally one got the notion that either the brothel's illegal status, his political power or a combination of both entitled him to behave in crass and boorish—or even violent—ways. Miss Edna termed this "showing their ass" and held it in contempt. One particular state senator from Houston who served in the early '60s stood out for his unpleasant reaction when Miss Edna called him on his bad behavior.

"He'd been up here some time or another and shown his ass. And nobody put up with it, and [we] run him off. He threatened 'I'll get even with you!'" Miss Edna said. "Okay, get even. Do your best. I'll tell them that in a minute.

"If that's what they think they're going to do to me…I'm *not* going to let any of them blackmail me into letting them mistreat those girls," she said. "I'm not going to be mistreated by anybody, and I'm not going to let them mistreat one of the girls, either."[367]

In the end, Miss Edna banned the state senator from the Chicken Ranch—as dire a fate anyone could face, in some opinions. Instead of expressing remorse for his abusive ways and apologizing or trying to make amends, he started badmouthing Miss Edna in the capitol, trying to enlist other state senators and representatives in an effort to shut her down. He found few supporters for his political temper tantrum.

"He was the real son of a bitch behind it all. I said, 'What the hell'd [the Chicken Ranch prostitutes] do? Did he come out to the whorehouse and they throwed his ass out because they wouldn't let 'em abuse them?'" Miss Edna said. "That was the only one I ever saw got so cutesy about that whorehouse. If he couldn't come out and mistreat somebody, and get away with it, well, then he wanted to try and close it up, huh?"[368]

When it came to enforcing standards of behavior, Miss Edna didn't cut anyone any slack. If someone didn't behave himself and treat the women right, she'd ban him fast and hard regardless of threats of reprisals. Not even people with power to arrest her and her women were immune from Miss Edna's wrath.

"One Texas Ranger showed his ass. He was off work, he was from over there in Columbus," she said. "He came over, drunk, raising static about different things. He went even down to the nigger joint—the beer joint, you know—giving them a bunch of shit and everything.

"Anyway, he was showing up, saying this and saying that, a bunch of crap. The whole thing in a nutshell was the sheriff had to get on him about some things," Miss Edna said. After that, the Ranger offered a heartfelt apology for his behavior, and everyone mended fences. "They didn't tell me every little detail that went on, but they told me enough to where you'd have to be an idiot not to know what was going on."[369]

In most instances, the threat of a ban got offenders to straighten up. If not, then the stigma of an outright ban worked wonders. Nobody wanted to get on Miss Edna's shit list.

"You banned them for a little while, then they came back acting nice. I'm not going to put up with it," Miss Edna said. "A young boy from over at Brenham came in showing his ass. I told him, 'You'd better behave or get your ass out of here. If you don't, I'm liable to kill you.'

"You know, he showed his ass to [a prostitute]. I finally got him out of there," she said. "A couple days later, here he comes. To this day, he's sober. Cool. Gave me an apology and everything. I told him he came as close to dying as he ever will in his life. I said, 'You've gone too far.'

"I wouldn't take it. Not going to take it. He apologized, and we accepted it. This time he's sober," she said. "I kinda felt like he was pilled up, to be honest about it. But I didn't know it, so I just called it drunk. I think he'd had a few drinks, it's true, but he acted more like a damn pill-head than he was drunk."[370]

It is easy to overlook the fact that the Chicken Ranch did not exist in a vacuum. Even though the officially sanctioned vice districts in various Texas cities disbanded prior to World War I, independent brothels flourished throughout the state. On San Angelo's notorious Concho Street, Miss Hattie's upscale bordello operated continuously for nearly fifty years until the Texas Rangers finally put an end to the shenanigans in 1946. Texarkana boasted four brothels in an area collectively known as Swampoodle. Famed madam Hattie Valdes (not to be confused with the Miss Hattie of San Angelo) operated a well-regarded brothel on Austin's South Congress Avenue for decades until it burned in the late 1960s. Prostitutes worked out of practically every flophouse hotel in Fort Worth's lower downtown. Even small-town Taylor had a notorious strip where almost any vice could be indulged for a price. Ready examples of all the oft-cited excesses and negative, dehumanizing effects of prostitution abounded.

"Boy, south side of Taylor was nothing but a string of black and Mexican beer joints. There were prostitutes running out of those of all ages and all types," one former patron remembered. "Taylor was a wild place. You could go over there and you could pick out fifteen-year-old girls and boys.

"I remember one night four of us went over there and were drinking and all. We got an old gal and took her out to a cotton field," he said. "I mean, we were actually out in a cotton field! One old boy took her panties and wouldn't give them back.

"She said, 'Well, if I get home I need my panties, because my momma is going to check me to see if I been whoring.'

"He said, 'No, you're going to have to screw one more time to get your panties back,'" he said. "So, we got a second round with her just to get her panties back!"[371]

Neither Miss Edna nor Aunt Jessie before her tolerated such dehumanizing treatment of their working girls. Anyone spouting foul language, groping breasts or treating the women in a rough, abusive manner faced immediate expulsion. Any offender who refused to leave on Miss Edna or Aunt Jessie's orders soon earned the singular privilege of explaining himself to the sheriff. Few, if any, of the many other brothels dotting the Texas countryside enforced such a strict zero-tolerance policy, which goes a long way toward explaining why so many held the Chicken Ranch in such high esteem. That also might explain why other brothels faced periodic raids and closure by law enforcement agencies, a problem the Chicken Ranch seldom encountered.

"In this section of Texas it has been well known there were houses of prostitution in Brenham and Sealy and Austin, and Post Office Street in

The Hollywood Dinner Club opened in 1926. Run by Sam Maceo, it was a glitzy casino that attracted top entertainment acts years ahead of Las Vegas. *R-462, Texas Department of Public Safety photographs, 1937–1965, undated. Archives and Information Services Division, Texas State Library and Archives Commission.*

Galveston, Mud Alley in Richmond…Of course, while that's not a general subject of conversation, almost everyone in this area knew about those things," said former district attorney Oliver Kitzman. "So, the role of the Chicken Ranch in connection with all that is sort of distorted. [It was] nothing unique for that community. People didn't go around talking about it. Everyone knew about it, whether they'd been there or not. But it was something all the people in this part of the state had grown up with."[372]

Even though the La Grange brothel had operated illegally since at least the World War I era—and its legal status prior to that is debatable—the general consensus held that it served a vital role in the community. The regular medical exams the prostitutes underwent kept venereal disease in check. The young men of the area found a safe outlet there for their raging libidos. The county's daughters maintained their virtue and avoided the risk of unplanned pregnancy. Anti-vice advocates mocked these claims as baseless, but whether those benefits to the community were real or imagined is irrelevant. The community *perceived* the Chicken Ranch as an asset, and that view held great sway in some quite surprising places.

"In my work with the National District Attorneys Association, I became acquainted with Bill McDonald, who was the state's attorney in

Winnemucca, Nevada. My wife and I visited with Bill and his wife on several occasions, and one of the things Bill and I talked about was the question of how best to address the ancient profession," Kitzman said. "In his situation, of course, in Nevada, prostitution is legalized. Along with that came to him the responsibility for oversight and the responsibility to see to the rules concerning medical care and all those things.

"It was not exactly a pleasant duty of his, but he accepted it and undertook to do it well. He was a very good man. But in contrasting—in our several conversations—the difference between what they did in Winnemucca, Nevada, and what Texas was doing here locally seemed to me to come out in favor of what Texas was doing," he said. "In Winnemucca, that business venture is visible to children, what business is going on. In Texas, there was always a respect for the public by the discreet way the people tried to operate their [brothels].

"They weren't high profile in the community, but again, anybody who lived there knew they were there. They tried to function discreetly, and if they had not done so, they would not have been there," Kitzman said. "I came to the conclusion—and Bill did too—that from a social standpoint and practical standpoint, that kind of problem under the care of responsible law enforcement officials was much more affordable than what goes on in his jurisdiction there."[373]

EVERYTHING CHANGED IN 1956 with the election of Will Reid Wilson as Texas attorney general. Wilson made a name for himself as a hard-charging, take-no-prisoners district attorney who cleaned up Dallas County and then parlayed that to election as a Texas Supreme Court justice. Attorneys general were far more proactive than justices, though, and once he made the jump, Wilson wasted no time in launching a statewide anti-vice crusade. Higher office clearly beckoned the ambitious Wilson—governor or US senator, it didn't matter—and the beginning, middle and end of his campaign consisted of cleaning up vice in Texas.[374]

The Lone Star State hadn't seen the likes of Wilson before, certainly not on such a large scale. From day one, Wilson set his sights on taking down the so-called Free State of Galveston. The island resort, a short drive from Houston, operated in flagrant disregard of state anti-vice laws under the longtime control of the Maceo crime syndicate. High-rolling casinos such as the Hollywood Club and Balinese Ballroom attracted A-list talent such as George Burns and Gracie Allen, Frank Sinatra, Bob Hope, Sammy Davis

By the time the Texas Rangers closed the casino under orders from Attorney General Will Wilson in 1957, the Hollywood Dinner Club was a shabby shadow of its former self. *R-462, Texas Department of Public Safety photographs, 1937–1965, undated. Archives and Information Services Division, Texas State Library and Archives Commission.*

Jr. and Duke Ellington to entertain their wealthy guests. The infamous Post Office Street boasted the highest concentration of upscale brothels in the nation. A well-financed network of payoffs and corruption kept the Maceos insulated from arrest and prosecution. Police Commissioner Walter Johnson bragged about payoffs he received from forty-six brothels. For sex, gambling, booze or any other indulgence the well-heeled might want to buy, Galveston prospered as a hedonist's paradise.[375]

"If God couldn't stop prostitution, why should I?" famously demanded Herb Cartwright, mayor of Galveston from 1947 through 1955.

One local religious leader observed, "To be respectable in Galveston, you have to support prostitution."[376]

Or so the conventional wisdom held. In reality, by the 1950s, Galveston's glory days were fading fast. Fierce competition from Las Vegas, with legal gambling, siphoned away much of the entertainment and gaming talent. Revenues fell rapidly, hurting the entire island's economy. The lavish,

Texas Ranger Captain Johnny Klevenhagen, along with Rangers Pete Rogers, Hollis Sillivan and Tully Seay, supervises workers moving confiscated gambling equipment stored in the old Hollywood Club in Galveston on June 20, 1957. *R-462, Texas Department of Public Safety photographs, 1937–1965, undated. Archives and Information Services Division, Texas State Library and Archives Commission.*

upscale Post Office Street brothels declined into seedy affairs, with girls aggressively shouting at passersby and fighting among themselves for customers. A tawdry shell of its former self, the Galveston machine had lost its invincible aura.[377]

That's not to say Galveston didn't put up a fight. Wilson marshaled sixty Texas Rangers for a daring surprise raid only to learn of the island's casinos and brothels abruptly closing shop well in advance. Clearly, the Maceos had informants within the DPS, forcing Wilson to change tactics. On the advice of Jim Simpson, a former candidate for Galveston county attorney, Wilson hired unknown undercover operatives to infiltrate various casinos and brothels on Galveston, collecting evidence for restraining orders and injunctions. Controversially, Simpson also argued that the Texas Rangers be cut out of the loop. The abrupt failure of the planned earlier raid involving the Rangers didn't pass Simpson's smell test. If a Ranger wasn't tipping off the suspects, then one of their support staff was. Either way, Simpson intended to put a stop to it.

"Will Wilson was a good man, totally honest," Simpson said, "but he was fundamentally naïve. I had a different view. I'd been an FBI agent in Chicago, and I understood corruption."[378]

The Texas Rangers weren't sidelined entirely. Even as Wilson fired off wave after wave of restraining orders, the Rangers continued mounting their raids against flagrant casinos. The Balinese Room, in particular, presented unique challenges. Built on a six-hundred-foot pier jutting out into the Gulf of Mexico, the casino occupied a large ballroom at the farthest end from shore. Whenever the Texas Rangers launched a raid, the band struck up "The Eyes of Texas" and all the patrons would stand and sing, impeding the lawmen's progress as they raced the length of the pier. By the time they reached the casino area, all the slot machines and gaming tables had vanished into concealed compartments. Ranger captain Johnny Klevenhagen put a damper on things by sending in Rangers whenever the Balinese opened, who sat in the casino area until the club closed late in the evening. With the ever-present Rangers looking on, the hidden gambling equipment stayed hidden, with customers and profits drying up. Later, with the casino's manager desperate to open up, Klevenhagen changed tactics, instead sending in Ranger Clint Peoples undercover as a high roller from South Texas. Once the gambling got up to speed, the Rangers launched their raid. Right on cue, the band began playing "The Eyes of Texas," but Peoples was ready. Pulling out a smuggled handgun, Peoples held the pit boss, workers and forty-eight guests until the raiding party arrived to seize the gaming tables and slots.[379]

The struggle over Galveston did little to distract Wilson from the rest of the state's vice problems. Texas didn't have any other gambling operations that compared with Galveston, but prostitution flourished. Wilson's agents, in cooperation with Texas Rangers, launched raids statewide and successfully pressured local officials to take meaningful action. Brothels in Beaumont, Big Spring, Cuero, Port Arthur, Richmond, Rosenberg, Texarkana, Travis County, Victoria and elsewhere soon closed permanently. The century-old tradition of widespread commercial sex in Texas abruptly came to a jarring end. Sealy's venerable brothel on Rice Street closed. Not even the Chicken Ranch escaped entirely unscathed.[380]

"Back in the Sixties, when Will Wilson was attorney general and got it in his craw to be governor, he closed 'er down," recounted one longtime La Grange resident. "Yeah, for about two weeks. They put up a big ole

Workers unload confiscated gambling equipment from a truck in Galveston on June 20, 1957, as Texas Rangers supervise the action. *R-462, Texas Department of Public Safety photographs, 1937–1965, undated. Archives and Information Services Division, Texas State Library and Archives Commission.*

'Closed' sign out front. Newspaper people came and snapped pictures. But if a regular customer went out there, he knew what back road to park on and the girls slipped him in the back door."[381]

To Big Jim, the attorney general's expansion of his anti-vice crusade beyond Galveston infringed on local sovereignty, under the unforgivable heading of "outsiders sticking their noses where they don't belong." The Fayette County sheriff offered only minimal cooperation, with Big Jim derisively mocking Wilson's initiatives as a "damned publicity stunt."[382]

Miss Edna, who had not yet bought the place from the ailing Miss Jessie, remembered Wilson's crusade well, dismissing it with contempt. The Chicken Ranch's simple gambit of pretending to close while continuing to admit customers through the back door worked only because the attorney general's effort didn't have nearly the popular support he thought it did.

"He tried his best [to close the Chicken Ranch], but he got defeated every point and time," Miss Edna said. "He didn't have no governor behind him, you know.

"I had no respect for him. I saw him in Austin one time, down at the cafeteria downtown," she said. "I was sitting at the table, eating. He came in, got his tray. I wasn't too far from him. That was the first time I'd ever seen him in person, besides on television. People like that are not much good."[383]

Galveston remained Wilson's prime target, and the relentless pressure finally won out. The brothels closed, and the prostitutes scattered to the four winds. Texas Rangers discovered the secret warehouses where the casinos stashed their gaming equipment. Thousands of slot machines and gaming tables shattered into useless scrap under the Rangers' sledgehammers. To add insult to injury, Wilson ordered the slot machines dumped into the deep waters of the Gulf of Mexico. The Rangers set up checkpoints along the causeway to the mainland to make sure none of the contraband slot machines or roulette wheels escaped destruction. The Free State of Galveston was, for all intents and purposes, dead and buried.[384]

Hollis Sillavan (left), along with another Texas Ranger, watch as confiscated gambling equipment burns in a Galveston field on June 20, 1957. *R-462, Texas Department of Public Safety photographs, 1937–1965, undated. Archives and Information Services Division, Texas State Library and Archives Commission.*

A little bit of the graveyard dirt landed surprisingly close to the Chicken Ranch, however. During the early stages of the crackdown, the Salvato family—which ran a number of casinos on the Galveston County mainland—managed to smuggle some of their gaming equipment out of the area. With gambling likely finished on the island, they saw an opportunity to rake in huge profits on the mainland. Despite facing a number of gambling indictments brought against him by Wilson in Galveston, P.J. Salvato used Eva D. Reynolds McCallum as a go-between to purchase a failed motel outside Sealy along US Route 90. The Salvato family invested a great deal of money in renovating the old motel, turning it into a stylish casino for Houston's oil millionaires, less than an hour away by car.

The gambit never had a chance. The Texas Rangers sniffed it out almost from the start. In one of the greatest displays of passive-aggression ever, the Rangers sat back and watched as the Salvatos invested tens of thousands of dollars to remodel the place, only to swoop in with axes and destroy the contraband equipment just as the improvised casino readied to open.[385]

That incident, interesting as it was, would have little bearing on the history of the Chicken Ranch were it not for the fact that Sealy's longtime brothel—closed a year or so earlier by Wilson—reestablished itself under new management in that failed motel on US 90 just a few miles west of town. The Wagon Wheel, like so many other Texas whorehouses, offered prostitution—sans gambling—to anyone willing to pony up a few dollars. Unlike so many other Texas whorehouses, though, the Wagon Wheel would play a direct and crucial role in the ultimate downfall of the Chicken Ranch.

Chapter 9

THE WAGON WHEEL

If the Chicken Ranch could be likened to an amorous aunt who, despite telling off-color jokes at family gatherings, was fondly accepted as the life of the party, then the Wagon Wheel played the role of the tacky cousin who drank too much, hit on the caterers and invariably made everyone uncomfortable. The Wagon Wheel never enjoyed the respect or fame afforded the Chicken Ranch, despite being one of only a handful of Texas brothels to survive into the 1960s and outlast Attorney General Will Wilson. Actually, outlast is probably the wrong word, because the Wagon Wheel didn't exist prior to 1960 or thereabouts. That's not to say Sealy didn't have prostitution or brothels before 1960—far from it. But the Wagon Wheel wasn't yet part of the equation.

Sealy's history developed quite differently than La Grange's. Modern Sealy is practically a bedroom community of ever-growing Houston, but it began as a railroad town in every sense of the word when the Gulf, Colorado and Santa Fe Railroad platted the community in 1875 and named it after the company director, George Sealy. The town grew steadily as a manufacturing center—the Sealy mattress corporation got its start there—but with the Civil War a fading memory by the time of its founding, the community lacked any real historic connection to the mythic early days of Texas.[386]

"Austin County was a little more commercial than Fayette County," said former district attorney Oliver Kitzman, whose territory encompassed Austin County and Sealy, as well as Fayette County and La Grange. "Austin County was not quite in the position that Fayette County was back then of losing population, but the City of Sealy has always been a very progressive town. I was surprised; one day, I sat down and checked and it was the largest city in my district."[387]

Sealy benefited from the railroad as well as its proximity to Houston and US Route 90 (and later Interstate 10), a major east–west highway through the middle of Texas. All that traffic provided a lot of potential customers, and prostitution soon followed. Unlike La Grange, Sealy lacked even an oral tradition to date the origins of the town's first brothel, but it was certainly well established by World War II. If the whorehouse enjoyed a fanciful name, few people alive today remember it. Located in the black part

Former district attorney Oliver Kitzman. *Author photo.*

of town, like so many other brothels of the era, the house was a large, fourteen-bedroom affair on Rice Street not far from the old gristmill. A madam by the name of Pat Roeper ran the house, but women who worked there referred to the owner—who tended to stay in the background—as Mr. Jones.[388]

"Sealy had one [a whorehouse] too, yes. We were delivering cars to Houston from a Ford dealership in Elgin one time, and me and a guy went," one former customer recalled. "I took the car and he followed me to pick me back up, and we stopped there in Sealy. Rumor had it, girls who went to Rice [University worked at the brothel], which I doubt seriously."[389]

As a teenager growing up in Sealy, David "Rusty" Rice delivered groceries to the brothel when he worked at the local grocery store. Once he turned fifteen, he ran away from home and started working at a truck stop on the highway. It didn't take Rice long to figure out he could be making a little extra on the side by giving directions to horny truckers.

"I got free pussy there all the time. I had these maps made up that showed how to get to the whorehouse—the one in town," Rice said. "I couldn't write 'whorehouse' so I wrote 'Hog Heaven' on there.

"I told them, 'You have to have this to get in the door,'" he said, a clever little lie that ensured the madam knew exactly how much business he sent their way. "After a while, the madam said, 'Go get you a girl.' I had a couple of specials in there, you know."[390]

During the early 1950s, the Chicken Ranch and the Sealy brothel had an informal working relationship. Whenever the Chicken Ranch had any openings, Aunt Jessie called on the Wagon Wheel for temporary replacements.

"We'd swap out sometime, some of the girls from Sealy would come over. They would work for Miss Jessie. They would trade out," said Ruth E. Pariseau, a former nurse at the La Grange clinic that handled the prostitutes' weekly checkups. "Mr. Jones owned the place in Sealy, and Miss Jessie's girls and his girls would trade out if they were short on girls.

"Most of the girls said that their husbands were either alcoholics or drug addicts and that they worked as prostitutes to support the habit," she said. "When the girls came in, they'd say, 'We're just pinch hitting, we're from Sealy.'"[391]

By the late 1950s, the good times in Sealy had come to a screeching halt. The old brothel—like so many others in Texas—met its match in Attorney General Wilson. The state's anti-vice initiative closed it down, and not enough local support existed to make reopening it a possibility. Enter Jerry McKay.

A wheeler-dealer from an early age, McKay rubbed shoulders with Galveston-style vice in the seaside town of Kemah, Texas, where he worked in a nightclub boasting both illegal gambling and prostitution. McKay knew and did business with many unsavory characters, probably even the Maceos themselves. Able to play the good old boy role when needed, McKay could be equally cold and cruel if it furthered his criminal enterprises. He found pimping lucrative and placed women in brothels across the state, including the Chicken Ranch and the old Sealy brothel. He'd earned enough of a reputation that state police developed a file on him, labeling McKay a "known criminal element." McKay's high-rolling life turned sour in early 1960 after a vicious rival from Houston shot him three times in an ambush.

Hospitalized and lucky to be alive, McKay decided he'd had enough of the dangerous turf wars around Galveston. He moved to Freeport in 1960, but if he had any intention of reforming and leaving vice behind, it didn't last.[392]

"He'd been a pimp all his life," said Rice, who worked for McKay a number of years. "A pimp shot him in the arm—he had a gimp right arm. I asked him one day, 'Whatever happened to Clyde, that guy that shot you?'

"He said, 'Aw, hell, he stole more chain than he could swim with.' I found out [Clyde] was in Galveston Bay on a boat and Jerry McKay went and shot him off the boat and killed him," he said. "[The police] never did nothing to him—pimps weren't worth a shit in them days. You were just trash, and they didn't worry about it."[393]

That nasty business taken care of, McKay turned his attention to Sealy. With the old brothel in town closed, he sensed a golden opportunity to start running prostitutes and fill the vacuum. The closed Wagon Wheel motel three miles west of Sealy on the north side of Route 90 offered the perfect location. P.J. Salvato, whose casino plans lay in ruins thanks to the Texas Rangers, proved to be a motivated seller. McKay went up the road to neighboring Columbus, Texas, and recruited a wealthy businessman as an investor. With Columbus money backing him, McKay used A.A. Pruitt as an intermediary and bought the Wagon Wheel from Salvato in February 1960. McKay immediately set to work opening it as a brothel.[394]

The new location consisted of a large main building with eight smaller sixteen- by thirty-two-foot lodges arranged in an east–west line on either side of it. The site offered easy access from Route 90 and later Interstate 10. Customers drove behind the motel, where the buildings and a fence screened the parking lot from the highway. They entered the main building, chose a prostitute from among those gathered in the lobby and then accompanied her back to one of the bedrooms in the lodges to conduct their business. Like the Chicken Ranch, blacks weren't allowed and Hispanics only occasionally. The women would eat their meals in the kitchen area of the main building. Normally, eight to twelve women worked at the Wagon Wheel, but at many as fourteen could be found there on occasion. Those road-weary travelers who mistook it for a legitimate motel realized their errors quickly.[395]

"It was a long, low-lying motel on the side of the road. [It was] probably built back when cars were first on the road, you know," said Larry Conners, who, as a young reporter, investigated both the Wagon Wheel and the Chicken Ranch. "It was a nondescript type thing, kind of a rundown, grungy thing.

"I don't remember much about the girls in there," he said. "We walked in. It was kind of a large room and a hallway that led off to the rooms. But I never did go back there, back in those rooms at that place."[396]

To handle the day-to-day operations of the Wagon Wheel, McKay leveraged his pimping background and offered the position of madam to one of his working girls, Linda Bartholomew. Tall, blond and pretty, Bartholomew had worked at the Sealy brothel before the attorney general closed it down. Although younger than was typical for a madam, her familiarity with Sealy and prior relationship with McKay cinched the deal for her. She adopted the name of "Miss Connie," and the Wagon Wheel was open for business.[397]

In the early 1960s, Rice worked at a truck stop outside Sealy that his buddy McKay owned. He also lived at the Wagon Wheel, as McKay let him

The Wagon Wheel quickly fell into disrepair following its closure. By 2009, the main building, which had housed the office, kitchen and lobby, was reduced to a cinder block shell. *Author photo*.

stay in the lodge on the easternmost end. For Rice, the proximity of so many prostitutes made him feel like a kid in a candy store.

"I *tried* to do them all, but I never got to do them all. The crew changed on me before I ever made the circle," Rice said. "There's some you never catch up on. You might get another one, but you'll never catch up on the two you lost."[398]

Life wasn't always fun and games for Rice at the Wagon Wheel, however. One time, the state mental hospital in Rusk, Texas, discharged an unstable black man who made his way to Sealy. The man spotted the Wagon Wheel, looking for all the world like a motel, and decided he'd take up permanent residence in Rice's rooms. Which is bad enough itself, but the fact that the man was armed and violent escalated the situation.

"He went there with a pistol and told the maid that was cleaning my room that he's taking my room over," Rice recalled. "A highway patrolman named Ben Havlicek, he was shooting at that crazy nigger through the window. Constable Buck Childers was out in front, and a bullet ricocheted off the cinder block walls, and it shot that cinder block and splattered. It went right through Buck's lip and stuck in his teeth. When I got there, his lip was bleeding and that nigger had shot him in the arm.

Of the eight free-standing Wagon Wheel cabins, by 2009, one had been razed and the other seven had fallen into ruin. *Author photo.*

"They finally got the nigger out; he run out of bullets, and they finally got him out," he said. "They couldn't shoot him or kill him because by that time it was too many people that drove up watching the shootout, so they had to take him back to Rusk."[399]

While the shootout had provided great entertainment for the spectators, it left the motel room in tatters. Rice, then a young twenty-something, approached Austin County sheriff Truman Maddox after the gunfight.

"I had my clothes hanging in the bathroom behind the door. Man, they shot it, and them bullets were ricocheting on that cinder block in there. I had shirts with five or six bullet holes in them," Rice said. "I said, 'Who's gonna pay for my shirts?' [Sheriff Maddox] said, 'You was damn lucky you wasn't in them!'

"That was the end of that deal."[400]

Not counting the unique situation of the Wagon Wheel, three longtime brothels survived into the 1960s: the Chicken Ranch in La Grange, Dutch Lane in Brenham and Hattie Valdes' M&M Courts in Austin—the last of several brothels she'd owned in the state capital. These three, along with the Wagon Wheel in Sealy, occupied an irregular triangle in East Central Texas within 120 miles of one another—and the Wagon Wheel, more of a Johnny-come-lately, enjoyed far less local favor than any of the others.

"It was run a little differently [than the Chicken Ranch]. There was a madam out there, but I don't know if the madam was doing anything other than [managing day-to-day operations]," said Herb Hancock, a former assistant attorney general under John Hill. "There appeared to be somebody other than the sheriff in control of it.

"It did not have the political power the other one had, from what I could gather. The ownership of that one could very well have been—that may be where I got a lot of the information that it had organized crime," he said. "It was a little bit more expensive to go there, and sometimes they'd have fifteen girls working there at one time. The other place was usually standardized at ten, from what I can gather from the report. When I went inside, I could not count. I just barely went in and left. I didn't get to see."[401]

Escaping Will Wilson's vice purges turned out to be hollow victories for two of those whorehouses, however. Valdes' M&M Courts on South Congress Avenue in Austin caught fire and burned in 1965. Valdes, by then getting on in years, chose not to reopen in another location. Her steady stream of business from the state legislature shifted completely over to the Chicken Ranch after that. Brenham's Dutch Lane, a small, quiet brothel that catered to Blinn College students as well as occasional Aggies and travelers along US 290, suffered a similar fate.

"About '64, when I was an insurance adjuster for the Insurance Company of North America while going to law school, I had a claim report on a building in Brenham that had burned down," recalled Kitzman. "Our company didn't have an agent in Brenham, and the case was assigned to me. I drove over to Brenham and went directly to the fire department. I talked directly to the fire chief, and when I told him why I was there, he behaved a little peculiar.

"Folks around Brenham aren't known to just bubble over with information, but he didn't seem like he wanted to talk about that. So I asked him to show me where the fire was," he said. "I went out, and there was a heap of ashes and a bunch of iron bedsteads there. Of course, it turns out that was the [brothel]."[402]

Kitzman found the circumstances of the blaze suspicious and ruled it arson, denying the claim. Eventually, the insurance company settled the dispute out of court, but Dutch Lane never reopened.

"It'd probably been there as long as the Chicken Ranch in some form or another. Maybe not in that location," Kitzman said. "There was nothing unusual about that. They call it the oldest profession. People have to figure out how they want to handle it. It is nonsense to try and stomp it out, because you can't do that.

"You need to have a plan, though, to keep it under control, keep it discreet and try not to embarrass your children or your mother with all that going on," he said. "Most people—and I'll say most people in the areas where they had this going on—were of Czech and German heritage. So, by all means, the Chicken Ranch had nothing materially different about it than any of those other places that were of no interest to law enforcement."[403]

FOR ALL PRACTICAL PURPOSES, the Wagon Wheel had—as did the Chicken Ranch—just one real concern when the subject of law enforcement came up. Unless organized crime showed its hand enough to attract the attention of the Texas Rangers, prostitution remained a local matter, handled as the county sheriff saw fit.

In Austin County, Truman Maddox served as sheriff from 1953 to 1987, winning reelection ten times. Although fifteen years junior to Sheriff Jim Flournoy in Fayette County, Sheriff Maddox cut no less an imposing figure. Standing tall at six feet, three inches—an unwritten rule apparently required all Texas sheriffs to tower over their constituents—Sheriff Maddox made as colorful a figure as any who wore a badge throughout Texas history. And he generally treated the Wagon Wheel with a hands-off policy.[404]

Sheriff Maddox was born in Madison County, Texas, on September 30, 1917. A short time after that, the family moved one county over, and Maddox grew up near Hearne, Texas. The Great Depression hit during his teen years, and he found work with the Civilian Conservation Corps. Unlike Big Jim, Maddox never aspired to be a cowboy or lawman. His path to the badge took a more circuitous route.[405]

"Sheriff Maddox grew up on a farm working cattle. He was in the [Civilian Conservation Corps], and in order to keep all these young men in line, they had to have a pretty rigid policy, some paramilitary organization. He was involved in that," said Kitzman. "When World War II broke out, he went into the army. He went to Africa and worked his way up into Germany, the whole war. He was in the Rapido River crossing in Italy with all the blood and gore that happened there."[406]

After the war, Maddox bought a grocery and meat market on Flowkes Street in Sealy. The meat market came with a barbecue pit out back, and on Wednesdays and Saturdays, he'd fire it up, selling as much as five hundred pounds of hot links and barbecue a day.[407]

With the meat market doing good, solid business, Maddox had no reason to go looking for other opportunities. But other opportunities came looking for him in 1949. Marcus Steck had won election as sheriff the previous year and needed a dependable deputy for Sealy. Austin County had no police radios, and the county commissioners frowned on even the ten-cent cost of a long-distance phone call from Bellville, the county seat, to Sealy. Sheriff Steck needed a deputy who could manage the southern half of the county on his own without depending on backup or even regular direction. Maddox's outstanding service record from World War II made him an easy choice for Sheriff Steck, but Maddox wasn't so easily convinced.

"I've been running from the law for 30 years, why should I change and start running with 'em now?" Maddox quipped before ultimately accepting the badge.[408]

As quick as that, Deputy Maddox found himself part of the Austin County Sheriff's Department, making the grand salary of $150 a month. Although technically a full-time deputy, Maddox worked most days in his meat market to pay the bills. That's where he was one busy Saturday afternoon when he heard two gunshots. Instantly, he knew they were pistol shots because he'd heard that exact sound far too often in the war. Deputy Maddox threw off his apron and grabbed up his Colt .45.[409]

"I ran to the front and looked, and laying in the front door of my market was this gentleman, Dallas Hibboldt," Maddox said. "He lay face down, with the screen door open, blood running down his back. He says, 'Forrest Ward shot me, go get him!'"[410]

Deputy Maddox went out onto the sidewalk, spotted Ward walking up the street toward the City Café and took out after him.

"I started down that way, young and brand-new, knowing that he's got a gun, knowing that he just shot a man, thinking, 'I'm going after him, but I don't exactly know what I'm gonna do,'" Maddox said. "That's just about what you got on your mind. You know you got to move on, 'cause that's your job, but he's got a gun, too. If he shot him, he's liable to shoot me!"[411]

As soon as Ward spotted the approaching deputy, he grabbed a passerby to use as a human shield and started firing. Maddox took cover until the hostage broke away and then returned fire. The normally bustling street cleared out instantly. Ward dove behind parked cars for cover. Maddox shot the windows out of four cars and a pickup, filling Ward's eyes with glass and forcing his surrender.

In the aftermath, Deputy Maddox got Ward to jail and Hibboldt to the hospital and clamped down on the feud that had started the whole mess, preventing the respective families from escalating the incident into a real bloodbath. After that dramatic shootout, nobody in Austin County dared question the new deputy's resolve.[412]

"That was where Truman Maddox became famous, the way he handled that gunfight in Sealy," Kitzman said. "He was a fascinating fellow."[413]

In 1953, worn down by the stress of the job, Sheriff Steck announced he wouldn't run again. Maddox threw his hat into the ring, and despite being perceived as an outsider by some locals, he campaigned hard and won the election.[414]

Some sheriffs cultivated a no-nonsense reputation. Sheriff Maddox didn't fit that mold. Sociable and quick with a joke, he projected an easygoing air, but the instant trouble started, he took care of business. With regard to the Wagon Wheel, nobody ever seemed to complain about it, so Sheriff Maddox contented himself with keeping an eye on the operation but left it alone. The resources necessary to close it down had better use elsewhere, practically speaking, and like Big Jim over in Fayette County, it occurred to Sheriff Maddox that the Wagon Wheel might prove a useful source of intelligence.

"We have to have informants to help us break cases," Sheriff Maddox said. "There's no way I can walk down the street and buy dope from somebody, they all know me. In fact, most of these thugs can smell a cop when he walks in the front door.

"You have to have somebody out there that's kind of on their level to really be of much good," he said.[415]

"I was well aware that Sheriff Maddox knew all he wanted to know about it," Kitzman said. "I didn't see any reason for me to ask a bunch of questions about it. I guess maybe from my experience in air force intelligence, you learn not to ask any questions unless you need to know!

"Likewise, I never had any constituent of mine complain about it," he said. The district attorney never took action against the Wagon Wheel.[416]

Although Sheriff Maddox saw more than his share of interesting, strange and even laughable cases come across his desk, for the most part his workload mirrored that of other Texas sheriffs of the time. A growing issue for law enforcement across the state was the increased prevalence of illegal drugs flowing into their counties, and Austin County was no exception. With the opening of I-10, access to Houston became that much easier, and drug-related arrests increased in Austin County.

One trait Sheriff Maddox shared with Big Jim in Fayette County was a loathing of the drug trade. Historically, vice attracted vice, and wherever prostitution flourished, gambling and drugs soon followed, if not vice versa. In the case of the Wagon Wheel, the Texas Rangers had decisively crushed all thoughts of gambling, but narcotics remained a growing concern.

"A man under dope is actually worse than a drunk," Sheriff Maddox maintained.

"When I first started I myself didn't know what marihuana was, I didn't know what coke was, I didn't know what heroin was," he said. "We made a buy off a man of four ounces of cocaine and seized a Mercedes automobile he was in, and two days later we made another buy off another man with 10 ounces of coke and seized his money and his automobile. Well, that's the difference in the type of crime that [there] was whenever I started here and what we're having now."[417]

Determined to keep the drug trade from taking root locally, Sheriff Maddox delivered an unsubtle warning to the Wagon Wheel—prostitution might be tolerated, but the presence and distribution of drugs would result in immediate and permanent closure.

The Wagon Wheel management received the message loud and clear. For all its other faults, the brothel took the sheriff's prohibition on drugs very seriously. Unfortunately, not everyone gave that message equal weight. Rice, for one, had to learn firsthand how dim a view Sheriff Maddox took on illegal drugs.

"They didn't do no drugs in there. I know that for a fact, because I used to work at a truck stop and I sold pills," Rice said. "I sold pills to them truck drivers to keep them awake.

"[McKay and Miss Connie] told me, 'Don't ever bring none in your pocket when you come in here.' I got busted on that, but that was my fault. I screwed up, you know?" he said. "I went to the penitentiary over it. That's why I had to leave.

"The deal over it, Sheriff Truman, [Texas Ranger] Hollis Sillavan and Jerry McKay, the guy that owned the whorehouse, they got me out, but the deal was I had to leave Sealy," he said. Convicted of selling amphetamines and sentenced to two years in prison, Rice got out in 1967 having served just a fraction of his term. "I got out in six months. I got a change of scenery."[418]

As far as cautionary tales go, Rice's experience illustrated the fact that Sheriff Maddox did not tolerate drugs, period. Not much ambiguity clouded the issue. Yet in late 1971 or 1972, a new prostitute—call her "Mary Jane" for clarity's sake—arrived at the Wagon Wheel from Houston, determined to test the rules. Mary Jane blended in with the other prostitutes, women with varied backgrounds but similar stories that always concluded with them trying to make a living in the illegal sex trade. She might have bragged about an important lawman in Houston she enjoyed a relationship with, but claiming intimacy with lawmen, politicians or celebrities was par for the course. Mary Jane worked at the Wagon Wheel for some months without incident—until she was caught dealing drugs to the other prostitutes, and probably to clients as well.[419]

Reaction came swiftly. Miss Connie kicked her out of the Wagon Wheel on the spot, forbidding her to ever return. Nobody knew if Sheriff Maddox would follow through on his zero-tolerance promise. Nobody dared put it to the test.

Mary Jane hit the road, Highway 71 to be exact, and within a short while caught on with the Chicken Ranch in La Grange. It didn't take long before she started the same racket—peddling her drugs to the other prostitutes and customers.

She couldn't have picked a worse brothel for such an operation. Miss Edna's hostility toward narcotics verged on pathological. None of the prostitutes who had lived at the Chicken Ranch for any length of time would cover for Mary Jane. In short order, her drug dealing came to light, and in the blink of an eye, Mary Jane found herself homeless and unemployed once again.[420]

Under normal circumstances, Mary Jane's story would end there. But in one of the universe's great ironies, that close relationship she claimed to have with a lawman proved very much true. In all likelihood, he profited from her drug-dealing operations. Regardless, Mary Jane's lawman refused to tolerate his chippie's dismissal by two pissant country whorehouses.

"[Texas Ranger sergeant] Johnny Krumnow told me about the background of how the Chicken Ranch thing got started. Things I didn't know at the time," Kitzman said. "He told me that there was a DPS intelligence officer [who] had a 'chip,' as he called it, who was a hostess at the house in Sealy. She was found to be using illegal drugs and encouraging the other hostesses to do the same thing. So she was dismissed. She went from there over to the Chicken Ranch, and the same thing happened. And she was dismissed.

"Well, the DPS intelligence officer tried to get the Chicken Ranch administration to take her back over there. And they refused to do it," he said. "Whatever his psychological problem was, he decided he needed to do something to the Chicken Ranch, who would not show him the respect to do what he asked them to do."[421]

The aggrieved DPS officer resolved to settle for nothing less than the permanent closure of both the Chicken Ranch and the Wagon Wheel. "Better men than you have tried," Miss Edna might as well have said once

Right: Texas Ranger Johnny Krumnow. *R-461, Texas Department of Public Safety photographs, 1937–1965, undated. Archives and Information Services Division, Texas State Library and Archives Commission.*

Below: In 2015, the owner of the property began a conversion of the remaining Wagon Wheel buildings into commercial storage lockers. *Author photo.*

again. After all, if Attorney General Wilson—who had brought the Free State of Galveston to heel—couldn't close the Chicken Ranch, what could one lone officer do?

But this new enemy had the experience of learning from others' mistakes. A frontal assault against the brothels was doomed to failure and amounted to career suicide. No, beating the Chicken Ranch meant outflanking the brothel and its allies, a strategic campaign that demanded patience and the cultivation of tactical allies.

The first step involved winning over the Houston office of the Department of Public Safety. The officers of the Houston region pretty much ignored the La Grange and Sealy brothels as a matter of course. The houses were remote and of little consequence to Houston, which had enough crime and vice to keep them plenty busy. But once the whisper campaign started, a subtle but distinct change overtook the Houston office of DPS Criminal Intelligence.

"About the Wagon Wheel, I had heard there was something going on around there in Sealy," said retired Texas Ranger Ramiero Martinez, who, at the time, was working in the Department of Public Safety's narcotics division in Houston. "But I was strictly in narcotics, and I let intelligence handle that, because that was their bailiwick. That was their specialty."[422]

By the 1970s, Texas had changed from the dusty, rural backwater of the 1950s. Without anyone actually noticing at the time, the Chicken Ranch—so long an accepted part of the good ol' boy culture—had transformed into a giant powder keg, just waiting for a stray spark to set it off. The renegade DPS officer spread his matches far and wide.

All that remained was to find someone willing to strike that spark, fireworks guaranteed.

Chapter 10

MARVIN ZINDLER,
EYE! WITNESS! NEWS!

News of the Chicken Ranch's closure quickly spread far and wide. Politicians, farmers and students alike reacted with anger and dismay at the report in the closing week of an unusually warm and rainy December 1971.

"Now it's reported that the farm's telephone number has been disconnected," reported Sam Kindrick in his regular column for the *San Antonio Express-News*. "A San Antonio man says when you drive up to the farm gate, a shotgun-packing guard steps forth and orders you to leave private property."[423]

The ensuing panic did not quite equal the stock market crash of 1929, but tremors reverberated throughout the state. Kindrick received a flood of inquiries and, less than a week later, published a retraction of sorts.

"Sorry if anyone was unduly alarmed by reports here that the La Grange chicken farm, Texas' oldest brothel, had closed down," Kindrick wrote. "Faithful farm customers say the shutdown was only for the Christmas holidays, allowing the working hens time off to visit their families and rest up for 1972."[424]

Even that clarification failed to allay the fears of some regular customers, who continued to write in. One particularly insistent patron from Schertz, Texas, took his concerns to comic heights, offering to bribe the writer for contact information on the supposedly displaced whores.

"The closing of the chicken farm (Texas' landmark brothel) near La Grange ruined the New Year's party I had planned to spend with Bonnie,

The May 1971 issue of *Men in Adventure* magazine claimed the Chicken Ranch was a place where prospective customers were regularly drugged and robbed. *Author's collection.*

the queen of the farm. I note in your column that you have received letters from the various pullets. If you can get an old cowhand in touch with Bonnie, I'll personally deliver you a fifth of I.W. Harper bourbon—100 proof!"[425]

For the Chicken Ranch, 1971 was a rough year—no two ways about it. Never before had the brothel received so much media attention, welcome or otherwise. That August, the Associated Press moved a major investigative series on prostitution in Texas. The in-depth package included an extensive question-and-answer-style interview with Edna Milton. Although she remained anonymous throughout and the brothel itself was identified only as "more than 50 miles from the capital of a southwestern state," anyone familiar with the Chicken Ranch instantly recognized it.[426]

A more damning piece came out in May of that year in the pages of the seamy, sensationalistic *Men in Adventure* magazine. Frank C. Reily's tawdry article, "The Half-Million Dollar Sex Salon the Texas Rangers 'Can't' Find," painted a picture of a garish den of sin fueled by booze, drugs and graft, with leering, menacing bouncers and thieving, scheming whores. Though almost entirely fictional, the article caught the attention of the Texas Rangers, no doubt because it mocked the agency for not closing the brothel and implicated them in payoffs and active cover-ups. The article went on file in the Rangers' Austin headquarters, joined by the AP story some months later.[427]

Miss Edna got walloped with a metaphorical two-by-four as well. Her marriage to John Dewey Luke—a man ten years her senior whom she'd married in 1962, just one year after purchasing the Chicken Ranch—fell apart in an ugly way.

"That husband lied so much to me. You know, you just look at him you knew he was lying—you didn't need to ask any questions," Miss Edna said. "He was that type of a liar that he wasn't a good liar at all. A good liar stays close to the truth. They change only a few facts. But he didn't do that at all. He was a bad liar. He'd sit there at the chair or at the table, hell, he'd have his head down looking at the floor. Lying son of a bitch. He'd make up a lie wasn't even close to being real.

"I'm tired of talking to people like that. Don't even want to talk to them," she said. "After a while you just finally get tired of it, and one day when they're out of town, you gather your personal things and leave. And have divorce papers waiting for them when they get back, because I just had them served. Hell, there's no point in going through that crap and trying to fight with them."[428]

Luke reveled in being the center of attention and went far beyond embellishment when it came to overstating his importance. To acquaintances in Austin, he presented himself as the silent partner in the Chicken Ranch, the money man whom Miss Edna had called in from Louisiana in 1961 to front her the $80,000 to purchase the brothel. He liked to flash money and handguns in casual conversation and more than once implied he was tight with various organized crime figures. He never mentioned his marriage to Miss Edna, nor did he offer any proof to his grandiose claims, not least of which was his wildly inflated price of the Chicken Ranch.[429]

On April 17, Miss Edna slapped Luke with a restraining order, forbidding him to go to their shared home at Route 2, Box 43, or contact her in any way. She followed that with a temporary injunction on May 7 and divorced him on June 23.[430]

The stress of the situation took its toll. Miss Edna collapsed and was rushed to the hospital. There, the attending physicians feared she'd suffered a stroke.

"I think I was closer to death than I realized. Dr. Michaelson said, 'You're gambling in every way I can think of,'" Miss Edna said. After extensive tests, they determined she hadn't experienced a stroke but suffered hypoglycemia instead. After going on a special diet, her health stabilized, but the whole experience unnerved her and led her to question her lifestyle.[431]

As rough as 1971 treated Miss Edna and the Chicken Ranch, a flamboyant, forty-nine-year-old deputy with the Harris County Sheriff's Department by the name of Marvin Zindler was having a banner year. Marvin, a publicity-craving dynamo who'd risen to the rank of sergeant in the public relations branch after previous stops in the civil, vice and fugitive divisions, convinced Sheriff Buster Kerns and the district attorney to allow him to set up a new consumer affairs division within the department. Nobody in Houston (or the entire state of Texas, for that matter) could match Marvin's oversized, in-your-face ego. He cheerfully owned up to his own egomania as well as a litany of other shortcomings, though, an unvarnished honesty many found disarming if not downright endearing.

Marvin—dragging his partner, Deputy E.L. Adams, along for the ride—set up shop in a tiny office with the goal of investigating the claims of ripped-off consumers previously dismissed by the police as civil matters. The Spartan office had one distinctly personal touch from Marvin that set the tone for his daily endeavors—on the wall he hung an inscribed sign: "Yea though I walk through the valley of the shadow of death I shall fear no evil. For I am the meanest S.O.B. in the valley."[432]

"I used to see dozens of people come up to the sheriff's department for help because they'd been cheated," Marvin explained. "But because they were cheated by business instead of robbed with a gun everybody always told them there was nothing that could be done. They were told it was a civil case and they'd have to sue. Hell, you could look at those people and know they didn't have the money to sue anybody."[433]

Marvin dove into his new role with gusto. He preferred David v. Goliath cases, championing the little guy from day one—a sort of Robin Hood with a badge. If Marvin couldn't find a particular statute to apply in a particular case, he'd often fall back on "false advertising" laws, which he applied in increasingly creative ways. If that failed to bring the offending business to heel, he'd mastered the art of bludgeoning them into submission by using bad publicity.

"He called news conferences, called stations and said, 'I'm going to be at such-and-such a place this morning and close them down,'" said Larry Conners, a young reporter at KTRK-TV in Houston at the time. "He'd circle the block waiting for the news crews to get there and then come roaring up. He'd always provide us great video."[434]

Marvin assailed anyone and everyone suspected of dishonest business practices. Used-car dealers who cranked back the odometers on vehicles were a favorite target, but in a few short months, Marvin made life rough on overbearing landlords, gas station owners who intentionally miscalibrated pumps, employers who illegally withheld back salaries of employees and a host of other merchants who used false advertising to sucker in customers for bait-and-switch sales.[435]

"It was nothing for Marvin to work 18 to 20 hours a day, seven days a week," said Adams. "Sometimes I'd just get out of the car and tell him I'd had enough, that I was going to go home to my family. He was determined to be the best officer in the department, and if it meant working around the clock that was what he'd do."[436]

From his earliest days, Marvin craved the spotlight. While the neighborhood kids roughhoused with his brothers in a game of football on the front lawn, Marvin himself provided impromptu halftime entertainment by alternately playing his piccolo and twirling a baton. He obsessed over his clothing far more than any other elementary school student would, always dressing stylish and formal. In school photos he stood out, snappily dressed. These nonconformist behaviors earned him scorn from other boys, who taunted him with the nickname "Marvina." By his teenage years, he'd shed some of his effeminate reputation by taking up boxing for a time.[437]

Born in 1921, Marvin grew up in relative affluence due to the efforts of his father, Abe Zindler. Abe, an industrious, hardworking man with deeply held ethics, turned an inherited tailor shop into Zindler's, one of the most successful clothing retailers in Houston. His success insulated the family from the worst hardships of the Great Depression, and in the mid-1930s, he won election as mayor of the then-suburb of Bellaire, quite a feat for a Jew in Houston, which never boasted a Jewish community comparable to cities on the East Coast.[438]

What should have unfolded as an idyllic, feel-good story was anything but. Abe lived a bitter, joyless life filled with an uncontrolled anger he often vented on his family. Demanding unquestioning obedience, he expected all five of his sons to work with him in the store and enjoy it. All of his sons rebelled against these demands to varying degrees, strong-willed Marvin most of all. Their epic battles raged on a nearly continual basis. While the fights rarely, if ever, turned physical, their verbal arguments tended toward the scorched earth variety, barbs so sharp they could draw blood.[439]

"He was a terror, plain and simple," Marvin said. "I was 19 years old before I knew my name wasn't 'Got-Damned Sonofabitch.'"[440]

Marvin dedicated his life to escaping his father's control but time and again fell back into Abe's orbit. When he graduated high school, Marvin took off for distant Stephenville, Texas. Enrolling at John Tarleton Agricultural College (now Tarleton State University) against his father's wishes, Marvin majored in music and became a drum major in the college band his freshman year but soon dropped out and returned to Houston to work in the family store. When World War II erupted, skinny, awkward Marvin enlisted in the marines but got shipped home on a medical discharge before he even completed basic training. Instead of fighting the Axis powers, Marvin joined the Houston auxiliary police, unpaid volunteers used to make up for the loss of regular officers to the armed forces—while continuing to work full time at his father's store. True to form, "Officer Zindler" had the store specially tailor a uniform to his exact specifications. Whenever Marvin made an arrest, he developed a habit of wandering by the HPD press room to share his exploits with any newspaper or radio reporters available. Other officers soon tabbed him as a publicity hound, undermining any credit he earned by putting in long hours on night patrol.[441]

After wrangling an appointment to vice, Marvin visited the Balinese Room at Galveston and won $200. Thereafter, he became a familiar face in the Free State of Galveston, shooting craps and playing blackjack with the best of 'em. He considered it harmless fun—until one night when the owner of one establishment slipped him an envelope full of cash.

During World War II, Marvin Zindler joined the Houston auxiliary police as an unpaid volunteer. *RGD0005F6251-004, Folder 6687, Houston Press Collection, Houston Public Library, HMRC.*

"It suddenly dawned on me what was going on. The gamblers owned the police department, or a big part of it. They owned the city. They just bought it. With that kind of power, there was nothing they couldn't do, if they wanted," Marvin said. "And they seemed to be wanting more all the time. I hadn't been gambling in Houston because it was more fun in Galveston. Until then I didn't realize the money I was losing was going to policemen and politicians to pay them off for helping the mobsters."[442]

As the war ended, Marvin's time with the police auxiliary ended, but his thirst for adventure did not. Still working at the store, he began to moonlight as a disc jockey at radio station KTHT before moving to KATL. *The MZ Show*, as he called it, strived to break new ground as a local, on-the-spot, weekly news program. In practice, lacking any real training, Marvin's crass, sensationalized reports epitomized yellow journalism at its worst. Marvin drove around Houston in a car decked out with police radios, ready to race to the scene of a crime on a moment's notice. If he beat the police to a traffic accident, he'd shove his microphone through any ethical concerns and into the faces of survivors to get the all-important interview.[443]

"How do you feel?" Marvin asked a bloody victim once. "Do you think you're gonna die? What's going through your mind right now?"[444]

His ratings stayed strong enough to keep Marvin on the air, but his antics did little to endear him to Houston's regular press corps. Veteran reporters viewed him as a rich kid playing at being a reporter without really understanding or respecting the Fourth Estate. His popularity made it all the worse. To them, Marvin represented everything journalism shouldn't be.

"Marvin Zindler and I were both police reporters in Houston years ago. I worked for the *Houston Post*. He worked for radio station KATL. He was a little jerk," said former Texas lieutenant governor Bill Hobby. "In any group, there is always someone who's the butt of all the jokes. Among the police reporters, Marvin was that person."[445]

Annoyed with Marvin's ego and self-importance, Jack Weeks of the *Houston Chronicle*, a twenty-year veteran of the police beat, oversaw a truce among himself and the reporters from the *Houston Post, Houston Press* and the three television stations. Gathering in the HPD press room one afternoon, they waited for Marvin to arrive so they could put their elaborate scheme into action.

Soon enough, Marvin arrived, setting down his audio equipment and launching into a grand story about his latest exploit. After a few minutes, one co-conspirator suddenly burst into the press room.

"Hey, did you hear what happened?" he shouted. "The police chief just went over to the courthouse and shot the county judge!"[446]

"The rest of us were in on it of course," Hobby said with a deep belly laugh. "Zindler went ape. He had—as all radio reporters did—he had that little microphone to put on the desk. But somebody had taken Marvin's microphone and taped it to the ceiling where he couldn't get to it. They should've left it there, let that son of a bitch get on the air without it!

"I didn't think much of Zindler when we were both twenty years old," Hobby said between chuckles. "He had the news judgment of an ant…A *retarded* ant."[447]

When KPRC began broadcasting as Houston's first television station in 1949, it didn't take Marvin long to realize the new medium offered an opportunity to get both his voice *and* his face in front of a vast new audience. He left his radio show and began working with Southwest Film Production Company, essentially doing the exact same thing he'd done for his radio program, except now he worked as a one-man film crew. By 1950, he had landed a contract with KPRC to provide film footage of after-hours wrecks and crime and other assorted police activity at the commission rate of twenty-five cents per foot of film used on-air. Unsurprisingly, Marvin worked his tail off for the fledgling news broadcast, and his first check totaled a whopping $2,500. Terms were quickly renegotiated, locking Marvin into a set monthly payout of $400.[448]

That turned into a series of running clashes with station manager Jack Harris. Marvin's contract stipulated he deliver silent film and just show the scene in simple terms—essentially "B-roll"—so that the studio anchors could report the story in voice-over. This ran counter to Marvin's thirst for fame, however, and he began inserting himself into the footage, including audio. When a film roll of Marvin interviewing Humphrey Bogart on-camera

Marvin Zindler embraced his inner yellow journalist as a photographer with the Scripps Howard–owned *Houston Press*. *RGD0005F6687-002, Folder 6687*, Houston Press *Collection, Houston Public Library, HMRC.*

turned up at the station, Harris reached his breaking point. He fired Marvin with a scathing condemnation: "You're too ugly for television."

Years later, Harris disavowed that infamous quote. Sort of.

"If I didn't say it," Harris allowed, "I probably should have."[449]

Again, Marvin landed on his feet—this time at the *Houston Press*, a struggling, distant third to the *Houston Post* and *Houston Chronicle* in terms of both prestige and daily readership. The *Press* survived and drew readers with in-your-face photos and screaming headlines. The understaffed newsroom made up for the long hours and lack of prestige by having a great deal of fun on the job, so much so that one former staff member likened it to "riding on a drunken trolley car." Marvin, naturally, fit right in.[450]

Or rather, Marvin fit in a little *too* well. Whereas the other journalists on staff liked to push the envelope in their pursuit of a tawdry story, they had basic lines their integrity wouldn't allow them to cross. Marvin, on the other hand, ignored such petty concerns. Once, while playing the role of paparazzi to the hilt, he set his sights on getting photo proof that tempestuous lovers and Houston's A-list jet-set celebrities Shepherd King and Samia Gamal had reunited. And get the shot he did, by breaking into their shared mansion and sneaking into their bedroom to photograph the couple, entwined in satin sheets, sleeping in each other's arms.[451]

If anything, Marvin behaved even worse at crime scenes. Once, when he didn't think a stabbing victim looked injured enough for a newspaper photo, he splashed a bottle of ketchup across the man's chest for the picture.

"He lied to me and told me he didn't do it," said Marvin's editor at the time, Vance Trimble. "But I knew he did. And he knew I knew. I don't think he ever did anything like that again."[452]

Such high-flying days couldn't last. In 1954, when the parent company learned of the extent of the *Houston Press'* outrageous coverage, the hammer came down, hard. Placed on a short leash, Marvin didn't find the newspaper business fun anymore. To make matters worse, his father offered him an ultimatum: come back to the store for $2,000 a month or get cut off entirely and try living on his $400 monthly paycheck from the paper. Marvin reluctantly accepted his father's offer. By that point, Marvin had burned through five different jobs in as many years.[453]

IN A PERFECT WORLD, time would have softened his father's ferocious personality some. But the world Marvin lived in was far from perfect. Abe hadn't mellowed one iota. Marvin felt trapped, with no hope of escape. He put his generous monthly income to good use as he saw it, however, by investing in cosmetic surgery. By the standards of the time, such a thing bordered on scandalous, but the cutting dismissal from KPRC stuck in Marvin's craw. He got a nose job, dramatically slimming and flattening his prominent nasal bridge. Surgically implanted cartilage built up his weak chin to a more dynamic profile. He also took to shaving the top of his head and wearing a hairpiece out of fear of someday going bald. By the end of the 1950s, Marvin literally looked like a new man, ready to start a fresh chapter in his life.[454]

The ferocious battles with his father, Abe, grew so bad that Marvin attempted to branch out with his own clothing store, just to escape. That the venture quickly failed in spectacular fashion did nothing to weaken Marvin's resolve to never work for his father again. In need of a job and wanting to get back into law enforcement, Marvin threw caution to the wind and asked longtime Harris County sheriff Buster Kern for a job. Marvin had campaigned for a Kern challenger several elections prior, so he viewed his

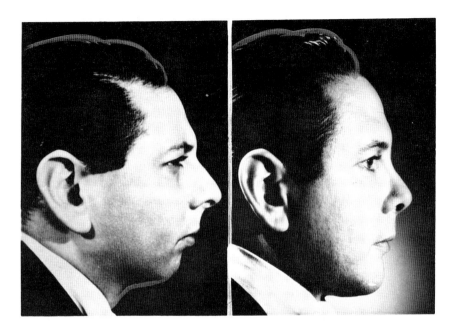

Reportedly fired from KPRC-TV for being "too ugly for television," Marvin Zindler responded in perhaps the most Marvin Zindler way possible—by undergoing extensive cosmetic surgery and documenting every step of the process. *RGD0005f6687-001, Folder 6687*, Houston Press *Collection, Houston Public Library, HMRC.*

prospects as slim. Surprising everyone—Marvin included—Sheriff Kern made him a deputy right away. It didn't come out until years later that Abe, in a rare moment of compassion, relented and put in a good word with the sheriff for his son. Perhaps he finally realized that his son would never make a good retailer, or maybe he thought Sheriff Kern would whip some maturity into his playboy son. Either way, Marvin landed feet-first back in the middle of the action.[455]

For a decade, Marvin reigned unopposed as the most flamboyant deputy in Harris County. He carried two pearl-handled six-shooters and had a whole wardrobe of tailored uniforms. Even his official business cards caused more than a few raised eyebrows—with his named printed in golden, Old English script over a glossy black background.[456]

Everything he did maximized his media exposure, no matter how menial the job. His first assignment with the sheriff's department involved serving papers, as routine as they come. Yet Marvin dominated every headline in the city when he seized a fully laden freighter ready to depart the Houston ship channel because of $900 in back pay owed one aggrieved seaman.[457]

During the years he worked in the fugitive division, shuttling around the country picking up and transporting prisoners, Marvin visited Fayette County several times, working closely with Sheriff Jim Flournoy. On one occasion, Marvin asked Big Jim about the Chicken Ranch and how it had operated openly for so many years.

"He told me that it was the way the people wanted it," Marvin said. "He was a pretty nice old fellow."[458]

After moving to vice, Marvin displayed his creativity and tenacity in a big way when he took on Houston's notorious X-rated movie houses. Prosecutors failed over and over again to close them on obscenity charges, but Marvin took a different approach entirely. State law forbade the sale of alcohol in porn theaters, but these movie houses got around the ban by serving brew with less than 2 percent alcohol—so-called near beer. Signage in the theaters merely listed "beer," so Marvin, with newspaper and television reporters in tow, made the rounds one night and shut them all down for deceptive advertising practices.[459]

Marvin's unshakeable belief in himself and the righteousness of his cause eventually caught up to him in 1971, when he executed a judgment against the wrong person. Papers in hand, Marvin arrived at the owner's business and served the papers—despite the man's protests of his innocence. Marvin, perhaps believing in his own mythology a bit too much, refused to accept the possibility he might be mistaken.

"The guy, the owner of the property, said, 'Please don't do this. Please don't put me out of business. Let me go to the bank and borrow the money to pay this off,'" said Oliver Kitzman. "It was something like $2,500. He took Marvin's execution papers with him, went to the bank and borrowed the money, then came back and paid it under protest, then later sued the county for it and the bonding company involved and all that.

"They tried the case without a jury in front of Judge Tom Stovall. During the course of the trial, it became clear that Marvin had wavered on his integrity a little in the testimony."[460]

When Judge Stovall called Marvin on his inconsistent statements, Marvin grudgingly allowed that he may have "misspoken" during his testimony. Judge Stovall ruled in favor of the plaintiff.[461]

Such misfires by Marvin made it easy for other officers to dismiss him as a poseur, an attention-seeking dandy hardly worthy to wear a badge. Around the sheriff's department, other officers showed their contempt by nicknaming him "Deputy Dawg." By the time Jack Heard defeated Sheriff Kerns in the 1972 election, Marvin had few defenders in the department

Working in the vice division under Harris County Sheriff Buster Kern, Deputy Marvin Zindler—shown here with Sidney R. Miller—succeeded in closing down many of Houston's notorious X-rated theaters and peep shows. *RGD0005f6687-003, Folder 6687, Houston Press Collection, Houston Public Library, HMRC.*

and nonstop complaints rolling in from the Houston business community. His days were clearly numbered.

Looking to jump before being pushed, Marvin made an appointment with Ray Miller, news director at NBC affiliate KPRC-TV, to talk about a job. Halfway to the interview, Zinder got called back for a meeting with the new sheriff. The meeting lasted more than two hours, ending with Sheriff Heard offing him a stark choice: resign or be fired. Marvin refused to resign and received his dismissal. True to form, Marvin promptly called a press conference to tell the world he'd been sacked.[462]

IN THE HOUSTON TELEVISION news market at that time, KPRC—channel 2— consistently finished first in the ratings, followed by CBS affiliate KHOU, channel 11. Dead last came ABC affiliate KTRK on channel 13. With poor ratings cutting into the bottom line, KTRK needed something—anything— that would force Houston viewers to give the news broadcasts a second look.

"I had just finished the evening's newscast. [Assistant news director] Gene Burke was sitting across from me. I was just winding down from completing the news and I looked up at Gene," recalled longtime news anchor Dave Ward. "Almost simultaneously we said something like, 'Why don't we get Marvin Zindler as a consumer reporter?' The idea, strange as it may sound, had hit Gene and me at the same time."[463]

Ward tracked down Marvin's phone number and made the call.

"The telephone rang several times, then Marvin picked up the phone," Ward said. "I told him what Gene Burke and I were thinking about. I asked Marvin if he would consider coming over to the station as a consumer reporter."

"Dave, you must have been reading my mind," Marvin replied. "It must be ESP. There is nothing I would rather do than come over and discuss that very thing with you."[464]

Marvin never rescheduled his interview with KPRC. Instead, he called a press conference to announce his future plans—which mainly consisted of making life difficult for KPRC and KHOU from that point on.

"All the stations went, because he'd always provide us great video," said Conners. "One of our photographers was there shooting, and he told me that when Marvin said, 'I'm going to go work for Channel 13!' the Channel 2 photographer said, '*Shiiiit*,' and turned off his camera!"[465]

The marriage of convenience between Marvin and KTRK was not a match made in heaven, though. Marvin drew eyeballs to the newscast sure enough—he'd been a minor celebrity in Houston long enough to guarantee a following. But his relentless self-promotion, which had grated on coworkers in the sheriff department—not to mention his media peers a decade before— showed no sign of abating. If anything, Marvin turned his bombastic approach up a notch for television. That, coupled with a lack of any formal journalistic training, made him the very definition of a loose cannon.

"You know, I liked Marvin, and we became friends, but when it came to doing anything on the air, we had to be real careful and double-check stuff," Conners said. "They put us together on a program called *Dial M for Marvin*. We were an ABC station, and they ran it on Saturday nights against Archie Bunker on CBS, which was obviously a hot program at that time.

"So we are teamed up, and it's a long table with Marvin at one end and I at the other, and whoever the guest was would sit in the center. The first program opened with a Houston madam, and she was going to tell her story," he said. "It became apparent to me that I can't control him. I finally had to tell the director, 'You've got to cut his mic and just come to me. There is no other way we can stop him.' We'd be in a commercial, and Marvin in the background would still be going on and on!"[466]

Dial M for Marvin lasted only part of one season. Its brief, tumultuous run presaged the reality TV craze that swept the nation's airwaves decades later, as well as audience-shocking talk shows driven by over-the-top personalities such as Morton Downey Jr. and Jerry Springer. *Dial M for Marvin* established the format they all eventually adopted.

"We followed that up with a program on the Klan. We had Klansmen come in all in this full regalia. Marvin wanted them to do the full bit. Again, it made for great TV," Conners said. "We had a doctor talking about venereal disease, gonorrhea and so forth and Marvin just—again, it was never clear where he would go—he asked the doctor, 'I want you to look into the camera and tell these kids watching that they can't get crabs from toilet seats. Tell them! Tell them they can't get it from toilet seats!' So, the doctor said, 'No, unless it's a hairy toilet seat they tend to slide right off.' That was kind of how the program went."[467]

Despite these experiments in expanding the Marvin Zindler franchise, his "Action 13" consumer affairs reports on the evening newscast remained KTRK's bread-and-butter. Negligent landlords, shady home repair vendors and crooked used-car dealers provided plenty of fodder for his never-ending crusade for the common man. The weekly restaurant report from the health inspector's office became a popular staple of his segments, and Marvin's full-throated roar of "*Slime* in the ice machine!" became his most enduring catchphrase.

"I know a lot of businessmen out there don't really understand me or what I'm doing," Marvin said. "And I know they talk about me and say a lot of tough things about what they'll do if I ever show up at their place.

"It doesn't bother me," he said, grinning impishly. "It's like a lot of people will say Muhammad Ali is a cowardly nigger sonofabitch.

Less than a year into his tenure as the consumer affairs reporter for KTRK-TV, Marvin Zindler set his sights on taking down the Chicken Ranch. *Courtesy Special Collections, University of Houston Libraries.*

"But they don't say it to his face."[468]

KTRK's ratings started climbing. Marvin's shtick played well and drew a steadily growing audience to the newscast. There was just one problem— as a consumer affairs reporter, his reach was limited. His fame might rival anyone else's in Houston, but exposing the double-dealings of local businesses would never amount to much on a national stage. Yes, he made a very real difference in the lives of those people he helped, but his insatiable ego craved more attention, more adulation.

For that, Marvin needed much bigger fish to fry.

Chapter 11

WHEELS WITHIN WHEELS

Many stories purport to explain the "real reason" Marvin Zindler targeted the Chicken Ranch: Sheriff Jim Flournoy ticketed Marvin for speeding through Fayette County, incensing Marvin; or, Marvin's son lost a considerable amount of money while gambling in Fayette County, and Sheriff Flournoy refused to intervene in the matter; or, Marvin got thrown out of the Chicken Ranch himself and vowed revenge.

One theory centers on an early '70s newspaper article about the Chicken Ranch written by a couple of Southwest Texas State University students, Bill Boe and Peggy Meek. The piece, published in the school newspaper, supposedly attracted Marvin's attention, alerting him to the brothel's existence.

The best of the bunch, however, held that Zinder went after the Chicken Ranch with such vigor because he visited as a customer one time, asked for "the best woman here" and his daughter walked out (or, alternatively, she enjoyed working there so much he couldn't get her to quit).[469]

None of those explanations is true. Simply put, Marvin investigated the Chicken Ranch because Assistant Attorney General Herb Hancock Jr. talked him into it.

MARVIN'S INVOLVEMENT DID NOT come about in a straightforward manner. Following the firing of the chippie "Mary Jane" from both the Wagon Wheel and the Chicken Ranch in 1971, the aggrieved DPS Criminal Intelligence officer from Houston set to make good on his threats to shut down the brothels. With carefully reasoned comments and suggestions, he planted the seeds that

Former assistant attorney general Herb Hancock. *Author photo.*

transformed perception of the Chicken Ranch from an amusing oddity to a malignant cancer. The strategy worked. The Houston criminal intelligence office—which to that point had ignored the distant country brothels because of more pressing urban crime than could reasonably be investigated in a lifetime—abruptly took a direct, even obsessive interest in the brothels.

Captain George E. Read headed up the regional office in the early 1970s. A well-respected special agent with DPS intelligence, Read made a name for himself through his exhaustive investigative work and testimony before the Texas legislature during the slant well oil field scandals of the 1960s. His top officers—Agent Thomas A. Davis Jr. (who would go on to head the office himself), Sergeant Charlie Whitcomb and Agent James R. Wilson—joined Captain Read in vocal opposition to the continued operation of the Chicken Ranch. Hancock, then a thirty-two-year-old assistant district attorney for Harris County, heard the complaints from the officers time and again. At the time, he assisted both the DPS and Houston Police Department vice squads in processing warrants for raids against the many peep shows then flourishing in the Houston area. Whenever Hancock worked with DPS Criminal Intelligence, though, the officers invariably complained about the double standard of enforcing vice laws in Houston while the Chicken Ranch and Wagon Wheel operated freely.[470]

"There was a number of officers that worked out of the Houston office at that time, and one of their biggest complaints was they could not get the ability to close the Ranch down," Hancock said. "They could not get the local authorities to assist them in closing the Ranch down. No one would accept charges.

"It was just a grumbling or an outcry by law enforcement that said, basically, 'There is a violation of the law in this area, and we can't take care of it.' I'd hear it. You, as a prosecutor, can't do anything about it. You can't convince the folks there is an unequal way of enforcing the law in Texas," he explained. "You enforce it in Beaumont, but you won't enforce it in Sealy and La Grange. You enforce it in Houston, but you won't enforce it in Sealy and La Grange. Those are the allegations that kept floating around, and I was not successful in getting anything done by the local officials.

"There's not much that you can do when you're fighting an institution that's been around for as long as [the Chicken Ranch had] been around," he said. "If it is, in fact, a violation of the law to run a whorehouse in Texas, then there should be no difference there than it is in any part of the state of Texas."[471]

Nobody in Houston pounded the war drums harder than Captain Read, however. Determined to end the DPS' long-standing tolerance of the Chicken Ranch and Wagon Wheel, Captain Read committed considerable criminal intelligence resources to the investigation of the brothels. On November 17, 1972, he dispatched a pair of DPS officers to conduct surveillance of the Chicken Ranch, and things quickly got interesting.

The officers set up shop in the middle of the afternoon in clear view of the turnoff to the Chicken Ranch, on the right-of-way beside Highway 71. A little after sunset, a Fayette County deputy drove past the stake-out and up to the house. Fifteen minutes later, the deputy returned, parking in front of the DPS officers and spotlighting them in his high-beams as he radioed in to the sheriff's office. At 8:15 p.m., the sheriff arrived.[472]

Sheriff Jim Flournoy, as an old-school lawman and former Texas Ranger, held the highway patrol in low regard. He didn't view them as serious officers but, rather, glorified traffic cops and made no secret of his displeasure when DPS reforms ended long-standing prohibition to their joining the Rangers.

"I have a great respect for the old Rangers. But today all they've got is a bunch of plain-clothed highway patrolmen, who'll never control anything but traffic," Big Jim groused. "Hell, I never wrote a traffic ticket in my life."[473]

Big Jim unfolded his towering six-foot, four-inch frame out of his sheriff's car. On the passenger side, a deputy unloaded himself, casually cradling a shotgun in the crook of one arm. Big Jim sized them up, introduced himself and demanded to know what they were doing in his county. The DPS officers, doubtless familiar with Big Jim's take-no-bullshit brand of law enforcement, felt more than a little vulnerable given the circumstances. They admitted they were taking pictures of the cars driving in to visit the Chicken Ranch.

"Well, who sent you down here?" Big Jim demanded.

"The boss did," they answered.

"Who is your boss?" Big Jim asked, certain that Colonel Wilson "Pat" Speir, director of the DPS, wouldn't authorize such an operation—certainly not without clearing it locally first.

"Out of Houston."

Houston. The pieces immediately clicked for Big Jim.

"You with intelligence?" Big Jim asked slyly, already sure of Captain Read's involvement.

"Yeah."

"It doesn't take very much intelligence to know what's going on up there. Every little farm boy knows what's going on up there," he unloaded on them. "I've been running this county for 65 years and we'll advise the Department of Public Safety whenever we need its help."[474]

Subsequent reports indicated Big Jim and his deputies held the DPS officers at gunpoint, but the sheriff dismissed the accusations. Even Hancock considered the claims overblown—and also a strong indication that the Chicken Ranch investigation was, in fact, a rogue operation.

"From my experience, if they were out there with the blessing of [Colonel Speir], that when he pulled out that shotgun, the next time he figured out what was happening was when they shot him," Hancock said. "I don't know if they were out there with anyone's blessing, because they folded their tent and left."[475]

The fact that a swarm of Texas Rangers didn't descend on Fayette County to bring Big Jim and his deputies in for threatening a Texas DPS officer on state business is pretty clear indication that 1) the threat never happened and 2) the officer wasn't conducting official state business, Hancock said. That Big Jim was a legendary sheriff and former Texas Ranger held in high esteem didn't enter into it. Professional deference only went so far.[476]

Despite the confrontation, the stakeout returned the following day before ending operations in Fayette County. The officers counted 145 vehicles driving up to the Chicken Ranch on Friday, with another 142 following suit on Saturday. One license plate was traced to a Fort Worth pimp and another to a man under investigation for drug trafficking and tax evasion.

The DPS estimated each vehicle carried two to three passengers and stayed at the brothel anywhere between twenty minutes and two hours. From these figures, Captain Read's men estimated that the Chicken Ranch grossed an eye-popping $1.5 million annually, although other estimates tabbed the cash flow at less than a third of that figure.[477]

For her part, Edna Milton scoffed at such high-flying estimates of annual cash flow at her "little country whorehouse."

"Anyone who saw my home would say that anyone making that much money wouldn't have my furniture," Miss Edna said, dismissively.

Likewise, Wagon Wheel owner Jerry McKay insisted his actual take from his Sealy brothel came nowhere near the DPS figures.

"If I was making a million dollars a year," McKay said, "I'd have quit after the first year, and I'd still be rich."[478]

In late 1972, John Hill won election as attorney general, and even before he officially took office in January 1973, he set up an organized crime task force to be headed by Assistant Attorney General Tim James. No such group had ever operated in Texas before, and the scope of James' powers under state law remained vague. Hill's entire career to that point had thrived under a strategy of aggressive enforcement, and with his eye on higher office, Hill saw no reason to back off on that approach.

"When you talk about fighting organized crime in Texas, John, you've got to look at the kind of people we'll be taking on," James warned Hill during

Texas Attorney General John Hill. *Courtesy Texas State Library and Archives Commission.*

an early meeting. "You're talking about people who have some standing and some prominence and wealth in the community. That's what organized crime traditionally had tried to do and very successfully had done. They've established leadership roles with those people of great substance in the community."

"Well, I think that I have great substance and worth and standing in this community," Hill answered, emboldened following his successful campaign. "Let's just take those suckers on, and we'll see who wins."[479]

At the time, Hill would have found the prospects of his organized crime task force spending the better part of a year investigating the Chicken Ranch laughable.

But Hill failed to give his task force much guidance or direction, leaving the door open for others to greatly influence James and his team.

Almost immediately, Otis Klar, a fourteen-year veteran DPS officer from Read's office, landed an assignment to the task force, along with former Houston Police Department vice officer Bobby Bell. Both men knew each other well and began working to convince James that the Chicken Ranch and the Wagon Wheel were the most pressing organized crime problems facing Texas.[480]

Not content with the influence his two men wielded on the task force, Captain Read wasted little time in setting up a one-on-one meeting with James, bringing the assistant attorney general to his Houston headquarters.

"Let me show you something," Captain Read said, picking up the phone to make a call. "Hello, I've got twelve guys coming in on a deer hunt this weekend, and I'm going to bring them over there Friday night. How many girls you gonna have?"

"I'll have ten that night and eleven the next," Miss Edna answered, her voice clearly audible. "I can handle everybody you've got, so c'mon."[481]

The casual, business-as-usual attitude of Miss Edna shocked James, who expected a more cautious, guarded response from an illegal brothel. The meeting with Captain Read, along with his long discussions with Klar and Bell, won James over and convinced him the Chicken Ranch had grown too powerful, too untouchable, too dangerous to ignore any longer.

"The Chicken Ranch was the one great festering, frustrating sore on the face of law enforcement in Texas," James later said, repeating the Houston DPS office's list of well-polished talking points. "Whenever people gathered and I talked about our efforts against crime, I always get the same, sorry question: 'If you're so worried about crime, why don't you do something about that wide-open whorehouse in La Grange?'"[482]

Nearly giddy at the prospect of taking down such a well-known target as the Chicken Ranch, James brought it up with Colonel Speir at his first opportunity. Expecting lavish praise, James received, instead, the equivalent of a cold shower.

"The Chicken Ranch? I sure hope you know what you're getting into," Colonel Speir said in a none-too-subtle tone of disapproval. "You'll be facing some of the most severe opposition you can imagine."[483]

Nothing if not persistent, James didn't let the meeting with Colonel Speir dissuade him. Klar presented James with the files the Houston office of DPS Criminal Intelligence had collected on the Chicken Ranch and Wagon Wheel—an investigation authorized by Read but, tellingly, not by Colonel

Edna Milton in the uniquely decorated parlor of the Chicken Ranch. Commercial ashtrays were strategically positioned after every second chair. *Courtesy Edna Milton Chadwell.*

Speir. Despite the massive amount of evidence already compiled showing the houses openly engaged in prostitution, James could not convince any prosecutor with jurisdiction to bring charges against them. Frustrated by the inaction, James decided to launch his own investigation, using the DPS file as a foundation. In February 1973, he brought in Hancock and Neal Duval from Houston as assistant DAs to head up the project, most likely on the strength of recommendations from Klar, Captain Read and others from Houston.[484]

No longer a mere spectator, Hancock dove right into his work. It didn't take him long to figure out he was fighting an uphill battle.

"The department had been monitoring the Chicken Ranch for years. I was amazed they couldn't shut them down," Hancock said. "Hell, if the Rangers couldn't do it, Jesus Christ himself couldn't."[485]

Once James' organized crime task force launched its formal investigation, Captain Read's men backed off and let the legal team take point. Hancock himself staked out both brothels, counting cars and taking down license plate numbers. One day while parked across from the Wagon Wheel, a highway patrolman pulled over to grill Hancock. After showing his identification, Hancock interviewed the officer instead.

"Say, do you know there's a whorehouse working right over there?" Hancock asked.

"Sure. Everybody knows about it," the confused officer answered.

"Do you know it's a violation of the law to run a whorehouse?" Hancock asked.

"Yes."

"Why isn't it closed down? Do you know if anyone is being paid off? Why don't the Rangers close it down?"

"There's politicians involved," the officer replied, surely thinking by now this must be some sort of a put-on. "DPS won't get involved because it's local folks in charge."[486]

Exasperated by the exchange, Hancock decided he needed witnesses to testify against the Wagon Wheel in court. When a bus from Houston pulled up to the brothel one night and disgorged thirty-five conventioneers, Hancock thought his case made. He'd simply wait for them to finish their revels and then pull the bus over as it left and take their names and statements. The bus drove around behind the Wagon Wheel to park, and Hancock waited all night for it to drive back out. It never did—instead, the bus sneaked away via a back road.[487]

"I thought I was a pretty good investigator, and I lost a damn bus with thirty-five folks on it. I didn't know where it went!" Hancock said, laughing at his own ineptitude. "That's the funniest thing that ever happened to me because we were going to stop it and see who was on board. We were so naïve as to believe they didn't know what we were doing or why we were there."[488]

Meanwhile, other agents working for James' task force had made contact with two brothers heavily involved in the Houston vice scene. The brothers told the undercover agents that Wagon Wheel owner Jerry McKay was looking to sell the Sealy brothel, and negotiations quickly began. Meeting in Houston with a certified public accountant, the brothers opened the brothel's books to the prospective buyers and named an asking price of $1 million. The agents countered with $300,000 before backing out of negotiations and turning their information over to the IRS.

"That really would have been nice for us to have gone ahead and done ourselves," James said. "They even showed our man how to manage the cash flow. They bought him hook, line and sinker."[489]

By April, James judged they had gathered enough evidence to shut down both houses a dozen times over. He presented the files to Attorney General

John Hill, who turned the case over to the local district attorney, Oliver Kitzman, whose district just happened to include both La Grange and Sealy. Kitzman, much to James' dismay, declined to pursue the case.[490]

"At the time all this was happening, the operation of a 'bawdyhouse,' as the law books say, was a misdemeanor. The responsibility for enforcing any laws in connection with that rested upon the county attorney and not the district attorney, because the county attorney prosecuted all misdemeanors," explained Kitzman. "Perhaps I could've done something about it—the power without the responsibility—if I wanted to, which I didn't. But I saw no reason to bring that point up with the press because it just would've caused the county attorney [to] be dragged into the thing unnecessarily and it would've been reported as an evasion of my responsibility. So I didn't mention it and let it go."[491]

Regardless of Kitzman's reasons for declining the case, Attorney General Hill regarded the matter as closed. He held no follow-up meetings with James, no strategy sessions to plan a new approach to take down the brothels. Privately, the attorney general likely breathed a sigh of relief that the whorehouse crusade ended so abruptly, without attracting any wider political or media fallout.

For James, Duvall, Hancock and the rest of the task force, the utter failure of their investigation came as a crushing disappointment. That months of effort, untold man-hours and who knows how much taxpayers' money spent investigating the brothels had gone for naught was too much to bear. Unwilling to accept defeat and discard all their hard-won evidence, a halfhearted idea emerged to continue monitoring both the Chicken Ranch and Wagon Wheel, gathering more evidence in the hope of uncovering a mythical smoking gun that might someday force prosecutors to act.

To Hancock, a former state trooper and Nacogdoches native, the prospect of continuing to bang his head into a brick wall held zero appeal. There had to be a different approach, he reasoned, a different strategy that could succeed where others failed. And suddenly, a name jumped out at him like a lighthouse beacon through the fog: Marvin Zindler.

"We weren't ever going to close the thing down unless somebody other than the local officials got involved in it. The governor wouldn't do it because the local representative and senator were not going to stand for it," Hancock explained. "So the only avenue left was just to get an aggressive person with the press to get involved in it. Marvin was new at Channel 13, and he was about as wild…he was a little bit *innovative* in the way he handled things, and he was not afraid of the old devil himself.

"Marvin was kind of an odd duck at best," he said. "I guess when I started out at the district attorney office [in Houston], he was one of my better friends. I was always attracted to oddballs, and he fit into that category."[492]

Still, getting Marvin involved amounted to a desperate, Hail Mary pass for Hancock. The task force investigation existed only on life support, if not already dead. Hancock, an idealistic—some might have said self-righteous—believer in equal justice under the law, couldn't bear to see all their hard work go for naught without one final effort, no matter how futile.

Certain that the infamous Chicken Ranch amounted to a hanging curveball for Marvin's swing-for-the-fences theatrics, Hancock met with his old friend at the coffee shop in Houston's venerable Rice Hotel in April 1973 and pitched the idea. Marvin listened patiently as Hancock spelled out the findings of the task force and of the prior criminal intelligence investigation. Then Hancock outlined the dead ends and road blocks thrown up in their way, preventing prosecution, and how media attention could make an end-run around the brothels' protection and turn the tide of public opinion. Marvin carefully considered everything Hancock told him before answering.

Marvin didn't say no, he said *hell no.*

Going after used-car dealers who rolled back odometers played well locally and did real good for those taken in by the scams, but who were the aggrieved victims of the brothels? Dissatisfied customers weren't exactly flooding Marvin's mailbox with complaints about whores shorting them five minutes out of a thirty-minute "date." Nobody would raise much of a stink if he went after the Wagon Wheel, but the Chicken Ranch had powerful political friends and popular local support. "Foolhardy" didn't begin to describe the folly of taking on the Chicken Ranch. To Hancock's utter disappointment, Marvin flat-out refused to get involved.

Hancock, fresh off four months of investigative work, didn't give up so easily. He continued to see Marvin socially whenever work took him back to Houston, often drinking coffee together in the mornings. At every opportunity, Hancock went after Marvin, much as the criminal intelligence officers had gone after him the previous year, adopting a strategy of shaming Marvin into picking up the investigation.

"Marvin had been down there himself as a youngster. I accused him of that. He never did admit to it, but I accused him of knowing of its existence," Hancock said. "I raised hell with him just as the officers raised hell with me.

"We were friends, but it became something of, 'You know about this. You are a news reporter yet you sit on your hands and won't say anything about it,'" Hancock said, explaining how he hammered Marvin over and over with an argument Marvin had no easy answer for. "It got to be, 'You won't do anything about it. You bitch because the law enforcement won't do anything about it. Who in the hell do you think's going to do anything about it?'"[493]

Hancock's verbal badgering took its toll. Even as Marvin refused, his resolve wavered. Hancock made a convincing case, and busting up a crime ring running out of the famous Chicken Ranch would easily make the biggest story of Marvin's career. His insatiable ego began warming to the idea. After all, the reports Hancock kept citing placed the Chicken Ranch at the center of as many as fifteen major prostitution circuits spanning the length and breadth of Texas. By cutting off the head of the snake, he could cripple organized crime statewide and send more than a few pimps scrambling for a different line of work. Wasn't that what heroes did? Wasn't that what *legends* did?[494]

And to become a legend, didn't one have to first kill a legend?

Finally, during one of Hancock's coffee shop harangues, Marvin reached his tipping point.

A frontal view of the Chicken Ranch as it looked in the early 1970s from the main right-of-way. *Courtesy* Dallas Morning News.

"All right, you son of a bitch, you get me something to work with and I'll get after it," Marvin abruptly blurted out. "I can't do anything unless you get me something solid, because this damn thing will come apart on me if I don't."[495]

If Hancock could produce those DPS files he kept talking about, Marvin said, then the story became more than just a couple of country whorehouses. The story became one of political corruption, the impotence of law enforcement and the power of organized crime. *If* he had the files, then the story had substance—and, more importantly, Marvin had a defense against any potential political fallout.

To provide the confidential files Marvin demanded meant breaking any number of state regulations, which would quite likely cost Hancock his job if discovered. The risk, though, was worth it, he judged. For his own protection, Hancock extracted a condition of his own—the source of the investigation report must remain anonymous, no matter how much heat ultimately came down on Marvin.

"Marvin had to have something concrete before he would get involved in it, so I somehow got my hands on an offense report from the Department of Public Safety that reflected some of their investigative work," Hancock said. "It involved the number of cars that were going in and out. It was an investigative report which indicated how much money that was in the operation, how many girls were usually working on a weekly basis, who did the physicals on the girls, where the circuit was for the girls coming in and out. Things that were important for a reporter to use when he started working on a story."[496]

It took a while, but Hancock managed to smuggle the investigation report out of DPS offices. The subterfuge hardly rose to Watergate levels, but Hancock took it very seriously, deciding to keep his plan secret from Attorney General Hill and other coworkers to protect them from retaliation if things went wrong. On July 4, 1973, he met Marvin again in the Rice Hotel and handed over the documents.[497]

"When I gave him that report, his eyes lit up like two damn flashlights," Hancock said. "[The files] were not something I could [normally] get my hands on. He could not or would not do anything until he got that. After he got that offense report, he kind of took it and run with it.

"He promised me at that time that he would not reveal his source, and he never did as long as I worked for the attorney general's office. He was a person of his word," Hancock said. "I started ducking and dodging for fear of losing my job. It was a very good job, one that I left the district attorney's office in Harris County for, and I certainly didn't want to embarrass John Hill or Tim James at the time this thing was going on. John Hill could've done anything from [telling me] 'Good boy' to 'Hit the road, Jack,' so I didn't take a chance in that respect."[498]

With that, Marvin finally had his hard evidence: the official report from the Houston office of DPS Criminal Intelligence filed by Captain Read in December 1972. The flames he fanned with that file would soon sweep across Texas.[499]

"I did not expect Marvin to really make any headway," Hancock admitted. "I knew Marvin was crazy, but I didn't know he was *that* crazy."[500]

Chapter 12

NOT WITH A BANG

KTRK-TV news producer Garvin Berry called Larry Conners into his office one afternoon in mid-July 1973. To Conners' utter astonishment, Berry offered him an unusual assignment, to say the least: team with Marvin Zindler in an undercover operation to bust the infamous Chicken Ranch in La Grange.

Conners had arrived at the Houston TV station from Amarillo a couple years before, and the management viewed the twenty-six-year-old as a reporter with a level head and sound news judgment. The fact that Conners was single, too, didn't go unnoticed.

Conners, an Austin native who'd grown up in West Texas, had heard of the Chicken Ranch all his life. It took him about two seconds to make up his mind.

"I thought it would be a great story. I thought it would be a blockbuster. I mean, it was a Texas tradition, obviously," Conners said. "Management knew [Marvin] needed someone to work with him, somebody they trusted on the intelligence side, because Marvin was a little flamboyant. You know, flamboyant is good TV, but he's not always under control and sticking to facts. So they kind of teamed us up together."[501]

Marvin brought Conners up to speed on the allegations of corruption, organized crime and money laundering that Hancock had passed along. The rumor that Sheriff Flournoy had threatened DPS officers seemed to confirm something much worse than prostitution had taken root in La Grange.

"The intelligence officers had gone in and said they were thrown down on by the sheriff and run off. They were ticked off and wanted to make an issue out of it—that's what I was told by Marvin," Conners said. "I think he later recanted that story and said it wasn't exactly set up like that. But that's what I was told at the time.

"It gave us an excuse," he said. "I mean, it wasn't in our coverage area or anything, but we knew it obviously had potential for statewide impact. To me, it was going to be a great story. Finally, something was going to be done about [the Chicken Ranch]."[502]

As the planning of the operation progressed, a sophisticated, cloak-and-dagger scheme took form, like something out of *Mission: Impossible*. At least, that's what it sounded like to Conners and cameraman Frank Ambrose, the team handling the fieldwork for the undercover investigation; Marvin would stay behind in the studio. To infiltrate the brothels, the station promised them a miniaturized Minolta spy camera, ensuring plenty of incriminating photos. The station also promised a stealthy, unmarked car suitable for investigative reporters intent on keeping a low profile.

Reality intruded rudely on the mid-July D-Day. The high-tech Minolta spy camera never materialized. Instead, Conners received a regular 35mm camera with a very large lens and was told to make do. And their stealthy undercover vehicle turned out to be a beat-up old van painted a garish orange with curtained windows. Conners felt a sinking feeling as he watched all the best-laid plans fall to pieces before even leaving the studio.

"So, they gave me this 35mm camera with a big lens on it, and I decided I had to wear an army field jacket. Here was this [summer] day, and it looks kind of stupid, but it was the only way I could conceal the thing," Conners explained. "I'd have it down in the pocket and kind of lift it up. I have to get more than half the camera out to get the lens out. When I fired it, to me it sounded like a shotgun. Every time. I just knew I'd get caught."[503]

Setting their misgivings aside, the newsmen climbed into the van and set out for La Grange and Sealy. Along for the ride was a Yankee friend of Ambrose's visiting from New York who thought it would be fun to see what real television journalism looked like.

"We're laying out what we're doing, and his friend…I don't even know if his friend *really* knew what we were doing 'til we're driving together and he realizes what's going on," Conners said, as he and Ambrose discussed their plan of attack all the way to La Grange. "We're just charged up. We think it's going to be a great story. Frank was charged up and ready."

As they approached La Grange, Conners uttered the most prophetic words of his life.

"I think this story will have legs," he said. "It will go quite a ways."[504]

The unlikely trio pulled into the dusty parking lot at the Chicken Ranch around 7:00 p.m., easing the big van up underneath a copse of oak trees. Their parking spot served two purposes: 1) it gave Ambrose a clear view of the front of the house and anyone coming or going, and 2) it offered a bit of shade from the brutal Texas sun, which wouldn't set for another hour and a half.

After taking a few moments to psyche themselves up, Conners and the Yankee made their way across the mostly empty parking lot to the front door, leaving Ambrose behind to shoot as much good footage as he could get. Conners climbed the steps and knocked on the front door. Trudy, working the door as usual, opened up and looked the pair over, as she'd done with thousands of other customers. Despite the oddity of Conners wearing a heavy jacket in the broiling heat, Trudy judged them presentable and ushered them in.[505]

"You seen a bunch of hell-raisers from the university down here?" Conners asked, doing his damnedest to sound like a college student from Austin—the only way, they'd decided, to possibly explain away the eyesore of a van they'd arrived in.

"Not yet, but come on in and have a Coke," one of the prostitutes in the parlor answered.

"Well, my pals oughta be along soon," he said. "We'll just wait a while here."[506]

Nervous and stalling for time, Conners pumped a bunch of quarters into the overpriced jukebox dominated by Hank Williams selections. Using the music as cover, he eased the camera out of his coat pocket to fire off a handful of blind shots. To Conners' ears, the crack of the shutter seemed to echo through the parlor. Fortunately for the reporter, the whores didn't notice and the handful of customers didn't care. Still, his tension grew, certain that discovery would come at any moment. He bought one of the overpriced Cokes and drank it down—anything to keep from sweating.[507]

Out in the parking lot, the sun was doing its best to roast Ambrose alive. Even with the front windows open, the van managed to absorb every bit of available heat. Dripping with sweat, Ambrose made a strategic decision—he stripped down to his boxers and lay down in the back just this side of stark naked to keep from boiling in his own juices. With his camera on his shoulder, he could pop up just enough whenever he heard a car drive up to get shots of the customers and license plates through the curtained windows.

Then Ambrose heard somebody right outside the van.

"Hey! There's somebody almost naked in there!" a man's voice said. "Look at him!"

Ambrose froze on the floor of the van, praying that the two cowboys peering in through the window would figure him passed out, drunk. More importantly, he prayed that they wouldn't notice the big TV camera beside him. After a minute, they lost interest and continued on to the house, laughing to themselves.[508]

Back inside, Conners was quickly running out of excuses. As the sun set, business picked up. Of the men coming into the parlor, only two—Conners and the Yankee—showed more interest in the jukebox than the women. The time had come to take one for the KTRK team.

"Obviously some of [the prostitutes] were a little chunky, some were striking and some weren't. They came in all different sizes, and all white, obviously, because that is the way it was," Conners said. "They would come in as guys were coming in. They'd sit on one side [of the parlor] away from them and look at the man and smile, and the guys would look. They'd finally go pick one out and say, 'Do you want to dance?' And they'd go back into the back rooms to dance.

"I mean, you're in there to do a job, but I couldn't help but notice these gals. They're obviously provocative looking. When they dress like that, you know what they're there for, and they'd do anything for you for the money," he said. "You don't get that out of your head. I was trying to make sure I stayed focused, and at the same time I wanted to make sure I didn't get caught. We're out in the middle of the woods. We're on our own there without anyone knowing other than our station—and they were hundreds of miles away."[509]

Conners approached a cute brunette with a nice figure, who looked like she would blend in on any college campus. She led him to one of the back rooms and asked what he wanted, explaining she could perform pretty much any type of sexual act he desired. They eventually settled on a straight date, and Conners paid her in the neighborhood of twenty-five to thirty dollars for her efforts—later claiming that KTRK-TV received a very interesting expense report for that particular piece of investigative reporting. While the girl deposited his payment in the office, Conners seized the opportunity to snap a few photographs of the room before she returned. When she returned, they stripped and completed the transaction with little fanfare.[510]

Conners quickly dressed and returned to the parlor, secure in his firsthand knowledge that prostitution did indeed take place at the Chicken Ranch.

KTRK's undercover reporter at the Chicken Ranch did not go unnoticed. "I know something's going on," Edna Milton thought at the time, "but I don't know what it is." *Courtesy Edna Milton Chadwell.*

By this time, night had fallen and the parlor was filled with lots of horny cowboys, many of whom were already drunk. The temptation to get a photo of the gathering throng proved too much for Conners. Positioning himself alongside the Yankee next to the jukebox, he eased the lens of the camera up out of his field jacket and squeezed off a couple more shots.

"What you got there, honey?" a woman asked from out of nowhere, rubbing up against him. "That feels like a camera. What you doing with that?"

"Uh, I thought I could buy a picture with some of the girls or something," Conners answered weakly. "You can do that, right? Buy a picture? You can buy anything else here, can't I buy a picture?"

"Let me go and ask Miss Edna to find out."[511]

Conners had pushed his luck too far. Miss Edna had noticed his odd lingering earlier, as had the other women. With his strange dress and furtive behavior, Conners' undercover operation fooled exactly nobody.

"He was in there in the parlor. You know, it was a night that it was all busy. Busy as hell, every damn chair was filled and people were standing," Miss Edna said. "Most of them were outside the place waiting to get in. It just happened to be a really busy night.

"He was going around, creeping around. You know how I can tell they was reporters, they almost crawl around on their knees doing different things. That was a habit they didn't get out of just because he was there," she said. "And he's crawling around and he's over there talking to [the Yankee], *whisper whisper*. I said, 'I know something's going on, but I don't know what it is.'"[512]

Conners didn't wait around to fill Miss Edna in. He grabbed the Yankee and made a break for the van. But word spread quickly.

Someone had a camera.

Who?

Someone up to no good.

As Conners scrambled into the van, he realized pickup trucks had filled the parking lot, and every single one of them boasted a rifle rack. In the yellow glow from the porch light over the front door, a crowd of men gathered. Some, ominously, were pointing at the orange van.

"They're all kind of gathering out there, and I can hear them talking, cursing and the girls are gathering," Conners said. "I'm trying to find out where the hell the key goes in the ignition because I don't recall if it's on the steering column or the console. *I don't know where it is*."

"Hurry up!" Ambrose shouted, starting to panic at the thought of all those gun racks. "Get us out of here! Get us out of here!"

"I can't find the ignition!" Conners shouted back, still fumbling with the unfamiliar van. "It's too dark!"

Suddenly, light exploded within the van. From the outside, it looked as if the sun blazed out from the front windshield. Ambrose, desperate to get away from what seemed like certain death, had turned on the oversized floodlights attached to his TV camera, blinding everyone in the process.

"*Bang!* I see great big dots in front of my eyes, but at the same time, I can see it enough to get the key in," Conners said. "As I'm driving out, hightailing it out, I see dots all the way to the highway."

"As soon as we get to the highway, a sheriff's car is whipping in headed down toward the ranch," he said. "We just kept going."[513]

The trio pulled up to the Wagon Wheel to finish the night's job, but the stress of the debacle in La Grange weighed heavily on them. Again, Conners went in with the camera concealed in the field jacket, but paranoia made him jumpy. What if the brothels worked closely together and the Chicken Ranch had sent a warning? In the end, they cut the evening short and retreated to Houston. They had more than enough material to forge ahead with the story anyway.[514]

COLONEL WILSON "PAT" SPEIR, head of the Texas Rangers and the Department of Public Safety, sat in his Austin office as Marvin and his cameraman set up for the interview. Colonel Speir, a lifelong lawman, dedicated his career to putting criminals behind bars. Working his way up through the ranks, once he assumed the position of top lawman in Texas he took on the equally challenging job of reforming and modernizing the state police. None of that accumulated experience came close to preparing him to deal with Marvin Zindler.

"Colonel, are you aware of prostitution that is going on in both La Grange and Sealy?" Marvin asked, going right for the jugular.

"We're aware that these places have been in operation for a certain period of time," Colonel Speir answered, the Stetson that had been a gift from Miss Edna the previous Christmas hanging on the hat rack in the corner, just outside the camera's field of view. "Certainly, we don't approve of this type of activity. Prostitution itself is only a misdemeanor. We have sought the aid of some local authorities in these areas to close them down, and we're also conducting, and will continue to conduct, investigations to see if the activities here have reached further."

"Define 'reaches further' for me, Colonel," prodded Marvin.

"We're particularly interested in any organized crime aspect, to see if indeed it does have any connection, and if so how much more and where. We've been conducting an investigation not only of these areas but several other areas for a long time—several months. Of course, we have to take what information we can get, evaluate it and see where we go from there."

"Colonel, do you think there are any political payoffs in any operations—both at La Grange and Sealy?"

Left: Colonel Wilson "Pat" Speir, director of the Texas Department of Public Safety. *Courtesy Texas State Library and Archives Commission.*

Right: Attorney General John Hill (center) considered the Chicken Ranch a "tar baby." *Courtesy Texas State Library and Archives Commission.*

"Not to my knowledge at this time. I'd not be in a position to speak on that. I do not have any information, myself."[515]

Marvin next approached Attorney General John Hill. Since Assistant Attorney General Herb Hancock had worked so hard to get him involved in the case, passing along the DPS investigation report, Marvin expected the interview to go well. Marvin half-suspected Hill put Hancock up to enlisting him. If he had a natural ally in Austin, Hill was that man.

Except Hill's interview didn't unfold as Marvin expected. Hill had no idea of Hancock's connection with Marvin. When Marvin brought up the brothels in La Grange and Sealy, Hill casually replied that his office planned to launch an investigation—so Marvin's follow-up completely blindsided him.

"Are you aware that your men have already conducted a full investigation of this?"

"Uh," managed the attorney general, like a deer caught in the proverbial headlights. "I am not aware that it is so. And I don't believe [it] to be so. You know that I have a group of lawyers who are investigators that are in my organized crime strike force, and they work with the DPS. I believe the facts to be that they have learned enough [in] discussion with the DPS that there has been an investigation under way for something, in the neighborhood of several months, into the possibility of organized crime activity."[516]

Attorney General Hill's confused, rambling answer perplexed Marvin. Was he playing dumb or really in the dark? Marvin began to wonder whose side the attorney general was really on. Annoyed by the stonewalling and evasions, Marvin decided the time had come to march into the lion's den and set up an interview with Big Jim in La Grange.

"Sheriff, we had a little conversation, and we talked about the house called the Chicken Ranch. A house of prostitution, or whatever you want to call it," Marvin asked. "How long has that been in operation?"

"It was there before I was born. It was there when I was a little boy. It was there when I was a deputy sheriff, and it is still there. It don't give nobody any trouble."[517]

Marvin and Big Jim went back and forth amicably a bit over estimates on the Chicken Ranch's annual income, with Marvin quoting $1 million or more and Big Jim dismissing such amounts as outlandish. Then Conners interrupted with a blunt question that dramatically changed the entire tone of the interview.

"Sheriff, you don't believe that it is linked to any organized crime, here or anywhere else?"

"I know damn well there is no organized crime connected in any way whatsoever," Big Jim shot back, his friendly demeanor gone in an instant.

"Has your office, or you or any of your deputies ever accepted any money from [Miss Edna] or in any way like that?" Conners pressed.

"Not a thing. There was no payoff anywhere in the world to anybody."[518]

Conners continued to press the sheriff, with Marvin content to cede the attack dog role to the younger reporter.

"Sheriff, when you speak about these figures, does the money go out of here into bigger organized crime? Who is right, you or the state investigating team?"

"The state is a goddamned liar if that is what they say."

"Well, let me ask you this. If the state comes down here and tries to close the Chicken Ranch down, and tries to find out where the money is going, what are you going to be doing?"

"If they can find out where that money goes, let them close it down. If they think that it is that kind of money. There is no such money as that spent out here. They are not taking in that kind of money out there."[519]

Marvin saw an opening and asked the sheriff point-blank if he'd assist state police if they moved in to close down the Chicken Ranch. Big Jim's reply brought Marvin and Conners up short.

"The only move it would take is just for me to pick the telephone up and tell them to shut it down," Big Jim said simply.

"You mean you can close down the Chicken Ranch by just making a telephone call?" Marvin asked, incredulous.

"That is right, yes sirree!"

"Why haven't you, Sheriff?"

"You hard of hearing, boy? Because, as I said, it has been there since when I was a little boy. It gives nobody any trouble. The majority of my constituents want it," Big Jim growled, his patience exhausted. "Inasmuch as there has been no trouble out there, I haven't shut it down. I would rather have them out there than in the back alleys over in nigger town and spreading venereal disease. We don't have no venereal disease at the Chicken Ranch. Those girls are examined once a week by a local doctor in downtown La Grange."[520]

Marvin and Conners left La Grange in a near state of shock. Big Jim hadn't given them evasive answers wrapped in political double-talk. Blunt and forceful, the sheriff showed absolutely no fear of the media. Indeed, he'd practically thrown them out of his office. But that fearlessness doubled as Big Jim's Achilles' heel—such blunt, brutally honest comments were a reporter's wet dream. It only took a few loose pebbles to start an avalanche, and Marvin and Conners could feel an entire mountainside start to give way.

Giddy at their good fortune, the KTRK team planned its next moves. Conners and cameraman Rick Armstrong would visit the Chicken Ranch again to confront Miss Edna on camera. After hearing about the narrow escape of Conners and Ambrose on their previous visit to the brothel, Armstrong refused to get out of the car once they arrived.

"He was afraid that she was going to have a gun and shoot us," Conners said. "So, he stayed in and was kind of hanging the mic out the window while he sat in there."[521]

Conners got out of the car, and minutes later, Miss Edna opened the front door, dressed in a purple and gold floral print housecoat. She told the reporters she owned the house and land and demanded they leave. Conners, instead, asked her what kind of business she operated out of her house while Armstrong continued filming from the safety of the car.

"I have a boardinghouse here," Miss Edna said.

"Is that all it is?" prodded Conners.

"That's enough."

"You're not operating a house of prostitution?"

"Whether I am or not doesn't come under the heading of your business," Miss Edna shot back, true to form. "I am not going to go for having a bunch of pictures unless you are definitely trying to close me personally."

"I'm not trying to close you. I want to know what you're operating here…"

"You know exactly."

"…and who's all involved in the money."

"I am involved in it and the bunch of others who are here are making it," she answered.

"Who all gets money other than that?" Conners asked, continuing to press for evidence of payoffs and government corruption. "Any law officials? Government officials?"

"Certainly the federal government," Miss Edna answered, a quick-witted response that caught Conners by surprise. "Certainly they get their pint of blood for every quart you get."[522]

Austin County sheriff Truman Maddox remained the last name on Marvin's short list to interview. The Wagon Wheel outside Sealy had received less scrutiny from KTRK's reporters, but that had to change. Like Big Jim and everyone else Marvin had called up to request a meeting, Sheriff Maddox agreed immediately. Maddox's quirky sense of humor, however, momentarily left Marvin speechless.

"Marvin sat down and the sheriff sat down, pulled his pistol and laid it down in front of him and asked him what he wanted to talk about!" Kitzman said, laughing. "Of course, it was all a big joke. Maddox had a way of taking charge a little more than Flournoy did."[523]

Marvin quickly figured Sheriff Maddox was having him on and dove right into the same list of questions that worked Big Jim up into such a lather. Maddox, perhaps benefiting from a different perspective than Big Jim, kept his cool for the duration of the interview.

"Sheriff, I am going to ask you this question," Marvin began. "Have you ever taken any money for protection as far as that place is concerned?"

"I certainly have not," Sheriff Maddox answered.

"Do you think that there is any organized crime connected with this establishment?"

"No! I don't think that there is any organized crime or any of that," said Maddox. "We have checked, along with the state and other agencies, to possibly see if there is, and we haven't found any indication whatsoever that there is any type of any organized crime."[524]

Sheriff Maddox's answers in the early going echoed what Marvin had already heard from Big Jim, Colonel Speir and the rest, so he decided to attack the issue from a different direction.

"Have the Texas Rangers ever asked you to close down your operation?" Marvin asked abruptly.

"Yes, I have had talks with them a few times, and we did close it down," Sheriff Maddox said, an admission that surprised Marvin.

"Did they ask you very often?"

"No, it was only once or twice as far as I know."

"Has Colonel Speir ever called you?" Marvin continued.

"Colonel Speir has talked to me one time, and the place was closed at that time," Maddox answered.

"Sheriff, do you think that if the state wanted to close it down, would you close it down, if they called you?" Marvin asked, trying to pin the sheriff down. This interview had taken a very different direction than Big Jim's.

"I would do my best to keep it that way if I thought there were complaints from the local people, and they don't want it there," Maddox said. "Yes, I would close it."

"Would you do it by civil injunction, or by criminal law?"

"I don't think that I would have to do either one," Maddox explained. "I think that I could just call them up. Tell them to close it down. Keep a watch on them pretty good. I believe that it would stay closed."[525]

Marvin left Sealy convinced that both Fayette and Austin County's sheriffs were either running the brothels behind the scenes or on the take, big time. How else could they both claim, with straight faces, that a mere phone call could close either operation down permanently? It echoed his epiphany at the gambling tables in Galveston years earlier. Suddenly, he saw corruption everywhere. Marvin couldn't conceive of the long-term détente between the law and the brothels in the rural counties. Couldn't believe the DPS and Texas Rangers viewed the whorehouses as mostly harmless and chose to let them operate because they served a useful purpose. Everything Marvin had uncovered reinforced what he'd read in the DPS report given to him by Hancock. He'd uncovered a dangerous nest of vipers deep in the heart of Texas.

Marvin huddled with the KTRK news staff on Friday, July 20. Armed with more than enough footage for a week's worth of explosive programming, the team decided the time had come to pull the trigger. Additionally, Marvin secured an appointment in Austin with Texas governor Dolph Briscoe for the following Monday. They laid out a plan—Marvin would interview

Governor Briscoe and then return to Houston in time for the 6:00 p.m. newscast, at which point he'd expose the bawdyhouses in La Grange and Sealy. Meanwhile, Governor Briscoe's footage would be prepped for the 10:00 p.m. broadcast. On paper, at least, it looked about as devastating as any one-two punch combo could get.

On Monday, July 23, 1973, Marvin sat at his Action 13 desk and, midway through the 6:00 p.m. newscast, proceeded to open a can of worms as big as any the state of Texas had ever seen.

"Action 13 received an anonymous complaint about two alleged houses of prostitution," Marvin thundered. "The complaint said the houses were operating in our neighboring towns of Sealy and La Grange. It's illegal to operate a house of prostitution in Texas, and past history shows they cannot function without someone in authority protecting them. I asked *Eyewitness News* correspondent Larry Conners to check out the report."

"I can state as fact that prostitutes are working there," Conners reported, solemn and straightfaced.[526]

With that broadcast, the proverbial shit hit the fan.

"DID YOU KNOW THERE is a *house of prostitution* called the Chicken Ranch operating in clear violation of the law over in La Grange?" Marvin demanded.

The interrogation completely blindsided Governor Briscoe. Despite the fact that Marvin had already grilled Attorney General Hill and Colonel Speir, nobody had thought to inform or warn the governor about Marvin's crusade.

"Staring into the glare of his camera lights, all I could say was 'no,' because I had never heard of this place," Briscoe said. "Marvin then asked me what the governor of Texas was going to do about it. Without hesitation, I said, 'Marvin, we are going to close it up.'"[527]

Governor Briscoe's commitment to Marvin played well for the cameras, but there was just one problem: under Texas law at the time, prostitution constituted a misdemeanor offense falling under local enforcement. The state police didn't have jurisdiction. The Texas governor, historically among the weakest executive officers of any of the fifty states, found himself impotent to do anything about the whorehouses.

"After Marvin left my office, I felt as though a bolt of lightning had hit me," Briscoe said. "I knew right away that I had a problem, because I had just stated on television that I would shut this place down, and I had absolutely no authority to do that. I knew I had to do something, of course, because prostitution is against the law and I had taken an oath to uphold the laws of the state of Texas, even if I had no power to do so."[528]

In the end, Governor Briscoe called a war room meeting with his top staff, including Attorney General Hill and Colonel Speir, for the following Tuesday. Late in the day, Attorney General Hill happened by the office of the governor's press secretary, Robert L. Hardesty, and stuck his head in the doorway.

"What's this [Tuesday] meeting all about?" Hill asked, suspicious.

"The Chicken Ranch," Hardesty replied simply.

"If Dolph thinks I'm going to touch that tar baby," the attorney general scoffed, "he's sadly mistaken."[529]

Colonel Speir proved equally reluctant to take on the Chicken Ranch, although he chose more measured words than Hill when Houston media cornered him about the scheduled meeting with the governor.

"We've been trying to see if there is any connection with organized crime," Colonel Speir explained carefully. "I envision an exchange of information on the subject, but I don't know exactly what shape the meeting will take."[530]

Clearly, Texas' top law enforcers looked forward to eradicating prostitution from the rural areas of the state almost as much as going to the dentist for a voluntary root canal.

La Grange transformed overnight into a three-ring media circus. Newspaper reporters from across the state showed up on the courthouse square, hungry for a story. They found plenty of support rallying behind the Chicken Ranch, with little indication anyone in the community wanted the brothel closed. Just the opposite, in fact. A petition drive spearheaded by *La Grange Journal* publisher Buddy Zapalac sprang up on the streets of La Grange, quickly garnering hundreds of signatures from community businessmen, teachers and even housewives demanding that Governor Briscoe allow the Chicken Ranch to remain open.[531]

"I grew up in this county and nobody I've heard has raised any objections to it. No one's even mentioned it in casual conversation," said Fayette County attorney Dan Beck. "My job is not to go looking for something. I wait until a complaint is filed."[532]

For the record, he confirmed his office had received no complaints.

The sheriff took his defense of the Chicken Ranch to another level entirely. Incensed at outsiders coming in and presuming to tell him how to run his county, Big Jim offered up a laundry list of the brothel's virtues.

"It's been here all my life and all my daddy's life and never caused anybody any trouble," Big Jim said. "Every large city in Texas has things 1,000 times worse."

Miss Edna, he pointed out, contributed generously to the local community. Like Miss Jessie before, Miss Edna donated $10,000 to the local hospital—in $1,000 annual installments—after she bought the Chicken Ranch. When one hospital board member untactfully suggested her donation be anonymous, Miss Edna replied that "Anonymous" sounded like a Greek name to her, and she wasn't Greek. She also donated $1,000 to the community swimming pool and sponsored a Little League team.[533]

"It's never caused no trouble 'round here. No fights or dope or nothin'. I ain't never got no complaints," Big Jim said. "There's never been no rapes while I been sheriff. Of course, that don't count no nigger rapes."[534]

Big Jim's justifications of the Chicken Ranch echoed what many in La Grange felt, but his words chafed the KTRK staff to no end.

"He makes that whorehouse sound like a damn non-profit county recreational facility," Conners groused.[535]

Even as the scandal grew, KTRK pressed ahead with its stories. Emboldened by early attention, the station upped the ante by outing customers during Marvin's broadcasts.

"Once we started running the story and started showing license plates and cars, I got all kinds of phone calls from guys saying, 'Hey, don't run that! My brother borrowed my car that night—it wasn't me!'" Conners said. "They're saying, 'If you run this I'll hunt you down,' or 'You're going to destroy my family.'

"There were all these threats, in addition to others just pleading. I imagine quite a few women got to go out and have dinners on some of those nights," he said. "They made a big point of saying that she was a great civic asset. 'All the girls were clean and inspected once a week, there was no rape or that kind of crime.' Basically, they endorsed it."[536]

Conners also noticed something away from La Grange that troubled him more than the hostility of the local sheriff and irate phone calls: his peers were laughing at him. None of the other television stations or newspapers in Houston picked up the story, although it was the talk of the town. Instead, the reporters and station managers chose to sit back and watch the sideshow spin wildly out of control. Whenever Conners brought up the specter of organized crime, colleagues rolled their eyes. Everyone knew about the Chicken Ranch—some had likely patronized the brothel—and very few people believed any kind of shady mafia figures lurked behind the scenes.

From their perspective, the exposé amounted to a cheap ratings grab and nothing more.[537]

Miss Edna finally gave up trying to maintain her anonymity since KTRK had broadcast her name and picture across half the state. She gave a number of interviews to various newspapers, her words conveying a beleaguered desperation, pleading for a reprieve of any kind.

"They're just having a problem confusing crime with sin. There are no drinks served here, no white slavery, no children involved," said Miss Edna. "If anyone was forced to do something, that would be different.

"If they are going to close us down, they should wait until the constitutional convention in January. If they want to make [prostitution] a crime, okay. Or if they just want to leave it as sin. But they should wait.

"I honestly hope they don't decide against us," she said. "At least they could give everybody a chance to find a job if they see the handwriting on the wall in January."[538]

In Austin, the scandal exploded like a tree burst, sending state legislators and lobbyists scurrying for any cover they could find, terrified their careers hung in the balance and praying Miss Edna wouldn't start naming names. The situation unfolded so quickly that State Senator Bill Moore of Bryan, otherwise known as the "Bull of the Brazos," couldn't martial any political defense of the Chicken Ranch. Despite his support of the brothel in the past, this political impotence at a critical time no doubt disappointed his constituents at Texas A&M in nearby College Station. State Senator William N. "Bill" Patman of Ganado, who represented Fayette County at the time, nearly broke the sound barrier in his urgency to distance himself from the brothel.[539]

"It's something I would certainly never seek to protect, if it does, in fact, exist. I had heard it was closed," Patman said, digging himself deeper with every denial. "I've never interceded on its behalf. I've been requested to.

"I consider a conversation I had once as one in which I was asked to intercede on its behalf," he continued. "It's a matter that as far as I'm concerned is closed."[540]

In the governor's office on the morning of Tuesday, July 31, the mood was somber and strictly business. The problem of how to extract Governor Briscoe from the rock-and-a-hard-place represented by Marvin Zindler and the Chicken Ranch made up the first, last and only item on the agenda. The gathered included Attorney General Hill; his first assistant, Larry York;

Colonel Speir; Secretary of State Mark White; Governor Briscoe's executive assistant, Charles Purnell; Director of the Governor's Criminal Council Mack Wallace; Hardesty; and the governor's wife, Janey Briscoe. Notably absent was Lieutenant Governor Bill Hobby.[541]

"I say this with all affection, because I'm very fond of Dolph," Hobby said, "but Janey, his wife…[the Chicken Ranch] is the kind of thing she would just go ape over. I think that had a good deal to do with Dolph's reaction."[542]

Hancock, too, felt that Janey Briscoe's ferocious opposition to the brothels dramatically limited the governor's options in responding to the situation.

"When Marvin started sticking that microphone in the governor's face, all hell [broke] loose because Janey was sitting in there when he was talking to Briscoe," Hancock said. "[Afterward] Janey was, you know, raising some hell. And when she started raising hell, things started happening."[543]

In any event, Janey's presence at the meeting wasn't coincidental. Once discussion turned to the whorehouses, "I thought Janey was going to choke," Hardesty recalled.[544]

After Hardesty summarized the unenviable position Marvin had placed the governor in—a third of the population of Texas would damn him if he closed the brothels, a third would damn him if he didn't and the final third would damn him either way—Speir reported on the DPS' position.

"We've had it under surveillance for some time. There were rumors that organized crime was involved, but we couldn't find any evidence of that," said Colonel Speir, coming as close to defending the Chicken Ranch as anyone in the meeting. "It's a very important part of the community. No complaints. And we didn't see any reason to close it down."

"Do you have the authority to close it down?" Briscoe asked.

"Well, we think so."

"It's operating illegally?"

"We assume so."

Governor Briscoe turned to the silent attorney general for clarification.

"John? They're operating illegally?"

"Well, Dolph, they almost certainly are, but I'd want to research it," Hill answered, making it very clear that he still considered the Chicken Ranch an untouchable "tar baby."[545]

Getting absolutely nowhere with the state's top two lawmen, Governor Briscoe finally pulled Mark White into the quagmire, asking for the secretary of state's input.

Texas Governor Dolph Briscoe (right) with his wife, Janey, during the 1973 inauguration parade down Congress Avenue in Austin. *Courtesy Texas State Library and Archives Commission.*

"Governor, I didn't go to UT or A&M. I went to Baylor University," White deadpanned. "I didn't know about places like the Chicken Ranch."

The gag worked, and the ensuing laughter cut the growing tension in the room…until Janey leaned over and said to White, "I'm so proud of you."

With that, the room fell deathly silent. Governor Briscoe pondered a moment to himself and then looked at Colonel Speir.

"Pat, we need to enforce the law."

"Yes, sir," Colonel Speir answered. "I'll call Sheriff Flournoy immediately."[546]

Colonel Speir made the call, but Big Jim wasn't having any of it. The sheriff announced that petitions on his desk had hundreds of signatures in favor of keeping the Chicken Ranch open and there was no way he would act against the wishes of his community. Colonel Speir fired back that the DPS was prepared to station state troopers outside the Chicken Ranch to record and publicize the license plate number of every vehicle arriving—a last-ditch move Governor Briscoe was loath to commit to, considering the fact that more than a few members of the legislature might get caught with their hands in the cookie jar.

Mark White, Texas secretary of state under Dolph Briscoe and future governor. *Courtesy Texas State Library and Archives Commission.*

Over in Austin County, Sheriff Maddox wasn't any more cooperative.

"I'm going on my twenty-fifth year here, and they haven't run me off," Maddox said, echoing Big Jim's insistence that he wouldn't move against the Wagon Wheel unless local citizens demanded it.

For the first time, the hornets' nest stirred up by Marvin threatened to get very, very ugly. At that point, State Representative John Wilson of La Grange intervened, setting up a meeting for 10:00 a.m. on Thursday, August 2, that would bring Big Jim, Sheriff Maddox and Kitzman to Austin to meet with the governor, Hill and Speir. The delay served to buy all sides some time, but only a little.[547]

"I came out of [the meeting] really disillusioned with Colonel Speir and John Hill leaving the governor to take all of the blame, because there wasn't going to be any credit, that's for certain. And that's what happened," Hardesty said. "[Governor Briscoe] didn't take any pleasure in it. I think it saddened him. Certainly he hadn't run for governor of Texas to shut down a whorehouse."[548]

Tossing a burning match into an open barrel of kerosene couldn't produce as big a firestorm. For the group most directly responsible for the blow up—the Houston Criminal Intelligence office—their dreams of victory quickly turned into a nightmare scenario. With the governor, attorney general and DPS director all caught in an embarrassing media spotlight, the consequences of their years-long campaign against the Chicken Ranch and Wagon Wheel suddenly loomed large. Captain George Read, Tommy Davis, Charlie Whitcomb, Otis Klar—all of the Houston-based officers who'd argued so passionately for a crackdown on the brothels—abruptly made themselves scarce.

"The local officers that were involved in it were kind of like me and sunk back into the woodwork because—pardon the French—the shit hit the fan when this thing came down," Hancock said, explaining that they most likely spent those last few days of July trying to erase any connection between them and the scandal. First to go was the intelligence reports they'd spent the latter half of 1972 compiling. "I think they probably shredded them because, to be honest with you, I don't know if this was ever an official investigation. There ain't a bit of telling."[549]

As more reporters found their way to La Grange, Zapalac did his best to personally meet as many of them as he could and share his own defense of the Chicken Ranch. At the same time, he told anyone who would listen he planned to devote a major editorial to supporting the continued operation of the brothel.

"I think it's all right. There's no organized crime attached to it, and it's beneficial to the community," Zapalac said. "I've never seen anything bad come from it and I've lived here all my life. The girls buy all their clothes here, their eats. It brings in business for the community.

"They pay taxes same as everyone else, city, county, federal income taxes. It's listed on the records as a rooming house," he said. "It keeps down rape, venereal disease. I think most of the people here are in favor of it."[550]

"Why don't you call Sheriff Flournoy yourself, Dolph?" Colonel Speir suggested out of the blue.

As the trying day turned into an equally trying night, Governor Briscoe continued to talk with Colonel Speir to find some way out of the impasse. During their discussion, the governor—a longtime South Texas rancher—realized he'd known Big Jim from way back, when the sheriff worked as the foreman of the McGill Brothers Ranch. Big Jim clearly resented outside interference in what he considered a strictly local matter, but Marvin had shone a glaring spotlight on it. Clearly, things could never go back to the wink-and-nod tolerance of before. The sheriff didn't accept that the DPS had any authority over him, but if Governor Briscoe *himself* gave the order…

"Sheriff, it's just too much. We'll just have to close it down," Governor Briscoe said as soon as he got Big Jim on the line.

"You know, there's a lot of furniture out there and we have to get those girls moved out," Big Jim answered in his slow drawl. "Why don't you let us run two more weeks just to let things taper off?"

"No sheriff, you're just going to have to shut it down. That's all there is to it. There's too much heat. Everybody's embarrassed by this thing," Governor Briscoe said. "Sheriff, I am *ordering* you to close what is known as the Chicken Ranch."

Big Jim paused a long moment and then answered with a simple, tired, "Okay."[551]

"He and I both knew that I had no authority to order him to close the place, but it was a practical way for us to get the law enforced in that county," Governor Briscoe said later. "For several days afterward I kept waiting for someone to point out that I had no legal authority to close the place down, but no one did."[552]

All that remained was for Big Jim to inform Miss Edna, a phone call he loathed to make. Miss Edna's nephew, Robert Kleffman, was visiting on the evening of July 31 when his aunt disappeared into her office to take the call. When she returned, her mood was grim.

"She said, 'Dang it, Robert, Mr. Jim's got to shut us down. He's got to. The governor's on his way,'" Kleffman said. "She sent all the girls home except for two. I went and got a shirt—Edna'd bought me some new shirts, she was always buying me clothes—and I pulled the cardboard out of it and I drew the block letters of *CLOSED*. I stuck it on the front screen door with a bobby pin and shut the door and locked it.

"Edna had everybody get their cars and took 'em around back. In a little bit, there was a knock on the door, and we just didn't answer it," he said. "We sat back in the back. There was a bottle of Cold Duck, and me and those two girls sat back there drinking that bottle of grape juice, watching TV in the dining room.

"Edna sat back there, kinda daydreaming and looking out the window, thinking the way she does. We just refused to answer the door," he said. "That was the end of it, because we were told the governor and the Texas Rangers—that's the story as I remember it—were coming down and were going to close the place. So we just put a closed sign on the front and didn't answer. We made like we weren't there."[553]

The news hit Miss Edna like a ton of bricks. She sent the few customers there that night home and then called the girls together and told them the story. Most of the women packed their bags that night and left by morning.

"One or two little girls—they were young but they were not kids—I got tickled with them. They came in and got in my lap and put their arms around my shoulders and neck and everything. I had to kind of grin," Miss Edna said, smiling at the bittersweet memory. "It was sweet of them, you know. They'd been there long enough where I was family to them. Those little girls, I'll remember forever.

"Later, another one came in I wasn't expecting and did the same thing, nearly. It wasn't quite rehearsed, but nevertheless it could've been," she said. "If something had happened and I could've reopened and gotten those girls back…well, I wouldn't have made pets out of them, but it would've been hard for me to ever raise hell with them [if they misbehaved]."[554]

Sheriff Maddox received a similar phone call from Colonel Speir and Governor Briscoe. Unlike Big Jim, the Austin County sheriff stopped short of drawing a line in the sand and pushing the issue further. Instead, he contacted the Wagon Wheel's owner, Jerry McKay, on August 1 and ordered the brothel closed. The next day, McKay telephoned the Wagon Wheel from his lawyer's office and told the madam, Miss Connie, to send the women away and lock the doors for good.[555]

Despite all of Marvin's publicity, Miss Edna never truly believed the Chicken Ranch might close down. Since the brothel claimed origins dating back to the 1840s—before Texas became a state—she believed the Chicken Ranch had a grandfathered exemption to any modern anti-prostitution laws. Armed with that, as well as a long list of powerful business and political clients that stretched from Austin to Washington, D.C., she considered fighting the order that long, dark night following Big Jim's call. Even if she didn't win, she could bring a whole bunch of cowardly hypocrites down with her—and probably take out half the Texas legislature and congressional delegations. By morning, though, Miss Edna had thrown in the towel.

"The whole damn thing, in a nutshell, was that I didn't want to keep it open and I sure didn't want to guilt somebody to mess up or sell to somebody even if they got somebody to finance it or otherwise. I was just tired," Miss Edna said. "It needed more hours than is humanly possible for a person to do. If you're putting in fourteen, sixteen and eighteen some days twenty hours. You get a little tired after a while. And it doesn't take very many years to kill you.

"After awhile you get so tired, and I did. Toward the last, so damn tired of everything. I was ready to get the hell out of there," she said. "If I hadn't been so terribly tired I might've fought them to keep it open. But I was just tired."[556]

Big Jim was tired, too, sick and tired of outsiders telling him what to do and reporters crawling all over La Grange, coming at him with notepads in hand asking him if he'd taken payoffs, and if not, why he'd let the brothel operate so long. He had one more opening to state his case to Governor Briscoe—the next day's 10:00 a.m. meeting in Austin. Big Jim let everyone know he intended to speak his mind at the meeting, as well as present the petitions to the governor. By the sheriff's count, more than seven hundred people were working to gather signatures throughout the county.

"That was one call I never wanted to make, but if I hadn't done it, the state would have," Big Jim complained bitterly. "The people want to let them in Austin know how the people and local officials feel about the closing.

"[The petitions have] as many as several thousands of names," he said. "I don't think it will do any good, but I plan to go with several people to see him."[557]

The sheriff didn't know that the petition drive had faltered. Fayette County residents who had eagerly signed their names Tuesday morning had, in the face of nonstop media scrutiny, lost much of their resolve by Wednesday evening. One by one they sought out the petition organizers and sheepishly asked to strike their names from the list. If the number of signatures ever numbered in the thousands, by Thursday morning it had dropped back down into the hundreds.[558]

Ultimately, circumstances rendered the question moot. The ballyhooed meeting never happened.

"This is the one time when I put my foot down," Kitzman said. "I was driving over there to meet with them to go to Austin. I heard on the radio that we were going over there, so I went to the sheriff's office and told him, 'Sheriff, we're not going over there.' I told him why, and he agreed.

"I called the governor's office and told them we weren't coming. He would've had the place full of news people, and Sheriff Flournoy, being such an imposing fellow—I think really the tide of public opinion was in support of [Flournoy] rather than the governor anyway," he explained. "If we had gone over there, it would've been disaster for the governor."[559]

Disaster of another sort awaited the sheriff, the kind that would have canceled the governor's meeting even without Kitzman's intervention. Lee Flournoy, Big Jim's elder brother, died abruptly in Baytown on August 2. After word reached Big Jim, he soon left town to grieve with his family and await the funeral.[560]

The governor's office, relieved by the cancellation of the meeting, judged (correctly) that Governor Briscoe had dodged a particularly messy bullet. Hardesty quickly arranged a press conference the morning of August 1 to make the official announcement, but even that turned into a surreal affair, with reporters openly laughing and Governor Briscoe struggling to maintain a straight face.

"[I spoke] with the attorney general and Colonel Speir and asked them for an investigation," Governor Briscoe said. "That investigation said it was in operation, so we requested the local law enforcement officer to enforce the law."

Dolph Briscoe
ultimately faced
the media alone in
an awkward press
conference regarding
the Chicken Ranch.
*Courtesy Texas State
Library and Archives
Commission.*

"Surely, if it's been in operation for over a hundred years, you've known about it before this last week?"

"Let me…There was some articles in papers about it, I think, several years ago. Whether it's been in operation or not, this year, since I took office as governor. I had no way, I had no knowledge of whether—" Governor Briscoe said, fumbling for a nonexistent safe answer. "I heard about it back when it was written up in the papers, when? Two or three years ago? There were some articles about it at that time. Since then, I've heard nothing about it."

"And you didn't know it was in operation until the television series?" the skeptical reporter pressed.

"I had no knowledge as to whether it was in operation or not in operation," Governor Briscoe insisted. "And I had had no one mention it until last week."

About that time, another reporter mercifully jumped in, asking if the governor had gotten any feedback on the scandal from the people of Texas.

"We have had quite a few calls here in the office, I don't recall any letters. And I say the calls, there's been some complaining calls, there've been some calls that…wanted it to remain open," Governor Briscoe said, laughter rippling across the room. "We've had some anonymous calls.

"I can't give you the exact number of calls that we've had, but we have had some calls."[561]

Hardesty concluded the conference by distributing a simple, terse press statement from the governor.

"The Chicken Ranch is permanently closed. This resolves the problem."[562]

Chapter 13

HELL TO PAY

M arvin Zindler celebrated his victory over the Chicken Ranch by taking a Caribbean vacation. Edna Milton shuttered the rambling clapboard farmhouse, darkening forever the welcoming porch light that promised sinful delight. The women who had worked there and called the place home scattered to the big cities of Houston, Austin and San Antonio, where they could continue plying their trade in relative anonymity.

Surrounding communities, which for so long took advantage of the local brothel's services, looked on with a mixture of amusement and resignation. The *Colorado County Citizen* in neighboring Columbus made hay with the over-the-top headline, "Zany Zindler's Zestful Zeal No Zany Zero." The August 3 edition of the *Fayette County Record* devoted all of four paragraphs on the front page to the brothel's closing. Inside, the paper reported the La Grange Demons, the Little League team Miss Edna once sponsored, had advanced to the state baseball tournament. Significantly, Big Jim opened his weekly "Sheriff's Report" column with the most understated lede ever: "I don't have anything special to write about this time other than the daily happenings."[563]

Truly, the Chicken Ranch existed no longer.

Few folks were buying it.

To farm boys and politicians alike who'd grown up hearing stories of the Chicken Ranch, it bordered on inconceivable that the brothel—which claimed origins dating back to the Republic of Texas, which had survived two world wars, the Great Depression and Attorney General Will Wilson's morality crusade—could be done in by a flamboyant television reporter in a toupee.

Customers continued to arrive in La Grange looking to spend their money on a good time. Some were returning clients, unwilling to believe reports of the brothel's demise. Others were first-timers, attracted in equal parts by curiosity and the national publicity. All left town disappointed, but more than two years passed before denial gave way to acceptance and the incoming pilgrimage of would-be customers petered out.[564]

"The old-timers around here that were familiar with the place for many years, they told me stories afterward. They were a little surprised the way that happened, because in the past when any heat started coming up, the sheriff would just go out there and say, 'Let's shut the door for a few days and let the heat blow over and forget it.' And for some reason they never chose that method on this occasion," recalled former Fayette County attorney Dan Beck. "The guys who told me about this believed if they had done that, just shut it down for a few days and let the heat fly by, [the Chicken Ranch] would've survived."[565]

Because the Chicken Ranch never resorted to a temporary, strategic closure like it had in the past, some longtime residents grew suspicious. Conspiracy theories sprang up to try and make sense of the uncharacteristic behavior by everyone involved.

"Their conspiracy theory was that Miss Edna and the sheriff *wanted* to close it, and they used Zindler as the scapegoat so they could get it shut down," Beck explained. "One of the stories was that Miss Edna had some reason that she wanted to get out of business. [The closure] was part of a concocted scheme to make everyone a few bucks."[566]

Robert Kleffman numbered among those having a hard time coming to terms with a post–Chicken Ranch world. The University of Texas student still went to his classes and lived in relative anonymity in his south Austin apartment. In practical terms, the scandal affected his life very little, beyond the fact that he no longer spent lazy weekends hanging out at his Aunt Edna's brothel in La Grange.

A couple of weeks after Big Jim's fateful phone call, Kleffman drove over to the Safeway supermarket on Riverside Drive as he'd done countless times before. He forgot all about groceries, though, when he spied none other than Governor Dolph Briscoe coming out of the store with a bag under his arm.

"Dolph!" Kleffman shouted, sprinting across the parking lot.

Briscoe stopped at his car, looking around to find who was calling him.

THE ORIGINAL CHICKEN RANCH PRINT

Following the closure of the Chicken Ranch, a variety of art prints were offered for sale in Texas. Al Bates, a successful commercial artist from Houston, produced one of the most enduring works, featuring the brothel as it may have appeared in the 1930s. This ad ran in the May 1975 issue of *Texas Monthly*. *Author's collection.*

"Dolph," Kleffman said, catching his breath. "What's the deal? Why are you getting on my aunt and trying to shut her place down?"

Briscoe looked him dead in the eye and said, "Robert, I don't have a choice. That's just the way it is."[567]

Then the governor got into his car and drove away, leaving Kleffman alone in the parking lot, no closer to understanding why events played out as they had. Only later did it dawn on Kleffman that Briscoe recognized him by sight and addressed him by name.

Decades later, the brief encounter remained frustrating to Kleffman. "I don't know how he knew my name," he said, considering the closure that remained elusive. "You know, I couldn't talk to him or nothing. I just wanted to ask him, 'Why? Why now?' The place had been there since Moby Dick was a minnow! Sam Houston probably got well there [after San Jacinto], you know what I mean?"[568]

If the larger question of why the Chicken Ranch had to close in 1973 remained elusive, the motivation behind Briscoe's decision appeared obvious.

"He was just put in a position where I don't think he thought he had any choice, because with all the publicity on TV," Kleffman said. "Everybody wants another term, you know?"[569]

In the blink of an eye, the Chicken Ranch transformed from a happily tolerated vice to a political liability. The scandal spooked the Powers-That-Be in Austin, and persistent rumors that the brothel had reopened dogged the state's law enforcement. The rumors came to a head in November, forcing Attorney General John Hill to call District Attorney Oliver Kitzman and demand action.

"The attorney general, who was a friend of mine for many years, called me and told me he had word that the Chicken Ranch was operating again," Kitzman said. "I told him, 'John, the sheriff said that it's closed.' He said, 'I don't care. I've got information it's operating.'"[570]

Kitzman left his office that day and drove the sixty-five miles over to La Grange. He found Big Jim was out of town on a hunting trip, but Deputy Charlie Prilop listened patiently to Kitzman explain why he was there. Prilop then stood up, reached for his hat and in his slow Texas drawl said, "Let's go see."

What Kitzman found hardly resembled the working brothel of years past. Two elderly ladies—a far cry from the young prostitutes who made the place famous—stayed on the property, acting as caretakers. Otherwise, the Chicken Ranch remained deserted. Kitzman placed a call to the attorney general, reporting what he'd found and confirming the Chicken Ranch was closed—permanently. For good measure, Kitzman then telephoned the local newspapers and gave them the same information.

"That," said Kitzman, "was the end of that."[571]

EXCEPT, OF COURSE, NOTHING ended at all. Facts seldom get in the way of a good story, and too many people in Texas wanted the Chicken Ranch back in business to let the rumors die.

While some Texans stubbornly remained in denial about the closing of the famous brothel, others were downright incensed. Fortunately for Briscoe, few of those angry voters blamed the governor much for the closure of the Chicken Ranch. They chose, instead, to direct their ire elsewhere.

"You see, there's a thin line between credit and blame. A *very* thin line between credit and blame," said Larry Conners, counting his lucky stars that his direct role in the Chicken Ranch affair got thoroughly eclipsed by Marvin Zindler. "In my view, it always has been. Marvin, because of his flamboyant approach, got most of the credit *and* blame."[572]

Blame never figured into KTRK's plans for the Chicken Ranch story. Marvin sold the newsroom on the exposé not as a crusade against prostitution but, rather, as one on political corruption, graft and organized crime, of which the country brothel was but a symptom of larger problems. Once Marvin's bombastic delivery put "bawdyhouse" on the tip of every wagging tongue between Houston and Austin, however, those lofty goals quickly fell by the wayside.

"It was well agreed before the series started that to get the house of prostitution closed and no more would be a cheap shot," said KTRK news producer Garvin Berry. "We knew we'd receive an awful lot of publicity, but we'd also get an awful lot of needling.

"So there was mutual agreement by everyone concerned that the real story was why, when the DPS reported things wrong in law enforcement, was nothing done?"[573]

Because KTRK abandoned the follow-through, Marvin never proved his oft-repeated claims of ties between the Chicken Ranch and organized crime. The Houston criminal intelligence officers, satisfied the Chicken Ranch had closed, did nothing to encourage further investigation. Those gray areas were never addressed, said Berry, who offered no explanation why the station completely shifted gears.

Marvin, on the other hand—after bearing the brunt of public scorn—didn't hesitate to pass out blame.

"Well, I only did my part. The other reporter didn't do his homework, that's all. He was immature," Marvin said. "And he's not an investigative reporter. Shit, man, he didn't know what the fuck he was doing! He was good at presenting the story, but he left most of it out."[574]

Luckily for Marvin, television personalities depended on ratings more than public approval to keep their jobs. Up the road in College Station, students at overwhelmingly male Texas A&M University cursed him and mocked his sign-off as "Marvin Meddler, Eye-Bulging News." Letters inundated the KTRK offices in Houston almost from the moment Kleffman's hand-lettered "Closed" sign went up on the Chicken Ranch's door. From all across Texas they came, by and large condemning Marvin for sticking his nose where it didn't belong.

"We got thousands and thousands of letters," Marvin said. "Even little old ladies wrote to us."[575]

Despite the stream of negative letters—or perhaps because of them—Marvin wasn't willing to let the Chicken Ranch story die a natural death. With no shortage of "tipsters" willing to swear that the La Grange brothel was back in business, Marvin used his *Eyewitness News* soapbox the first week of June 1974 to announce that prostitution still thrived in La Grange:

The Chicken Ranch in La Grange is back open again and Marvin Zindler found out about it. There was a great deal of publicity over the closing of the La Grange house of prostitution, but it appears that the talk is lasting longer than the action. We have been receiving reports that the Chicken Ranch is back in business and today Texas Attorney General John Hill admits he's been receiving similar information.

"On a given day, there have been two prostitutes at the Chicken Ranch. We then passed that information on to the Texas Department of Public Safety."

The Attorney General said the reports don't actually name the Chicken Ranch as open, but we have to question just how concerned he is with really finding out. My sources state Department of Public Safety Intelligence officers have told the Attorney General that for the past few weeks, the back side of the Chicken Ranch has been open for business and that the Attorney General has been asking to seek an injunction to close the Chicken Ranch, which would close the Chicken Ranch by court order—not at the whim of the local sheriff.

"I think we always go on the assumption that the local law enforcement officers are enforcing the law and that statement we put out jointly the other day, I think, makes clear that if it is not done, we will consult with them and request them to enforce the law. If they do not, the state will take appropriate action."

It is time for appropriate and immediate action. We are not just talking about a house of prostitution, we are talking about law officials and disregard of law that equals malfeasance in office which leads to graft and corruption.[576]

Once again, Marvin's claims against the Chicken Ranch stirred up a hornets' nest in the attorney general's office. The damned place wouldn't stay closed—or the rumors wouldn't, at any rate. This time Hill didn't turn to the local DA but rather called on his big guns, the Texas Rangers, to investigate and settle the matter once and for all.

On June 4, Texas Rangers James F. Rogers and Hollis Sillavan—no stranger to the Chicken Ranch as an intelligence resource—traveled to La Grange to investigate. They didn't meet with Big Jim, who was away in Austin on business, but found the Chicken Ranch itself locked up and deserted.

Ranger Sillavan returned on June 10 and this time met up with Big Jim. The two examined the property and met with the new caretaker, W.D. McKeller, who stayed busy shooing away sightseers, reporters and would-be customers. Big Jim assured Ranger Sillavan the brothel would never reopen as such, invited the Rangers to follow up anytime and announced plans to install steel gates to keep the curious away.

"We went through the entire place, bed rooms, bath rooms, closets, kitchen area and waiting rooms," reported Ranger Sillavan. "There is no evidence of this place being used except for the small area used by the watchman. Dust

Rural garbage collection did not exist in early 1970s Texas, so refuse was often heaped onto large trash piles, where it was burned. The remnants of the Chicken Ranch trash pile hint at the predominant activity on the property. *Author's photo.*

along with the condition of the furniture, bath rooms and drink dispenser have not been used for quite some time."

Sillavan made two more unannounced visits on June 12 and 18, each time finding the place deserted. By July, the Texas Rangers closed the files on the case. As far as the Texas Department of Public Safety was concerned, the Chicken Ranch remained dead and buried.[577]

It might have stayed that way, too, if Marvin hadn't tried to milk the story for one last into-the-lion's-den feature. After the fact, Marvin maintained that he'd never wanted to set foot in Fayette County ever again out of fear of what Big Jim or the irate community might do to him. Even though the Chicken Ranch story had boosted his career to national prominence and he'd willingly revisited the topic on-air over the previous eighteen months, Marvin insisted KTRK news director Walter Hawver actually came up with the idea of staging a story in La Grange. By showing the town's economy hadn't collapsed following the loss of the brothel's revenue, they'd debunk one of the big arguments used by supporters of the Chicken Ranch. If they *also* planned to address the abrupt increase of Fayette County gonorrhea cases during the months following the closing of the Chicken Ranch, Marvin made no mention of it.[578]

Marvin clearly understood that returning to La Grange amounted to playing with fire, and right away he attempted to secure a Texas Rangers detail for protection. The response came swiftly and without ambiguity: no Rangers were available. After enduring Marvin's mockery and harassment over the Chicken Ranch for the previous year and a half, Colonel Wilson Speir and the rest of the Texas Department of Public Safety—at least, those not based out of the Houston Criminal Intelligence office—finally had the opportunity to administer a little passive-aggressive comeuppance. If Marvin insisted on provoking a showdown with Big Jim, he wouldn't have the Rangers to hide behind.[579]

The rebuff by the DPS only strengthened Marvin's resolve, and he recruited Mark Vela, a respected lawyer and former assistant DA for Harris County, to accompany him. Marvin's other legal backup, Neil Duval, an assistant attorney general with the Organized Crime Division, canceled abruptly on the eve of the expedition due to a medical emergency. Despite the change in plans, Marvin decided to press ahead.

Marvin, Vela and cameraman Frank Ambrose—who'd accompanied Conners to La Grange during the undercover investigation the previous year—departed Houston in Marvin's black Lincoln Continental Mark IV the morning of Monday, December 30. After stopping for lunch in Columbus, the party arrived at the Chicken Ranch in the early afternoon. They found a steel gate barring the front approach, so they drove around the back road to the house, which was padlocked. Ambrose shot footage of the abandoned building and surrounding land for several minutes before McKeller, the caretaker, arrived to order them off the property.[580]

Marvin's arrival in town in his long, black Lincoln wasn't exactly subtle. People in small towns tend to notice big, expensive cars. Marvin spotted people watching him, and a degree of paranoia began to take hold. Years later, Marvin claimed someone had run a license check on his car during the drive up from Columbus. As he drove through La Grange, time and again he thought he'd seen Big Jim's police car tailing him at a distance.

In actuality, Big Jim was comfortably holed up in the soda fountain on the courthouse square, shooting the breeze with a few acquaintances as he sipped a cup of coffee to ward off the chilly December weather.[581]

Marvin's Lincoln pulled up in front of the Sears Catalog Store, just a few steps down from the soda fountain. Ambrose pulled out his camera and began filming footage of the businesses surrounding the courthouse square to illustrate the fact that the La Grange economy hadn't collapsed due to the closing of the Chicken Ranch.

"The sheriff heard that Marvin was out there doing that," said District Attorney Oliver Kitzman, "and he was *not* amused."[582]

From Big Jim's perspective, the Chicken Ranch affair amounted to nothing less than a malicious act of public humiliation. Marvin, an outsider from Houston, had usurped the sheriff's authority in Fayette County for no good reason and taunted the entire town of La Grange with his showboating broadcasts. The hordes of reporters who'd descended on La Grange in the weeks following stung like salt rubbed into the wound, while the regular visits from the Texas Rangers and the attorney general's office chasing rumors of the Chicken Ranch's reopening served as constant reminders that *"Marvin Zindler won."*

Marvin showing up in La Grange, now…he was rubbing the sheriff's nose in it. That proved more than a man of Big Jim's rough-hewn, frontier Texas character could stomach.

"Marvin Zindler was wanting to create a problem, and he kept getting on Jim's ass about different things," said Edna Milton. "Finally, Jim just got mad."[583]

The seventy-one-year-old sheriff burst out of the soda fountain riding a wave of hellfire and damnation. Marvin instantly locked his car door but couldn't get the window rolled up in time. Big Jim—all six feet, four inches of him—dove through the window after Marvin.

"I made up my mind that the sheriff was going to have to kill me to get me out of that car," Marvin said. "He had nothing to get me out of that car for except he came looking for me, and he had his mind made up he was going to kill my ass."[584]

While murdering Marvin probably *did* rank fairly high up on the sheriff's to-do list, his *immediate* goal was to disarm the newsman. Since his days as the most flamboyant deputy in Harris County, Marvin had been reputed to carry a concealed weapon everywhere he went, plus a loaded M1 carbine in his car. Big Jim had zero intention of getting into a shootout with his foe.

"He reached in his car, because he knew Marvin carried a shoulder holster," said La Grange resident Leerie Giese. "[Big Jim] reached in there and grabbed him to see if he had that damn pistol on him because he knew he carried a shoulder holster."[585]

The gunfight never materialized, but the few spectators who gathered around the courthouse square did witness the most surreal tug-of-war ever, with Big Jim heaving Marvin partway out through the car window only to have Marvin fight to pull himself back in. Over and over they went, with the combatants screaming and cursing each other all the while.

"What'd you get mad at me about, Sheriff?" cried Marvin.

"You goddamned—"

"Well, I'm not—"

"Get out! Get out!" demanded Big Jim.

"It's not my fault!" protested Marvin. "I was sent down here on assignment."

"You goddamned son of a bitch…" Big Jim growled between heaves, "…every one of…mother-fucking son of a bitch…"

"But Sheriff, don't get mad at me…Sheriff! Don't do that to me!"

"Sheriff, please Sheriff…" begged Ambrose, desperately trying to defuse the situation. "Sheriff, stop."

"Oughta…" Big Jim clutched wildly at Marvin, struggling to get a solid grip so he could pull him out of the car once and for all. His hand caught a fistful of hair, and Big Jim gave a mighty pull, staggering back from the car. Standing in the middle of the street, the sheriff stared at the silver toupee in his hands. "Son of a bitch…"[586]

Harvey Dipple, working in his father's grocery store when he heard the commotion out on the street, stepped outside to get a better look. In doing so, he became one of the few witnesses to the improbable showdown.

"I was in the store. I just happened to look out the window, and I seen them, that they were arguing out there," Dipple said. "Oh, boy, they had it out there. And [Big Jim] finally just pulled [Marvin's] wig off!"[587]

If Marvin had built up his TV career by humiliating the sheriff over the preceding eighteen months, well, turnabout was fair play. Big Jim waved the toupee triumphantly in the air, whooping and hollering in celebration. Then he threw it to the street and jumped up and down upon it, shouting out, "This is MAAR-vin ZIND-lerr, MAAR-vin ZIND-lerr" over and over in mockery of the newsman's trademark sign-off.

His righteous fury played out, Big Jim went back to the car and seized the television camera from Ambrose and a tape recorder from the front seat of the car, then gave Marvin one last parting bit of advice: "You son of a bitch, don't you come back anymore. I'm done warning you that I don't want you running in this county."[588]

The short, furious battle left Ambrose and Vela speechless.

"Frank later told me, 'I've been with Marvin through all the stories. And when the sheriff ripped off his toupee, I'm looking at this bald little guy in the car and I didn't recognize him,'" Conners said.[589]

Shaken by the attack, with his dignity in tatters, Marvin turned to Vela with a request that summed up the whole encounter: "Go get my hairpiece, will you?"[590]

"I seen him when he pulled that wig off and threw it on the ground," Dipple said. "Marvin picked it back up again and put it back on. Then they had a few words and then they split."

"The sheriff did comment to me, [Marvin] was holding his wig on like that," said Kitzman, laughing. "In a rare attempt at humor, the sheriff told me he *really was* ugly without his toupee."[591]

News of the fight spread quickly, despite the scarcity of witnesses. Even as Marvin made his way back to Houston, the phone in Kitzman's office started ringing off the hook, and in short order, Kitzman learned the whole story. KTRK demanded the return of its camera, and Big Jim, naturally, refused to do any such thing.

"Well, I knew the sheriff couldn't possibly hold that camera, so I made a trip over to La Grange and explained to the sheriff he couldn't do that," Kitzman said. "I just felt I had to put some kind of a lid on that problem."[592]

Marvin, never one to look a gift horse in the mouth, seized the incident and ran with it like an All-Pro back for the Houston Oilers.

"I wanted to do a follow-up, show people that with the prostitution house closed the economy hadn't crumbled," Marvin said during his *Eyewitness News* report that night. "I saw busy streets and good business.

"The sheriff jumped in front of my car, he started cussing me and he reached through and hit me. He tried to get me out of the car," he said. "We got sound of it and our camera was rolling, but he went around to the other side of the car, grabbed the camera and smashed it. Then he smashed the recorder."[593]

The following morning, Big Jim appeared in the county attorney's office, still fuming.

"Did you see Zindler on TV last night?" Big Jim growled.

Dan Beck hadn't, but he'd heard enough to piece the story together. Besides, when the sheriff wanted you to answer a certain way, it was best to cooperate.

"Yeah, I did," said Beck.

"I just want you to know," Big Jim said, deadly serious, "if I'd hit that son of a bitch, he wouldn't've been on television last night!"[594]

Later that day, New Year's Eve, Kitzman collected the camera and tape recorder from Big Jim and, with a friend of his, lawyer Tom Roberson of Houston, returned the confiscated equipment to KTRK.

"We took the camera out there, and Marvin was there with *no sign* of any injury," said Kitzman. "They treated me courteously—except the weather guy. He was a jerk. I gave them the camera, and I stayed there until they'd processed the film."[595]

Once Kitzman handed over the camera, Conners went to work. The sheriff had destroyed the cassette from the tape recorder and exposed the film from the camera, but Conners suspected there might still be something of value to be had from the ruined footage.

"I run the film through the processor, and of course, I know that they've exposed it," Conners said. "There's not going to be anything on it. So it comes out just as white as a sheet of typing paper, but I set up a room where we could watch it together.

"The news director was in the room, I believe. I can't recall if Marvin was there or not," he said. "Marvin had claimed the sheriff had attacked him, and *they* were claiming Marvin had attacked the sheriff, and they were filing an action against Marvin."[596]

As Kitzman, Roberson and the KTRK people gathered in the viewing room, Conners explained they were going to watch the exposed film—much to everyone's surprise.

"I said, 'There won't be any footage, because it looks like it's been exposed by *accident*. I'm sure that you see this little brown stripe along the side of the film? That's a magstripe. *It records all the sound*.' And they went almost as white as paper," Conners said. "Once I start rolling it, sure enough, there is no video, but then you start hearing it play out on the sound just as Marvin had described it. Pleading with the sheriff, 'Please, Sheriff, don't do that. Don't do that.' And the sheriff hollering, 'MAAR-vin ZIND-lerr,' the way Marvin and Frank had described it. It backed up Marvin's story on what happened."[597]

"It didn't have any pictures, but it did have the soundtrack," Kitzman agreed. "There were some harsh words there!"[598]

Wasting little time, Marvin, promptly announced his intent to file a federal civil rights suit against Big Jim and Fayette County, as well as an assault-and-battery suit for $3 million. In addition to the audio of the fight between himself and the sheriff, a visit to Memorial Downtown Hospital resulted in a diagnosis of fractures to the seventh and ninth ribs, as well as mild pleurisy. Marvin secured letters attesting to this from the attending physicians to use as evidence.[599]

"He filed assault charges, and didn't he also file criminal charges? But either one—civil or criminal case—I have this big picture of a Fayette County jury indicting Jim Flournoy!" said Texas lieutenant governor Bill Hobby, laughing at the absurdity.[600]

Big Jim, like Marvin, was unshakably confident in his ultimate vindication. "I didn't hit him or strike him and didn't hurt him," Big Jim maintained.[601]

"Of course, Marvin claimed to have been injured," said Kitzman. "Marvin sued, complaining he had ribs broken and whatever, which certainly would be inconsistent with the way he handled himself when I went down there on New Year's Eve.

"I went back to Fayette County the following week and got the names of as many people as I could who'd been witnesses to that [fight]," he said. "I guess I interviewed about a half dozen of them, and none of them would confirm the sheriff had hit Marvin."[602]

Few people lined up to defend Marvin in public. Once again, he found himself cast in the role of villain, and it frustrated him to no end. Particularly galling was the deafening silence from the Houston Criminal Intelligence office of the DPS. Captain George Read, Agent Thomas A. Davis Jr., Sergeant Charlie Whitcomb, Agent James R. Wilson…all of those officers who'd argued so forcefully to get the Chicken Ranch closed down developed a deep interest in covering their own asses once Marvin's started getting kicked.

"They told me it would create a lot of heat for me and I might even lose my job as a result. I didn't worry about that," Marvin said bitterly. "But I'm sure as hell mad at them now, because later when I got my ass whipped by the sheriff they got scared and couldn't stand the heat. When they needed me it was all kissy-kissy. But when I got hurt they hid. I won't forget it, either."[603]

This latest chapter in the Chicken Ranch saga had people statewide shaking their heads in disbelief. The story that many felt should never have seen the light of day in the first place simply refused to die. Not only that, but it grew more outrageous as each new chapter unfolded. If Fayette County resented Marvin's original exposé on the Chicken Ranch, that hardly compared to the galvanizing effect of Marvin's lawsuit. Almost instantly, the county united in support of Big Jim, ready to take on Marvin one more time.

"The real trouble came when Marvin came back to take pictures of the closed Chicken Ranch and to gloat," complained L.A. Giese, a retired Fayette County farmer. "Big Jim did what any good sheriff would do—he protected the town from harassment."[604]

Nobody doubted that court proceedings would be even more knock-down-drag-out than the earlier clashes between Big Jim and Marvin. Big Jim intended to win, securing famed criminal defense attorney Richard "Racehorse" Haynes to represent him. Haynes boasted a well-earned reputation for taking—and winning—high-profile cases, including the notorious Cullen Davis murder trial.[605]

Of course, such high-powered legal counsel came at a price considerably steeper than a rural Texas sheriff could readily afford. Bumper stickers

Campaign cards from one of Sheriff T.J. "Jim" Flournoy's early campaigns (left) and a ticket to the barbecue fundraiser organized to help support the sheriff in his ongoing legal battles with Marvin Zindler. *Courtesy La Grange Visitors Bureau.*

proudly declaring "I'm a Friend of Sheriff Jim" and T-shirts emblazoned with "Sheriff Jim—A Living Legend" became common sights around the state as fundraising for the sheriff's legal defense supplanted Little League baseball as the most popular summer pastime in Fayette County. Supporters held massive barbecues in La Grange and Schulenburg, with more than 1,800 people packing the La Grange Fairgrounds on June 28, 1975.[606]

"This dinner is to support the sheriff," explained Elton Kaase, a supermarket owner from Schulenburg. "It's not catered, you know. The people did it all themselves. We slaughtered 23 calves and two hogs for the event. Those men over there are cooking 125 pounds of beans."[607]

Well-wishers included Lieutenant Governor Bill Hobby and a troop of twenty men from Louisiana with fond memories of the Chicken Ranch. Although one busload arrived carrying a banner emblazoned with "Chicken Ranch Alumni Association," the organizers took great pains to make it clear the event was a rally in support of Big Jim, not the closed brothel.

At $10 a plate, the single event raised a war chest for the sheriff's defense approaching $20,000. Adding in proceeds from T-shirt and bumper sticker sales, by the beginning of July the fund held at least $40,000.[608]

"As far as the people in Fayette County were concerned, until all this arose they were of the common culture of this community. They knew [the Chicken Ranch] was there, and I'm sure to a man knew that if they ever wanted it gone, all they had to do was tell Sheriff Flournoy," said Kitzman, explaining the fierce outpouring of loyalty during the lawsuit. "If his people had changed their minds about that, there would not have been a problem.

"You have to understand they had absolute confidence in Sheriff Flournoy. His integrity was totally intact," he said. "He was respected. They were proud of their famous sheriff. He didn't abuse their devotion. He didn't take all that for granted. He tried his best to be a good sheriff and tried to protect them, and did."[609]

Following the widely publicized barbecue fundraiser, Marvin seized upon the most prominent name on the guest list: Bill Hobby. The lieutenant governor lived in Houston, and if he could be drawn into the ongoing story, Marvin could benefit from a whole new wave of attention and the ratings that would bring.

"Marvin, he knew somehow that Jim and I were friends," Hobby said. "He came up to my office at the *Houston Post* one time with a camera.

"I told him to go fuck off," he continued, laughing hard. "He came charging at me, mainly because he knew I was a friend of Jim Flournoy. I probably made some remark to somebody that caused him to get mad."[610]

Bumper stickers announcing "I'm a friend of Sheriff Jim" were sold to raise funds to support the sheriff in the lawsuit Marvin Zindler filed against him. Years later, they were still a common sight around Fayette County. *Courtesy La Grange Visitors Bureau.*

The dead end of the Hobby lead was the least of Marvin's problems. KTRK quickly found its "slam-dunk" case becoming a logistical headache. Apart from the irate letters continuing to flow in, Baker and Botts, the law firm initially hired to represent the station and Marvin, abruptly withdrew from the case.

"The law enforcement fraternity is very closely knit," the firm explained. "This ties into the bar widely. Any of our lawyers' advice might be colored by their not wanting to get into open confrontation. It could affect referrals, witnesses, services and so on."[611]

Big Jim couldn't celebrate any tactical advantage, however, because he had lawyer problems of his own. Haynes resigned as his legal counsel to concentrate on the defense of Duval County district judge O.P. Carillo, who was facing impeachment in the state senate and indictment on money laundering and tax evasion charges.[612]

About that time, Kitzman traveled to Houston on business and stopped by the Old Capitol Club in the Rice Hotel. The club took its name from its location: the spot occupied by the capitol of Texas during the 1830s. In the 1970s, it served as the nexus of political activity in the city, frequented by lawyers, businessmen and politicians.[613]

"Even though I wasn't a member, I walked in there and they made me welcome. Of course, they got to asking me about the encounter of Zindler with the sheriff," Kitzman said. "The great attorney Percy Foreman walked in, and as he came in one of the lawyers asked him, 'Percy, are you going to represent Sheriff Flournoy in his lawsuit with Marvin Zindler?' And he, in his magnificent drama, said, 'I have offered my services to him, but he has not accepted.'

"He had his own table in there with his telephone on it, where he conducted a lot of his practice. I sat down with him and we kept talking," he said. "Finally, I told those guys that every witness I could find said the sheriff *did not hit* Marvin Zindler.

"And Percy said, 'You tell the sheriff if he *didn't* hit him, I *won't* represent him!'"[614]

The lawsuit, which seemed like a surefire path to vindication against the sheriff in January, resembled a quagmire by July. Marvin suffered a humiliating setback when the attorney general in Washington, D.C., refused to pursue his much-talked-about civil rights complaint. The sheriff remained defiant as ever, and worse, the entire state seemingly rallied behind him. The prevailing opinion allowed that Big Jim may very well have stepped over the line, but Marvin himself provoked the confrontation and got what he deserved. Faced with a growing public relations nightmare, KTRK floated the possibility of a settlement to make the entire mess go away.[615]

Since both Marvin and Big Jim belonged to the Shriners, the initial settlement offer proposed dropping the lawsuit in exchange for the sheriff donating the entirety of his defense fund to the Shriners' Crippled Children's Fund. When this fell through, KTRK put a second offer on the table: Marvin would end the suit for $10,000 if the sheriff agreed to a public reconciliation.[616]

"I told the lawyers they could have the Sheriff give me a check for $10,000 and we'd kiss and make up," Marvin said. "They said he wouldn't appear with me because he was afraid of what I might do. I told them, 'Hell, I wouldn't call the bastard a sonofabitch, or anything.'"[617]

Despite the intense animosity, both parties came to see a settlement as the only way to avoid years of courtroom battles, unwanted publicity and, at best, a no-win scenario. By September, Big Jim ended all fundraising on his behalf. Negotiations dragged out, but in March 1976, the antagonists finally settled out of court for an undisclosed sum.[618]

"I was, of course, representing the county at the time with help from a prominent federal court lawyer from Houston," Beck said. "The settlement was supposed to be secret, but the amount was not very much.

In addition to the barbecues and bumper stickers, a set of three cardstock images was printed up in Austin and sold in Fayette County to support Sheriff Flournoy against Marvin Zindler. The cards featured a front view of the Chicken Ranch, the sheriff being honored at the Fayette County Fairgrounds and five topless women purported to be former employees of the brothel. *Courtesy William "Trigger" Rogers.*

"The understanding of the settlement was that it was all going to charity, prearranged by, pre-picked by Zindler," he said. "I believe the sheriff wrote the check out of his account, and I think that check was written directly to the charity."[619]

Neither party ever revealed terms of the settlement, but Marvin hinted the amount approached $15,000. At least some of that money eventually found its way to charity, with Marvin pegging the size of the donation at somewhere between "some" and "all" over the years.

"I didn't want to break the county," Marvin said, explaining why he finally dropped his suit. "Besides, I didn't think the old sheriff would live long enough to get to court."[620]

The reaction in Fayette County was far less conciliatory. Many bitterly considered the settlement nothing less than outright victory for Marvin.

"I asked Jim Flournoy one day, 'Why didn't you shoot the son of a bitch right there? No damn grand jury would have indicted you,'" Leerie Giese said. "He said, 'Well, that's probably right.'"[621]

"I don't think Marvin should've won because Marvin had no business doing that," Dipple said. "It was Marvin that shut it down. He put Governor Briscoe on the spot, and they had to shut it down. I know the people over here, most of them were upset about having it closed down, because it was a good place."[622]

A grim sense of betrayal by their champion settled over La Grange. They'd rallied around the sheriff and poured their time, sweat and money into his defense, only to be rewarded with capitulation. Big Jim's reasons for settling with Marvin, though, ultimately had little to do with the community, Marvin or even the Chicken Ranch.

"You may be aware there was a lawsuit filed against him for assault, and contrary to the wishes of his constituents, he settled that case," Kitzman said. "I never discussed the case with him or why he settled it.

"I venture that the reason he settled it primarily was that he just did not want his wife to have to endure any more of that. One of the toughest things that ever happened to Sheriff Flournoy was the fact that his wife had to endure what took place over there in '73. That's why I say the reason he brought it to an end was that he couldn't bear seeing his wife suffer through it any more than was absolutely necessary.

"They raised thousands of dollars, and a lot of those people were very disappointed that he settled a lawsuit when they wanted him to fight it out to the bitter end. That's what his people really wanted," he said. "But it was a wise decision. The turmoil that would have grown out of that would have just made things much worse."[623]

By the time of the settlement, the "Chicken Ranch Affair" had already taken on elements of mythology. The handful of people who had witnessed the confrontation on the town square miraculously grew over the years to a great throng who watched Big Jim "beat Marvin up." To those too young to remember the actual events, the stories became a part of Texas folklore. At the time, though, Texans across the state simply scratched their heads, chuckled a bit to themselves and tried to make sense of the pitched battle being waged between the Old West sheriff and the publicity-seeking newsman.

"As crusades go, Zindler's one against the Chicken Ranch was probably not among his most popular with the populace," wrote newspaper columnist Dave McNeely. "But the sheriff's action, to say the least, was uncalled for.

"Somewhere here there is a moral. If anyone can figure out what it is—other than chickens coming home to roost—please let me know."[624]

Chapter 14

DIDN'T SEE *THAT* COMING

During the wee hours one September morning in 1973, somebody snuck up to Edna Milton's home and keyed her car.

Following her divorce from John Luke in 1971, Miss Edna had moved out of the home they shared outside town. Just a few months before Marvin Zindler began his television broadcasts exposing the Chicken Ranch, she'd placed a down payment on a modest, ranch-style house on South College Street in La Grange. A member of the community and major contributor to local charities for more than two decades, Miss Edna figured she'd earned acceptance enough to live in town.

That acceptance lasted only until the unwelcome media attention arrived with Marvin Zindler. Overnight, Miss Edna became a pariah.

"I went to get my car, and somebody keyed it. I didn't even know the word keyed—I just kept looking at it and looking and it and I thought, 'Well, somebody's gone and put some serious scratches on my car,'" she said, anger rising at the memory. "If you get in an accident that's one thing, but for somebody to come to your home and do that, that's terrible."[625]

Miss Edna had thought she could start over and make a new life in La Grange, the one place she'd called home longer than any other. La Grange had other ideas. Emboldened by the closure of the brothel, longtime opponents came out of the woodwork, determined to run her out of town. Under such pressure, the bank returned her down payment and asked to void the mortgage contract. Miss Edna got the message, loud and clear.[626]

Enter a newly licensed realtor from Austin, full of ambition. Flush with the boldness of youth, he drove up to the Chicken Ranch in early October and knocked on the door. Miss Edna just happened to be there at the time, and after her initial wariness eased, the realtor talked her into letting him broker a sale. Miss Edna, surprisingly enough, hadn't seriously considered selling the defunct brothel before that moment, but the realtor's sales pitch, coupled with losing her house in town, convinced her the time had come to get the hell out of Dodge.

With Miss Edna on board, the realtor wasted no time in driving to the Houston offices of two lawyers he happened to know, "Bill" and "Mike." The lawyers hadn't been looking for a defunct brothel to buy, but by the end of the meeting, they'd agreed to take a look at the property just for the novelty of it. They set up a meeting for late October, when they'd be traveling to Austin for a golf tournament being held in conjunction with a University of Texas football game.

"We stopped by about eleven o'clock in the morning, something like that. We knocked on the door, she answered and said she'd be glad to talk to us but it was too early, could we come back?" Bill said. "So we went in [to La Grange], had lunch and came back out in the early afternoon. We looked around, thanked her and went on to our golf outing.

"My partner—who didn't play golf—came back later that day, and he made a deal with her. He arrived [at the golf tournament] and called me off to the side," he remembered. "Mike said, 'Okay, I've made a deal. Are you in or are you out?'

"I said, 'Yeah, I'm in.' The price was very reasonable," Bill said. "That's why we bought it! We thought, 'You can buy history for $31,000? It should have a national landmark!'"[627]

Miss Edna made the deal quickly, selling the eleven acres and rambling nine-bedroom, nine-bath farmhouse for almost exactly what she'd paid for it a decade earlier. She'd grown weary of La Grange and tired of the constant headaches that now plagued the Chicken Ranch—an attitude plainly obvious to the Houston lawyers. With $31,000 in hand, she departed La Grange for the East Texas town of Gladewater, where her latest husband, Glenn Davidson, operated a mobile home business.[628]

"It was just a lark. Just pure lark. We didn't have any idea what we were doing," Bill said. "One of the interesting stories is that this golf outing was mostly put on by a banker for other bankers and bankers' lawyers. There were twelve banks represented.

"After Mike and I made our deal between ourselves, we went in after the party had been going for a period of time and called everybody's attention. 'Okay, we're buying the Chicken Ranch. And we want you guys to finance it. The deal is, everybody here gets to participate, and we'll draw high card for who gets to be lead bank,'" he said. "Because *all* of them wanted the loan file, just thinking the examiners would think it'd be a hoot to have this tiny, little bitty loan secured by the Chicken Ranch.

"We said, 'Here's how we're going to pay your loan back: For $500 we'll name a room after you. For $1,000 we won't,' Bill said. "We had our big laughs."[629]

By January, word had leaked of their purchase, and the phone calls started coming fast and furious. Writers, movie producers, talent agents—countless people approached then with surefire moneymaking plans for books, television shows, motion pictures, the works. There was only one catch: each of the interested parties wanted the Houston lawyers to put up the lion's share of financing, up to half a million dollars.

"Hey look, we bought this on a lark! We're not putting up any more money! If you want to do something, we'll sign a deal and *you* pay *us*. We're *not* going to pay you," Bill recalled, laughing at the absurdity of the situation. "We didn't buy this for an investment; it was a pure lark. Gosh, I even had a very well-known movie producer that came by our house and spent the night. He produced some really big movies."[630]

Ownership of the Chicken Ranch occasionally made things uncomfortable on the homefront as well. In one instance, Bill's ten-year-old daughter went to school and proudly announced to the class that her father had bought a chicken ranch in La Grange, which prompted a telephone call from her concerned teacher. It also made for some awkward moments when Bill was a candidate for the vestry of his church.

"I told the priest, 'Look, if this is any kind of embarrassment, I'll just drop out,'" Bill said. "[The priest] said, 'Heck no! Somebody with that kind of creativity, we need you on the vestry! We need money for the school. There are all sorts of things you can help us with!'"[631]

Owning a brothel—even a former brothel—came with more problems than Bill and Mike expected. Rumors abounded that Miss Edna had returned and reopened the Chicken Ranch for business, secretly admitting longtime customers. In fact, organized prostitution did indeed return to La Grange, albeit briefly, in February 1974. Buddy Zapalac—the publisher of the *La Grange Journal* and one of the most vocal defenders of the Chicken Ranch—and Jim Woods Jr. took it upon themselves to fill the void left by Miss Edna's departure by starting up a call girl service based out of the La Fayette Inn on Highway 71 east of town. This enterprise ended abruptly when Sheriff Jim Flournoy told them, in no uncertain terms, that if Miss

Edna could not operate a brothel in Fayette County, then by God, they couldn't either.[632]

Constant vandalism and looting soon forced the new owners to hire a full-time caretaker to live on the property to keep sightseers and souvenir hunters away. The man they hired, Bill McKellar, found the steady trickle of would-be clients knocking on the Chicken Ranch door too much to resist.

"A Texas Ranger came to my partner's office one day and said, 'Do you know that your caretaker has sort of reopened…?'" Bill said. "I didn't find out about that until my wife's hairdresser said, 'Did you hear that the Chicken Ranch has been reopened?' Then I went and asked Mike, and he says, 'Well, I wasn't going to tell you about the visit from the Texas Ranger…'"[633]

Meeting with DPS captain George Read, Bill realized he'd actually met the alleged prostitute—or one of them, at least. During a prior visit, McKellar introduced a young woman at the house with him as Sherrie, his niece. According to Captain Read, Sherrie was just one of a series of prostitutes working there, with McKellar rotating them out each Wednesday to keep the offerings fresh. Captain Read warned Bill and Mike that they would face charges if prostitution continued on the property.[634]

"So we did fire the caretaker," Bill said. "We never heard if the guy actually did [run prostitutes], because [Captain Read] just said this is what he'd heard. We just decided we needed to get rid of that caretaker."[635]

With the brothel safely back out of business, the lawyers found themselves pondering what in the world they would do with a property bought in jest that was rapidly losing its humor.

Across the country, Pete Masterson, an actor who'd grown up in Angleton, Texas, by chance picked up the April 1974 issue of *Playboy*. Now, despite the disbelieving chuckles such a statement normally provoked, Masterson really did read the articles—or at least one. A Texas journalist by the name of Larry L. King had penned a sometimes jaunty, sometimes caustic, sometimes wholly tangential article about the closing of the Chicken Ranch, and Masterson found it captivating.

Way back in August of the previous year, King had received a call at his Manhattan apartment from a friend in Texas, giving him a heads-up on the big Chicken Ranch blow-up. The friend suggested it would make a good article and suggested King fly down to cover it. King did so, but only grudgingly. He'd churned out reams of high-profile magazine articles over the years and

The Chicken Ranch's closure inspired an unusual amount of music—much of it stemming from the Broadway musical production of *The Best Little Whorehouse in Texas*. That Broadway show inspired a 1982 motion picture starring Dolly Parton and Burt Reynolds, a short-lived 1994 Broadway sequel titled *The Best Little Whorehouse Goes Public* and a 2001 national tour starring Ann-Margret. *Author's collection.*

grown burned out on the form. Plus, he was sick of being "that Texas writer" called upon to write quirky Texas pieces for East Coast publishers.

By his own admission, King farted around in Austin, partying with longtime drinking buddies, and didn't get to La Grange until a week after the brothel had closed. By then, even Johnny Carson had made La Grange the punchline on *The Tonight Show*, and townsfolk weren't too keen on reporters. A chance encounter with Big Jim did not go well, and King left town quickly with little more material than he'd arrived with.

It didn't matter. King wrote up a folksy, entertaining piece that made up for its lack of hard news facts with a heavy dose of irony. Rampant drinking, drug use and wanton sex in nearby Austin played a prominent role in the article, casting a stark spotlight on the hypocrisy inherent in the closure of a relatively straight-laced brothel that went out of its way to play by the rules, unwritten though they may be. He couldn't think of a suitable title for it, however. When it came time to mail the manuscript off, he scribbled the only thing that popped into his head across the first page: "The Best Little Whorehouse in Texas."

"It was as nice a little whorehouse as you ever saw," the article began. "It sat in a green Texas glade, white shuttered and tidy, surrounded by leafy oak trees and a few slim renegade pines and the kind of pure, clean air the menthol cigarette people advertise."[636]

King pocketed his $3,000 check from *Playboy*, the story ran and raised a few eyebrows here and there and that was that.

Until Masterson got ahold of it.

"I read it and I was moved by it. I thought it might make a good movie at the time, that's what I was thinking," Masterson said. "I put it away and thought about it. I talked with some people about it as a movie. I never thought about it as a musical."[637]

In the spring of 1976, he ran into composer and lyricist Carol Hall, an Abilene, Texas native. They, along with their spouses, attended an off-Broadway showing of *Vanities*, and the play's subject matter of three Texas women growing through life sparked a conversation.

"Have you ever thought about doing a Texas musical?" Hall asked.

The question caught Masterson off guard, as he'd never given much thought to doing *any* musical. Instead of blurting that out, he responded with a more cautious, "What did you have in mind?"

"I thought *The Last Picture Show* might make a good musical," she said.

Masterson thought about it for a moment and then shook his head. "I don't think that's as interesting as a musical," he said, "but I read something that Larry King wrote that might lend itself to a musical."[638]

Masterson didn't have a copy of the article to show her. He was performing in *That Championship Season* at the time, and someone had stolen the *Playboy* from his dressing room. To find another copy, he ended up going from porn house to porn house on Forty-Second Street to find a copy of the back issue. When he finally got the article to Hall, she loved it and gave King—who she happened to know—a call to pitch him the idea.[639]

"Carol, I don't know diddly-shit about musical comedy," King answered with his legendary understatement. "And only a dime's worth about the theatre."[640]

A meeting between the three confirmed King's complete lack of theatrical competence, but in short order, Masterson and King worked out a plot outline. Masterson's wife, actress Carlin Glynn, joined the group to play the lead role of the madam, Miss Mona Stangley, based loosely on Miss Edna. After the meeting, King wished them well with the project and planned to have nothing more to do with it. Inspiration intervened, however, and King returned a few days later with a sprawling, thirty-page opening scene based on an idea of Masterson's.[641]

"I rewrote the scene with another character, the character of Shy, who wasn't in Larry's script," Masterson said. "I staged it at the Actors Studio with no music yet. Carol saw this.

"The first time she was involved, she saw the scene we did, and based on that she wrote the first song of the musical based on the emotional response of the characters, called 'Girl, You're a Woman,'" he said. "We went from there. We built the show at the Actors Studio over a year. That's how it got started."[642]

Fits and starts came closer to the truth. *The Best Little Whorehouse in Texas* brought three strong-willed creative types together, and friction flared immediately. King had little use for song and dance and bristled every time Hall introduced a new song to the narrative. Masterson, when not playing referee to King and Hall, earned King's wrath by rewriting scenes on the fly. And when it came time to hammer out a collaboration agreement, more friction blossomed. The fact that the meager box office take from the Actors Studio showcase performances went directly to the actors because of union rules escaped King's understanding until late in the process, leaving him baffled and irate about all the blood and sweat he'd invested thus far for darn little return. And the clashes over music continued unabated.[643]

"Those song memos you keep sending," Hall confronted King one day. "*I'm* the songwriter. Why do you keep making them rhyme?"

"Hell, I dunno. It just seems easier."

"I am *not* putting any of your lyrics to music, Larry King."

"You don't seem to object to lifting lyrics from my article and script."

"I don't 'lift' them. I fold them in. That's standard practice. And I'm doing far less of it than most lyricists. I take one of your lines and then write two dozen of mine and you make it sound as if I'm stealing from you!"[644]

Much of what they put together for their Actors Studio run didn't work, but enough *did* work to inspire everyone involved to keep going. The production landed veteran actor Henderson Forsythe to play Sheriff Ed Earl Dodd, loosely based, naturally, on Big Jim. Tommy Tune, a six-foot-six Houston native, signed on to handle the choreography and co-direct with Masterson. Slowly but surely, the play took shape and developed some seriously biting social commentary in the process.[645]

"Well, for the Angelettes number we were going to do a sort of drilling tribute to the Chicken Ranch—you know how they make pictures of things during halftime at football games? But when we got to that point, there were only 10 girls available and I needed 16, so I said I can't do it," said Tune. "I didn't want to let the idea go, but I didn't know what else to do.

"Meanwhile, I had sent our stage manager down to 42nd Street to get me all sorts of sex games and objects and devices, because I was working on a number called 'Two Blocks from the Capitol Building.' It was about all the kinky sex you could get on this whole seamy street in Austin as opposed to this simply clean, pristine little whorehouse out in rural Texas," he explained. "That number got cut—it was just too seamy—but I had all these trinkets. And among them were these two inflatable dolls—they call them Love Dolls, you know, with artificial vaginas and mouths and everything? So I inflated these dolls and I was holding one on each arm, and I looked in the mirror and started dancing with them. Suddenly, I thought, 'My God, that's how we can do the Angelettes!'

"The point we were making, eventually, is that these girls on television are coarser and more vulgar and showing more to Americans on the TV set—and it's being accepted—than Miss Mona would allow her girls to do in public at the whorehouse. That's the double standard that is so easily recognizable in Texas and America," Tune said. "Also, if you were coming to see a show called *The Best Little Whorehouse in Texas*, you would expect to see all sort of lascivious writhing by the girls in the home, and we didn't choose to do that."[646]

By November 1977, the Actors Studio production had attained a level of buzz that prompted author and screenwriter William Goldman and his wife, Ilene Jones, to invite their friend Stevie Phillips along to a performance.

Phillips, who'd recently joined Universal Pictures to scout and acquire properties for the studio, liked what she saw. A lot. After the show, she offered to buy the rights on the spot. Universal had never bankrolled a theatrical production before but saw it as a good bet, with an eye toward adapting it as a motion picture in the future. Within a few days, a deal was in place, and *Whorehouse* appeared on the fast-track to opening off-Broadway, with the possibility of moving to Broadway if success warranted.

About this time, the parties realized they'd made one small oversight that could derail the entire production: they hadn't secured story rights from either Miss Edna or Big Jim, the two people at the heart of the play.[647]

OVER IN LA GRANGE, the Chicken Ranch itself received a new lease on life, of sorts. Once word spread that they had purchased the property, Bill and Mike had several entrepreneurs contact them about moving the building—lock, stock and barrel—to Houston and converting it into a theme restaurant. Like the various movie and book deals they fielded, these restaurant plans were pie-in-the-sky schemes, with no business plan or financing to back them up. But things changed in late 1976, when businessman Bill Fair approached them with an idea to move the building to Dallas, where he would transform it into a combination disco and chicken-themed restaurant on the site of the former Sportspage Club at 7136 Greenville Avenue.[648]

"This friend called and said he wanted to open a restaurant in Dallas, and could we make a deal?" Bill said. "So we agreed. I can't even remember what all he took, but whatever he took, we had some interest in the restaurant."[649]

Fair put his money where his mouth was, hiring interior designer Fred Merrill to plan the restaurant look and layout. Rather than move the entire building to Dallas, Fair and Merrill decided to only move the front parlor. As the largest room in the house, the parlor was also the most readily identifiable, with its semicircular bay window projecting from the right side of the structure. In the spring of 1977, they cut the parlor away from the house and loaded it onto a tractor-trailer rig. They also went through the remaining rooms, stripping away anything and everything that caught their attention—including furniture and drapes—before piling it onto the truck. With "Wide Load" flags flying, they hauled the whole shebang up to Dallas.[650]

"The location may have changed," crowed Fair once the parlor reached its new home, "but the notorious graffiti-covered walls have been carefully dismantled and reconstructed in the bar, remaining permanently preserved under coats of polyurethane plastic. Other relics may be purchased at the disco's gift shop and we plan to have memorabilia auctions periodically."[651]

"The Chicken Ranch on Greenville" opened to much fanfare on September 28, 1977. The parlor served as the main entrance and bar area, with the kitchen, restrooms and everything else located in the adjoining Sportspage Club building. Fair brought in Marvin Zindler for the grand opening, and Don Embry, Elvis Presley's studio and concert sound technician, handled the disco end of things. Dissatisfied with the brothel's rather plain, utilitarian furnishings, Fair installed bar stools supported by shapely women's legs carved of wood to increase the kitsch factor. Outside, a large circular sign depicting silhouettes of a rooster and hen beneath a heart proudly identified the new business.[652]

Diana Wilson, for one, watched as the new restaurant took shape on the Greenville strip among such party spots as Hornblower's and Humperdinck's and thought it looked like a promising place to work. She remembered the media attention when Marvin Zindler had it closed down and enjoyed ZZ Top's song "La Grange." She lived closer to the new place than Kellar's, the club she'd waitressed at on the Northwest Highway, so she applied for a job at the Chicken Ranch and got it.

"Greenville was a great place to party—plenty of band bars—but the Chicken Ranch was certainly different. There was stuff on the walls from its days as a whorehouse. Stuff like, 'Mike was here,' or, 'I Love Sandy,'" Wilson said. "You know, hooker graffiti. The owners didn't want to paint over it because it was part of the atmosphere. But there was lots of curiosity, walking around and seeing what was written. I know we did it as waitresses.

"My friends at the time had a lot of laughs over this. They said the customers were all going to be hitting on me as a hooker. I told them it wasn't going to be like that at all."[653]

Unfortunately, it turned out to be exactly like that. For some reason, many of the men coming in believed the new Chicken Ranch remained a brothel somehow able to operate openly in the middle of Dallas, with the restaurant aspect merely a cover. The uniforms the waitresses had to wear didn't help—a tight-fitting T-shirt with a deep-cut V-neck that had the waitress' name centered right between her breasts, an outfit that made Hooters girls look demure by comparison. The menu, too, helped set the tone with plenty of double entendres—a suspicious number of entrees emphasized hot thighs and huge breasts.

"Lots of men showed up thinking it was still a brothel. I got propositioned all the time," Wilson said. "We were told by the management and stuff,

Edna Milton stands outside the short-lived Chicken Ranch restaurant in Dallas. The owners hired Miss Edna as a hostess, thinking her presence would spur business. It didn't. *Courtesy* Dallas Morning News.

'These guys are going to think it's still that, and you just tell them it is now a restaurant and all you are serving is food and drink.'"[654]

Deciding the restaurant needed an extra boost, Fair tracked down Miss Edna and hired her to act as hostess.

"The madam introduced herself to us. She was a very nice woman. She struck me as a strong woman," Wilson said. "She was the one who gave us a lot of [advice], you know, 'If they come on to you, do this,' or 'If you had any problems, talk to so-and-so.'"[655]

It wasn't enough. Wilson quickly realized the Chicken Ranch had turned into a circus with tips wholly dependent on how much flirting and skin she'd share with the customers. Fed up, she resigned.

"It was a week and a half, two weeks, and I was, 'Nah.' That's because the business wasn't that good," she said. "And then when you get men thinking it's still a brothel on top of it? It's not a cool environment. Because they were, 'Okay, after dinner, you want to go meet?'"[656]

Miss Edna didn't stick around much longer, either. With Universal Pictures on the verge of backing *The Best Little Whorehouse in Texas*, Larry

King tracked her down to Dallas and had a brief sit-down meeting at the restaurant. When the subject of rights and compensation came up, King asked where he could reach her for future negotiations.

"Try me here," Miss Edna answered, then added in a conspiratorial tone, "but this sumbitch's likely to fold any day. People come out and drink whiskey but the food's not worth a shit. I don't like the job, nohow. I'll probably quit in a week or two."

A patron interrupted their conversation, requesting a photo with Miss Edna. She agreed but returned to the table in a sour mood.

"A few nights ago a man was doing that and the people with him went to sniggering," she explained. "I looked up and he was holding a five-dollar bill over my head.

"I snatched it out of that sumbitch's hand and run him off this place. He asked for his five dollars back. I told him, 'Hell, no, Mister. That's your bad-manners tax,'" she said. "That's why I won't stay at this damn job long. I'm tired of people treating me like some monkey in a circus."[657]

True to her word, Miss Edna jumped ship shortly thereafter. The Chicken Ranch on Greenville limped along for a few more months, finally giving up the ghost in January. Inadequate heating for the drafty old building, coupled with a limited menu—chicken spaghetti, chicken livers, Swiss chicken, etc.—and customers persistently more interested in bedding the wait staff did it in.

"There's no way it's going to stay closed. The Chicken Ranch is part of Texas history, and people aren't going to let it die. I guarantee it," insisted Merrill the following week. "It might take a rich Texan or a rich Arab to come up with the money. It might take moving the whole thing to Minneapolis, Minn. It might take someone who wants it for their little stud son. But there's no way the Chicken Ranch is going to stay closed."[658]

The Chicken Ranch needed more than Merrill's bravado to survive, though. After several investment deals fell through, Clyde Cromwell of the Small Business Administration ordered the property auctioned off to recoup some of the federally guaranteed loans backing the failed venture. Maybe two hundred people turned out for a three-hour auction on June 28 that netted $18,000. Among the items that sold were the svelte-legged barstools; sixteen used mattresses; a bag of brass brothel tokens; three thousand bumper stickers proclaiming "Bring it back! The Chicken Ranch"; and a stack of Gaylen Ackley's 45 single "Hello, Marvin Zindler."[659]

"It was a cancer in La Grange and it was a cancer here in Dallas," said Marvin, who attended the auction in person. "It lost money here, so I don't

Foreman I.T. Jarvis oversees the demolition of the Chicken Ranch restaurant in Dallas on September 11, 1978. "They told me it used to be the biggest whorehouse there ever was in Texas," Jarvis said. "To me it's just another job." *Courtesy* Dallas Morning News.

know why anyone would want to save it. When you come down to it, it was only good for one thing."[660]

Even so, it briefly looked as if the Chicken Ranch would rise from the ashes yet again when oilman V.A. "Boss" Hrbacek, one of the wealthiest citizens in La Grange, announced his intent to buy the parlor and move it back to Fayette County.

"I fly all around the world on business, and every place I go it's the same thing. Not a day goes by without somebody asking about it and saying it should never have been moved," Hrbacek explained. "I go to church and nice ladies, high-class, tell me it should be brought back to La Grange."[661]

The Chicken Ranch's white knight turned out to be a fleeting mirage. Hrbacek could never come to terms with the property owner, Stanley Kline. An investor with little concern for history or nostalgia, Kline ordered the building razed in order to clear the property for a strip mall development.

"It's completely gone, completely gone. It's just trash. It no longer exists," an annoyed Kline said as he watched over workers tearing the building apart in September, two weeks shy of the one-year anniversary of the restaurant's opening. "I don't want to sound rude, but it's just a nuisance to me. It's of no interest to me whatsoever."[662]

For a building with so much Texas history behind it, hosting celebrities, governors and presidents, the demolition came as an ignominious end, one final, spit-in-your-eye triumph by the vindictive DPS agent from Houston and his agent of vengeance, Marvin Zindler.

Miss Edna took a slightly more philosophical perspective.

"It's like when a person you care about dies, you can't mourn about it forever," she said. "When an old building dies, it dies."[663]

UNIVERSAL'S ALARM AT THE lack of any rights agreements with Miss Edna and Big Jim grew rapidly over the ensuing months, to the point where all work ceased on the musical. Marvin Zindler, being a self-promoting public figure, was fair game for the show's satire, but work could not resume on *The Best Little Whorehouse in Texas*, lawyers informed everyone, until both the madam and sheriff signed releases.

"Oh, shit," said King. "That goddamned old sheriff won't likely be inclined to sign."

"We'll deal with Miss Edna first. From all you've told me I'm sure she could use a tidy sum of money," Phillips said. Then, showing some of her instincts as a Hollywood horse trader, she added, "We'll make the offer contingent on her delivering the sheriff's signature, too."[664]

After a week of phone calls and searching, King tracked down Miss Edna and set up a meeting with her in Dallas. From there, they piled into Miss Edna's Cadillac to make the drive to La Grange for a meeting with Big Jim.

"We sent Larry to meet him and the producer, Stevie Phillips. They basically went to talk to them to get the release from them so we could use their characters in the musical," Masterson said. King, Phillips and Miss Edna sat down with Big Jim at the Cottonwood Inn to work out an agreement. "The sheriff said, 'I don't want no money, but I want you to make a promise that you won't come within a hundred miles of my town, and whatever you think is coming to me, you can give it to this little lady here.'"[665]

In the end, Miss Edna got $40,000—her $25,000 cut plus Big Jim's $15,000—plus an additional $50,000 if a movie ever got made. In return, Big Jim extracted promises that neither La Grange nor Fayette County would be mentioned in any stage or film version of the story and that any film crews would steer clear of Fayette County. Just like that, La Grange and

The Chicken Ranch never produced brass tokens during its long history, but that did not stop entrepreneurs from creating modern versions to sell. The earliest print evidence for these tokens found by the author dates to only 1977. Other tokens incorporate 1975 pennies. There is no evidence of Chicken Ranch tokens existing prior to 1975. *Author's collection.*

Fayette County transformed into the fictional Gilbert and Lanvil County. The ease of Big Jim's signing came as a surprise, as did the gift of his payout to Miss Edna. That was the first substantive evidence that the madam and sheriff had shared a deeper relationship that went beyond professional acquaintances—and served as a validation of Masterson's instincts.[666]

"When we were writing the show, I said, 'I think the sheriff and the madam should've had a past history,'" Masterson said.

"There's no evidence of that," complained King.

"Well, they *should've* had," argued Masterson. "They *should* have gotten together. Let's use it, it makes a good story.

"So the truth is…it probably *was* true," Masterson said. "They didn't seem to mind."[667]

Before they left La Grange, King and Phillips rode with Miss Edna to pick up Trudy, the black woman who guarded the Chicken Ranch's door for so many years. The foursome drove out to take a look at the remains of the Chicken Ranch—a homecoming far more bitter than sweet.

"Bastard lawyers," Miss Edna said, staring at the gutted remains of the Chicken Ranch. "They cut the goddamn house right half in two to open their fucking restaurant."

"Oh, that don't be looking right," Trudy said softly. "It makes me sad."

Weeds and brush had grown up in the intervening years. Scattered concrete blocks marked the outline of where the parlor once stood. The long hallway where the parlor connected with the rest of the house lay exposed to the elements like a long scar. Glass from broken windows covered the floors, along with peeling linoleum and water-damaged mattresses and books. Vandals had knocked holes in the ceiling and walls and torn out lighting fixtures, reducing the famed Chicken Ranch to a filthy ruin.

"Shit, I wish I hadn't come out here," Miss Edna said after surveying the damage. "This makes me ashamed. Let's go, y'all."[668]

With *The Best Little Whorehouse* in Texas barreling full-tilt toward an off-Broadway debut at the Entermedia Theatre in downtown New York, inspiration suddenly struck Masterson: why not cast Miss Edna herself in the play? She could have a non-speaking role as Miss Wulla Jean, the elderly madam, and later take part in crowd scenes. She could also pull double-duty as "technical advisor." Her notoriety would surely generate additional press coverage, he reasoned.

"I wanted to make her an extra. She could talk to the girls and add some reality to the background of the characters," Masterson said. "She had a mouth on her. She could cuss with the best of the sailors. She would shock me sometimes. She'd lean over and tell me a line the girls ought to say, and it would be unprintable!

"I realized I needed another character, so we hired another girl, and she came in the second day," he said. "Miss Edna went over to her and felt her, like she was feeling the goods. Just like a piece of [meat] or something. She was checking out the merchandise: 'She'll do fine.'"[669]

Miss Edna signed on for $280 a week plus a $150 weekly living stipend. While her arrival in New York did generate a flurry of press coverage as expected, her technical advisory role didn't go quite so smoothly.

"Miss Edna, how involved did your girls get in their…work?" actress Becky Gelke asked during what probably ranked as the most awkward cast meeting of her career.

"I warned 'em against getting involved," Miss Edna answered. "Worst damn thing a working girl can do is fall in love with some John."

Chicken Ranch–themed glassware likely originated with the failed Dallas restaurant or with the short-lived Original Chicken Ranch Company's failed attempt in 1984 to establish a museum in La Grange. *Author's collection.*

"No, that's not what I meant. I wasn't talking about love," Gelke clarified. "I mean, okay, if they're…entertaining…oh, several customers *a night*, then how do they—?"

"Oh, I see what you mean," Edna said. "I always told my girls to turn their minds off: 'Just grease and slide, hunny, just grease and slide…'"[670]

After that, there were no more cast meetings with Miss Edna, although she by no means faded into the background. If she saw something she didn't like, Miss Edna started raising hell, and she got several changes made to the play.

"I changed some names. They had my mother's name on a nigger gal, and I got that changed," Miss Edna said. "Larry King wanted to use Pearl—that was my mother's name. I stopped that. So they called her Jewel. I don't give a damn. Call her 'Jewels in a Crown' as far as I'm concerned.

"One of the girls' names they had in the show, they called her April. Larry King, he'd found some letters out there in the trash dump, and April's name was there," Miss Edna said. "'Oh, you liked that name and decided to use it? I don't think so.' That was her real, legitimate name, and I don't think it would be right to do her that way. She was a nice person. After the place closed, she went on to nursing school and became a registered nurse. I said, 'No. Call her Amber then on the show.'"[671]

In April 1978, *The Best Little Whorehouse in Texas* finally opened. After the first night's performance, odds were pretty strong that there wouldn't be many more. Phillips gave away hundreds of tickets in desperation, the only reason the show hadn't performed in front of a bunch of empty seats. Unlike the ill-fated Chicken Ranch in Dallas, though, *Whorehouse* refused to go down without a fight.

"A wonderful accident happened. Apart from the fact that the show was terrific, Jacqueline Kennedy came on the third night," Phillips said. "My press agent was alert enough to get a photographer there quickly and get a picture of her entering under the word 'whorehouse' on the marquee. It appeared on the front page of *The New York Post*, and we were sold out thereafter.

"Within six weeks we moved to Broadway and the cost of our doing so was $750,000, all in," she said. "We paid it back in two and a half months; there isn't a show that I can think of that can do that anymore. And we ran for five years."[672]

Miss Edna only stuck with the production for a few months. New York didn't sit well with her—she hated climbing the six flights of stairs to her apartment and complained that the city's pollution irritated her breathing. On top of that, she never really developed the acting bug.

"Boring. Boring as hell," Miss Edna said. "I didn't have a speaking role anyway, so I just did the same thing every day. You step here today, you step here tomorrow and the next day and the next year and the year after.

"You do the thing over and over and over. If you wear your hair a certain way, you wear your hair that same way every day. Every month," she said. "You went in with that hairdo, that's the hairdo you're going to be stuck with the rest of your life. That's what you feel like. I just got bored."[673]

Once Miss Edna made up her mind, it stayed made up.

"One day, the stage manager called me at home after we'd moved to Broadway. He said Miss Edna quit," Masterson remembered. "I said, 'You mean she gave her notice?' He said, 'No, she quit and went home.'

"I said, 'She's supposed to give two weeks' notice according to actor's equity," he said. "He said, 'I told her that, but she told me what I could do with the equity rules!' She was gone. She'd had enough of New York."[674]

The play hardly skipped a beat. Momentum favored *Whorehouse* now, and the strange, raunchy and oddly emotional musical about the last days of a country brothel found itself the hottest ticket in town. The main narrative—

A wide array of Chicken Ranch "artifacts" appeared after the brothel's closure—the bottle opener and money clip pictured being among the most common. Other items include brass hat racks, boot jacks, bells, nut crackers, lamps, bed warmers, etc. Most are stamped "Chicken Ranch Texas Do Not Remove from Bedroom." All are modern fakes. *Author's collection.*

efforts by crusading reporter Melvin P. Thorpe to close the whorehouse—served as a framework from which to develop character sketches through song, sharp dialogue and humor. Prostitutes Amber and Shy, black housekeeper Jewel and wistful waitress Doatsy Mae took on added depth as the play paused to delve into their personal histories and motivations, even as it continued on to the inevitable conclusion. A song-and-dance routine by the Aggie football team combined sex and sports in a surprisingly entertaining way (to the delight of Texas A&M alumni everywhere), and the antics of a particularly evasive governor offered plenty of political satire.

While the entire musical hinged wholly on audiences buying into the "prostitute with a heart of gold" trope, the finale came across as surprisingly poignant and melancholy for a comedy. It was no more a historically accurate account of the closing of the Chicken Ranch than *Inherit the Wind* was of the Scopes Monkey Trial, but the quirky juxtaposition worked. Within a few months of moving to the 46th Street Theatre, it became clear Hall, King and Masterson had scored quite possibly the most unlikely hit in Broadway history.

"The three of us, all from Texas, always said our show was *not* about prostitution—it was about hypocrisy," said Carol Hall.[675]

Once awards season rolled around, the scrappy musical gave a good accounting of itself. Although it lost out to *Sweeney Todd* for Best Musical at

The Best Little Whorehouse in Texas boasts enduring popularity in the Lone Star State. Theatre Under the Stars' 2012 revival in Houston's Hobby Center proved so popular that the company brought the production back for the 2014 season at Miller Outdoor Theatre. *Author's collection.*

the 1979 Tony Awards, Carlin Glynn and Henderson Forsythe both won for Featured Actor and Actress in a musical.

The musical's success wasn't hailed and cheered from all quarters. In La Grange, more than a few folks had more than their fill of publicity stemming from the Chicken Ranch.

"I wouldn't go across the street to see that play," Big Jim growled.[676]

Orders from Governor Dolph Briscoe had closed the Chicken Ranch five years earlier. The property's new owners chopped the building to pieces and left it a ruin. A wrecking ball in Dallas buried the relocated parlor, once and for all. Despite such steep odds, *The Best Little Whorehouse in Texas* gave the Chicken Ranch the one thing its detractors never wanted and could never take away: immortality.

"One of the things when we made the show, a number of people—including Universal Pictures—wanted us to change the title because they wouldn't take our ads at first, the newspapers and television. On buses in New York. They wouldn't put our ads in the tube stations in London," Masterson said. "I said, 'That's a deal-breaker. I'm going to make whorehouse a household word.'

"And we kinda have."[677]

Chapter 15

ENDURING LEGACY

Texas' Eagle Ford shale oil boom of the 2010s echoed the Austin chalk boom of the 1980s. Drilling fever hit Fayette County in 1981, when technology and demand intersected to make exploitation of the Austin chalk formation economically viable. More than one thousand new wells began pumping throughout the rolling hills of East Central Texas, with drilling rigs popping up on farms and cattle pastures. But when the roughnecks came to La Grange, they dubbed their first well—pumping out low-sulfur crude to the tune of 107 barrels a day—"Chicken Ranch No. 1."

Those oil field workers trucking in equipment heard ZZ Top's blues-drenched "La Grange" often enough over the radio, but if they listened closely, they might catch local stations spinning Gaylen Ackley's elegiac single "Hello Marvin Zindler" or Austin favorites Man Mountain and the Green Slime Boys' "The Ballad of the La Grange Chicken Ranch." Later on, singer-songwriter Dale Watson alluded to the Chicken Ranch in his popular cut "Truck Stop in La Grange," Willis Alan Ramsey hinted at it in "Northeast Texas Women" and Billy Joe Shaver threw subtlety to the wind for an Old West take with "Aunt Jessie's Chicken Ranch," while the Austin Lounge Lizards sang about getting "laid low in La Grange" in their song "Jalapeño Maria." Clearly, to the delight of some and the horror of others, La Grange's identity only grew more tightly associated with the brothel over the course of the previous decade, not less.[678]

The runaway success of *The Best Little Whorehouse in Texas* played no small part in that notoriety. The musical opened in Houston to large and enthusiastic

The members of ZZ Top weren't the only musicians inspired by the closing of Texas' oldest brothel. Singer-songwriter Gaylen Ackley self-published his recording "Hello Marvin Zindler," and legendary Austin live music venue Armadillo World Headquarters produced "The Ballad of the La Grange Chicken Ranch" by Man Mountain and the Green Slime Boys. *Author's collection.*

crowds and soon launched a national tour even as the original production on Broadway continued playing to sell-out crowds. By the time Chicken Ranch No. 1 began pumping black gold in Fayette County, *Whorehouse* had struck box office gold in Australia, Greece, South Africa and New Zealand. An ambitious production scheduled to open in London's famed West End in February boasted Tony-winning Carlin Glynn, reprising her role as Miss Mona. Since many Britons were unfamiliar with the story of the Chicken Ranch, the show's promoters decided to bring in Edna Milton for a round of publicity interviews with London's famously sensational tabloids. The plan hit a snag right away, though: nobody could find Miss Edna.[679]

Following her abrupt departure from Broadway, Miss Edna hightailed it straight back to Dallas, where she made the rounds of all the local media and announced she'd signed with author Robin Moore—who had collaborated with Xaviera Hollander on *The Happy Hooker*—to write her memoir.

"It's going to be a history of the Chicken Ranch," Miss Edna said. "I'd only read one book about a madam, and I didn't like it. It was *A House Is Not a Home*, you know, about Polly Adler. She said she never hustled herself. I can't believe that. So I never finished the book."

She and her husband of seven years, Glenn Davidson, also announced their plans to open a club. Her less-than-stellar experience with the failed Chicken Ranch on Greenville didn't seem to give her pause.

"I've never owned a club before, but I don't think it will be much different," she said. "I'll just be there to talk to people and act as hostess."[680]

"Miss Edna's Chicken Ranch" opened at 5404 Lemmon in Dallas in October 1978, serving pan-fried chicken and steaks, with Freddy King Jr. performing in the lounge area. Miss Edna invested most of her Broadway money into the place, but running a bar turned out to be more complicated than running a brothel. The place closed a year or so later. On top of that, the deal with Moore to write a Chicken Ranch memoir also fell through, ending any hope of a literary income.[681]

Bank accounts empty, Miss Edna separated from Davidson and struck out on her own once again. When the British *Whorehouse* people finally tracked her down, they found her working in a Midland, Texas massage parlor. It took little to entice her into a short publicity tour of London, and predictably, the British tabloids loved her—especially when Miss Edna reacted with distaste to the thriving sex shops in the Soho District.

"This really isn't very nice, you know," she observed.[682]

While Glynn eventually won an Olivier Award for her West End portrayal of Miss Mona, the real excitement was brewing stateside. Universal Pictures—flush with $67 million in profits from the Broadway run and touring companies—put a movie version on the fast track. Larry L. King went to work on the screenplay while co-directors Pete Masterson and Tommy Tune threw themselves into pre-production work. Early on, Universal fixated on Dolly Parton for the Miss Mona role and began negotiations. For the role of Sheriff Ed Earl Dodd, the cussin'est lawman in Texas, the producers initially courted the legendary country singer Willie Nelson with much enthusiasm. Masterson and Tune scouted locations across Texas for the film. Hallettsville landed the role of fictional Gilbert, and the Chicken Ranch itself would be portrayed by the historic Murchison House outside Pflugerville. In fact,

The Chicken Ranch Dance Hall existed for several years in the tiny Fayette County community of Nechanitz, just a few miles outside La Grange. *Photo by Lisa Elliott Blaschke.*

pretty much everyone in Texas seemed to fall over themselves to be part of the production. Texas A&M University agreed to allow filming at its football stadium, Kyle Field, and the state had no problem allowing filming in the capitol in Austin. Even Southwest Texas State (now Texas State University) got into the act by providing the entire Bobcat Marching Band for the show-stopping "Sidestep" number.[683]

Just about the only location in Central Texas that didn't have a piece of the action was La Grange itself, and that didn't go over too well in some quarters.

"There's only one La Grange," complained chamber of commerce spokeswoman Marian Butts. "I really think they will be missing something. I'm from La Grange, and I don't think they could find a better place than La Grange."[684]

Despite the protests, the film crew honored the handshake agreement with Sheriff Jim Flournoy and never came near the county. In truth, King, Masterson and Tune had far bigger headaches to deal with than hard feelings in La Grange. The studio abruptly dropped its negotiations with Nelson and instead signed Burt Reynolds to play the sheriff. Parton insisted on writing her own songs. Reynolds demanded rewrites that emphasized macho action and an expanded romance between the sheriff and madam.

"I think Burt Reynolds wants to make *Smokey and the Bandit Go to a Whorehouse*," King groused.

Before the dust settled, Universal forced King, Masterson and Tune off the production, and half of Carol Hall's songs from the play were scrapped. Colin Higgins, who came on to direct, extensively rewrote King's script. The $20 million production finished its cinema run with gross box office receipts totaling nearly $70 million—a decent take but somewhat disappointing considering the runaway success of the original play.

The movie enjoyed one big advantage over the play in that once the cinema run, television broadcasts and home video were all taken into account, exponentially more people saw *that* version of the story than any other. Consequently, people thought more of Burt Reynolds and Dolly Parton than anything else whenever the topic of the Chicken Ranch came up.

"I don't think they ever intended to let us direct it," Masterson said. "They used us to get the basic script, to scout locations and do all the shit work, and then kicked us out."[685]

A decade later, Hall, King, Masterson and Tune reunited in an attempt to capture lightning in a bottle one more time. In 1990, the IRS seized the Mustang Ranch—a legal brothel in Nevada—and subsequently auctioned it off for tax fraud. Like the Chicken Ranch before, that little bit of true history sparked an idea for a play. The resulting musical, *The Best Little Whorehouse Goes Public*, opened on Broadway in 1994 but lasted just sixteen performances. Even so, it garnered Tony Award nominations for Dee Hoty as Lead Actress in a Musical as well as for Orchestration and Costume Design.

"What we concocted was that this guy ran off with all the assets of the Mustang Ranch, and he left a big debt to the government. There wasn't any way to pay it off, so they got Mona to run it. They recruited her from Chicken Ranch fame and brought her to Reno, Nevada, to run it," Masterson explained. "There was no way to make enough money running a whorehouse to pay the government back, so they sold shares of stock. The government didn't like it because it didn't look good. And they closed them down for good.

"It didn't have the heart the first one did. I think that's basically it," he said. "It was still pretty good. I liked it a lot. The critics hated it."[686]

Jim Flournoy retired as Fayette County sheriff on January 1, 1981, at the age of seventy-eight. Big Jim, still an imposing figure despite his advanced years, indicated he would have retired before the previous election but ran one last campaign out of respect for his constituents. Enforcing the law, he complained, had grown too onerous.

"It's getting to where we get sued so often for violating some criminal's rights," Big Jim said, wistful for the days when a Texas sheriff wielded much more power and faced much less oversight. "We got a big oil boom going. Lots of outside people are coming in. The new sheriff is going to have a big job."[687]

Big Jim—inducted into the prestigious Texas Rangers Hall of Fame in 1976—didn't hesitate to share his thoughts on the state of Fayette County and law enforcement in general. The only thing that brought conversation to a halt was mention of the Chicken Ranch.

"I don't want to hear that name again," he said, his voice carrying a clear warning. "My wife is sick of hearing about it, and so am I."[688]

Retirement did not last long for Big Jim. He died in his home on October 27, 1982, at the age of eighty. Lieutenant Governor Bill Hobby and a contingent of nearly one hundred lawmen from across the state attended his funeral. His obituary ran in newspapers from Los Angeles to New York, and the venerable *Times* of London devoted a full story to his passing, celebrating him as the legendary sheriff who defended the Chicken Ranch from closure.[689]

Even Big Jim's arch-enemy, Marvin Zindler, confessed to keeping a photo of Sheriff Jim on his desk at KTRK and praised his one-time nemesis as "a great sheriff who thought he was doing the right thing with the house of prostitution.

"The old man was really a great guy."[690]

The other sheriff involved in the brothel controversy, Austin County's Truman Maddox, managed to avoid questions about Marvin Zindler and the Wagon Wheel the rest of his career. He retired in 1987. Although homebound by declining health in his later years, Sheriff Maddox regularly entertained friends until his death on March 19, 2000. Obituaries made no mention of his involvement with Marvin Zindler's great prostitution exposé three decades before.[691]

Although the Chicken Ranch gained national notoriety in 1973 that went on to spawn a hit play and movie, it took a fellow by the name of Walter Plankinton to figure out a way to capitalize on the defunct brothel's reputation in a more *direct* manner.

A dreamer with loads of ambition and an inferiority complex to match, the thrice-divorced Plankinton could spot business potential in almost any situation. During his life, he'd launched careers in garbage collection, mining, dairy farming, trucking, politics (losing badly in the Colorado governor's race) and even operated a shrimp boat for a time. The business ventures took him from Texas to Colorado to California to Belize. Unfortunately, he didn't possess the discipline or business acumen to succeed at any of them. After battling severe heart disease for years, Plankinton essentially retired to the quiet desert town of Pahrump, Nevada, in 1976.[692]

Almost immediately, Plankinton ran afoul of local politics. A man with an insatiable appetite for attention, upsetting the apple cart came naturally to him. He railed against local graft and corruption and, during a failed bid for a seat on the county commission, made enemies of Nye County sheriff Jay Howard and district attorney Peter Knight. He entertained himself by regularly visiting the legal brothels that dotted the rural Nevada landscape. He soon realized that Pahrump, at the very edge of Nye County, was the closest location a brothel could legally operate in proximity to Las Vegas, sixty miles away. By September, Plankinton determined that Pahrump had never incorporated, so no local ordinances prevented him from opening a brothel. He purchased two mobile homes for $14,000 and, remembering the national publicity generated just a few years before by the closing of the Chicken Ranch in Texas, appropriated the name for his new venture.[693]

Naming his bare-bones brothel the Chicken Ranch was an act of genius by Plankinton, a man never lacking in chutzpah. Miss Edna considered "Chicken Ranch" a simple nickname and never used it in any legal dealings. Likewise, subsequent owners of the property never thought to trademark the name. Plankinton, with no connection to the Chicken Ranch whatsoever, didn't ask permission or make any effort to buy the name. He simply claimed it, and nobody questioned him.

"That's precisely what happened. He was just a liar," Miss Edna said. "It was just a dumpy trailer house. That's all. I saw a bunch of them from Las Vegas on, and I didn't see any of them that was anything to brag about."[694]

The result was instant legitimacy and a track record dating back to the 1800s—at least as far as potential clients were concerned. To the local power

A menu of services offered from the Chicken Ranch of Pahrump, Nevada. Founder Walter Plankinton chose to name his brothel after the La Grange landmark because of the national notoriety stemming from its high-profile closure. Beyond that, there is no connection. *Author's collection.*

brokers, it mattered not one bit. Nye County, Plankinton soon found out, existed in a universe far removed from Fayette County.

The day before the Chicken Ranch opened, Plankinton drove his only prostitute to Tonopah, the county seat, for age verification and registration. Sheriff Howard, an obese man who enjoyed his power a bit too much, spotted Plankinton and confronted him.

"Plankinton, you still plannin' to open that whorehouse over there, even though I told you not to?" Sheriff Howard demanded. "Well, Plankinton, I'll be down to getcha, and when I do, don't you resist me."

True to his word, the sheriff arrested Plankinton the next day and hauled him in front of the justice of the peace. Despite his protests, the justice of the peace found Plankinton guilty of violating a nonexistent ordinance prohibiting prostitution in the phantom town of Pahrump.

That might have been the end of the second incarnation of the Chicken Ranch had Plankinton not noticed a property outside the hypothetical city limits. Secretly bankrolling his son to purchase the desert property for $16,000 so as not to alert his enemies, he closed the deal and moved his two trailers before anyone could stop him. After battling the utility companies for electricity and water service for months, the Chicken Ranch finally reopened on March 18, 1978.[695]

Despite ongoing legal battles with the county political machine—the so-called Tonopah Mafia—Plankinton's brothel flourished due to its proximity to Las Vegas and the steady flow of gamblers and conventioneers. By mid-1978, the Chicken Ranch had expanded and employed a dozen full-time prostitutes who earned in the neighborhood of $1,000 a week. Plankinton himself grossed nearly half a million dollars annually by then, a situation Nye County's reigning brothel king, Bill Martin, found intolerable. Because of its location, the Chicken Ranch intercepted traffic from Las Vegas and severely cut into the business of Nye County's more established brothels. The Shamrock, 80 miles from Vegas; Fran's Star Ranch, 113 miles away; and Bobby's Buckeye Bar, 200 miles off—all lost patrons to Plankinton and his upstart Chicken Ranch. Impatient with the slow pace of ongoing legal harassment against Plankinton, in June 1978, Martin hired three thugs to burn the Chicken Ranch to the ground.[696]

During an overnight trip to Las Vegas, a frantic 5:00 a.m. phone call from his son, Doug, woke Plankinton.

"Dad, the Ranch is gone," Doug shouted, nearly incoherent on the other end of the line. "Someone just burned the Ranch to the ground."[697]

Three armed men violently forced their way into the brothel after closing, dousing the trailers with fuel and setting them ablaze. Fifteen people barely escaped the inferno that consumed all six double-wides and vehicles on the property. Miraculously, nobody died, and only a handful suffered relatively minor injuries in escaping from the blaze. Sheriff Howard, though, refused to investigate—until he learned two FBI agents had arrived on the scene.

"He jumped out of his car as fast as he was ever capable of jumping, and waddled toward the roped area intending, obviously, to step right over the rope. As he lifted his huge leg, the agent in charge stepped right in front of him and ordered him to stay behind the rope barrier," Doug said. "The sheriff arrogantly informed the agent that this was his county and he was there to take charge.

"The agent, in an uncompromising and authoritative voice, enlightened him fully, saying, 'This is now the business of the FBI. Please return to your office and remain there until you are summoned, because you, too, are under suspicion, Sheriff,'" he said. "Visibly shaken by what the agent said, the sheriff obeyed. He sheepishly walked away, got into his car and quietly drove off."[698]

Plankinton, once he got over the shock, milked the publicity for all its worth. Within five days, he'd moved several new mobile homes to the property, placing them adjacent to the burned-out crime scene, and reopened for business with much fanfare. The arson attack made national news. In Texas, most people hearing about the fire naturally assumed the stories referred to the original building. The confused story that someone had burned the La Grange Chicken Ranch to the ground persisted for decades.

The war between Plankinton and the Tonopah Mafia continued unabated. The arson investigation stalled. Death threats and armed robberies followed. Plankinton discovered a bomb wired into his car. The situation grew ugly, to say the least. Unexpectedly, a political novice, Marcia "Joni" Wines, defeated Sheriff Howard in the next election. Despite stiff opposition, Sheriff Wines reopened the investigation into the Chicken Ranch fire. In December 1979, Martin, Jack Tatum and Kenneth Kolojay were indicted in federal court on counts of arson, perjury and conspiracy, with the arson team leader, Elbert Easley, as the prosecution's star witness. The arson and conspiracy charges were dismissed due to jurisdiction issues, but on December 31, 1980, the jury convicted all three of perjury.[699]

Seemingly victorious, Plankinton soon opened a small airstrip at the Chicken Ranch to fly in high rollers from Las Vegas. This garnered additional national media attention. When the national touring production of *The Best Little Whorehouse in Texas* opened in Las Vegas, Plankinton and seventeen prostitutes from the Chicken Ranch attended a show with much fanfare, generating even more press for the brothel. But the legal battles with the Tonopah Mafia didn't ease in the slightest. Exhausted from nearly six years of nonstop harassment—some of it life-threatening—Plankinton abruptly sold the Chicken Ranch to a group of investors in December 1981 for a tidy $1.1 million.[700]

The new owners, led by Kenneth Green, quickly established détente with the Tonopah Mafia. Green brought in Russell Reade to manage the brothel, and Reade, a former science teacher and football coach from Sebastopol, California, quickly won over a lot of skeptics with his easy manner.

"I loved teaching, but it had become very frustrating for me," Reade said. "I put in a lot of hours and the kids were eager to learn there. They come from the country so they're polite. But there was just never enough money."[701]

He landed the job after responding to an ad in the *Wall Street Journal* and soon became known as "Mr. Madam." On his final day of teaching, his students gave him a send-off by decorating his classroom with pink and blue condoms they'd inflated.[702]

By 2015, the Nevada Chicken Ranch boasted seventeen bedrooms and seventeen baths on forty acres surrounded by peach orchard. A free-standing bungalow was geared toward overnight stays. The airstrip closed in 2004. The brothel employed up to twenty-five women at a time, explained Debbie Rivenburgh, Chicken Ranch madam since 1987, but they rotated in and out weekly, so at any given time between eight and fifteen women were available for clients.

"We like to connect ourselves to the original Chicken Ranch," Rivenburgh said. "People are curious. A lot of tourists stop in here. They've seen the movie, *The Best Little Whorehouse in Texas*. We have the history of the original Chicken Ranch written up in our menu, so we like to think we do carry on some of the traditions of being a place where men can come and relax and enjoy and spend time with beautiful women and walk away with an experience they might not have had if they had not stopped in here."

On occasion, they've even hosted customers who patronized the original brothel in La Grange decades before.

"It's uncommon, because I think most of them would be older by now. But we encounter people that are from that area, from Texas in general, and they know the original Chicken Ranch was in Texas. So we like to think we are keeping a lot of the original Chicken Ranch's traditions alive."[703]

THE CHICKEN RANCH'S POPULARITY continued to grow over the years. In 1981, a Dallas-based clothing company, Peddlers II, launched "The Chicken Ranch Collection," a line of apparel featuring a tweaked version of the circular "Chickens in Love" logo initially used by the ill-fated Chicken Ranch restaurant. Despite shipping twelve thousand nightshirts early on, limited distribution kept the fashion statement from widely catching on. In La Grange itself, Todd Hoffman and his partner, Bob Burns, imagined a greater future for the Chicken Ranch. They saw the decaying La Grange brothel as a potential tourist attraction. They bought the eleven acres in

1986, and in September "The Original Chicken Ranch, Inc." went public with their plans—and what grand plans they had.[704]

On the eleven-acre site, they planned to build an elaborate, two-story museum patterned loosely after the style of the Murchison House in Pflugerville. Although the museum would look more like the house from the movie version of *The Best Little Whorehouse in Texas*, lumber from the remains of the actual Chicken Ranch would be used in the construction. Later, once the museum opened, a more faithful replica of the rambling, jerry-built brothel would go up on land behind the museum. To finance the ambitious, half-million dollar vision, they subdivided a section of the property into forty-five million one-inch square plots, which initially sold for $8.00 (later $9.95) each: the same cost as a "date" with one of the girls at the Ranch back in the 1950s.[705]

"It's really a piece of history. It will be like a national monument," Hoffman said. "It will be first class, a place to bring the wife and kids. It will be a bordello atmosphere, but it's not going to be a dirty book store."[706]

An artist's rendering of the Original Chicken Ranch Company's proposed museum. The building more closely resembled the brothel from the movie *The Best Little Whorehouse in Texas* than the actual Chicken Ranch. It was never built. *Author's collection.*

Initial reactions to the announcement were positive. The La Grange Chamber of Commerce endorsed the plan, and the Fayette County Commissioners Court—which now included Dan Beck, the former county attorney who had spoken up in favor of the Chicken Ranch during Marvin Zindler's broadcasts more than a decade earlier—reacted positively. Buoyed by the show of support, the Original Chicken Ranch opened a temporary office in town near Highway 71 where the one-inch plots were sold, along with other memorabilia. While the brothel never sold souvenirs, the failed restaurant in Dallas had produced some faux brass tokens, similar to ones used at some brothels in the Old West. These proved popular, and the Original Chicken Ranch ordered a bunch with the now-familiar "Chickens in Love" design, as well as other trinkets and souvenirs with "Chicken Ranch" emblazoned on them.[707]

Hoffman soon began planning for phase two of his grand plan: a five-day "Chicken Fest" held annually on Memorial Day weekend at the Fayette County Fairgrounds. The event would be huge, attracting upward of 250,000 people and featuring headlining musical acts such as ZZ Top, Willie Nelson and Dolly Parton. A barbecue cook-off would boast a whopping $40,000 purse.[708]

Such pie-in-the-sky plans came crashing back to reality soon enough. By January, the La Grange Ministerial Association, led by Monsignor Harry Mazurkiewicz, blasted the plan, condemning "any attempt to glorify, memorialize or otherwise celebrate…an immoral and illegal house of prostitution."

Mazurkiewicz called on all residents to join the town's clergy in "openly and strongly opposing this blight on our homes, our families and the generation to come."[709]

Mayor Charlie Jungmichel, who had complained loudly back in 1981 about the damage he believed the *Best Little Whorehouse* movie would do to the town's reputation, showed no mellowing during the intervening years, calling the plans "a slap in the face to the people in our county."[710]

The scathing attacks stunned Hoffman, who had expected widespread support. He didn't see a historical museum as glorifying anything. His increasingly frustrated explanations that the planned museum would be a tasteful examination of a colorful episode of Texas history and not an actual working whorehouse fell on deaf ears. Pointing out the economic benefit of Chicken Fest—and that others already profited from the Chicken Ranch's fame—got him nowhere.

To raise money to fund construction of the proposed museum, the Original Chicken Ranch Company sold one-inch square plots of land for $9.95 each. The Fayette County Appraisal District maintained a separate book for the novelty deeds. *Author's collection.*

"We're not interested in the money," Jungmichel sniffed. "I think our morals are a little better than that."[711]

The La Grange City Council lined up behind the mayor in opposition, denying Hoffman the permits needed to hold Chicken Fest at the Fayette County Fairgrounds. The chamber of commerce meekly withdrew its support for the museum and Chicken Fest. The commissioners court fell silent. Hoffman, by this time as angry as he was frustrated, vowed Chicken Fest '87 would happen come hell or high water and threatened to take the event elsewhere. He claimed sales of thirty to forty thousand one-inch lots, and each Chicken Ranch "owner" would have free admission to the festival.

Chicken Fest never happened. In the face of relentless opposition, Hoffman lamented that 10 percent of locals opposed the plans, another 10 percent approved and as many as 80 percent just didn't care one way or another. The Original Chicken Ranch withered on the vine.

"The Chicken Ranch is a part of Fayette County's history," Hoffman said. "I'm not interested in bringing pornography into this operation…only history."[712]

Hoffman's vision didn't go completely unrealized, however. It just took another town to see the historic value in a long-departed brothel. The popularity of *The Best Little Whorehouse in Texas* inspired San Angelo, Texas, to embrace its own local brothel. Founded in 1896, Miss Hattie's operated openly on wild and woolly Concho Street until the Texas Rangers closed it for good in 1946. When the city launched a major urban renewal effort to clean up Concho, Evelyn Hill purchased the old building that once housed Miss Hattie's and was amazed to find the upstairs rooms filled with the original furnishings, as well as trunks of clothes and other personal items that once belonged to prostitutes.

After a three-year restoration, Miss Hattie's reopened as a museum, complete with a turn-of-the-century gold-gilt pressed-tin ceiling, velvet drapes and a red-light signal system, used to warn guests and employees whenever the law showed up. The elderly Miss Hattie herself approved of the restoration when she paid a visit with her granddaughters shortly before her death. A steady stream of visitors, young and old, queued up for the daily tours. When it came to embracing unvarnished local history, San Angelo grabbed a nearly four-decade—and counting—head start on La Grange.[713]

IF THOSE WHO WANTED to whitewash La Grange's history thought the demise of the Original Chicken Ranch marked the end of the town's association with the brothel, 1990 proved to be a very disappointing year. Unexpectedly, the Chicken Ranch became the most talked-about political topic in the state.

Oliver Kitzman ran for a seat on the Texas Court of Criminal Appeals as a Republican, challenging long-serving Democrat Sam Houston Clinton. Kitzman ran as a law-and-order candidate, criticizing Clinton as out of touch and too focused on technicalities. Clinton wasted no time in blasting Kitzman for hypocrisy, pointing out that Kitzman looked the other way when he served as district attorney for Fayette and Austin Counties during the early 1970s when both the Chicken Ranch and Wagon Wheel operated openly.

"My opponent is fond of speaking nowadays of strong support for law enforcement," Clinton said. "But as a longtime district attorney he seems to have followed a policy of selective enforcement of the law, ignoring madams of notorious houses of prostitution in his own jurisdiction."[714]

The tactic proved effective. Clinton won a sixth term before eventually retiring from the court in 1996. But the judicial race only counted as an undercard to the main event for most Texans. The Texas governor's race strutted onto the main stage and instantly sucked all the air out of the room.

Clayton W. Williams Jr., an oil man and Texas A&M alum raised in West Texas, took on Democratic state treasurer Ann Richards in an attempt to become only the second Republican governor since Reconstruction. The race, amusingly dubbed "Claytie and the Lady," promised—and delivered—spectacular political fireworks. Despite enjoying a double-digit lead over his opponent early in the race, a series of self-inflicted gaffes disrupted Williams' campaign.

Running as a "Good Old Boy," Williams put his foot in his mouth with ill-timed sexist jokes, and rumors that he'd visited brothels in his younger days dogged him. The rumors became such an issue that his campaign announced he'd address the matter after returning from an out-of-state trip. Reporter John Gravois made up his mind not to wait and tracked Williams down in Scottsdale, Arizona. Rather than offer the standard "No comment," Williams instead spoke openly and at length about his experience at brothels—the Chicken Ranch in particular.

"I've never claimed to be a perfect man. It's part of growing up in West Texas…It's like the Larry McMurtry book *The Last Picture Show*," Williams explained. "As a teen-ager, it's part of growing up in West Texas. You go to Mexico. It's part of the fun."[715]

Republican candidate Clayton Williams, Jr. lost his 1990 bid to the Texas governorship due, in part, to his admission of frequenting the Chicken Ranch while he was a student at Texas A&M. The news attracted national attention and provided much fodder for political cartoonists. *Courtesy Jimmy Margulies.*

"What he did before we were married is certainly his business," his wife, Modesta, chimed in. "That doesn't bother me at all. Everybody has a past, and for the West Texas boys, that was part of their growing up. I hope no one is offended."[716]

And, naturally, Williams visited the Chicken Ranch in La Grange during his years as an undergraduate at Texas A&M, as so many other Aggies had done before and after him.

"It was kind of what the boys did at A&M," he said. "It was a lot different in those days. The houses were the only place you got serviced then."[717]

Reaction came swift and fierce. Bill Kenyon, Williams' press secretary, tried his best to defuse the situation, explaining, "One of Clayton's greatest strengths as a person is one of his greatest weaknesses as a politician. He always tries to be honest."[718]

"He implies that women are here to 'service' men," Richards' campaign spokesman Glenn Smith shot back. "That kind of attitude is as insulting to men as it is to women."[719]

The national media, until then content to largely ignore the Texas gubernatorial race, jumped on Williams with both feet.

"The most you can say for the contest for the governorship of Texas is that the voters cannot claim to be bored," wrote Mary McCrory for the *Washington Post*. "In Texas, where excess in pursuit of higher office is no vice—as volume two of Robert Caro's biography of Lyndon Johnson, *Means of Ascent*, so vividly attests—the focus has been on sex and drugs and personal history. In an era of exceptionally rotten and negative politics, the Lone Star State seems to be going for the gold in slander and bad taste."[720]

Houston's Billie Carr, a member of the Democratic National Committee, directed more pointed words at Williams.

"I'm so mad I don't know what to do. It's not that he did something years and years ago. It's his attitude," Carr said. "Not only does he condone prostitution, he seems to think it's an important part of growing up. That's an unbelievable attitude for the 1990s."[721]

Times had indeed changed. In 1972, the Chicken Ranch directly helped Bill Hobby win election as lieutenant governor, but in 1990, brothels were a political liability. Williams lost the election to Richards by almost 100,000 votes.

ALTHOUGH NOT APPARENT AT the time, the strange turn of events in the Texas gubernatorial race established something quite clearly in retrospect: the Chicken Ranch's legacy simply refused to go away. Like a Boris Karloff or Bela Lugosi horror movie, just when audiences thought they'd seen the last of the monster, Universal Studios would surprise everyone a year or two down the line with another sequel. So, too, went the Chicken Ranch. Anyone willing to wait patiently would be rewarded when the legendary brothel staggered from its grave yet again to dominate headlines across the state—typically in stories skewed toward the absurd.

For proof, one need look no farther than Longview, Texas, as far removed from La Grange and claims to the Chicken Ranch as any place in the state. That didn't stop a group of investors from opening a steakhouse in May 1994 dubbed the East Texas Chicken Ranch. Unlike the failed restaurant in Dallas, the East Texas Chicken Ranch didn't restrict its menu to chicken-themed entrees. It also featured totally nude dancers.

"We're not breaking the law," said David Sudduth, one of the restaurant's owners. "We're not forcing anyone to come in here.

"It's just normal guys stopping in here, looking for a break. It's just a sexual outlet where no one gets hurt," he said. "It beats dating a hooker or soliciting a hooker."[722]

Unsurprisingly, a nude steakhouse didn't go over terribly well with the community, possibly exacerbated by the fact that Longview didn't have a tradition of naked-themed eating establishments dating back to 1844. Locals quickly formed a protest group, Citizens Against Pornography in Texas, or CAP-IT, and started photographing customers entering the restaurant, keeping files of license plate numbers and videotapes.

"They are real big in saying they have a right to be here, but so do we," said Bruce Edge, a co-founder of CAP-IT. "Would these people be objecting if we took photos of them going into a grocery store or mall? Probably not. I think it's not us that has created the problems, rather it's their actions that are causing the problems."[723]

Lawsuits, counter-suits and a flurry of city ordinances followed over the ensuing year as the controversy raged. Finally, in May 1995, both sides reached a settlement in which the nude steakhouse would close and not reopen anywhere else in Gregg County, and the county wouldn't pursue court costs and attorney fees. The East Texas Chicken Ranch closed for good, putting an end to the year-long controversy.[724]

Maybe jealousy over Longview's stealing of the notoriety or perhaps long-simmering resentment of the Nevada brothel finally boiling over is what prompted La Grange to remind everyone that, for good or ill, the one and only *real* Chicken Ranch resided in Fayette County. Whatever the cause,

Civic organizations such as the Texas Jaycees (left) and the Optimist Club have produced commemorative pins featuring the Chicken Ranch when they've held annual meetings in La Grange. *Author's collection/courtesy Ralph Rosenberg.*

unthinking knee-jerk reactions of local residents landed La Grange a whole lot of unexpected media coverage regarding the Chicken Ranch, coinciding with nothing less than the turn of the century. And, naturally enough, the bizarre episode involved Aggies.

Toward the end of 1999, a group of former Texas A&M students decided to throw a Y2K party for one hundred of their closest friends. Aggies being Aggies, during the early planning stages someone suggested they hold the party on the site of the old Chicken Ranch, as a nod toward the historical ties between the brothel and student body.

"I come from a long line of Aggies who have been reputed to have visited the Chicken Ranch in its glory days," said party organizer Ray Prewitt, explaining the allure of the long-closed brothel. "My father and all my uncles went to A&M, and just being around them and their classmates, some story always pops up."

Just for the hell of it, Prewitt tracked down Ron Jeffrey, the owner, and asked if they might rent the property for the party. To Prewitt's surprise and delight, Jeffrey said yes.[725]

The back entry to what was formerly Aunt Jessie's bedroom and later Miss Edna's office presents an illusion that the Chicken Ranch isn't as ruined as it actually is. Four decades of neglect have left the building a rickety shell. *Author photo.*

Jeffrey had acquired the place some years before from the investors of the Original Chicken Ranch. He'd only visited the property twice, and as long as the party planners got insurance for the event, he was happy to let the Aggies sit around drinking beer from dusk 'til dawn, ringing in Y2K with style. After a brief negotiation, they agreed on a $500 rental fee to cover the party as well as set-up and take-down time.

"The guy was really helpful. He was into the idea, and he wasn't really using the property," Prewitt said. "He was out of Houston, so it was just money in his pocket. We got a bond so that if anything happened, he'd be off the hook. We tried to do everything real professional, and he appreciated that."[726]

The Millennium Chicken party, as it was soon named, quickly evolved into the most "professional" event ever planned for the Chicken Ranch. They capped the guest list at one hundred, with $100 tickets to defray expenses. They rented a heated, five-thousand-square-foot event tent from Austin; three electric generators; and enough portable toilets to serve the expected crowd. Because of limited parking and expected heavy drinking, they hired a shuttle bus to transport partygoers to and from local hotels. They promised hot tubs, catered barbecue and an open bar with lots and lots of liquor. Like a Hollywood game show, every guest would receive souvenir mugs as a parting gift. A website dedicated to the party listed a start time of 8:00 p.m. on December 31, with a vague ending sometime January 1.

About this time, Sue Owen, a party invitee and reporter at the *Austin American-Statesman*, mentioned the shindig to humor columnist John Kelso. Kelso wrote up a typically jokey column, which appeared in the December 29 edition of the *Statesman*. Reaction in La Grange came instantaneously.[727]

"We were out there while they were erecting [the tent] and having the port-a-pottys delivered, and not too long after everything was set up and paid for, we got a visit from pretty much every local official in La Grange," Prewitt said. "The sheriff said more than once that if anybody showed up for the party, we'd all be arrested and thrown in the Fayette County Jail.

"They were serious about not letting this thing go on."[728]

The phalanx of local officials confronting them read like a who's who of La Grange: Fayette County sheriff Rick Vandel, county judge Ed Janecka, agents from the Texas Alcoholic Beverage Commission and the neighboring landowner, Violet Mischer. Mischer, in particular, was livid. She'd fenced off the original 1915 right-of-way granted to the Chicken Ranch. Prewitt and his friends, thinking the section belonged to Jeffrey, had removed the barbed wire to get to the property. Mischer accused them of trespassing and fence-cutting and insisted the Chicken Ranch property was landlocked

Texas grocery store chain H-E-B had some fun with Chicken Ranch mythology in 2015 when it began selling "Texas Chicken Ranch" eggs "from the best little hen house." The tongue-in-cheek packaging was proof that the chain 1) knew its market and 2) had an active sense of humor. *Author's collection.*

with no easement. The only way to reach it, she claimed, was to cross her property—and she adamantly refused to grant permission.

"This is a landlocked piece of property," said Judge Janecka, "and the owner of the adjacent property, for whatever reason, didn't want people going through there."[729]

News of the abortive party annoyed Jeffrey as soon as he heard about it. But Mischer's claims of no easement and trespass infuriated him. A gate existed on the old "back road" to give access, but apparently Mischer claimed ownership of the bar ditch as well.

"The property is *not* landlocked," Jeffrey insisted, explaining that the first time he'd visited the site, he'd driven up the dirt road that made use of the historical easement. "Subsequently, the Mischer family, on their own, put up a fence on that property to cut off access.

"One of these days I am going to sue them for that. You can't close off access to an easement. That easement's been there for a hundred years. I'm sure there are people in the community who would love for it to be closed off and forgotten."[730]

An irate Jeffrey made it clear to the judge and sheriff that if his property was indeed completely landlocked with no access other than, say, helicoptering in, then the property value amounted to exactly zero. If so, Jeffrey expected a full refund of property tax from his previous years as owner. The sheriff and judge quickly changed their reasoning for halting the party.

"The sheriff and judge came in saying, 'It's a hazard to have a party out here. It's too dry. It's going to burn down the county,'" Jeffrey said. "Well, of course, that wasn't the reason they wouldn't let them have their party. Let me tell you, they wish it would just go away."[731]

Some of the La Grange officials gathered to stop the party recognized, belatedly, the arbitrary unfairness of the situation and tried to help the Aggies find another local venue for the shindig. But, being New Year's, every suitable facility was already booked. Plus, La Grange city ordinances required events to stop serving alcohol and end by midnight—which pretty much defeated the entire purpose of an all-night New Year's Eve bash.

In the end, the party relocated to Austin on a subdued note, a disappointing ending, no doubt, for those flying in from Seattle and Canada for the event. The thousands spent on the tent, port-a-pottys, insurance, generators and the rest was a total loss, but Jeffrey refunded the Aggies' $500 property rental fee as a gesture of goodwill.[732]

Clearly, the Millennium Chicken affair was not La Grange's finest hour.

"There's a lot of stigma in that town associated with the notoriety of the Chicken Ranch in La Grange," Prewitt said. "If they're happy with them thinking they can suppress this fact about their town, more power to 'em. They just kind of live in their own world."[733]

IN A SANE WORLD, the Millennium Chicken fiasco would easily qualify as the most surreal Chicken Ranch–related event of the decade—regardless of whether it's the 1990s or the 2000s in question. Of course, the Chicken Ranch itself proves this isn't a sane world at all. The East Texas Chicken Ranch likely trumps Millennium Chicken for weirdness in the '90s, and in the post-millennium decade, the Y2K party that never happened finishes a distant second to a Conroe, Texas production of *The Best Little Whorehouse in Texas*.

A production that tried to sanitize the script to make it *family-friendly*. Or at least inoffensive. A play about a *whorehouse*.

The board of directors of Conroe's amateur acting troupe, the Crighton Players, approved a production of *The Best Little Whorehouse in Texas* in 2002. After rehearsals began, the board got cold feet about the nonstop profanity and subject matter. The board voted to remove all instances of "goddamn" and "fuck" and came up with ways to "soften" the other swear words such as "shitass." The decision incensed director David Fernachak, who resigned in protest. Then thirty-two of the thirty-four cast members resigned in solidarity.[734]

"They were stunned," said Erin Maxey-Wilhite, cast in the role of Jewel in the production. "What's really cool is that [Fernachak was] the high school drama teacher. I thought that was a very brave thing to do in that position. When the rest of us found out what was going on, we all stood with him except for maybe three or four people.

"And so [the board] scheduled a substitute production with very few cast members," she said. "Then we started looking into how we could stage it ourselves."[735]

The battle lines formed quickly and, as with all things Chicken Ranch–related, attracted swarms of media. The *Houston Chronicle* and *Dallas Morning News* ran big stories about the fight, as did NPR and CNN. Marvin Zindler waded into the fray, opining that since he had to say "bawdyhouse" instead of "whorehouse" on his broadcasts thirty years before, changing swear words shouldn't be a big deal.

"I feel like they could change that word…to goddanged," Marvin said. "When he says, 'You goddanged little pissant,' which is what he said, you get the sense of what he said.

"I have seen 40 versions of *The Best Little Whorehouse* in Texas, and they leave out a lot of stuff."[736]

Nothing doing, fired back playwright Larry L. King.

"Marvin Zindler is full of shit," King said. "We try to watch [script changes] very carefully.

"Ann-Margaret has been on tour with it for 16 months, and here these people are acting like this is something new and dangerous," he said, and then threatened to call in the Dramatists Guild of America. "There will be no production if they change a damn word."[737]

The Conroe cast, encouraged by the broad support, banded together to put on their own show without the support of the Crighton Players. Paul Tetreault, managing director of the Alley Theatre in Houston, offered to host a fundraiser in support of the actors. Peter Masterson, co-director and co-author of the original Broadway production, flew in to help with the fundraiser. At the end of June, just like Mickey Rooney and Judy Garland, the Conroe actors put on their do-it-yourself show in a cavernous building that formerly housed a gymnastics studio.[738]

"I can't tell you if we broke even or not. I think we did, I think we had a little left over," Maxey-Wilhite said. "I don't know what [the board] was thinking. I can't imagine. Certainly, the dances were provocative, and *my* song ['Twenty Four Hours of Lovin''] was hot.

"You've got *G-D* and *S-* and all of the sudden it's going to be 'Happy Family Time?'" she said, laughing. "What were they thinking?"[739]

MARVIN ZINDLER DIED ON July 22, 2007, at the age of eighty-five after a sudden, unexpected battle with the only opponent he couldn't best: pancreatic cancer.

Marvin signed a lifetime contract with KTRK-TV in 1988, taking it to literal extreme by filing his last report from his hospital bed days before his death. Although he never had a story as big as the Chicken Ranch again, he continued his one-man crusade as consumer advocate in Houston, successfully defending his title as "The Loudest Man on Television" for the thirty-four years he worked for KTRK. Along the way, he founded Marvin's Angels, which provided free medical care to Houston children, and the Agris-Zindler Children's Foundation, which provided free reconstructive surgery to children worldwide.

Marvin's signature catchphrase, "*Slime* in the ice machine!," proved so popular that Houston's Theatre Under the Stars added it to its sold-out 2012 production of *The Best Little Whorehouse in Texas*, to knowing laughter.[740]

Still, despite four-plus decades of public interest crusades and philanthropic work, media across the country identified him in obituaries first and foremost as the man who closed the Chicken Ranch.

In 2015, ZZ Top performed at the Fayette County Fair to a crowd of twenty thousand fans eager to hear that little ole band from Texas play "La Grange" for the first time ever in La Grange.[741]

For her part, bad investments quickly burned through the $50,000 Miss

Edna received for the movie version of *The Best Little Whorehouse in Texas*. She ended up in Oklahoma City managing a massage parlor downtown. She met her future husband, Clayton Chadwell, during this time. When police closed the massage parlor in 1984, she and Chadwell married and moved to Phoenix, Arizona. For the next twenty-three years, Miss Edna lived a quiet life of retirement in an unassuming ranch-style home with a swimming pool in back. Her neighbors had no idea of her infamous history, an anonymity she worked to maintain.[742]

She developed osteoporosis in her later years, breaking her hip in a fall at home. A chain smoker, Miss Edna burned through two packs of cigarettes a day. In September 2011, she suffered severe head trauma in a

Edna Milton Chadwell, age eighty-one, February 2009. *Photo by Lisa Elliott Blaschke.*

traffic accident, which affected her memory. Institutionalized from then on, Miss Edna died of complications from her injuries on February 25, 2012, outliving all five of her husbands—ex and otherwise—as well as Sheriff Flournoy, Marvin Zindler and Governor Dolph Briscoe.[743]

NO CHARGES WERE EVER filed against anyone involved with the Chicken Ranch. Repeated claims that organized crime called the shots at the brothel remained unsubstantiated forty years later. Even Assistant District Attorney Herb Hancock—thoroughly convinced in 1973 that the brothel was out of control—admitted to concerns about the accuracy of the DPS files emphasizing the brothel's ties to money-laundering in Mexico.

"I really am not confident there was [organized crime involved]," Hancock said. "From what I've heard since then and what I learned, if there was any money leaving that location and going to Mexico…there were never any ties that I saw that would indicate that."[744]

But times change. The Chicken Ranch had already outlived most of its contemporaries, and Texas of the 1970s bore little resemblance to Texas of the 1930s. The Chicken Ranch existed on borrowed time.

After the removal of the parlor section in 1977, the elements—along with looters and vandals—took a heavy toll on the remains of the Chicken Ranch. The ruined kitchen is one of only two remaining rooms that haven't completely collapsed. *Author photo.*

"If you fast-forward, it probably couldn't have survived more than fifteen or twenty years," Hancock said. "Some reporter would've picked up on it, but I don't know it would ever have been closed down through the legal process."[745]

Larry Conners, whose undercover reporting directly led to the Chicken Ranch's downfall, viewed the brothel's closure as an ironic loss of innocence. Texas—and, by extension, the nation—traded a humble vice for a crass morality.

"It's interesting, as I can also see a cultural shift. You know, sex is more open and readily available. Now you've got something like Craigslist existing, and it's just amazing how far we've come," Conners said. "It's because sex became freer and more open, and guys don't really have to pay because girls are willing to do anything all the time.

"But either way, it was probably doomed at some point. No doubt about it," he said. "Now, you still have prostitution, but that's an entirely different level. That doesn't compare. No, you go to Vegas. You walk down the street. They're passing out these pictures of these gals to anybody walking by, and they're throwing the rest of them on the ground so kids walking by are seeing them and everything else. There is something wrong with that."[746]

As of 2022, the Chicken Ranch lies in ruin, a splintered, rotting husk slowly collapsing in upon itself. Vandals damage and deface whatever survives exposure to the elements. Occasional curious sightseers slip over the gate to gawk at the remains, and sometimes they're confronted by a stern Fayette County deputy. Most of the time, though, the Chicken Ranch is left alone, abandoned and forgotten amid overgrown yaupon, cedar trees and the odd coral snake.

For Hollywood, though, the old brothel remains big business. In 2010, Universal Pictures announced plans for a lavish remake of *The Best Little Whorehouse in Texas*, produced by Marty Bowen and Wyck Godfrey, the team behind the insanely popular *Twilight* vampire romance films. The announcement promised a modern update to the story, with new music and songs, but a decade later, all parties had moved on to other projects. In 2014, Tony, Emmy and Olivier Award winner Rob Ashford announced he would direct and choreograph a revival of the musical—its first return to Broadway since the original run three decades earlier. Ashford followed up that announcement in 2016 with a staged reading featuring Kristen Chenoweth as Miss Mona Stangley, Kevin McKidd as Sheriff Ed Earl Dodd and Jennifer Holliday as Jewel. Despite the all-star lineup, financing never came together, and the revival was mothballed.[747]

The concrete foundation blocks of the long-gone front parlor lie scattered in this 2013 view of the front of the Chicken Ranch ruins. The west wing (left) and south wing have both completely collapsed, leaving only the original 1915 section marginally stable. As of 2015, efforts were underway to secure a historical marker for the property, but very little remains that otherwise merits preservation. *Author photo*.

Hollywood and Broadway will do as Hollywood and Broadway always do, but no matter how successful any future version of the story, it cannot wholly define the unlikely tale of the Chicken Ranch. Impossibly, the little country brothel slipped the confines of fact and fiction long ago, passing into the realm of folklore. It may not share the revered dignity of the Alamo or the lonesome romance of bygone cattle drives, but the Chicken Ranch *has* earned its place in Texas mythology. One way or the other, the Chicken Ranch legacy—truths, falsehoods and everything in between—will endure.

Appendix A

This edited version of Miss Edna's Chicken Ranch rules of conduct is sourced from Ken Demaret, *The Many Faces of Marvin Zindler* (Houston, TX: Hunt Company, 1976), 142–47. The original set of rules was printed up in a mimeographed booklet and distributed to all new hires at the brothel. Miss Edna also had a truncated version of the rules painted on plywood and displayed prominently in the kitchen area. Miss Edna confirmed that the rules as presented here are accurate. Regarding the deleted list of businesses her prostitutes were permitted to go to, Miss Edna said, "They could go into any place they wanted to, except bars. If they wanted to go to a bar, wait until they get off and go out of town to do that, because I don't want them on my floor drunk."

Chicken Ranch Rules and Regulations for Boarders

I, Edna Milton, a femme sole trader own this building and all the furnishings, also 11.32 acres of land duly recorded in the Fayette County Courthouse, La Grange, Texas 78945.

This place nor I have any connection what so ever with any other place, mob, or syndicate of any type.

This place is individually owned by me.

To whom it may concern to all living on these premises.

If any one here is an illiterate or of sub normal intelligence they had better have someone read and explain this to them.

Read this book regularly (about once a month) if you want to live here.

These rules will be followed by all boarders no exceptions.

Any one having no intentions of following these rules might just as well leave now.

Absolutely no narcotics are permitted on these premises. If any narcotics are found or suspected the law will be called immediately.

Drinking is not permitted during visiting hours and any one doing so will be asked or ordered to leave.

In short dope heads, pill heads and drunks are not permitted to live here regardless of who they are.

Thieves, liars and robbers are not needed or wanted here when I ask a boarder a question I demand an honest to the point answer.

What you do away from here and away from this county is your business as long as it has no reflection on me or my business.

I don't like cliques in my house and I don't want to walk into anybodies room and see a group of people on a bed, chairs or the floor. The shinning room parlor have a sufficient number of chairs to accommodate every one here for discussions and other get togethers. Beds are not to be wallowed in. That is what hogs do. I expect all boarders to take care of my furniture even if they don't know how to take care of their own.

There are nine rooms here and I consider it as hiring short of boarders where there are only boarders here. If I had three more rooms and had boarders in every room at all times I wouldn't consider it as having too many boarders for the amount of company coming here. There are times when things are slow, but the same holds true with any occupation anywhere in the world. Any occupation has its off season.

No boarder will have a regular room unless I have told her otherwise also at my discretion there may be two boarders in one room, this comes under my business and I don't care to discuss the reason for doing so with any one. Any time a boarder regardless of who she may be decides to interrogate me in any manner she may show proper credentials and a badge authorizing her to do so and then get out.

I expect all regular boarders to be here at least ¾ of the time otherwise she will be considered a transit boarder.

When a boarder is off I expect a phone call the day before she returns if for some legitimate reason a boarder is not able to return as scheduled. I expect a phone call advising me so I can make arrangements if necessary. I don't always appreciate being caught short of boarders due to somebody else's negligence and irresponsibility on the day a boarder returns to work after being off she is expected to be here no later 6 p.m. bus schedules excluded and only then if the bus arrives at a reasonable hour.

When a boarder plans to leave I want to know in advance, unless they are leaving permanently, as well as when they plan to return. Anytime a boarder leaves this house without my knowledge or permission she will pack her things.

If a boarder has a pimp that comes under the heading of her business if she does not have a pimp it still comes under the heading of her business not mine or any other boarder living on these premises as long as a boarder takes care of her business does not interfere into my business and the business of other boarders she can live here, her business is hers and my business is mine. I consider myself quite capable of taking care of my own business and I will do just that.

If a boarder has people she should advise them to keep their nose out of my business. I won't want my business as well as their business in a mix master.

This is not and never will be a house of (white slavery) as long as I continue to operate this boarding house, no pimp will ever own it. If they ever get that idea they do sin as much as they could possibly sin.

As I said this is not a white slavery place and never will be as long as I have any thing to do with it therefore I will not have a boarder in my house with an excess amount of bruises and a lot of tattoos on their body. Cattle are branded for identification, tattoos are much the same as brands. I can remember my name without them, can you?

Boarders are permitted to see their pimp or lover one night a week (never more than that). Boarders may call the [deleted] Inn or [deleted] Motel for reservation when their lovers come into town.

A boarders lover may pick her up on week nights at 3:15 a.m. She is to return no later than 3 p.m. except by permission.

All boarders and pimps are to stay off the back road.

The phone is to be used by everyone here I don't want any boarder to receive more than one phone call per day and that is from home, three minutes is sufficient time for any one to talk concerning family or their business.

Anyone caught discussing my business on the phone won't live here. Money is not to be discussed on the phone at any time. Phone calls are subject to be monitored. Remember don't let your mouth overload your capabilities.

Phone calls are to be made between the hours of 12:00 noon and 3 a.m. No exceptions.

The cook comes to work at 11:00 a.m. and breakfast is served shortly there after. Food is removed from the table by 12:30 p.m.

Dinner is served at 4 p.m. or shortly there after.

No one is to skip a meal because they have company and then expect their food later, they can always excuse themselves when dinner is served or make arrangements with the cook to put their dinner away for them. I don't pay the cook to cater to anyone interference with the cook irregardless of which boarder they will leave here as soon as I know about it.

Decent or reasonable manners are expected of everyone eating at my table suitable subjects are to be discussed while eating. Not everyone can eat while filthy talk is going on in fact as far as I am concerned the filthy talk can wait forever.

No boarder is to leave the dinner table until she has finished eating.

All boarders dressed and properly made up by 1 p.m. when guest are permitted into the house. Casual dress is appropriate for daytime. Hair should be combed or at least covered with an attractive scarf.

All boarders are to be dressed in dinner dresses, cocktail dresses or evening pantsuits no later than 7 p.m. Absolutely no casual clothes permitted at night except by special permission.

The house closes at 3 a.m. so if a boarder expecting an overnight guest they should arrive on week nights about 3:15 a.m. Exceptions by permission only. Overnight guest on Saturday night should arrive at 3:30 a.m. never earlier.

When the call bell rings that there are guest in the parlor all boarder are expected to go into the parlor immediately. Exception to this rule are only permissible if the boarder is eating dinner, taking a bath, using the commode or else busy entertaining a guest. Long sad faces look like hell to me and I don't like them in my parlor. A smile doesn't cost anything but it could prove expensive not to smile. Unpainted faces and stringy hair is unattractive and being unattractive due to self negligence and laziness can prove costly.

Boarders are expected to act like adults in the parlor at all times as well as in any other room here.

The guest that come here are from all walks of life they are very much families with being treated as a guest should be treated. If any one doesn't know how to treat a guest properly they haven't been educated in the right way as perhaps they need a refresher course else where no training are available here. I don't always agree with the old motto, the customer is always right, but I don't ignore it altogether either not anyone can please everyone in the world all the time but it sure would be nicer if everyone tried to always do right.

Anytime a boarder has a friend in the parlor she is to sit with him until he is ready to leave or until she is busy with another friend. I don't want any man to be left alone in the parlor just so a boarder could go to her hen session.

Also when any boarder has a friend waiting on her the man is to be permitted to wait for her as long as he desires, if the man decides to change his mind it is his own decision. I don't want another boarder trying to coax another boarders friend into waiting for her. A boarder caught doing so will only be here long enough to get her things together and get out.

Boarders are to go to the doctor on Monday, Tuesday, or Wednesday before 11:30 a.m. or after 2:30 P.M. Boarders are to go to another doctor only when the regular doctor is on vacation or can't handle the case.

Any laxity on the part of any boarder in adhering to medical rules will result in immediate check out.

When going to the doctor or shopping every boarder will wear a street dress of reasonable length. Not shorter than 2" above the knee and a complete set of undergarments including hose, pants and shorts are absolutely prohibited.

Boarders are not permitted to go into any beer place in town or any café in town.

Listed below is a list of permissables for boarder to go when town. [Deleted]

I could stay here writing forever but I consider the foregoing rules sufficient at this time, there are of course many other things to be considered and I expect a girl to ask me or whomever is in charge.

Appendix B

This partial, heavily edited copy of the investigation report (Kent Demaret, *The Many Faces of Marvin Zindler* (Houston, TX: Hunt Company, 1976), 149–51) is apparently the only version that survives. Herb Hancock believes that all other copies within the DPS were destroyed at the time the scandal broke to protect those who authorized the investigation. Zindler's copy still existed into the early 1980s (Joseph Agris, *White Knight in Blue Shades* [Houston, TX: A-to-Z Publishing, 2002, 227–28], but multiple inquiries to the Zindler estate through Marvin Zindler Jr. went unanswered.

DPS Criminal Intelligence Report on the Chicken Ranch

The Chicken Ranch is located two miles Southeast [*sic*] of La Grange, off state highway 71, one-half mile off the roadway. It is located in Fayette County, Texas. The surveillance at this location was conducted on November 17, 1972, from 3:00 p.m. until 3:30 a.m. and on November 18, 1972 from 1:45 p.m. until 3:00 a.m. The [Texas] Department of Public Safety [DPS] intelligence surveillance equipment was parked, on both dates on highway right-of-way in front of said location. On November 17, 1972, a Fayette County deputy…admitted…to [agents] that there was a whorehouse located at this particular location. On said same date at 7:05 p.m. Texas exempt license number (Registered to county sheriff's department) went into the house, came out at 7:20 p.m., drove to the surveillance vehicle and kept his bright lights on, making several transmissions via his police radio. At 8:15 p.m. Texas exempt license plate (another sheriff's department vehicle) arrived with two men. One was a deputy sheriff…with a shotgun, the other was identified as Sheriff J.T. Flournoy.

The Sheriff wanted to know what DPS personnel were doing at said location. Advised said personnel that he had been running said county for 65 years and would so advise the Department of Public Safety if he needed their assistance in enforcing the laws in his county. He also advised he would call Austin, and the attorney general's office and that he would call the capitol and visit with the governor.

On Friday night, November 17, 1972, one hundred and forty-five (145 vehicles) went into said location. In each vehicle there were between two and three people…On Saturday, November 18, 1972, one hundred and forty-seven vehicles went into said location again with two or three people per car. The length of time each of these vehicles stayed in said location was from 20 minutes to two hours.

It is estimated by DPS personnel that approximately one and a half million dollars ($1,500,000) a year goes through said location.

Sheriff Flournoy and his deputy, during the conversation with DPS personnel, were very hostile in their contact with said personnel.

Also the deputy with Sheriff Flournoy had a shotgun that was pointed at DPS personnel.

It is my opinion that these operation should be closed down and permanently put out of business in the following manner: that each location should be raided on at least two occasions…and injunctive proceedings should be instituted in district court…

Please keep in mind that law enforcement personnel in each of the counties (which have overlapping criminal prosecution jurisdictions) will strenuously oppose any such operation.

But keep in mind also that the laws that are being violated are of the State of Texas.

It is my opinion that this operation is a constant embarrassment to the law enforcement personnel in this state in that everywhere they go, of when three or more law enforcement agencies get together, eventually their conversation comes around to why we are not enforcing the law against prostitution in Sealy or La Grange, Texas.

One might also take into consideration that there will be a lot of heat generated by any type of enforcement proceedings against these… locations…but please keep in mind that we would not generate any type of pressure if we stayed at home and did not try to enforce the laws of our state.

The heat possibly could come from high state officials, senators, state representatives or other public officials.

At this time it is not known whether or not any public officials are taking any type of payoffs to allow the whorehouses…to stay open…

However, it is highly suspected that such is going on.

As long as these operations are allowed to continue it would be a mockery of our laws to enforce the prostitution laws in Houston, Galveston, Dallas or any other area of the state…

It is my opinion that it is our duty and responsibility, regardless of the amount of pressure, to first be right and then enforce the laws of our state.

If this procedure is not followed, who next will decide what laws shall or shall not be enforced.

Notes

Introduction

1. Ruth, former employer of Edna Milton, interview by author via phone. Digital recording, Duncan, Oklahoma, September 28, 2016; Ruth, interview by author via phone, digital recording, Duncan, Oklahoma, September 29, 2016; Ruth, letter to author, October 11, 2016; Ruth, interview by author via phone, digital recording, Duncan, Oklahoma, July 7, 2022.

Chapter 1

2. David C. Humphrey, "Prostitution," in *The New Handbook of Texas*, vol. 5, ed. Ronnie C. Tyler, Douglas E. Barnett and Roy R. Barkley (n.p.: Texas State Historical Association, 1996), 357–59.
3. David C. Humphrey, "Prostitution in Texas: From the 1830s to the 1960s," *East Texas Historical Journal* 33, no. 1 (1995), 27–43.
4. Thomas Matocha, "Indians of Fayette County," in *Fayette County: Past and Present*, ed. Marjorie L. Williams (La Grange, TX: Fayette County Historical Commission, 1976), 3–4; Julia Lee Sinks, *Chronicles of Fayette: The Reminiscences of Julia Lee Sinks* (La Grange, TX: Fayette County Historical Commission, 1975), 33–48; Daphne Dalton Garrett, "Fayette County," in *New Handbook of Texas*, vol. 2, Tyler, Barnett and Barkley, 969–71.

5. Garrett, "Fayette County," 969–71; "La Bahia Road," in *New Handbook of Texas*, vol. 3, Tyler, Barnett and Barkley, 1180.

6. Sinks, *Chronicles of Fayette*, 33–38.

7. Ibid., 45.

8. John Leffler, "La Grange," in *New Handbook of Texas*, vol. 4, Tyler, Barnett and Barkley, 6–7; "Moore, John Henry," in *New Handbook of Texas*, vol. 4, Tyler, Barnett and Barkley, 821–22.

9. Sinks, *Chronicles of Fayette*, 55; Leffler, "La Grange," 6–7.

10. Thomas Supak, Charles Hensel and Ricky Dipple, "German Settlers in Fayette County," in *Fayette County*, Williams, 22–23; Louis E. Brister, "Adelsverein," in *New Handbook of Texas*, vol. 1, Tyler, Barnett and Barkley, 30–31; Daphne Dalton Garrett, "Nassau Farm," in *New Handbook of Texas*, vol. 4, Tyler, Barnett and Barkley, 939.

11. Diane Polasek, "Early Bohemian Settlers of Fayette County," in *Fayette County*, Williams, 26–27; Clinton Machann, "Czechs," in *New Handbook of Texas*, vol. 2, Tyler, Barnett and Barkley, 465–66; Albert J. Blaha Sr., "Bergmann, Josef Arnost (1798–1877)," *Handbook of Texas Online* (Texas State Historical Association, updated March 16, 2018), https://www.tshaonline.org/handbook/entries/bergmann-josef-arnost, retrieved June 19, 2022.

12. Oliver Kitzman, former district attorney for La Grange, interview by author. Digital recording. Brookshire, TX, June 26, 2009.

13. Supak, Hensel and Dipple, "German Settlers," 24–25, 28.

14. Sinks, *Chronicles of Fayette*, 91.

15. Jan Hutson, *The Chicken Ranch: The True Story of the Best Little Whorehouse in Texas* (n.p.: Author's Choice Press, 2000), 33–34. It is here we have issues with the veracity of Jan Hutson's chronicle. In addition to the dubious existence of Mrs. Swine, multiple additional assertions made by Hutson are flatly contradicted by this author's research. Ultimately, the value of Hutson's work in a historical context is marginal at best.

16. Ibid. While it is impossible to pinpoint the exact time when the book ceased being viewed as a reliable source, by 2000, historical researchers were openly calling it into question: Stephen Hardin, PhD, Victoria College, Victoria, TX. E-mail to Gary McKee, Fayette County Historical Commission, January 7, 2000.

17. Edna Milton Chadwell, former owner and madam of the Chicken Ranch, interview by author and Lisa Blaschke. Digital recording. Phoenix, AZ, February 20, 2009.

18. Ibid.

19. Ibid.; Gerald D. Saxon and John R. Summerville, "The Chicken Ranch: A Home on the Range," *Red River Valley Historical Review* (Fall 1982): 33–44.

20. Pete Looney, letter recounting conversation with Walter P. Freytag (La Grange Chamber of Commerce), October 28, 1992; Kathy Carter, unpublished history of the Chicken Ranch (Fayette Heritage Museum and Archives).

21. "Soiled Doves," *La Grange Journal*, February 18, 1897; Saxon and Summerville, "The Chicken Ranch." A similar problem exists with the work for Saxon and Summerville as with Hutson. That is, their article exists with no substantiating documentation. The article as published does cite primary and secondary source interviews as the basis of the article, and the authors take Hutson to task in their footnotes for failing to provide such in her book. Yet when this author contacted Saxon seeking access to his interview material, Saxon stated all materials were disposed of by the authors, believing that because they were conducted anonymously, such interviews were worthless. Establishing a timeline of the Chicken Ranch's early decades is dubious at best.

22. Sinks, *Chronicles of Fayette*, 63–65, 69–70; "Black Bean Episode," in *New Handbook of Texas*, vol. 1, Tyler, Barnett and Barkley, 560; Robert Burton and Randy Heger, "The Story Behind Monument Hill," in *Fayette County*, Williams, 33–34.

23. Sinks, *Chronicles of Fayette*, 69–70; Burton and Heger, "Story Behind Monument Hill," 33–34.

24. Neal Miller, "The Secession Movement and War Participation in Fayette County," in *Fayette County*, Williams, 393–95.

25. Miller, "Secession Movement," 38; Garrett, "Fayette County," 970.

26. Garrett, "Fayette County," 970; Supak, Hensel and Dipple, "German Settlers," 24.

27. Garrett, "Fayette County," 970; Hutson, *Chicken Ranch*, 40.

28. Anne M. Butler, *Daughters of Joy, Sisters of Misery: Prostitutes in the American West, 1865–90* (Champaign: University of Illinois Press, 1987), 4–5.

29. Humphrey, "Prostitution in Texas," 27–43.

30. Amy S. Balderach, *A Different Kind of Reservation: Waco's Red-Light District Revisited, 1880–1920*, master's thesis, Baylor University (Ann Arbor: ProQuest/University of Michigan, 2005), Publication No. 1430809.

31. Anne Seagraves, *Soiled Doves* (Hayden, ID: Wesanne Publications, 1994), 23; Butler, *Daughters of Joy*, 8–9, 15.

32. Michael Rutter, *Upstairs Girls: Prostitution in the American West* (Helena, MT: Farcountry Press, 2005), 4–5, 63–64.

33. Ibid., 67–68.

34. Ibid., 11, 76–77.

35. Ibid., 75–77; Gene Schulze, MD, "Miss Jessie's Place" (1998), 47, 160. Unpublished manuscript, Gene Schulze Papers, 1978–2000, Dolph Briscoe Center for American History, University of Texas at Austin; *A Handbook of Useful Drugs* (Chicago: Press of the American Medical Association, 1914), 120–21. archive.org/stream/handbookofuseful00co uniala#page/120/mode/2up/search/Salvarsan; Julius Wagner-Jauregg, "The Treatment of Dementia Paralytica by Malaria Inoculation," Nobel lecture, December 13, 1927. www.nobelprize.org/nobel_prizes/ medicine/laureates/1927/wagner-jauregg-lecture.html.

36. Seagraves, *Soiled Doves*, 58.

37. Randy Gardiner, Bradley Kalmus and Joe Wessels, "The Kreische Brewery," in *Fayette County*, Williams, 47–49; Jeff Carroll, "Monument Hill–Kreische Brewery State Historic Site," in *New Handbook of Texas*, vol. 4, Tyler, Barnett and Barkley, 807–8; "Monument Hill–Kreische Brewery State Historic Site," Texas Parks and Wildlife Department.

38. Gardiner, Kalmus and Wessels, "Kreische Brewery," 49; Edwin Bartek, "The Glidden–La Grange Southern Pacific Spur," in *Fayette County*, Williams, 52.

39. Sharon Vanek and Charles Schulz, "Overflows of Fayette County," in *Fayette County*, Williams, 44–45.

40. Saxon and Summerville, "Chicken Ranch," 33–44; "Soiled Doves," *La Grange Journal*.

41. Saxon and Summerville, "Chicken Ranch," 33-44.

42. Leerie Giese, La Grange resident and banker, interview by author. Digital recording. La Grange, TX, August 17, 2009.

43. "Soiled Doves," *La Grange Journal*.

Chapter 2

44. Sharon Vanek and Charles Schulz, "Overflows of Fayette County," in *Fayette County*, Williams, 45–46.

45. Ruth Rosen, *The Lost Sisterhood: Prostitution in America, 1900–1918* (Baltimore: Johns Hopkins University Press, 1983), 5.

46. Al Reinert, "Closing Down La Grange," *Texas Monthly*, October 1973, 52; Rosen, *Lost Sisterhood*, 9.

47. Rosen, *Lost Sisterhood*, 8.

48. Ibid., 15; Butler, *Daughters of Joy*, 56–57; Karen Abbott, *Sin in the Second City* (New York: Random House, 2007), 29–30; Richard Zelade, *Guy Town by Gaslight* (Charleston, SC: The History Press, 2014), 47.

49. Butler, *Daughters of Joy*, 36–37.

50. Rosen, *Lost Sisterhood*, 62–63.

51. Abbott, *Sin in the Second City*, 246–55, 278–84.

52. 1890 U.S. Census Report, Waco, Texas (Ancestry.com); 1900 US Census Report, Waco, Texas (Fayette Heritage Museum and Archives; John Kamenec, letter to author, December 17, 2018. Stewart's name is alternately spelled "Faye" or "Fay" on a variety of surviving documents. The author chooses to use the former spelling, as this is the earliest version found.

53. Hutson, *Chicken Ranch*, 45–47; relative of Fay Stewart, interview by author via phone. Digital recording. La Grange, TX, November 22, 2013; Reinert, "Closing Down La Grange," 48; Carter, unpublished history of the Chicken Ranch.

54. Saxon and Summerville, "Chicken Ranch," 33–44.

55. Kamenec, letter; James Pylant and Sherri Knight, *The Oldest Profession in Texas: Waco's Red Light District* (Stephenville, TX: Jacobus Books, 2011), 272–73.

56. Pylant, Knight; "In The Police Court," Austin Daily Statesman, July 14, 1903, 5.

57. Ibid.; 1910 US Census Report, Austin, Texas (Fayette Heritage Museum and Archives). The 1910 census form lists Jessie Williams as being a married boarder, but there is no further reference to a husband on the census form. Indeed, this is the only reference the author has ever come across indicating that Miss Jessie may have ever been married, even for a brief time. The listing may be accurate, but it is just as likely to be a clerical error or an outright fabrication on Miss Jessie's part. "A Card of Thanks," *Austin Daily Statesman*, March 23, 1908, 8.

58. David C. Humphrey, "Prostitution and Public Policy in Austin, Texas, 1870–1915," *Southwestern Historical Quarterly* 86 (April 1983): 473–516; "Women of District Leave," *Austin Daily Statesman*, October 2, 1913, 2; Zelade, *Guy Town by Gaslight*, 142.

59. Leerie Giese, La Grange resident and banker, interview by author. Digital recording. La Grange, TX, August 17, 2009.

60. Deed of trust, vol. 99, 561–62, July 31, 1915. Fayette Heritage Museum and Archives. Curiously, almost every article the author has found on the topic places the Chicken Ranch either south or southeast of La Grange, often in proximity to the Colorado River. The location of the Chicken

Ranch is actually east-northeast of town, more than a mile north of the Colorado's closest approach. One wonders if this is a result of an early error being repeated by subsequent writers or a deliberate misdirection by wary locals.

61. Chadwell, interview, February 20, 2009.
62. Deed of trust, vol. 104, 339, February 15, 1917. Fayette Heritage Museum and Archives; Hutson, *Chicken Ranch*, 49; Saxon and Summerville, "Chicken Ranch," 33–44.
63. Giese, interview.
64. Thad Sitton, *Texas High Sheriffs* (Austin: Texas Monthly Press, 1988), 1–6.
65. Milton Synnott, Mark Steinhauser, Douglas Kristoff, Phyllis Washington and Rebecca Schneider, "The Loessin Brothers," in *Fayette County*, Williams, 215–16.
66. Ibid.
67. Ibid.; Schulze, MD, "Miss Jessie's Place," 118.
68. Giese, interview.
69. Synnott, Steinhauser, Kristoff, Washington and Schneider, "Loessin Brothers," 215–16.
70. Giese, interview.
71. Ibid.; "Raymond Hamilton Captured in Texas Posing as a Tramp," *New York Times*, April 6, 1935, 1.
72. Giese, interview.
73. Reinert, "Closing Down La Grange," 46–53.
74. Saul Friedman, "The Chicken Ranch," *Texas Observer*, June 21, 1968, 8–9; Walter F. Pilcher, "The Chicken Ranch," in *New Handbook of Texas*, vol. 5, Tyler, Barnett and Barkley, 74.
75. Giese, interview.
76. Reinert, "Closing Down La Grange," 46–53.
77. Humphrey, "Prostitution in Texas," 27–43.
78. Giese, interview.
79. Ibid.
80. Tony Murello, e-mail to author. May 18, 2012.
81. Friedman, "Chicken Ranch," 8; Pilcher, "Chicken Ranch," 74; Carter, unpublished history of the Chicken Ranch.
82. 1920, 1930 Federal Census Reports, La Grange, Texas (Fayette Heritage Museum and Archives); Carter, unpublished history of the Chicken Ranch.
83. Relative of Faye Stewart, interview.
84. Ibid.

85. Giese, interview; Saxon and Summerville, "Chicken Ranch," 33–44.
86. Giese, interview.
87. Ibid.
88. Ibid.; Herbie Friemel, Sandra Sulak and Gloria Wood, "Fayette Memorial Hospital," in *Fayette County*, Williams, 266–67.
89. Giese, interview.
90. Ibid.
91. Ibid.
92. Chadwell, interview, February 20, 2009.
93. Schulze, "Miss Jessie's Place," 174.
94. Relative of Faye Stewart, interview.
95. Friedman, "Chicken Ranch," 9; Reinert, "Closing Down La Grange," 49.
96. Chadwell, interview, February 20, 2009.
97. Kent Biffle, "Madam Pays a Visit to Displaced Bordello," *Dallas Moring News*, October 30, 1977, 32A.
98. Chadwell, interview, February 20, 2009.

Chapter 3

99. Chadwell, interview, February 20, 2009.
100. Ibid.
101. Ibid.
102. Ibid.
103. Ibid.; Humphrey, "Prostitution in Texas," 27–43.
104. Chadwell, interview, February 20, 2009.
105. Ibid.
106. Ibid.
107. Ibid.
108. Ibid.; Chip Orton, "Texas Madam Makes It on Broadway," *US*, August 8, 1978, 74.
109. Chadwell, interview, February 20, 2009.
110. Ibid.; Larry L. King, *The Whorehouse Papers* (New York: Viking Press, 1982), 143.
111. Chadwell, interview, February 20, 2009.
112. Ibid.
113. Ibid.
114. Ibid.; Tony Freemantle, "Last Madam of Infamous Chicken Ranch Has Died," *Houston Chronicle*, February 29, 2012.

115. Chadwell, interview, February 20, 2009.

116. Ibid.

117. Ibid.

118. Ibid.

119. Ibid.

120. Ibid.

121. Ibid.

122. Ibid.

123. Ibid.

124. Robert Kleffman, e-mail to author, December 21, 2011.

125. Chadwell, interview, February 20, 2009.

126. Ibid.

127. Kleffman, e-mail.

128. Chadwell, interview, February 20, 2009; Kleffman, e-mail to author, December 18, 2011. Kleffman writes, "She gave me hints as to who the father was, but never came out and told me. She said she'd take that info [to] the grave with her."

129. Chadwell, interview, February 20, 2009.

130. Ibid.

131. King, *Whorehouse Papers*, 146.

132. Chadwell, interview, February 20, 2009.

133. Ibid.

134. Ibid.; Ruth E. Pariseau, former nurse for Dr. John Guenther, interview by author via phone. Digital recording. San Antonio, TX, March 13, 2012.

135. Chadwell, interview by author via phone. Digital recording. Phoenix, AZ, August 24, 2009.

136. Robert Kleffman, nephew of Edna Milton Chadwell, interview by author via phone. Digital recording. Berryville, AR, May 13, 2009.

137. Chadwell, interview, February 20, 2009.

138. Ibid.

139. Relative of Faye Stewart, interview.

140. Pariseau, interview.

141. Chadwell, interview, February 20, 2009.

142. Deed of trust, vol. 333, 139, November 27, 1961. Fayette Heritage Museum and Archives. Miss Edna filed a certificate of assumed name in December 1963, officially changing the brothel's name to "Edna's Ranch Boarding House."

143. Chadwell, interview, February 20, 2009.

144. Ancestry.com Texas Death Index 1903–2000; Pylant and Knight, *Oldest Profession in Texas*, 278–279.

145. Chadwell, interview, February 20, 2009.

Chapter 4

146. Ibid.

147. Ibid.

148. Robbie Davis-Floyd, interview by author via phone. Digital recording. Austin, TX, July 29, 2009.

149. Chadwell interview, February 20, 2009.

150. Robbie Davis Johnson, "Folklore and Women: A Social Interactional Analysis of the Folklore of a Texas Madam," *Journal of American Folklore* 86, no. 341 (July–September 1973): 211–24. Robbie Davis-Floyd (since remarried) revised the original article to restore the identity of Miss Edna and the Chicken Ranch, which were obscured in her original publication. The updated document was subsequently published online at davis-floyd.com/the-folklore-of-a-texas-madam1/. Apart from the restored identities, it does not differ substantially from the *Journal of American Folklore* article.

151. Ibid.

152. Ibid.

153. Ibid.

154. Ibid.

155. Ibid.

156. Davis-Floyd, interview.

157. Davis Johnson, "Folklore and Women."

158. Saxon and Summerville, "Chicken Ranch," 36.

159. Giese, interview.

160. Reinert, "Closing Down La Grange," 49.

161. Darla J. Blaha, "The La Grange Chicken Ranch Revisited," *Touchstone, a Journal of the Walter Prescott Webb Historical Society* 17 (1998): 62.

162. Chadwell, interview, August 24, 2009.

163. Giese, interview.

164. Ibid.

165. Chadwell, interview, August 24, 2009. According to Miss Edna, Estelle had two brothers, one of whom took over the dry cleaning business after Estelle's stepfather died, while the other operated a factory that produced

women's clothing. "He'd make her dresses and send them to her every once in a while. That was nice of him, you know. He didn't have to. They were not a wealthy family."

166. Ibid.

167. Ibid.

168. Ibid.

169. Chadwell, interview, February 20, 2009. Miss Edna used this exchange to establish dominance during the interview. When Lisa Blaschke sought clarification as to whether the quoted number meant 500 prostitutes or 500 customers, Miss Edna responded with a wholly unexpected broadside: "You said girls, didn't you? You didn't say boys, did you? I didn't say anything about customers, did I? I'm gonna talk to you just like I talked to those girls, because you pull that stunt on me, huh? That they pulled on me. Who owns this place? Who runs this place? Who gives the orders around here? See what I'm talking about now? I think you got it plain and clear."; "Prostitution in Texas," Associated Press, August 20, 1971. The report didn't claim only 764 prostitutes were working in Texas at the time; rather, investigators identified that many. Most of the madams operated call girl operations rather than brothels—in this, the Chicken Ranch and Miss Edna were genuine relics of the past.

170. Chadwell, interview, February 20, 2009. Most other writings on the Chicken Ranch indicate the brothel offered free room, board and medical services, an idea Miss Edna found ludicrous. She charged her boarders for everything: "They're the ones making the money, why not?"

171. Chadwell, interview, February 20, 2009.

172. Ibid.

173. "Penny," former Chicken Ranch prostitute, interview by author. Digital recording via phone. Pasadena, TX, September 8, 2013.

174. Ibid.

175. Ibid.

176. Ibid.

177. Ibid.

178. Chadwell, interview, February 20, 2009.

179. Kleffman, interview.

180. Penny, interview.

181. Chadwell, interview, February 20, 2009.

182. Ibid.

183. Penny, interview.

184. Ibid.

185. Ibid.

186. Ibid.

187. Ibid.

188. Davis-Floyd, interview.

189. Ibid.

190. Penny, interview.

191. Chadwell, interview, August 24, 2009.

192. King, *Whorehouse Papers*, 123.

193. Linda Hass, e-mail to author, March 2, 2012. In the 1980s, the State Highway 71 Bypass around La Grange bisected the old "back road" to the Chicken Ranch. The northern half, which led to the site of the closed brothel, was named Rocky Creek Road. The southern half, which led to town, was named Truesdale Road.

194. Chadwell, interview, August 24, 2009.

195. Chadwell, interview, February 20, 2009.

196. Ibid.

197. Ibid. See Appendix A.

198. Robert Heard, "Prostitution in Texas: Brothel Madam," Associated Press, August 20, 1971, Company A files, Texas Ranger Division records, Texas Department of Public Safety records. Archives and Information Services Division, Texas State Library and Archives Commission. The Associated Press positively identified Miss Edna as the subject of the interview in 1973; "Governor May Get Petition to Let Chicken Ranch Reopen," *Austin American-Statesman*, August 2, 1973, 6A.

199. Penny, interview.

200. Ibid.

201. Chadwell, interview, February 20, 2009.

202. Ibid.

203. Heard, "Prostitution in Texas."

204. Chadwell, interview, February 20, 2009.

205. Ibid.

206. Heard, "Prostitution in Texas."

207. Chadwell, interview, February 20, 2009.

Chapter 5

208. Henry C. Dethloff, "Texas A&M University," in *New Handbook of Texas*, vol. 6, Tyler, Barnett and Barkley, 274–75.

209. Willie Pankoniem, interview by author via phone. Digital recording. College Station, TX, December 21, 2009.

210. Richard "Dick" Ghiselin, interview by author via phone. Digital recording, February 6, 2012.

211. Ibid.

212. Ibid.

213. Ibid.

214. Pankoniem, interview. Surprisingly, despite anecdotal evidence that University of Texas students visited the Chicken Ranch as much as, if not more than, Texas A&M students, only Aggies tended to respond to interview solicitations put forth by the author through various methods.

215. Ibid.

216. Davis-Floyd, interview; Ken Walters, interview with author via phone. Digital recording. Freeport, TX, August 11, 2009.

217. Walters, interview.

218. Chadwell, interview, February 20, 2009.

219. Pankoniem, interview.

220. Chadwell, interview, February 20, 2009.

221. Jim Dent, *The Junction Boys* (New York: Thomas Dunne Books, 1999), 23.

222. Red O'Neill, interview with author via phone. Digital recording. Corpus Christi, TX, August 10, 2009.

223. Davis Johnson, "Folklore and Women," 211–24.

224. Chadwell, interview, February 20, 2009.

225. Ibid.

226. Ibid.

227. Pankoniem, interview.

228. Ibid.

229. Jim Walton, interview with author via phone. Digital recording. Stephenville, TX, August 5, 2009.

230. Ibid.

231. Walters, interview.

232. Reinert, "Closing Down La Grange," 46–53; Chadwell, interview, February 20, 2009.

233. Chadwell, interview, February 20, 2009.

234. Wilbur Evans and H.B. McElroy, *The Twelfth Man: A Story of Texas A&M Football* (Huntsville, AL: Strode Publishers, 1974), 119–23. If the student health center at A&M did start offering penicillin shots, it was more likely the result of students patronizing the poor, black streetwalkers

who worked nearby Bryan, Texas. Most basic medical care was already covered by student fees, so the "freeness" of any shots may well be an embellishment.

235. Ibid.

236. Author's personal experience.

237. Krista Smith, Association of Former Students, Texas A&M University, e-mail to author, May 18, 2009.

238. Walters, interview; Walton, interview; Pankoniem, interview; Ghiselin, interview; Chadwell, interview, February 20, 2009. *The Best Little Whorehouse in Texas* was a 1978 Broadway musical later adapted as a motion picture that depicted, in loose terms, the circumstances surrounding the Chicken Ranch's closure in 1978. For more information on this, see chapter 14.

239. John Walvoord, e-mail to author, July 27, 2009; Friedman, "Chicken Ranch," 8–9.

240. Ghiselin, interview.

241. Pankoniem, interview; Chadwell, interview, February 20, 2009.

242. Chadwell, interview, February 20, 2009.

Chapter 6

243. William P. "Bill" Hobby Jr., lieutenant governor of Texas, 1973–91, interview by author. Digital recording. Austin, TX, September 25, 2009. Comparisons to L.B.J. weren't just idle chatter, either. Jim Flournoy once secured rooms for his traveling party in a sold-out hotel because the manager mistook him for Lyndon Johnson; Virginia McMillion, "Sheriff Jim: What Becomes a Legend Most," *Austin American-Statesman*, December 10, 1977, B1.

244. Kitzman, interview, June 26, 2009.

245. Elizabeth Weidner, Linda Hrncir, Bart Bade, Donnie Griffin and Genevia Faison, "Thomas James Flournoy: A Fayette County Peace Officer," in *Fayette County*, Williams, 185–89.

246. "Chicken Ranch Sheriff Retires," *Odessa American*, June 5, 1980, 3A. Brother Mike Flournoy eventually won election as sheriff of Wharton County, and brother Royce served as a Texas Ranger until his death in 1957.

247. Weidner, Hrncir, Bade, Griffin and Faison, "Thomas James Flournoy," 186.

248. Ibid.

249. Ibid.; Bob Banta, "La Grange to Lose Lawman: Flournoy's Famous Career Spans Half a Century," *Austin American-Statesman*, June 1, 1980, A9.

250. Weidner, Hrncir, Bade, Griffin and Faison, "Thomas James Flournoy," 186; Mark Seal, "Sheriff Jim," *Scene Magazine: Dallas Morning News*, July 8, 1979, 9.

251. Seal, "Sheriff Jim," 9.

252. Weidner, Hrncir, Bade, Griffin and Faison, "Thomas James Flournoy," 186.

253. Banta, "La Grange to Lose Lawman," A9.

254. Ibid.

255. Weidner, Hrncir, Bade, Griffin and Faison, "Thomas James Flournoy," 189.

256. Banta, "La Grange to Lose Lawman," A9.

257. Weidner, Hrncir, Bade, Griffin and Faison, "Thomas James Flournoy," 189.

258. Kitzman, interview, June 26, 2009.

259. Chadwell, interview, February 20, 2009. Several sources indicated that Gladys was not always an easy person to get along with. Chadwell, through the confidences Jim Flournoy shared with her over the years, developed an unflattering opinion of the sheriff's wife: "I wouldn't have liked her. Because to me, you're supposed to show some respect to the man you're married to, whether you love him or not. If you're going to sit there, sleep in his bed, sit at the table, share food together, at least show him the courtesy of being a human being toward him."

260. Giese, interview.

261. Ibid.

262. Larry L. King, "The Best Little Whorehouse in Texas," *Playboy*, April 1974, 220.

263. Weidner, Hrncir, Bade, Griffin and Faison, "Thomas James Flournoy," 187.

264. Virginia McMillion, "Sheriff Jim: What Becomes a Legend Most," *Austin American-Statesman*, December 10, 1977, B1.

265. Seal, "Sheriff Jim," 13–15.

266. Weidner, Hrncir, Bade, Griffin and Faison, "Thomas James Flournoy," 187; "Jury at La Grange Gives Man Life in Carmine Holdup," *Victoria Advocate*, May 12, 1933, 4.

267. Banta, "La Grange to Lose Lawman," A9.

268. Weidner, Hrncir, Bade, Griffin and Faison, "Thomas James Flournoy," 187; Banta, "La Grange to Lose Lawman," A9; McMillion, "Sheriff Jim."

269. McMillion, "Sheriff Jim."

270. Banta, "La Grange to Lose Lawman," A9.

271. Weidner, Hrncir, Bade, Griffin and Faison, "Thomas James Flournoy," 187; Banta, "La Grange to Lose Lawman," A9.

272. Banta, "La Grange to Lose Lawman," A9. Buddy Zapalac recalled, "The next day, they closed all the schools so all us kids could go by the funeral home and see that dead bank robber. We learned early that crime didn't pay in La Grange."; Seal, "Sheriff Jim," 15.

273. "Raymond Hamilton, Bank Robbing Expert of Barrow Gang, Is Captured," *Lubbock Morning Avalanche*, April 26, 1934, 1, 11; "Hamilton Says People Have Him All Wrong; Declares He Is No Killer and Would Always Give Up at a Showdown," *Lubbock Morning Avalanche*, April 26, 1934, 1, 11.

274. "Hamilton Says People Have Him All Wrong," 1.

275. Giese, interview; Weidner, Hrncir, Bade, Griffin and Faison, "Thomas James Flournoy," 187.

276. Giese, interview.

277. Ibid.

278. Weidner, Hrncir, Bade, Griffin and Faison, "Thomas James Flournoy," 187; John Neal Phillips, *Running with Bonnie and Clyde: The Ten Fast Years of Ralph Fults* (Norman: University of Oklahoma Press, 1996), 294–95.

279. Kitzman, interview, June 26, 2009. In later years, Flournoy would show off the Thompson machine gun and say, "This is the gun I had since Bonnie Parker and Clyde Barrow days, and it was sure turrible not being able to use it on 'em!"; Seal, "Sheriff Jim."

280. Banta, "La Grange to Lose Lawman," A9.

281. Jim Carlton, "After 54 Years, 'Sheriff Jim' Has Decided to Step Down," *Houston Chronicle*, January 21, 1980; Weidner, Hrncir, Bade, Griffin and Faison, "Thomas James Flournoy," 187; Randy Sillavan, "Remembrances of My Dad: Hollis Milton Sillavan," *Texas Ranger Dispatch*, www.texasranger. org/dispatch/Backissues/Dispatch_Issue_05.pdf, Fall 2001.

282. Weidner, Hrncir, Bade, Griffin and Faison, "Thomas James Flournoy," 187; Banta, "La Grange to Lose Lawman," A9.

283. Weidner, Hrncir, Bade, Griffin and Faison, "Thomas James Flournoy," 187; Banta, "La Grange to Lose Lawman," A9.

284. Banta, "La Grange to Lose Lawman," A9.

285. Carlton, "After 54 Years."

286. Kitzman, interview, June 26, 2009; Weidner, Hrncir, Bade, Griffin and Faison, "Thomas James Flournoy," 188.

287. Weidner, Hrncir, Bade, Griffin and Faison, "Thomas James Flournoy," 188.

288. Ibid.

289. Kitzman, interview, June 26, 2009.

290. Thad Sitton, *The Texas Sheriff: Lord of the County Line* (Norman: University of Oklahoma Press, 2000), 48.

291. Sitton, *Texas Sheriff*, 48; Weidner, Hrncir, Bade, Griffin and Faison, "Thomas James Flournoy," 188.

292. Weidner, Hrncir, Bade, Griffin and Faison, "Thomas James Flournoy," 188.

293. Kleffman, interview.

294. Gary E. McKee, Fayette County Historical Commission vice-chair, e-mail to author, March 3, 2012.

295. Kitzman, interview, June 26, 2009.

296. Ibid. Curiously, Edna Milton Chadwell denied ever cooperating with the sheriff's office or any other law enforcement agency. She responded to the line of questioning defensively and unconvincingly, abruptly changing the subject. One might assume her denial of a well-known cooperative relationship independently confirmed by multiple law enforcement sources stems from the stigma of being labeled a snitch.

297. Seal, "Sheriff Jim," 15.

298. Ibid.

299. Ibid., 16.

300. Ibid.

301. Sitton, *Texas Sheriff*, 181.

302. Ibid.

303. Seal, "Sheriff Jim," 10.

304. Ibid.

Chapter 7

305. John Kelso, "Chicken Ranch 'Just a Way of Life' in La Grange," *Austin American-Statesman*, April 17, 1977, B1.

306. Oliver Kitzman, interview by author via phone. Digital recording. Brookshire, TX, early May 2009.

307. Kitzman, interview, June 26, 2009.

308. Marilyn Schwartz, "Sheriff Jim: They Love Him in La Grange," *Dallas Morning News*, June 29, 1975.

309. Heard, "Prostitution in Texas." The Associated Press positively identified Miss Edna as the subject of the interview in 1973; "Governor May Get

Petition to Let Chicken Ranch Reopen," *Austin American-Statesman*, August 2, 1973, 6A.

310. Heard, "Prostitution in Texas."

311. Robert Anderson, e-mail to author, Austin, TX, August 5, 2009.

312. Robert Anderson, interview by author via phone. Digital recording. Austin, TX, August 5, 2009.

313. Kleffman, interview.

314. Ibid.

315. Ibid.

316. Ibid.

317. Ibid.

318. O'Neill, interview.

319. Ibid.

320. Stephen Harrigan, "Main Street," *Texas Monthly*, February 1983, 156.

321. Anonymous 1, interview by author via phone. Digital recording. December 4, 2009. In the early 1960s, Hope joked about the Chicken Ranch during a performance at the University of Texas, establishing his awareness of the brothel; "Bordello Money to Be Traced," *San Antonio Light*, August 3, 1973, 14A.

322. Robert Draper, "The Great Defenders," *Texas Monthly*, January 1994, 99; John Gravois, "Williams Paid Prostitutes as Youth," *Houston Post*, April 22, 1990, 1A.

323. Glenn O'Brien, "Life at the Top," *SPIN* 1, no. 10 (February 1986): 72. Curiously, the 1973 release of the "La Grange" single came several months before the Chicken Ranch's closure. Many people erroneously assume the song was written after the fact as a memorial to the closed brothel.

324. Gary Cartwright, interview by author via phone. Digital recording. Austin, TX, February 7, 2012.

325. Ibid.

326. Ibid.

327. Ibid.; Gary Cartwright, *Heartwiseguy* (New York: St. Martin's Press, 1998), 10–11.

328. Blaha, "La Grange Chicken Ranch Revisited," 67; Chadwell, interview, August 21, 2009.

329. Chadwell, interview, February 20, 2009.

330. Kleffman, interview.

331. Bill Anders, Apollo 8 lunar module pilot, interview by author via phone. Digital recording. San Diego, CA, February 25, 2012.

332. E.P. Stein, *Flight of the Vin Fiz* (n.p.: Arbor House, 1985), 217–22.

333. Ibid., 222–23. A marvelously entertaining story, it is, nevertheless, almost certainly embellished with revisionist history after the fact. In 1911, prostitution in La Grange remained a decidedly unglamorous affair, and the Chicken Ranch would not acquire its distinctive name and statewide reputation for at least another two decades. The primitive conditions of Texas roads in 1911 meant that many would be muddy and impassable after the heavy rains experienced earlier in the day, rendering the sixty-mile trek to La Grange exceedingly difficult if not impossible. It is more plausible that the randy ground crew instead drove fifteen miles back to Austin to find their entertainment at the far more convenient and notorious Guy Town vice district.

334. Pankoniem, interview.

335. Kleffman, interview; Herb Hancock, former assistant attorney general for the state of Texas, interview by author. Digital recording. Kenedy, TX, June 4, 2009; King, *Whorehouse Papers*.

336. Frank X. Tolbert, "Tolbert's Texas: Poem Written About 'Edna's Chicken Farm,'" *Dallas Morning News*, August 12, 1973, 39A.

337. Chadwell, interview, August 21, 2009.

338. Chadwell, interview, February 20, 2009.

339. Kleffman, interview.

340. "Penny," interview.

341. William P. "Bill" Hobby Jr., former lieutenant governor of Texas, e-mail to author, August 17, 2009.

342. Hobby, interview.

343. King, *Whorehouse Papers*, 6.

344. Hobby, interview.

345. Robert A. Caro, *The Years of Lyndon Johnson: Master of the Senate* (New York: Vintage Books, 2002), 121. Multiple attempts by the author to contact Caro regarding specific references to L.B.J. visiting the Chicken Ranch went unacknowledged.

346. Wesley O. Hagood, *Presidential Sex* (Secaucus, NJ: Citadel Press, 1996) 181–95.

347. Chadwell, interview, August 21, 2009.

348. Ibid.

349. "Penny," interview.

350. Ibid.

351. Ibid.

352. Kleffman, interview. In the author's judgment, both of Miss Edna's stories are likely true. When the question of L.B.J.'s visit to the Chicken

Ranch was first put to her, Miss Edna began to answer and then diverted the interview with a long tangent unrelated to the question. Nearly an hour later, she abruptly returned to the subject with the story of L.B.J.'s failed attempt to visit. There is nothing confrontational in her answer, unlike other episodes where it is clear she is being less than truthful and defying the author to call her on it. It is the author's belief that Miss Edna used the time bought by her tangential response to compose a partially truthful response. The photograph referenced by Kleffman would lend credence to the second story, but to the best of the author's knowledge, it has not turned up in the effects of Miss Edna's estate.

Chapter 8

353. Saxon and Summerville, "Chicken Ranch," 33–44.
354. Ben Gill, *Stumbling Up the Stairway to Heaven* (self-published, 2015), 129–30; Ben Gill, letter to author, February 21, 2018.
355. Marie W. Watts, *La Grange*, (Charleston, SC: Arcadia Publishing, 2008), 120; Hutson, *Chicken Ranch*, 72.
356. Sillavan, "Remembrances of My Dad."
357. Ibid.
358. Ibid.
359. Kleffman, interview.
360. Gill, letter.
361. Saxon and Summerville, "Chicken Ranch"; King, "Best Little Whorehouse in Texas," 224; Friedman, "Chicken Ranch," 8–9; Assistant Attorney General Fletcher, Austin, Texas, letter to Frank Maloney, November 9, 1961, Texas State Library and Archives Commission.
362. Davis-Floyd, interview.
363. King, "Best Little Whorehouse in Texas," 132.
364. Friedman, "Chicken Ranch," 8.
365. Chadwell, interview, February 20, 2009.
366. Ibid.
367. Chadwell, interview, August 21, 2009.
368. Chadwell, interview, August 21, 2009; Chadwell, interview, February 20, 2009.
369. Chadwell, interview, February 20, 2009.
370. Ibid.
371. Anonymous 1, interview.

372. Kitzman, interview.

373. Ibid.

374. Gary Cartwright, *Galveston: A History of the Island* (Fort Worth, TX: TCU Press, 1991), 249–61; Friedman, "Chicken Ranch," 9; Reinert, "Closing Down La Grange," 51.

375. David G. McComb, *Galveston: A History* (Austin: University of Texas Press, 1986), 184–87; Cartwright, *Galveston*, 249–61.

376. Humphrey, "Prostitution in Texas," 36.

377. McComb, *Galveston*, 184–87; Cartwright, *Galveston*, 249–61.

378. Cartwright, *Galveston*, 249–61.

379. Sitton, *Texas Sheriff*, 146; Robert Nieman, "20th Century Shining Star: Capt. Johnny Klevenhagen," *Texas Rangers Dispatch*, www.texasranger.org/dispatch/Backissues/Dispatch_Issue_10.pdf, Spring 2003; "Legendary Lawman Peoples to Retire," *Houston Chronicle*, March 16, 1987, 7A.

380. Humphrey, "Prostitution in Texas," 37; Randy Sillavan, former ballistics expert with the Houston Police Department, e-mail to author, July 21, 2009.

381. King, "Best Little Whorehouse in Texas," 224.

382. Saxon and Summerville, "Chicken Ranch."

383. Chadwell, interview, February 20, 2009.

384. Cartwright, *Galveston*, 249–61; McComb, *Galveston*, 184–87.

385. Stanley E. Babb, "Gambling Charges Quashing Asked," *Galveston Daily News*, November 20, 1957, 1, 5; Deed of Trust, vol. 720, 396, August 6, 1991, Austin County Clerk's Office, Bellville, Texas; Sillavan, "Remembrances of My Dad."

Chapter 9

386. Charles Christopher Jackson, "Sealy, Texas," in *New Handbook of Texas*, vol. 5, Tyler, Barnett and Barkley, 954.

387. Kitzman, interview.

388. Pariseau, interview; David "Rusty" Rice, interview by author via phone. Digital recording. Danbury, TX, May 14, 2012. According to Rice, the owner of the Sealy brothel is alive as of 2012: "I ain't gonna mention who owned the sonofabitch, because he'd kill me. He knows me, knows where I live. He's eighty-six or eighty-seven years old, and he lives in League City. He knows where I live in Danbury, and I don't need that shit."

389. Anonymous 1, interview.

390. Rice, interview, May 14, 2012.

391. Pariseau, interview.

392. Dan Grothaus, "Former Operator of Brothel Tried to Avoid Notoriety," *Houston Post*, September 15, 1985, 5D; Rice, interview, May 14, 2012. Jerry McKay died in 2009.

393. Rice, interview, May 14, 2012.

394. Ibid.; Deed of Trust, vol. 720, 396, August 6, 1991, Austin County Clerk's Office, Bellville, Texas.

395. Rice, interview, May 14, 2012; Anonymous 1, interview; Austin County Appraisal District account details for R000013022. A dearth of information regarding the history of the Wagon Wheel exists, and the author has attempted to reconstruct a plausible, if not probable, history of the brothel. Because of the large gaps in the relevant information available, the author acknowledges the possibility of other interpretations.

396. Larry Conners, interview by author via phone. Digital recording. St. Louis, MO, May 14, 2009.

397. Rice, interview, May 14, 2012; Joseph Agris, *White Knight in Blue Shades* (Houston, TX: A-to-Z Publishing, 2002), 179.

398. Rice, interview, May 14, 2012.

399. Ibid.

400. Ibid.

401. Hancock, interview.

402. Kitzman, interview.

403. Ibid.

404. "Sheriff Truman Albert Maddox," *Houston Chronicle*, March 22, 2000; Kitzman, interview.

405. "Former Sheriff Maddox Dies," *Sealy News*, March 21, 2000, 1; Kitzman, interview.

406. Kitzman, interview.

407. Ibid.; *Houston Chronicle*; Sitton, *Texas High Sheriffs*, 185; Frank "Bo" Krampitz, "Truman Was 'The Sheriff,'" *Sealy News*, March 24, 2000, 4.

408. Sitton, *Texas High Sheriffs*, 185–86. During World War II, Maddox rose to the rank of sergeant, earning the Bronze Star with Combat V and oak leaf clusters for his service with the US Army Thirty-sixth Division.

409. Sitton, *Texas High Sheriffs*, 186, 192; Krampitz, "Truman Was 'The Sheriff.'"

410. Sitton, *Texas High Sheriffs*, 187–90.

411. Ibid.

412. Ibid.

413. Kitzman, interview.

414. Sitton, *Texas High Sheriffs*, 191–93.

415. Ibid., 208–9.

416. Kitzman, interview.

417. Sitton, *Texas High Sheriffs*, 206, 211.

418. Rice, interview, May 14, 2012; David "Rusty" Rice, interview by author via phone. Digital recording. Danbury, TX, May 20, 2012.

419. Oliver Kitzman, interview by author via phone. Digital recording. Brookshire, TX, May 22, 2009; Kitzman, interview, June 26, 2009; Randy Sillavan, e-mail to author, Trinity, TX, July 12, 2009.

420. Kitzman, interview, May 22, 2009; Kitzman, interview, June 26, 2009; Sillavan, e-mail to author, July 12, 2009.

421. Kitzman, interview, June 26, 2009.

422. Ramiro Martinez, former Texas Ranger, interview by author via phone. New Braunfels, TX, February 8, 2012.

Chapter 10

423. Sam Kindrick, "Offbeat: Texas' Oldest Brothel Has Closed Down," *San Antonio Express-News*, December 29, 1971, 3B.

424. Sam Kindrick, "Offbeat: Violence Ignores Geography," *San Antonio Express-News*, January 3, 1972, 5D.

425. Sam Kindrick, "Offbeat: Old City Ordinance Could Control Dogs," *San Antonio Express-News*, January 10, 1972, 9A.

426. Heard, "Prostitution in Texas." The Associated Press positively identified Miss Edna as the subject of the interview in 1973; "Governor May Get Petition to Let Chicken Ranch Reopen," *Austin American-Statesman*, August 2, 1973, 6A.

427. Frank C. Reily, "The Half-Million Dollar Sex Salon the Texas Rangers 'Can't' Find," *Men in Adventure*, May 1971, 27–59, Company A files, Texas Ranger Division records, Texas Department of Public Safety records. Archives and Information Services Division, Texas State Library and Archives Commission. The author of the piece currently lives in the Texas Hill Country and goes by the pseudonym "Old Jules" in homage to the author Mari Sandoz and maintains an online presence at sofarfromheaven.com as of 2012. He alludes to the inaccuracies in the piece and confesses to inventing the Reily identity to disassociate himself with such questionable markets.

428. Chadwell, interview, February 20, 2009.

429. Anonymous 2, interview by author via phone. Digital recording. Austin, TX, March 5, 2012.

430. District clerk records vol. 14, 248; District clerk records vol. 14, 261; Texas Divorce Index, 1968–2002, Ancestry.com; Carter, unpublished history of the Chicken Ranch.

431. Chadwell, interview, February 20, 2009.

432. Kent Demaret, *The Many Faces of Marvin Zindler* (Houston, TX: Hunt Company, 1976), 86–93.

433. Ibid., 93

434. Conners, interview.

435. Demaret, *Many Faces of Marvin Zindler*, 93–94.

436. Ibid., 86.

437. Ibid., 20.

438. Ibid., 29–31.

439. Ibid., 31–33.

440. Ibid., 29, 32.

441. Ibid., 35–39.

442. Ibid., 40.

443. Ibid., 41–42.

444. Ibid.

445. Hobby, interview, September 25, 2009.

446. Ibid.

447. Ibid.

448. Agris, *White Knight in Blue Shades*, 63; Demaret, *Many Faces of Marvin Zindler*, 42–43.

449. Demaret, *Many Faces of Marvin Zindler*, 43.

450. Ibid., 62.

451. Ibid., 65–66.

452. Ibid., 64.

453. Ibid., 67–68.

454. Ibid., 74–77.

455. Ibid., 74; Agris, *White Knight in Blue Shades*, 41.

456. Agris, *White Knight in Blue Shades*, 42.

457. Ibid.

458. Demaret, *Many Faces of Marvin Zindler*, 91.

459. Gary Taylor, *I, the People: How Marvin Zindler Busted the Best Little Whorehouse in Texas* (Los Gatos, CA: Smashwords edition 1.0, October 2009; Revised January 2012), www.smashwords.com/books/view/123620.

460. Kitzman, interview, June 26, 2009.
461. Ibid.
462. Demaret, *Many Faces of Marvin Zindler*, 93–99.
463. Agris, *White Knight in Blue Shades*, 78–79.
464. Ibid.
465. Conners, interview.
466. Ibid.
467. Ibid.
468. Demaret, *Many Faces of Marvin Zindler*, 9.

Chapter 11

469. William Rogers, La Grange native, interview by author. College Station, TX, February 6, 2010; Rice, interview, May 14, 2012; Bill Boe and Peggy Meek, "'Chicken Ranch' Delight of La Grange Visitors," *University Star*, February 11, 1972, 6. While the article by the Southwest Texas students might be daring for college writers of the time and did garner positive attention from columnist Sam Kindrick of the *San Antonio Express* ("Offbeat: College Reporting in Changing Times," *San Antonio Express*, February 28, 1972), the piece did not contribute to the downfall of the Chicken Ranch in any meaningful way. Of the handful of newspaper and magazine articles written about the Chicken Ranch in the early 1970s, the *University Star* write-up is the only one that did not make it into DPS or Texas Ranger files on the brothel.

470. Molly Cost, Texas Department of Public Safety Assistant General Counsel, e-mail to author, March 30, 2012; "Grand Jury Opens Slant Well Probe," *Big Spring Daily Herald*, October 18, 1962, 1; Texas legislature, House of Representatives, General Investigating Committee, official report to the House of Representatives of the 58th Legislature of Texas, Book, 1963, 12. digital images (texashistory.unt.edu/ark:/67531/metapth5869), University of North Texas Libraries, The Portal to Texas History, texashistory.unt.edu; crediting UNT Libraries, Denton, Texas; Texas legislature, House of Representatives, General Investigating Committee, official report to the House of Representatives of the 58th Legislature of Texas, Book, 1963, 89. digital images (texashistory.unt.edu/ark:/67531/metapth5869), University of North Texas Libraries, The Portal to Texas History, texashistory.unt.edu; crediting UNT Libraries, Denton, Texas; Herb Hancock, former assistant attorney

general for the state of Texas, interview by author via phone. Digital recording. Kenedy, TX, April 23, 2012. Other Houston-based DPS intelligence agents directly involved in the Chicken Ranch investigation included Sergeant Wayne Henscey, Sergeant Tommy Thomas and Lieutenant John J. Kiljan.

471. Hancock, interview, June 4, 2009.

472. Demaret, *Many Faces of Marvin Zindler*, 149–50.

473. Seal, "Sheriff Jim," 16.

474. Rick Fish, "La Grange's 'Chicken Ranch' May Have to Close Down," *Austin American-Statesman*, August 1, 1973, 6; Taylor, *I, the People*.

475. Hancock, interview, June 4, 2009.

476. Ibid.

477. Demaret, *Many Faces of Marvin Zindler*, 149–50.

478. Randy Fitzgerald, "La Grange 'House' a Landmark," *Houston Post*, August 1, 1973, 2A; Grothaus, "Former Operator of Brothel," 5D.

479. Taylor, *I, the People*.

480. Ibid.

481. Ibid.

482. Ibid.

483. Ibid.

484. Ibid.

485. Ibid.

486. Ibid.

487. Ibid.

488. Hancock, interview, June 4, 2009.

489. Taylor, *I, the People*.

490. Ibid.

491. Kitzman, interview, June 26, 2009.

492. Hancock, interview, June 4, 2009.

493. Ibid.

494. Taylor, *I, the People*.

495. Hancock, interview, June 4, 2009.

496. Ibid.

497. Ibid.; Agris, *White Knight in Blue Shades*, 181.

498. Hancock, interview, June 4, 2009.

499. See Appendix B.

500. Hancock, interview, June 4, 2009.

Chapter 12

501. Conners, interview.

502. Ibid.

503. Ibid.

504. Ibid.

505. Ibid.

506. Taylor, *I, the People*.

507. Ibid.; Conners, interview.

508. Conners, interview.

509. Ibid.

510. Conners, interview; Taylor, *I, the People*.

511. Taylor, *I, the People*.

512. Chadwell, interview, August 21, 2009.

513. Conners, interview.

514. Ibid.

515. Agris, *White Knight in Blue Shades*, 184–85.

516. Ibid., 186–87.

517. Ibid., 188–92.

518. Ibid.

519. Ibid.

520. Ibid.

521. Conners, interview.

522. "The Best Little Whorehouse in Texas," KTRK-TV, February 29, 2005, abclocal.go.com/ktrk/story?section=resources/inside_station/station_info&id=3300910.

523. Kitzman, interview, June 26, 2009.

524. Agris, *White Knight in Blue Shades*, 196–97.

525. Ibid.

526. Saxon and Summerville, "Chicken Ranch," 42; Taylor, *I, the People*; Carter, unpublished history of the Chicken Ranch. There is some doubt as to the exact date of Zindler's first Chicken Ranch broadcast. Most references are general: "the end of July" or "the last week of July." Darla J. Blaha gives a plausible alternative date of Thursday, July 27, in "La Grange Chicken Ranch Revisited," 71. Complicating matters is the fact that KTRK does not have records of the broadcasts or a readily accessible film archive from that time period (at least, none that it chose to make available to this author).

527. Dolph Briscoe and Don Carleton, *Dolph Briscoe: My Life in Texas Ranching and Politics* (Austin: Center for American History, University of Texas at Austin, 2008), 220–21.

528. Ibid.

529. Robert L. Hardesty, "Hardesty: Gov. Briscoe and the Chicken Ranch," *Austin American-Statesman*, July 30, 2012. Hardesty writes that the meeting with Briscoe occurred on Monday, July 30, but newspaper accounts indicate it happened Tuesday, July 31. The later date also supports Briscoe's contention Zindler's questions caught him unawares. Hardesty and other published accounts maintain that the governor was briefed on Zindler's intentions in advance.

530. "'Bawdy' Report Slated Today," *Houston Post*, July 31, 1973, 4A.

531. "Governor May Get Petition to Let Chicken Ranch Reopen," *Austin American-Statesman*, August 2, 1973, 1A.

532. Mike Kelley, "Merits of Brothel Matter of Opinion," *Austin American-Statesman*, August 1, 1973, 6.

533. Ibid., 1; Chadwell, interview, August 21, 2009. Miss Edna discontinued her support of the Little League a year or so prior to Zindler's broadcasts, annoyed that her donations were used, in part, to fund team parties.

534. Reinert, "Closing Down La Grange," 52.

535. Ibid.

536. Conners, interview.

537. Taylor, *I, the People*.

538. "Texas Prostitution Crackdown Due," *San Antonio Light*, August 1, 1973, 14-A.

539. Hancock, interview, June 4, 2009.

540. Rick Fish, "La Grange's Chicken Ranch May Have to Close Down," *Austin American-Statesman*, August 1, 1973, 6.

541. Hardesty, "Hardesty"; Hobby, interview by author, September 25, 2009.

542. Hobby, interview by author, September 25, 2009.

543. Hancock, interview, June 4, 2009.

544. Hardesty, "Hardesty."

545. Ibid.

546. Ibid.

547. Briscoe and Carleton, *Dolph Briscoe*, 222–23; Fish, "La Grange's Chicken Ranch," 1A; Kitzman, interview, June 26, 2009; Fitzgerald, "La Grange 'House' a Landmark," 2A.

548. Hardesty, "Hardesty"; Robert L. Hardesty, former press secretary for Governor Dolph Briscoe, interview by author via phone. Digital recording. Austin, TX, August 19, 2010.

549. Hancock, interview, June 4, 2009.

550. "Governor May Get Petition to Let Chicken Ranch Reopen," 6A.

551. Taylor, *I, the People*; Briscoe and Carleton, *Dolph Briscoe*, 223–24. Different sources conflict on who initially suggested that the governor call the sheriff personally. Taylor writes that Briscoe came up with the idea, whereas Briscoe and Carleton write that Sheriff Jim Flournoy himself called Colonel Speir with the suggestion. Other sources point to Speir, and as the DPS director is central to each version and served as the primary contact with Flournoy to that point, the author judges the latter most probable.

552. Briscoe and Carleton, *Dolph Briscoe*, 224.

553. Kleffman, interview.

554. Chadwell, interview, February 20, 2009.

555. Grothaus, "Former Operator of Brothel," 5D.

556. Chadwell, interview, February 20, 2009.

557. "Famed 'Chicken Ranch' House Closed, Reluctantly," *San Antonio Light*, August 2, 1973, 10A; "Pressure from Austin Closes Texas' Oldest Bawdy House," *San Antonio Express*, August 2, 1973, 6A.

558. "Chicken Ranch Closing Stirs Different Views," *Weimar Mercury*, August 9, 1973, 6. The petitions themselves disappeared shortly thereafter, in all likelihood thrown away in frustration or discarded as pointless.

559. Kitzman, interview, June 26, 2009.

560. "Lee Flournoy," *Fayette County Register*, August 7, 1973, 1.

561. Texas Archive of the Moving Image, www.texasarchive.org/library/index.php?title=2010_03736.

562. Randy Fitzgerald, "La Grange 'Chicken Ranch' Saga Ends," *Houston Post*, August 3, 1973, 4A.

Chapter 13

563. "Zany Zindler's Zestful Zeal No Zany Zero," *Colorado County Citizen*, August 9, 1973, 1.

564. Walter F. Pilcher, "The Chicken Ranch," in *New Handbook of Texas*, vol. 5, Tyler, Barnett and Barkley, 73–75; Agris, *White Knight in Blue Shades*, 224.

565. Dan Beck, former Fayette County attorney, interview by author. Digital recording. La Grange, TX, December 12, 2012.

566. Ibid.

567. Kleffman, interview.

568. Ibid.

569. Ibid.

570. Kitzman, interview, June 26, 2009.

571. Ibid.

572. Conners, interview.

573. Demaret, *Many Faces of Marvin Zindler*, 152–53.

574. Ibid., 154.

575. Pankoniem, interview; Demaret, *Many Faces of Marvin Zindler*, 154.

576. Broadcast transcript, Box 1998/097-2, Company A files, Texas Ranger Division records, Texas Department of Public Safety records. Archives and Information Services Division, Texas State Library and Archives Commission.

577. Investigation report, Box 1998/097-2, Company A files, Texas Ranger Division records, Texas Department of Public Safety records. Archives and Information Services Division, Texas State Library and Archives Commission.

578. Agris, *White Knight in Blue Shades*, 206; Stevi Jackson and Sue Scott, eds., *Feminism and Sexuality: A Reader* (Edinburgh: Edinburgh University Press, 1996), 351. The argument that the Chicken Ranch reduced sexually transmitted disease was a common argument made by proponents and one dismissed by opponents. However, the increase in sexually transmitted disease infection parallels similar outbreaks following brothel closures in 1917–20.

579. Agris, *White Knight in Blue Shades*, 208.

580. Ibid., 208–10.

581. Ibid; Giese, interview.

582. Giese, interview; Agris, *White Knight in Blue Shades*, 211; Kitzman, interview, June 26, 2009.

583. Chadwell, interview, August 20, 2009.

584. Demaret, *Many Faces of Marvin Zindler*, 155.

585. Ibid., 187; Giese, interview.

586. Demaret, *Many Faces of Marvin Zindler*, 156. The transcript in Demaret's book is edited to remove the profanity while still making clear what the actual words are ("bluck" and "blit" instead of "fuck" and "shit"). The author has taken the liberty of translating this coy affectation back to the original swearing.

587. Harvey Dipple, La Grange resident, interview by author. Digital recording. La Grange, TX, August 17, 2009; Harvey Dipple, interview by

Jamie Rapp, September 8, 2005 (pacweb.alamo.edu/InteractiveHistory/ projects/rhines/StudentProjects/2005/LaGrange/dipple.htm).

588. Demaret, *Many Faces of Marvin Zindler*, 156–57; Agris, *White Knight in Blue Shades*, 212; Kitzman, interview, June 26, 2009; Giese, interview.

589. Conners, interview.

590. Demaret, *Many Faces of Marvin Zindler*, 157.

591. Dipple, interview, August 17, 2009; Kitzman, interview, June 26, 2009.

592. Kitzman, interview, June 26, 2009.

593. "Newsman Finds He Isn't Best-Liked Man in Town," *Los Angeles Times* (1923–Current File), December 31, 1974, search.proquest.com/docview /157681774?accountid=5683.

594. Beck, interview.

595. Kitzman, interview, June 26, 2009.

596. Conners, interview.

597. Ibid.

598. Kitzman, interview, June 26, 2009.

599. Ibid.; "Newsman Finds He Isn't Best-Liked Man in Town"; Agris, *White Knight in Blue Shades*, 214; Demaret, *Many Faces of Marvin Zindler*, 156.

600. Hobby, interview.

601. Agris, *White Knight in Blue Shades*, 215.

602. Kitzman, interview, June 26, 2009.

603. Demaret, *Many Faces of Marvin Zindler*, 149.

604. Maryln Schwartz, "Sheriff Jim: They Love Him in La Grange," *Dallas Morning News*, June 29, 1975, 37A.

605. Agris, *White Knight in Blue Shades*, 216; Kitzman, interview, June 26, 2009; Gary Cartwright, *Blood Will Tell: The Murder Trials of T. Cullen Davis* (New York: Harcourt Brace Jovanovich, 1979), 115.

606. Schwartz, "Sheriff Jim."

607. Ibid.

608. Agris, *White Knight in Blue Shades*, 217–19.

609. Kitzman, interview, June 26, 2009.

610. Hobby, interview.

611. Agris, *White Knight in Blue Shades*, 217.

612. Justia.com, cases.justia.com/us-court-of-appeals/F2/561/1125/419154/ #fn1.

613. Kitzman, interview, June 26, 2009.

614. Ibid.

615. Agris, *White Knight in Blue Shades*, 217.

616. Ibid., 218-219; Demaret, *Many Faces of Marvin Zindler*, 157.

617. Demaret, *Many Faces of Marvin Zindler*, 157.

618. Agris, *White Knight in Blue Shades*, 219; Civil action 75-H621; "Man Settles with Sheriff Out of Court," *Dallas Morning News*, March 31, 1976, 12A.

619. Beck, interview.

620. Demaret, *Many Faces of Marvin Zindler*, 157; Agris, *White Knight in Blue Shades*, 219.

621. Giese, interview.

622. Dipple, interview, August 17, 2009.

623. Kitzman, interview, June 26, 2009.

624. Dave McNeely, "Marv's Second Visit Was Bigger Mistake," *Dallas Morning News*, January 20, 1975, 3D.

Chapter 14

625. Chadwell, interview, February 20, 2009.

626. Agris, *White Knight in Blue Shades*, 189.

627. Bill (last name withheld by request), former owner of the Chicken Ranch, interview by author. Digital recording. Sugar Land, TX, March 8, 2010.

628. Chadwell, interview, February 20, 2009; Bill, interview; George E. Read, captain, Texas Department of Public Safety, interoffice memorandum to W.A. Cowan Jr., agent in charge, April 5, 1974 (Michele Freeland, Texas Department of Public Safety legal assistant, e-mail to author, June 7, 2012).

629. Bill, interview.

630. "Edna Sells Her 12-Bedroom 'Chicken House,'" *Los Angeles Times*, January 22, 1974, 2; Bill, interview.

631. Bill, interview.

632. Ibid.; Read, interoffice memorandum, April 5, 1974.

633. Bill, interview.

634. George E. Read, Captain, Texas Department of Public Safety interoffice memorandum to W.A. Cowan Jr., agent in charge, June 24, 1974 (Michele Freeland, Texas Department of Public Safety legal assistant, e-mail to author, June 7, 2012).

635. Bill, interview.

636. King, *Whorehouse Papers*, 2–7; King, "Best Little Whorehouse in Texas," 130–32, 219–26; Craig McGinty, "Fun, Money and Freedom Come to Larry L. King," *Odessa American*, March 4, 1979, 2A.

637. Peter Masterson, interview by author via phone. Digital recording. Kinderhook, NY, November 12, 2010.

638. Ibid. Amusingly, this version of events differs from the two competing versions of the story King recounts in *The Whorehouse Papers* and reads as an amalgam of the alternative King versions.

639. Ibid.

640. King, *Whorehouse Papers*, 9.

641. Masterson, interview; King, *Whorehouse Papers*, 12–17.

642. Masterson, interview.

643. King, *Whorehouse Papers*, 29, 37–43, 62–63.

644. Ibid., 45.

645. Ibid., 65, 125.

646. Don Shewey, "Tommy Tune: Hoofers, Hookers and Hollywood Dreams," *Soho News*, July 2, 1980 (www.donshewey.com/theater_articles/tommy_tune.html). Carol Hall wrote many more songs that didn't make it through development into the final production. In addition to "Two Blocks from the Capitol Building," songs such as "Doin' It and Sayin' It Are Two Different Things," "Goddamn Everthang," "The Memory Song" and "Pussy" all were part of the musical for a while before falling by the wayside. The only discarded song among these to ever see release was "Have a Memory On Me," performed by Dee Hoty on the *Lost in Boston IV* album. Hall also contributed a new song, "A Friend to Me," for the 2001 touring production starring Ann-Margret.

647. King, *Whorehouse Papers*, 104–8, 113.

648. "'Chicken Ranch' Brothel May Rule Roost Once More," *Dallas Morning News*, January 23, 1974, 3D; "Chicken Ranch Has New Set of Feathers," *Dallas Morning News*, April 5, 1977, 4D; "Fowl Play Key to Disco's Fame," *Dallas Morning News*, September 25, 1977, 7D.

649. Bill, interview.

650. Ibid.; "Fowl Play"; Lon Cooper, "Disco Down to the Chicken Ranch," *Austin American-Statesman*, October 12, 1977, 1B.

651. "Fowl Play."

652. Ibid.; Cooper, "Disco Down."

653. Diana Wilson, interview by author via phone. Digital recording. Grand Prairie, TX, July 29, 2009.

654. Ibid.

655. Ibid.

656. Ibid.

657. King, *Whorehouse Papers*, 109–11.

658. Peter Applebome, "Chicken Ranch Closing Won't Last, Owners Say," *Dallas Morning News*, January 22, 1978, 34A.

659. Peter Applebome, "Lock, Stock and Mattress," *Dallas Morning News*, June 29, 1978, 1A; "Texas Institution, Chicken Ranch Boarding House, Auctioned Off," *Lakeland Ledger*, July 23, 1978, 21A.

660. Applebome, "Lock, Stock and Mattress," June 29, 1978.

661. Peter Applebome, "La Grange Oilman Seeking Roost for 'Chicken Ranch,'" *Dallas Morning News*, July 27, 1978, 40A.

662. Peter Applebome, "Death of Texas' Celebrated Cathouse 'Just Another Job' to Wrecking Crew," *Dallas Morning News*, September 12, 1978, 1D.

663. Ibid.

664. King, *Whorehouse Papers*, 113–14.

665. Masterson, interview.

666. King, *Whorehouse Papers*, 115–20.

667. Masterson, interview.

668. King, *Whorehouse Papers*, 122–24.

669. Masterson, interview.

670. King, *Whorehouse Papers*, 146–47.

671. Chadwell, interview, February 20, 2009.

672. Robert Ast, "Stevie Phillips, '58," *The Owl Magazine*, 2010, 23 (www.gs.columbia.edu/owl-article?ntitle=4812&mgid=4802).

673. Chadwell, interview, February 20, 2009.

674. Masterson, interview.

675. Carol Hall, e-mail to author, February 29, 2012.

676. Seal, "Sheriff Jim," 11.

677. Masterson, interview.

Chapter 15

678. "The Best Little Oil Well," *Time*, vol. 117, February 16, 1981, 73; Hank Card, e-mail to author, April 27, 2012; Man Mountain and the Green Slime Boys, "The Ballad of the La Grange Chicken Ranch," written by Ron Rose, Armadillo Records, Austin, TX; Gaylen Ackley, "Hello Marvin Zindler," written by Gaylen Ackley, Dream Land Records, Industry, TX.

679. Lawrence Christon, "Cathouse Purrs Over Nine Lives," *Los Angeles Times*, December 28, 1980, O58; Masterson, interview.

680. Connie Hershorn, "Ranch's Miss Edna Planning to Open Club," *Dallas Morning News*, August 29, 1978, 8A. Author Robin Moore himself confirmed that he and Fred Halliday were working on the "definitive history" of the brothel, to be titled simply *The Chicken Ranch*. "We're mining a new motherlode of gold—we hope," Moore said. The project was eventually abandoned without explanation; "The Chicken Ranch: A Legend," *Florence Times–Tri Cities Daily*, November 6, 1978, 3.

681. Chadwell, interview, February 20, 2009; "10 Ways to Celebrate Friday," *Dallas Times Herald*, November 24, 1978.

682. "Tut! Too Blue for Madam," *Daily Mirror*, February 19, 1981, 10; "Confessions of a Happy Hooker," *Daily Star*, February 19, 1981, 3; Masterson, interview; Chadwell, interview, February 20, 2009. Beyond the porn district, Miss Edna was generally unimpressed by her visit to Britain: "England was about like America to me. Because when I looked out the window at the hotel, what do I see? Woolworth's."

683. Masterson, interview; Christon, "Cathouse Purrs Over Nine Lives"; King, *Whorehouse Papers*, 263–72.

684. "'Best Little House' Not Good Enough," *Amarillo Globe-Times*, October 6, 1981, 9.

685. King, *Whorehouse Papers*, 263–71; "The Best Little Whorehouse in Texas," Box Office Mojo (www.boxofficemojo.com/movies/?id=bestlitt lewhorehouseintexas.htm). Despite the fact that Miss Edna thought the musical misrepresented the reality of life at the Chicken Ranch, she liked it overall. The movie version, however, she held in contempt.

686. Masterson, interview; Alexa Albert, *Brothel: Mustang Ranch and Its Women* (New York: Random House, 2001), 244; "The Best Little Whorehouse Goes Public," Internet Broadway Database (www.ibdb.com/production. php?id=4609).

687. Jim Carlton, "After 54 Years, 'Sheriff Jim' Has Decided to Step Down," *Houston Chronicle*, January 21, 1980; "Chicken Ranch Sheriff Retires," *Odessa American*, June 5, 1980, 3A.

688. Banta, "La Grange to Lose Lawman," A9.

689. Albin Krebs, "Notes on People," *New York Times*, January 2, 1981, D8; Michael Hamlyn, "Texas Mourns Reluctant Sheriff Who Closed Its Best Little Whorehouse," *The Times*, October 30, 1982, 6.

690. United Press International, October 29, 1982.

691. "Former Sheriff Maddox Dies," *Sealy News*, March 21, 2000, 1; Frank "Bo" Krampitz, "Truman Was 'The Sheriff,'" *Sealy News*, March 24, 2000, 4; "Honoring a Hero," *Sealy News*, March 24, 2000, 1.

692. Wendy Cole, *Whoremaster* (Las Vegas, NV: Abacus & Quill Books, 1997), 3–56; Jeanie Kasindorf, *The Nye County Brothel Wars* (New York: Linden Press/Simon & Schuster, 1985), 8–9, 17.

693. Cole, *Whoremaster*, 57–65; Kasindorf, *Nye County Brothel Wars*, 13–18.

694. Chadwell, interview, February 20, 2009; Chadwell, interview, August 21, 2009.

695. Cole, *Whoremaster*, 66–72.

696. Steve Oney, "The Little House in the Desert," *New York Times*, September 1, 1985, BR6; Kasindorf, *Nye County Brothel Wars*, 11.

697. Cole, *Whoremaster*, 151.

698. Ibid., 151–56.

699. Ibid., 158–97; Kasindorf, *Nye County Brothel Wars*, 51–60, 104–7.

700. Cole, *Whoremaster*, 179–81, 202–4; Ellis E. Conklin, "Town Keeps a Wary Eye on Brothel," *Los Angeles Times*, August 10, 1986, A3.

701. Linda Helser, "Mr. Madam: Brothel 'Overseer' Means Business," *Arizona Republic*, September 5, 1987, E1; Steve Harvey, "Ex-Teacher Happy with His 'Chicks,'" *Los Angeles Times*, September 7, 1983, SD A2; Henry Brean, "Famous Brothel Near Pahrump on Market for $6.5 Million," *Las Vegas Review-Journal*, June 8, 2004.

702. Helser, "Mr. Madam"; Debbie Rivenburgh, madam of the Pahrump, Nevada, Chicken Ranch, interview by author via phone. Digital recording. Pahrump, NV, July 13, 2009.

703. Rivenburgh, interview. Filmmaker Nick Broomfield completed an eighty-four-minute documentary on the Nevada Chicken Ranch in 1983 that offers some insight into the daily workings of the current incarnation of the Chicken Ranch, an operation that differs markedly from both the brothel Plankinton established and the original in La Grange.

704. "Listen," *Los Angeles Times*, March 6, 1981, I3; Dottie Meinardus, "Hoffman Plans to Revive the Historic Chicken Ranch," *Banner Press*, January 8, 1987, 1, 12.

705. "Entrepreneurs Want to Revive Texas Bordello as Museum," *United Press International*, November 3, 1986; "Entrepreneurs Want to Sell Pieces of 'Best Little Whorehouse,'" Associated Press, November 2, 1986.

706. "Entrepreneurs Want to Sell Pieces of 'Best Little Whorehouse.'"

707. "Chicken Ranch Plan Draws Pecks," *Waco Tribune-Herald*, January 23, 1987; Bill Fowler, "Texas Facts & Fantasies," *TAMS Journal* 19, no. 5 (October 1979): 190; Chadwell, interview, February 20, 2009. All Chicken Ranch tokens, as well as other memorabilia, are latter-day replicas (or, more bluntly, fakes). The earliest token documentation located by the

author is an ad from the *Dallas Morning News*, October 10, 1977, page 18 of the classifieds section: "Baudy house tokens depicting chicken ranch La Grange. 271-2533 after 5 p.m. or weekends."

708. Meinardus, "Hoffman Plans to Revive," 1; "Plans to Commemorate Famous Bordello Draws Criticism," Associated Press, January 22, 1987.

709. "Plans to Commemorate Famous Bordello Draws Criticism"; "Chicken Ranch Plan Draws Pecks"; Beck, interview.

710. "Chicken Ranch Plan Draws Pecks."

711. Ibid.

712. Meinardus, "Hoffman Plans to Revive," 12.

713. Vera Foss Bradshaw, "Texas Scenes—Miss Hattie's Bawdy House Becomes Museum," *Houston Chronicle*, October 16, 1988, T3; Susan Bayer Ward, "Hattie's House of Ill Repute is Back for a Second Run," *Austin American-Statesman*, April 12, 1993, D1.

714. Bruce Hight, "'Chicken Ranch' Brothel Hatches New Controversy," *Austin American-Statesman*, November 1, 1990, A1.

715. Mike Cochran, *Claytie: The Roller-Coaster Life of a Texas Wildcatter* (College Station: Texas A&M University Press, 2007), 270–72; John Gravois, "Williams Paid Prostitutes as Youth," *Houston Post*, April 22, 1990, 1A.

716. Gravois, "Williams Paid Prostitutes as Youth," A26.

717. Ibid.

718. John Gravois, "Williams' Candor Surprising," *Houston Post*, April 23, 1990, 1A.

719. Cochran, *Claytie*, 273.

720. Ibid., 272–73.

721. Gravois, "Williams' Candor Surprising," A7.

722. Mark Smith, "What's the Beef? Try Sex/Protesters Focusing on Adult Businesses," *Houston Chronicle*, August 21, 1994, State 1.

723. Ibid.

724. "Time Running Out on Ranch," *Houston Chronicle*, May 15, 1995, 15A. Arguably, the dispute wouldn't have risen above a local issue had "Chicken Ranch" not been a part of the restaurant's name. The tenuous Chicken Ranch connection added a level of infamy and, frankly, humor to the ongoing story that attracted more statewide media attention than the story truly warranted.

725. John Kelso, "Best Little Y2K Party in Texas?" *Austin American-Statesman*, December 29, 1999, 1B.

726. Ray Prewitt, interview by author via phone. Digital recording. Oklahoma City, OK, July 13, 2009; Ronald W. Jeffrey, interview by author via phone. Houston, TX, March 9, 2010.

727. Kelso, "Best Little Y2K Party in Texas?"; Prewitt, interview.

728. Prewitt, interview; John Kelso, "Party Plans Run Afowl of the Law," *Austin American-Statesman*, January 7, 2000, 1B.

729. Kelso, "Party Plans Run Afowl of the Law"; Frances Schramm, "New Year's Chicken Ranch Party a Bust in Fayette County," *Banner Press*, January 6, 2000, 1-2.

730. Jeffrey, interview.

731. Ibid.; Kelso, "Party Plans Run Afowl of the Law."

732. Prewitt, interview; "Best Little Y2K Party in Texas Did Not Happen," *Fayette County Record*, January 4, 2000, 1, 5.

733. Prewitt, interview. As these things go, opposition to the Millennium Chicken party proved counterproductive to the anti–Chicken Ranch brigade, generating far more publicity and attention than had they simply grumbled at Kelso's original column and gotten on with their lives.

734. Harvey Rice, "New Trouble Back at the Ranch: Cast Quits Musical after Conroe Board Cries Foul Language," *Houston Chronicle*, April 18, 2002, 1A. The Conroe kerfuffle was the biggest blow-up over a local production of the play since a 1991 battle in Glens Falls, New York, over whether the word "Whorehouse" could be publicly displayed to advertise the community theater's production, although other incidents have occurred across the United States. (John Kelso, "Producers of 'Whorehouse' Not Really Having a Banner Day," *Austin American-Statesman*, October 15, 1991, A20.)

735. Erin Maxey-Wilhite, interview by author via phone. Digital recording. Bryan, TX, August 11, 2009.

736. Ibid.; Rice, "New Trouble Back at the Ranch"; Mike Maza, "Show Can't Go On without Profanity—'Little Whorehouse' Playwright King Won't Let the Script Be Altered," *Dallas Morning News*, April 19, 2002, 37A.

737. Maza, "Show Can't Go On without Profanity."

738. Harvey Rice, "The Show Goes On and On…" *Houston Chronicle*, June 22, 2002, 35A; Maxey-Wilhite, interview.

739. Maxey-Wilhite, interview.

740. Joe Holley, "Marvin Zindler; Showy TV Personality, Exposed Notorious Brothel," *Washington Post*, August 5, 2007; Eric Harrison, "Channel 13's Marvin Zindler Dies at 85," *Houston Chronicle*, July 29, 2007, 1A. The 2012 Theatre Under the Stars production of *The Best Little Whorehouse in Texas* also incorporated Texas governor Rick Perry's infamous "Oops" blunder

during the 2012 Republican presidential primaries. Although the topical gag drew much laughter, certain sections of the audience reacted with disapproving silence. For the record, the author found it hilarious.

741. "ZZ Top Will Play 'La Grange' in La Grange," KHOU-TV, June 3, 2015, www.khou.com/article/entertainment/zz-top-will-play-la-grange-in-la-grange/411635595, accessed July 14, 2022.

742. Chadwell; Ruth, interview by author via phone. Digital recording. Duncan, Oklahoma. September 28, 2016; Ruth. Letter to author, October, 2016.

743. Chadwell, interview, February 20, 2009; Kleffman, e-mail to author, September 16, 2011; Kleffman, e-mail to author, October 4, 2011; Aileen Loehr, "Last 'Madam' of LG Chicken Ranch Dies," *Fayette County Record*, February 28, 2012, A2.

744. Hancock, interview, June 4, 2009. Although Hancock maintains a firm belief that he ultimately did the right thing, he confesses, "It's not a part of my history I feel proud about."

745. Ibid.

746. Conners, interview, May 14, 2009.

747. Masterson, interview; Tatiana Siegel, "Universal to Remake 'Best Little Whorehouse,'" *Variety*, February 10, 2010 (www.variety.com/article/VR1118015028); "Breaking: Brand-New Production of THE BEST LITTLE WHOREHOUSE IN TEXAS Coming to Broadway; Rob Ashford to Direct!" *BroadwayWorld.com* (www.broadwayworld.com/article/Breaking-Brand-New-Production-of-THE-BEST-LITTLE-WHOREHOUSE-IN-TEXAS-Coming-to-Broadway-Rob-Ashford-to-Direct-20140807#); Nicole Rosky, "Kristin Chenoweth, Kevin McKidd, Christopher Sieber, Jennifer Holliday & More Lead THE BEST LITTLE WHOREHOUSE IN TEXAS Reading," BroadwayWorld.com, www.broadwayworld.com/article/Kristin-Chenoweth-Kevin-McKidd-Christopher-Sieber-Jennifer-Holliday-More-Lead-THE-BEST-LITTLE-WHOREHOUSE-IN-TEXAS-Redaing-20160629, accessed July 11, 2022.

INDEX

Z

ABOUT THE AUTHOR

A native Texan, Jayme Blaschke grew up less than twenty miles from the former Chicken Ranch and heard stories about it his entire life. He was the only person to conduct extensive interviews with its former madam, Edna Milton Chadwell, prior to her death in 2012. Later that year, he presented a paper to the East Texas Historical Association titled "The Last Madam: The Unexpected Life of the Chicken Ranch's Edna Milton (1928–2012)."

Blaschke has published in fiction, nonfiction and graphic arts for nearly two decades, with his writing appearing in *Electric Velocipede*, *Cross Plains Universe*, *Interzone*, the *Brutarian* and *San Marcos Mercury*, among others. He is a member of the Science Fiction and Fantasy Writers of America, Authors Guild and a former member of the East Texas Historical Society. He earned his bachelor's degree in journalism at Texas A&M University and studied fine art photography at Texas State University, where he is currently the director of media relations.

OTHER BOOKS BY JAYME LYNN BLASCHKE

Ghosts of the Chicken Ranch (with Lisa Elliott Blaschke)
Voices of Vision: Creators of Science Fiction and Fantasy Speak